THE ORIGIN OF THE JEWS

The Origin of the Jews

THE QUEST FOR ROOTS
IN A ROOTLESS AGE

Steven Weitzman

PRINCETON UNIVERSITY PRESS

PRINCETON & OXFORD

Published by Princeton University Press,
41 William Street, Princeton, New Jersey 08540

In the United Kingdom: Princeton University Press,
6 Oxford Street, Woodstock, Oxfordshire OX20 1TR

press.princeton.edu

Jacket art courtesy of Shutterstock

ISBN 978-0-691-17460-0

Library of Congress Control Number: 2016960228

British Library Cataloging-in-Publication Data is available

This book has been composed in Miller

Printed on acid-free paper. ∞

Printed in the United States of America

10 9 8 7 6 5 4 3 2 1

To the memory of

Liba Feuerstein

CONTENTS

ILLUSTRATIONS

THE ORIGIN OF THE JEWS

Introduction

It is precisely because people are aware of the fearful distance that separates us from our beginnings that so many embark upon a search for the roots, the "deeper causes" of what happened. It is in the nature of roots and "deeper causes" that they are hidden by the appearances which they are supposed to have caused. They are not open to inspection or analysis but can be reached only by the uncertain way of interpretation and speculation.

—HANNAH ARENDT

IF WE WERE SOMEHOW able to conduct a survey of Jews around the world today, I have no doubt they would tell the story of their origin in many different ways. Jews, of course, come from many different parts of the world. Some Jews would be able to trace their ancestry back only a few generations—personally, things get murky for me beyond the generation of my grandparents. Others can claim lineages that go back to the Middle Ages or even earlier, and those who have chosen to become Jews might tell origin stories that go back to a recent conversion experience rather than to a distant ancestor. For many Jews, however, the story of their people predates the history of their particular community, going back to founders, a homeland, or a formative experience in the distant past. It is that common origin we are after in this book: the origin that connects all Jews into a single people, religion, or community; the very beginning of their collective story.

Many people assume the answer to the question of Jewish origin is already known: it is to be found in the Hebrew Bible/Old Testament, more precisely, in the Five Books of Moses or Torah. The narrative that begins with the Book of Genesis does not concern the Jews per se but is focused on the people of Israel, tracing their descent from Abraham through his grandson Jacob (who is later given the name Israel). The Israelites as depicted in the Torah are related to each other as members of an extended family—twelve tribes descended from Jacob—but their connection is not only genealogical. They undergo a series of trials and tribulations together—enslavement in Egypt, deliverance at the hands of Moses, a harrowing trek across the Sinai desert—and jointly commit to a covenant at Mount Sinai that imposes on them shared responsibilities to each other and to God. Nowhere does the Torah refer to "the Jews" as we understand that term today, but it does single out for special attention Jacob's son Judah—the eponymous ancestor of the tribe of Judah, which plays a special role in the biblical account, going on to produce the royal dynasty that would rule the Israelites under David and his successors, and emerging as the sole survivors, along with the tribe of Levi, of the catastrophes of the Assyrian and Babylonian conquests. Jews identify as the descendants of those who survived these catastrophes, tracing their origins to the Judahites who returned from exile to rebuild a life in the land of their ancestors and renew their covenant with God.

One reason we cannot begin with this narrative is that, from the perspective of modern scholarship, it cannot be relied on for an understanding of history. The story told of Abraham, Isaac, and Jacob in Genesis, most biblical scholars would agree, is an attempt by much later authors to explain the origin of their people: they might preserve certain kernels of genuine experience, but for the most part, many scholars believe, they do not reflect historical reality, having been composed in a much later period and projecting on to the past the experiences and perspectives of much later authors. Similar considerations have led scholars to conclude that the Exodus probably did not happen, or at least not in the way the Torah describes, and they have their doubts as well about the Israelite conquest of the land of Canaan, the existence of a kingdom ruled by David and Solomon, and other events and people mentioned in the biblical account especially in the formative period of Israel's history. There is plenty of debate about the history that lies behind the biblical account, about what really happened, but scholars generally agree that there is more to the story of how the Jews came to be than we can glimpse in the Bible.

For these and other reasons, this book must begin by acknowledging that we do not already know the origin of the Jews. But if we cannot look to the Bible for an answer, what can we say about where the Jews come from or how they came to be? The main goal of this book is to describe how scholars answer these questions. It is not a history of the Jews but an attempt to chronicle an intellectual quest, to explore scholarship's efforts to answer a question that emerged into view only after people began to doubt the veracity of the Bible and to think in new ways about how people and cultures originate. This book cannot promise a definitive answer to the question of Jewish origin, but it seeks to help the reader to think more deeply about the question by surveying what scholars have learned so far, and wondering aloud about why it is that this origin has proven so hard to pin down.

Some readers might be suspicious of such a project as an attempt to discredit the Jews. Going back to antiquity, anti-Jewish animosity has sometimes expressed itself in the form of counter-origin stories that seek to mock and discredit the Jews by negating their own understanding of their origin. The Roman historian Tacitus, writing in the second century CE, preserves a number of such stories that trace the Jews back to various origins (Tacitus, *Histories*, 5.1–4). Some describe them as fugitives from Crete, Ethiopia, Assyria, or Asia Minor, but most authors, Tacitus tells us, agree that they descend from a group of lepers driven from Egypt by its king. The distinctive customs that distinguished the descendants of this group from other peoples, the historian explains—their strange sacrifices, their avoidance of pork, the practice of circumcision and other rites that Romans like Tacitus deemed barbaric—were invented by Moses to secure the allegiance of his people. Tacitus was by no means the last author to disparage the Jews by ascribing to them a suspect origin different from the one Jews claim for themselves, and it would certainly be understandable if there were readers wary of a book that potentially gives license to anti-Jewish stories by calling into question the traditional account.

But the proliferation of origin stories, including many that are hostile to the Jews, is to my mind a reason to pursue an investigation like this, not an argument against it. While there are plenty of reasons not to ask about the origin of the Jews, the world still has need of origin stories and is still developing them about the Jews. Precisely because some of these narratives invoke scholarship to give them an aura of authority, it is important to make an effort to assess the various theories, to weigh them against one another, and to factor in criticisms. According to modern scholarship, what Jews have long believed about themselves is based on a myth, but Jews have also suffered from origin myths imposed on them by secular scholarship. Is there a way to get to the bottom of how the Jews came to be?

Many decades ago, I chose to specialize in ancient Jewish history because I believed it would be through that field—by studying the formative era of the biblical period—that I would find answers about who I was and what connected me to the past, a belief I now recognize as naïve but which has shaped my professional life and which I can't quite let go of even now. In a certain sense this search to understand the origin of the Jews is really an attempt to examine that belief. Can scholarship, especially scholarship focused on ancient history and long-dead people, help us understand who we are—where our sense of identity comes from, how we have been shaped by the past, what connects us to other people? This book happens to focus on the Jews, but a similar question can be asked of any person whose sense of identity depends on a certain understanding of origin. Is not our sense of common humanity tied to a sense of shared origin? The focus of this inquiry is the origin of the Jews, but it can also be read as a case study of the origin of group identity, with lessons that can be applied to other religions, ethnicities, and nations.

Along the way I also reflect on a larger subject that goes beyond Jewish studies—our relationship to origins in a general sense. The last two centuries have seen tremendous strides in our ability to address questions of origin—cosmic origins, human origins, the origins of thought—but it has also been an era in which many scholars grew disenchanted with the search for origin, and with the very concept of origin itself. The problem from this perspective was not just with particular origin accounts but with the underlying thinking that produces such accounts, the belief that one can understand a thing by grasping its origin. The most influential critiques of origin came from thinkers now identified with postmodernism, but the intellectual opposition to the search for origin goes beyond a particular school of thought, arising as a kind of generalized reaction against the preoccupation with origin that marked earlier generations of scholarship. By no means has scholarship today abandoned the search for origins, but for those who have absorbed the lessons of late twentieth-century intellectual history, a search of the sort we are embarking on here will seem naïve, suspect, a chasing after a chimera, as one historian puts it.

If I nonetheless persist in this quest, it is not because I wish to ignore those lessons or do not think they are important; it is because, for all their influence, they have not stopped the scholarly search for the origin of the Jews. The suspicion of origin that characterizes so much of late twentieth-century historiographical and literary theory has waned in influence—in fact, it has provoked a backlash, for there is now a resurgence of interest in questions of origin under way, a renewed curiosity about ancestry, inheritance, and what some now refer to as "deep history": the tracing of the origin of human behavior in the remote past. Much of this book is devoted to tracing the history of the search for the origin of the Jews, but the ultimate objective is to assess the future of this search, to determine whether it has any chance of leading anywhere; and that future will be shaped by how scholars balance the promise of new discoveries from fields like archaeology and genetics against the antiorigin skepticism bequeathed by postmodernism.

The Elusiveness of Origin

I cannot recall when exactly it occurred to me to undertake this inquiry, but if I had to single out a particular moment of origin, it was a bout of writer's block, my struggle to begin an earlier book about the history of the Jews. My portion of the book, which was written with three other scholars, was the initial section that covered the beginnings of Jewish history. All the material was familiar to me, and yet for some reason, I could not figure out how to begin. Like so many would-be authors, I find it very difficult to start a book, and that was part of the struggle, but there was an additional problem that went beyond ordinary writer's block. I realized that, despite years of research into ancient Judaism, I really had no idea how the Jews originated, and that all the scholarly theories I had digested had made things only more puzzling. It proved so difficult to commit myself to a particular theory of the Jews' origin that the only way I could begin the book was to simply acknowledge the problem without solving it, and I have been troubled ever since by the fact that this was the best all my years of learning and reading allowed me to do.

But my interest in the question of Jewish origin goes beyond the questions of geography and chronology, where and when to start Jewish history. An origin is not just a beginning; it is a "beginning that explains," not just the first point in a sequence of events but the answer to a question about how something came to be or why it exists. What really bothered me about not knowing where to start Jewish history was that I could not answer this most fundamental of questions. It is not that scholarship hasn't tried to address it—in fact, it offers an excess of answers—but those answers are inconsistent and conjectural, and it isn't hard to challenge them. I did not presume to think I could answer a question so many previous scholars have failed to resolve, but I at least wanted to have a better understanding of why it had proven so difficult to answer. This is what led me to undertake the present book, which is not an attempt to answer the question I struggled to address in the earlier book but an effort to explore and reflect on the history of the search and the directions it is now taking.

Why is it so difficult to pinpoint an origin for the Jews? I have already mentioned one reason. As I have noted, for most of their history—and to this day for many—Jews looked to the Five Books of Moses to understand where they came from, but the authority of its narrative came into question in the eighteenth and nineteenth centuries with the onset of a critical scholarship that treats the biblical text as a humanly authored document. One of the most consequential accomplishments of this scholarship (and a major reason many reject its findings) is its successful challenge to the Bible as a description of how things originated, and that challenge includes not just the Bible's creation account but its explanation for the origin of people, including the Israelites to whom later Jews would trace their ancestry. I could spend the better part of this book elaborating all the reasons scholars are now skeptical of the Bible as a historical source. Suffice it to say for now that it is not the secure starting point for Jewish history that it is often assumed to be. To this day we do not know the circumstances in which biblical literature was composed, though it is clear that the story told in the Five Books of Moses was not written by an eyewitness to the events it describes. While we certainly cannot dismiss its testimony out of hand, scholars are especially skeptical of how the Bible depicts the earliest history of the Israelites, the age of Abraham and Moses. To embrace the testimony of Genesis and other biblical books as the narrative of how the Jews originated is not only to accept events that are implausible by the standards of modern historiography but to risk missing what is not registered in its text, the part of the story unknown to its authors.

If the problem was simply one of how to reach beyond our sources, however, that by itself does not distinguish the question of Jewish origin from any other question we might ask about ancient Jewish history. Among the particular challenges posed by a search for the origin of the Jews, there are two I would highlight. The first is the difficulty of defining what we mean by the Jews. Do we have in mind a group of people united by a common lineage, an extended tribe that descends from the same small set of ancestors? Are we referring to a community constituted through a shared religious experience or a common set of beliefs and ritual practices? The Jews have been defined by scholars in many different ways—as a nation, a race, a religion, an ethnicity—and polling suggests that Jews themselves differ in how they would define themselves, some emphasizing their religious observance, others indicating their parentage, still others defining Jewishness as a set of cultural characteristics. The problem these differences pose for us is that each of these definitions connotes something different about the origin of the Jews. If the Jews are to be defined by their ancestry, a search for their origin might involve a quest to identify those ancestors. If we are focused on Judaism as a faith, we might focus instead on trying to understand the origin of the beliefs and practices that shape Jewish religious life. If we take seriously how people define their own identity, it is not clear even that the word "Jew" is the right label for this people. In certain periods of history, the Jews referred to themselves as "Israel" or used other self-designations like "Hebrew," terms that imply different things about their origin in their own right. There is no clear way for a scholar to decide among these different conceptions of Jewishness without arbitrarily or anachronistically privileging one definition over the others, and that builds into our quest an irresolvable ambiguity about when and where to begin, what evidence to look for, and what will count as an answer.

A second major challenge is the difficulty of pinpointing what we mean by an origin. The dictionary defines an origin as a point or place where something begins, and that is sometimes what scholars are referring to when they talk about the origin of the Jews—an origin in a particular period or part of the world. But the meaning of an origin runs much deeper than that, and the concept is perplexing in ways that continue to confound well-trained philosophers. Sometimes we use the word "origin" to mean roots—the things or conditions out of which something grows or emerges. With that conception of origin, we would investigate what happened prior to a thing's emergence: the ancestry from which it descends, for example. Often, however, we use the word "origin" to refer to a breaking free from the past: something originates at the point at which it becomes discontinuous with what has gone before. In that case we are looking not to trace continuity but to understand what happens after a moment of discontinuity or rupture. By the origin of the Jews do we mean how Jews developed out of what preceded them or the process that distinguished them from that which existed before? The concept of origin encompasses both possibilities.

Many of us who use the term "origin" may not think very carefully about what we mean by the term—I know I did not prior to taking on this project—and our confusion about the concept is part of what makes origins so difficult to pin down. Since everything is rooted in what precedes it, going back to the beginning of the universe, it is always possible to push an origin further and further in the past, and there is no clear-cut rule for how to distinguish an origin from a mere transitional moment—that decision is always going to depend on our starting point as interpreters of the past. Some of us are looking to understand what a thing was like in its initial or earliest form. Others are trying to understand a process by which something becomes something else. Some treat origins as little more than a departure gate, as a point from which something begins but ultimately is to be left behind. For Charles Darwin the origin of life was this kind of origin; what interested in him was not the question of how life first appeared but the ongoing process of natural selection that began after this moment of origin. For others origins predetermine what originates from them. A thing's origin exerts an influence over it, and remains a part of it, for the duration of its existence; and knowing that origin is therefore essential for understanding what that thing is or is capable of becoming. There is no way to reach a definitive understanding of origin because the concept itself is so hazy, so hard to pin down, and has been understood in so many different ways. This is why we cannot begin this study with a definition of origin. It would certainly be nice to begin with a clear understanding of what we are talking about, but scholarship has never been clear or consistent about what it means by origin, and we would be artificially narrowing our search if we decided that only certain ways of thinking about the topic deserve attention. We will therefore have to try to sort out what we mean by origin as we go along.

But maybe this is a reason not to undertake a study like this. The search for origins poses so many evidentiary and philosophical problems that there have long been scholars who have rejected the search for origin as a futile or misguided quest. Already in 1866, for example, the Société de Linguistique de Paris, one of the first great academic societies devoted to the scientific study of language, prohibited further discussion about the origin of language because the question had led so many scholars on a wild goose chase in pursuit of an original mother tongue, and linguists were not the only ones fed up with excessive conjecture. In *The Elementary Forms of Religious Life*, published in 1912, the sociologist Émile Durkheim (1858–1917) dismissed the search for the origin of religion as a nonscientific pursuit that "should be resolutely discarded." "There was no given moment when religion began to exist," he observed, "and there is consequently no need of finding ourselves a means to transport ourselves thither in thought." The anthropologist Bronislaw Malinowski (1884–1942) was similarly dismissive of the search for origin in his field—in his words, "a search in the nebulous realms of

the undocumented, unrecorded historic past . . . [where] speculation can roam freely, unhampered by fact." By the early twentieth
century, there were also historians dismissive of the search for origin as a delusional quest, an "embryogenic obsession" in the words
of the early twentieth-century historian Marc Bloch, and one can
find a similar attitude in fields ranging from psychology (William
James's preference for understanding the fruits of religious experience as opposed to its roots) to philosophy (Friedrich Nietzsche's
rejection of the search for the origin of values) to literary studies
(W. K. Wimsatt, Jr. and Monroe Beardsley's notion of the "intentional fallacy," judging a work in light of conjectures about the au-
thorial intentions that motivated its composition).

It bothered many of these scholars that the search for origin was
hopelessly speculative, but that was not the only issue. Scholars like
Durkheim and Malinowski also rejected the search for origin as beside the point for understanding social, religious, and cultural life.
The primitive societies Malinowski studied were preoccupied with
origins, producing various kinds of mythology to explain and justify
the institutions of the present. In his view scholarship should have
a different focus, explaining social institutions not by turning to an
imagined origin but by seeking to understand their function and
meaning in the context of living communities. Bloch's objection to
"the idol of origin" had to do with its confusion of beginnings with
causes, ancestry with explanation, which he thought had to be more
clearly distinguished. Later generations of scholars—I have in mind
figures like Roland Barthes, Maurice Blanchot, Jean Baudrillard,
Judith Butler, and many other thinkers active in the second half
of the twentieth century—went further in their critique, arguing
variations of the idea of origin as something that isn't really there,
an illusion or an errant form of thought in need of correction. For
these and other scholars, the search to understand origins represents scholarly thinking gone astray. The curiosity at work seems
deeply wired into how people think about things, and yet there is
something misconceived or futile about it: it can never find what it
is looking for; its vision is distorted by delusion.

According to some of this kind of scholarship, origins elude de-
tection not because they are hidden or remote but because they do
not really exist in the world out there. It is a mistake to think of an

origin as something that can be recovered, tracked down, or dug up, they argue, because it arises from the mind and how it grasps reality. The description of origin as a chimera or an obsession implies that it is a mental projection, and the only way to illumine an origin in this sense is to turn inward to understand what impels the mind to think in this way. As we will see over the course of this book, in fact, some scholars today, drawing on psychology or cognitive science, focus on the mental or cognitive mechanisms at work in the human attachment to origins, tracing people's desire for information about their ancestors or their place of origin to prerational psychological need. Others treat origin as an act of imagination, posing questions drawn from literary studies or folklore analysis: What cultural and social functions do origin stories play? What meanings do they superimpose on reality? From these kinds of perspective, it makes no sense to investigate origins empirically, to look for them as if they were events that happened in the past: the subject requires inquiry into the workings of consciousness, reason, or imagination.

It is one thing for scholars to apply this kind of perspective to Genesis or the creation accounts that have survived from other ancient cultures. Scholarship has long been accustomed to treating such narratives as "myths," false or fictive accounts of origin, which means that it no longer treats them as sources of information about origin and instead focuses on what they reveal about their authors and their perceptions of origin. It is another thing to apply a similar approach to the origin narratives produced by modern scholarship itself, narratives that claim to be an accurate representation of reality, that are grounded in facts, that adhere to the critical or scientific standards we now rely on to distinguish truth from falsehood. One of the great ambitions of reason is to illumine the origin of things— the origin of the world, the origin of species, the origin of language, the origin of understanding itself. Think of all the prodigious works of scholarship that have emanated from the scholarly ambition to understand the origin of things: Darwin's theory of evolution, Alfred Wegener's effort to account for the origin of continents and ocean basins, Georges Lemaître's notion of the Big Bang, and on and on. The quest to understand the world by going back to the moment of origins goes back to ancient Greek philosophy, and it would seem self-defeating for scholars to renounce their power to offer that kind of insight. And yet scholars in recent years have been doing precisely that by treating the origin accounts emerging from scholarship as fictions or secular creation myths.

An example is a book that made a lot of waves in the field of paleontology when it was originally published in French in 1994, *Explaining Human Origins* by Wiktor Stoczkowski. The main thesis of the book is that *all* scholarly accounts of human origin, no matter how scientific they might be, are fictionalized. To draw disjointed pieces of evidence into a meaningful account, they enlist common-sense ideas of causality devoid of empirical support and draw the structure of their narratives from preexisting storylines. They do enlist data, but those data can support many different kinds of narrative, which is why, in Enlightenment-era accounts, the origin of humanity is a story of technological progress; in Soviet-era accounts, a story of communal cooperation; and in feminist narratives, a story of matriarchal rule. In Stoczkowski's view, there is no way to determine the origin of humanity; the questions that drive the search for human origin can be addressed only through myth or theology, not by appeal to reason or to the data.

The intellectual trend I am describing here has influenced a number of fields—anthropology, history, art history, linguistics, even archaeology—and so it should not be a surprise that there are scholars of Jewish studies who have developed a similar aversion to the search for origin. An example of what I have in mind is an argument developed by the historian Amos Funkenstein in an essay titled "The Dialectics of Assimilation," published in 1995. On the surface the essay is an attempt to correct how scholars understand the process of assimilation, but it is also an attempt to disabuse the field of a certain concept of origin that Funkenstein finds implicit in the thinking of some of the founding figures of the field—Heinrich Graetz, Yitzhak Baer, and even the great scholar of mysticism Gershom Scholem. According to these scholars, a clear separation can be made between what is original in Judaism and what is secondary and superficial, between what was there in its earliest form and what developed later on as a result of interactions with other cultures. The original dimension of Judaism refers to qualities emerging organically from within its culture or religion. These qualities were there from the beginning, which makes them a source of authenticity, and without them, Judaism ceases to be Judaism. Secondary characteristics, by contrast, are acquired characteristics that Judaism has picked up from external sources, the foreign cultures with which the Jews have interacted over the course of their history. Original components of Judaism include the monotheistic idea and the Hebrew language, enduring qualities that persist throughout its history; secondary characteristics include the use of German, in the form of Yiddish, by Jews in Eastern Europe. Funkenstein rejects any distinction between original and secondary; that is, he rejects the idea that there was a period at the beginning of Jewish history when the Jews existed in an original form uncontaminated by external influences.

Whether or not Funkenstein is fairly describing his predecessors is less important for our argument than the fact that his critique reflects the broader suspicion of origin that had taken root by the time he wrote this essay. According to Funkenstein, this perspective on Jewish history suffers from the "fallacy of origin," something like Bloch's notion of the "idol of origins"—the idea that, by uncovering the origin of a nation, you lay bare its nature, essence, and true character over against less authentic aspects of its culture picked up later through borrowing and imitation. Any idea of a discrete origin for the Jews assumes that their culture once existed in some form separate from its environment, and Funkenstein rejects such an idea, which may explain why he does not offer his own account of the origin of the Jews. To understand Jewish culture, he argued, one should treat it as the result of an ongoing process rather than interpreting it in light of an imagined beginning that cannot be shown to have existed to begin with.

If this critique of the "fallacy of origin" is correct, is there any point to a search like this? This is the question that drives this book. On the one hand, scholars have not ceased trying to understand the origin of the Jews, and have proven remarkably perseverant and resourceful in their search for new insights. They may have gone astray, but they have learned from their mistakes, acknowledging their biases, adopting new tools and methods from other fields, amassing additional evidence, and proposing more sophisticated hypotheses. Simply disregarding all that research would represent a form of self-imposed ignorance. On the other hand, critics like Funkenstein cannot be ignored when they argue for something misguided about the search for the origin of the Jews.

What are we to make of the contradiction between these different kinds of scholarship? Is the search for the origin of the Jews a mistake? Are the skeptics too quick to dismiss what such a search can reveal? One of the central problems I wrestle with in this book is the idea that origins might be a fallacy. In scholarship today there are basically two approaches to origin that are in conflict with one another, what we can think of as an objective and a subjective approach to the question. The objective approach treats origin ontologically and empirically, as a real thing in the world— something that happened long ago or that involves processes that are difficult to observe and comprehend but that can be treated as an object of knowledge, as something to be understood about the world. The subjective approach treats origin from a psychological, phenomenological, or postmodern perspective, approaching it as a product of how the mind thinks about reality. The mind might feel impelled to seek out origins, but there is nothing to be discovered, not at least in the world beyond the thinking self. Most of the approaches we survey in this book fall under the objective category of origin—they treat the origin of the Jews as a hidden truth that can be uncovered—but they all come up against critiques that reject the premise that there is an origin hidden somewhere in the past to be uncovered. To search for the origin of the Jews in a way that embraces the full range of scholarly perspectives, modern and postmodern, means we will have to contend with the differences between these perspectives, and that is no mean challenge given that one is a direct rejection of the other.

The Politics of Origin

The conceptual slipperiness of origin is not the only challenge we will face in our search for the origin of the Jews. We will also have to reckon with an aspect of this subject that goes beyond the kind of problem that scholarship is in a position to resolve through inquiry and reasoned debate, a political dimension that makes the subject highly emotional, ethically fraught, irresolvably contentious, and sometimes very hurtful for many people. The scholarly search for the origin of the Jews is more than two centuries old, and for the entirety of that history, it has been tied to the political status of the Jews—to their status within European society and, more recently, to the legitimacy of the State of Israel. The politics has produced competing origin accounts of the Jews that mirror the conflicts between the Jews and their enemies. Some would turn to scholarship in the hope of overcoming the partisanship and prejudice at work in these conflicts, putting their trust in historical inquiry or the scientific method, but others would argue that scholarship itself is a part of these conflicts, that there is no way even for scholars to be politically neutral about the origin of the Jews no matter what method they use or how many facts they marshal.

The particular search described in this book was shaped by political debates in eighteenth- and nineteenth-century Europe. This was the age when today's nation-states emerged from the empires and kingdoms that had ruled much of Europe in earlier centuries, and those new nation-states often defined themselves by an appeal to genealogy, a shared ancestry: the French understood themselves to be the descendants of the ancient Gauls; the Italians were successors to the ancient Romans; the Germans traced their roots back to Aryan invaders from Persia. The nation being revived was usually an ancient or prehistoric people, distant ancestors who had always lived in the land or migrated there thousands of years ago; and scholarship's role, accomplished through philology, historical inquiry, archaeology, and other approaches, was to reconnect to the past, to resuscitate the ancient identity of the nation by ferreting out information about its ancestors, uncovering what they were like, and thereby reminding the nation who it truly was or was meant to be.

Scholarly interest in the origin of the Jews was a part of this process of national identity construction—in fact, the question of Jewish origin was at the center of this scholarship because of the Jews' role as a kind of foil for the Germans and other national groups. The various theories that scholars developed to account for the origin of the Jews were often tied to the "Jewish question" that emerged in the wake of the Enlightenment and its call for the modernization, emancipation, and integration of the Jews—the question of how exactly to fit the Jews into the European political system and social order. Prior to the Enlightenment and the onset of the modern nation-state, Jews in Europe were treated as a separate population by the Christian majority, and Jews saw and governed themselves in this way as well. The rise of modernity brought with it the question of what to do with these semiautonomous communities—whether to leave the Jews as a separate minority governed by its own laws or to try to assimilate them into the larger society. The political debate over the Jews' role in society is part of what motivated scholars of the period to investigate their origin, with the goal of understanding what had made the Jews so different from non-Jews. Was such difference an inherent and enduring racial characteristic, an indelible quality that could not be changed, or was it more recent and reversible—a consequence of social conditions like anti-Semitism that could be changed if those conditions were changed? The scholarship we are focused on is pretty much coterminous with the modern nation-state, and what was at stake in it in the nineteenth and early twentieth centuries was the political question of how the Jews fit into the emerging political structure of the European nation-state system: whether there was a place for them within that structure, whether they could be assimilated into it or had to be treated as a separate community within the European state, or whether they needed to develop a state of their own.

The political dimensions of the study of Jewish origin remained central in European intellectual culture throughout the nineteenth and early twentieth centuries, especially in Germany, where the debate culminated horrifically, in the 1940s, when the Nazis implemented their "final solution" to the Jewish question. The way this scholarship abetted or allied itself with the Nazis is yet another reason that scholars today have misgivings about the search for Jewish origin, but the search itself did not end after World War II. Scholars revised their approaches in a way meant to overcome the distorting effects of political allegiance and prejudice, and they developed new approaches—new forms of textual, archaeological, and biological study—that were much more refined from a methodological and factual perspective than what earlier scholars had relied on. According to critics, however, the scholarly search for origin remained just as political as it had been before the war. The chief issue, as the reader might guess, is the establishment of the State of Israel in

1948 and its conflict with the Palestinians, a conflict that involves competing claims about the geographic origin of the Jews and their relationship to the ancient inhabitants of Judea, and whether those ancestors or the ancestors of the Palestinians were there first. The driving force is still nationalism, but late twentieth-century nationalism, and the question is no longer how the Jews fit into Europe but how the Jewish state and Palestinians fit into the global political order that has been in place since World War II.

One of the differences between the situation today and the situation prior to World War II is the rise of the notion of "indigenous people," a legal status that entails certain rights. In a process that began at the beginning of the twentieth century but has taken off since the 1970s, the world (in the form of the United Nations) has come to recognize that indigenous communities—communities with a historical connection to precolonial or presettler societies—have rights that need to be recognized. What sometimes engenders conflict is the fact that the term "indigenous" is extremely hard to pin down—it can refer to descendants of the earliest inhabitants of the land and also to the most recent inhabitants prior to European colonization—and its ambiguity has led to differences over who should be counted as an indigenous people. The Jews who live in Israel have some of the attributes of an indigenous people. They can claim an ancestral connection to ancient inhabitants of Judea, and they have suffered the kinds of experiences that other indigenous peoples have suffered. But from a legal perspective, they do not fall clearly into the category because, with the exception of the small Jewish population present in Palestine prior to the nineteenth century, they were not present in the land at the time of its colonization—in fact, they are the ones accused of being the European colonizers. The challenge of defining who counts as indigenous is not limited to the conflict between Jews and Palestinians. Groups like the Marsh Dwellers of Iraq have gone on and off official listings of indigenous groups for no apparent reason, and many groups who see themselves as indigenous must struggle to have the rights that come with that status respected. The Israeli-Palestinian conflict, now about a century old, predates the rise of indigenousness as an officially recognized status, but the question of who counts as a native and who is an outsider, who was there first and who came later, has long been one of the historical issues at the core of the conflict.

This is where scholarship has been drawn into the fray: the question of whether a given people were the original occupants of the land or have some direct connection to such occupants would seem to be a historical one, and people on each side of the conflict have turned to scholarship to affirm their self-perceptions. Many Israelis in the 1950s and 1960s became interested in archaeology as a way to connect to their history, seeing in its discoveries confirmation of their ancestors' presence in the land in ancient times; and while archaeology has much less significance in contemporary Israeli society, it has been embraced by some settlers to establish their primacy in the West Bank, serving to uncover the presence of biblical ancestors who were there prior to the region's Palestinian population. A corresponding field of Palestinian archaeology never developed in the same way, but there did emerge other kinds of scholarship, including biblical studies like Keith Whitelam's *The Invention of Ancient Israel* from 1996, which asserted the Palestinians' status of original or first inhabitants of the land by arguing against the historical existence of a biblical Israel in Iron Age Canaan. Just as nineteenth-century scholars theorized about the origin of the Jews in support of different positions on the Jewish question, scholarship today is marshaled in support of different positions in the Israeli–Palestinian conflict.

Indeed, the influence of the conflict may have seeped into how scholars think about the concept of origin itself. One of the most influential works to reflect in a deep way on the concept of beginnings and origins is a book by Edward Said (1935–2003), *Beginnings: Intention and Method*, which he published in 1975 prior to his more famous study, *Orientalism*. Said's argument depends on an opposition he draws between the concepts of origin and beginning. For Said an origin is a kind of metaphysical starting point, an initial state beyond history from which a later reality derives. The most famous articulation of origin in this sense is Genesis, but it can take a secular form in the guise of any philosophical or political system that purports to derive reality from a foundational moment, a founding figure, a first principle, or an inaugural state. In contrast a "beginning," according to Said, does not arise from an established starting point. There is no one way to begin, as the history of fiction demonstrates: one can start in the middle of things if one likes or begin in one way and then start over at a later point. Said detects something authoritarian in origins: they dictate the way reality is supposed to be, hold sway over what comes after them, and impose a distinction between the chosen and the unchosen. Beginnings, by contrast, are secular, modern, and self-determining, born of a mind that embraces its power to create its own reality and chooses how its story will unfold.

Although Said was one of the world's most prominent Palestinian activists, nowhere in *Beginnings* is there any reference to the Israeli-Palestinian conflict: the work seems on the surface at least to be very detached from the conflict and from Said's identity as a Palestinian, and yet some of his commentators see a connection. This was how Said's work was read by his disciple Joseph Massad, for example, a professor of modern Arab intellectual history at Columbia University, where Said taught for forty years. Although Said was born in Jerusalem, Massad argues, he had no interest in Palestine as a point of origin in a Saidian sense, since that idea was tainted for him, and he preferred to think of Palestine as a "beginning," a point of departure for the creation of something new. By reading Said's biography into his distinction between origins and beginnings, Massad suggests that a description of origin that seems to have nothing to do with the Israeli-Palestinian conflict was actually born of that conflict, reflecting Said's opposition to Zionism and his aspiration to develop an alternative Palestinian identity that rejected not only the Jews' historical claims but also what he took to be the origin-centeredness of Zionism. Massad's analysis suggests that the Israeli-Palestinian conflict not only is influencing how scholars think about the question of Jewish origin but also has shaped one of the most important works of relevant academic theory from the past fifty years, a book routinely cited in contemporary discussions of origins and beginnings. We will see other examples where the concept of origin has become entangled with Zionism and where resistance to origin is allied with resistance to Israel.

If the scholarly search for the origin of the Jews is unavoidably political, if it played a role in anti-Semitism, and if it is helping to feed the Israeli-Palestinian conflict today, does that mean there is something inherently corrupted or even harmful about such a search? Are its results always going to be skewed by the prejudices and allegiances of the scholars doing the research, or is there some way to depoliticize the topic and to pursue it in a way that isn't serving the interest of either the Jews or their enemies? The answers to these questions depend on one's underlying conception of scholarship. Especially since the 1960s many scholars have become very conscious of the political dimensions of their guild: every society has its "general politics of truth," argued Michel Foucault, and scholarship is a kind of technique by which it controls the difference between the true and the false. From this perspective we could never hope to discover the origin of the Jews in an absolute sense: we can understand it only as conceived within a particular "regime of truth." But it should be noted that only some scholars are persuaded by this view. Others are pursuing the question of Jewish origin in earnest, uncovering new evidence and proposing new theories. They put their faith in the methodologies of modern scholarship, empirical evidence, and the checks and balances of peer review; and they reject the idea that the results of such scholarship are irredeemably tainted by politics, ideology, or the scholar's self-interest.

I find it impossible to dismiss the argument that the scholarship of Jewish origin, certainly as practiced in the past but also as it is being pursued today, is really at its core a form of political self-positioning. But then again if the search for the origin of the Jews is political, so too, one presumes, is the decision not to undertake the search. One of the reasons I am pursuing this quest is because it has given me a way to reflect on scholarship's rejection of origin as a politicized form of inquiry. Why is it that a question once seen as capable of being answered by scholars in an illuminating way—a question that drew me to the kind of scholarship I practice—now feels too contentious to pose? And does acknowledging the political dimensions of the question mean that we should give up trying to answer it? Maybe it is best in the end to treat the question of Jewish origin as a taboo subject, a field of inquiry too politically heated to pursue in a constructive way; but from my perspective ruling a question out of bounds for political reasons is significant—a renunciation of forms of reasoning used to understand not only the origin of the Jews but the origin of other peoples as well. If we are to give up on this search, we should at least understand as best we can why we are closing that door.

After Origin

Given all the reasons there are *not* to investigate the origin of the Jews, what is there to learn by revisiting the question? More than two centuries of research have not yielded certain conclusions or even a stable consensus. Over the course of its history, the scholarship has been skewed by theological bias and anti-Semitism and has become entangled in the Israeli-Palestinian conflict. Funkenstein and other scholars have argued that ascertaining the origin of the Jews does not tell us anything important about the Jews anyways. Why pursue a quest that has proven so irresolvable and quixotic, that has been used to validate prejudice, that is arguably beside the point for understanding the Jews?

One reason is that there is still a lot of curiosity about the origin of the Jews. There are many different kinds of people interested in the origin of the Jews—Jews themselves seeking to better understand the origin of their own identity or culture; Christians and Muslims seeking to understand the prehistory of their own religious traditions; Palestinians and others whose own sense of origin is tied in some way to that of the Jews despite the antagonism, not to mention anti-Semites who think the origin of the Jews validates their prejudices. Of course, many people could not care less what scholarship has to say on the subject, or reject its conclusions on religious or political grounds, but many look to scholarship for answers, and the scholarship would seem to support many different and contradictory accounts. Whether scholarship can provide the kind of insight that people seek from it is an open question, but it may at least be helpful to clarify what it has been able to uncover about the subject, why scholars reconstruct the origin of the Jews in such different ways, and why it has proven so difficult to get to the bottom of things.

What's more, there is no reason to completely despair of scholarship's potential to illumine the origin of the Jews. There has been continued research and reflection on the subject, scholarship that has expanded the evidence, introduced new perspectives, and refined the picture. There now exists a robust critique of the search for the origin of the Jews, scholarship that questions the motives and objectivity of those who have tried to address the question, but even that critique advances the search in a way, introducing alternative conceptions of origin that should be factored into the equation if our goal is to gain a comprehensive understanding of the subject, and often proposing its own alternative origin accounts of the Jews. A good portion of what follows is an attempt to sketch in a history of the scholarly search for the origin of the Jews as it has unfolded over the past two centuries, but that search is by no means over, and indeed, in some respects, it has been reenergized in the past two decades, and some of this scholarship is very cutting- edge, intriguing, and provocative. It seems worth asking what this continued research is revealing even as we wrestle with all the reasons there are to be skeptical of it. What has it uncovered about the origin of the Jews? Have scholars found a way to overcome the kind of obstacles and objections described earlier in this chapter? Where is the search going?

The following book is an exploration of what we know or think we know about the origin of the Jews. Scholars have literally written hundreds of books on the topic and come up with scores of explanations, theories, and historical reconstructions, but this book is a first-of-its-kind effort to trace the history of the different approaches that have been applied to the question, including genealogy, linguistics, archaeology, psychology, sociology, and genetics. I cannot offer the reader definitive conclusions, but I do see what follows as an attempt to push our understanding forward, to deepen how we think about the question.

Beyond wanting to illumine the history of the Jews, however, I must confess to having another reason to pursue this inquiry, one that is tied more to the concept of origin than to the Jews per se. My own perspective as a scholar was formed in an academic culture influenced by Michel Foucault (1926–1984), Jacques Derrida (1930–2004), and other thinkers associated with postmodernism: scholars who treated the search for origin as a false, restrictive, irrelevant, or even dangerous way of thinking and who developed alternative forms of inquiry that were premised on the absence of origin, the denial of anything that might count as a starting point, a foundation, or a source. While I could not decipher all their arguments at the time, the message came through loud and clear that it was a kind of intellectual sin to be wondering about origins in the way I was inclined to do. Almost twenty-five years later, I see that graduate students in my field are still highly distrustful of origins. As I was completing the first draft of this book in 2015, there appeared a volume edited by the scholar of religion Russell McCutcheon, *Fabricating Origins*, that was born of this distrust. As the title of the volume suggests, many of the essays featured in it, written by young scholars fresh out of graduate school, treat origins as fictions, as something the imagination makes up. By no means has academia in general given up on the search for origins as a way of understanding why things are the way they are, but an attitude of dismissal—and a disdain for or distrust of the kind of scholarship that seeks to recover origins—remains ingrained in much of humanistic scholarship.

Beyond wanting to explore what we know about the origin of the Jews, this book is an attempt to wrestle with the distrust of origins that I have inherited from earlier scholars and that is being passed on to the next generation. The most basic question I am posing in this book is this: can scholarship today answer people's questions about origins—can it satisfy their curiosity—or are the skeptics right to dismiss this kind of inquiry as a chasing after a chimera? Many scholars see the value of this kind of intellectual quest, pursuing it through archaeology, genetics, and other fields; many other scholars are highly critical of such inquiry; and I happen to be one of those torn between these perspectives. This book is an attempt to think aloud about the contradiction between these approaches, to look at a question of origin from the vantage point of those hoping to illumine it *and* from the perspective of those dismissive of the question in as balanced a way as I know how to develop, and to see what we might learn by juxtaposing them. I am not proposing to revive the search for origin; neither am I giving it up. My hope is to help readers better understand the different ways that scholars today frame the origin of social identity, not just of the Jews but of other religious and ethnic groups as well. Whether there is any way beyond those differences is something we will wrestle with in the conclusion, but the point of our quest is not to reach a definitive answer but to better understand what it is that we are asking—to situate present-day efforts to address the question of Jewish origin in light of the history of scholarship, to compare and contrast different approaches and theories, and to examine the motives, premises, and prejudices that color how scholars think about this subject. I certainly cannot promise that we will figure out once and for all how to begin the story of the Jews, but I will feel that I have succeeded to some extent if this book leads readers' thinking about questions of origin to a different place from where it started.

CHAPTER ONE

Genealogical Bewilderment

LOST ANCESTORS AND ELUSIVE LINEAGES

*Genealogy becomes a mania, an obsessive struggle to penetrate the past
and snatch meaning from an infinity of names. At some point the search
becomes futile—there is nothing left to find, no meaning to be dredged out
of old receipts, newspaper articles, letters, accounts of events that seemed so
important fifty or seventy years ago. All that remains is the insane urge to
keep looking, insane because the searcher has no idea what he seeks. What
will it be? A photograph? A will? A fragment of a letter? The only way to
find out is to look at everything, because it is often when the searcher has
gone far beyond the border of futility that he finds the object he never knew
he was looking for.*

—HENRY WIENCEK

ORIGINS ARE OFTEN DESCRIBED as lost or hidden away, a buried treasure to be sought after, a secret to be penetrated or a lost
memory to be retrieved, as demonstrated by book titles like *The
Mystery of Life's Origin, Hidden History: The Secret Origin of the
First World War*, or *Philology: The Forgotten Origin of the Humanities*. One of the key insights of modernity was the realization that
we live in a world where the origin of almost everything is veiled
from us: the origin of the world, the origin of life, the origin of the
reasoning that impels us to inquire into origins.

This is where scholarship has an important role as an agent that
can help to reconnect us to our hidden origins. Where people once

turned to religion and myth to satisfy their curiosity about origins, many of us now turn to science and historical scholarship for answers about how things truly began, and these fields can claim some major advances. Darwin's insight into the origin of species involved the uncovering of a common ancestry hidden in the background of living species that earlier scientists had supposed to have originated independently of each other. To hypothesize a Big Bang at the beginning of the cosmos, an event that took place fourteen billion years ago, scientists had to work backward from what they could see of the universe today, from the distances between heavenly bodies and the speeds at which they were moving, and it took another feat of detective work to figure out that the continents all originated from the breakup of a supercontinent hundreds of millions of years ago. The origin of the Jews also lies in the realm of the unseen, and if scholars have had any success in uncovering it, it is because they enlist the same techniques used to uncover the origin of species, language, and religion, methods by which the mind traverses gulfs of time and discerns invisible causes.

The irony here is that if anyone bears responsibility for "losing" the origin of the Jews, it is probably the modern scholar. It was the critical study of the Bible that called the biblical account into question in the first place and questioned the continuity between the ancient Israelites and later Jews. In the same period geologists, biologists, and scholars of the ancient Near East greatly expanded the length of the past, making it much murkier and harder to penetrate, and the critical study of creation myths and foundation legends showed that such stories often conceal the truth of how things originate. But having introduced the problem, modern scholarship also promised a solution by introducing new ways of searching for the origin of the Jews. The following chapters survey these various approaches, examining a range of methods and theories that come from different disciplines but that all have the goal of finding origins that are lost, hidden, or forgotten.

This and the next chapter are devoted to methods that frame the search for origin as a research for roots, for distant ancestors. The root is one of the oldest and most pervasive metaphors for origin in use today; it depicts whatever is being understood as a tree or plant that branches out from something buried in the ground, and implies the existence of something flowing from the root into the trunk and branches—identity, culture, DNA—that connects everything together into an organic whole. As Christy Wampole has pointed out in a recent study of the metaphorical thinking involved, the root captures a number of the qualities that people associate with origins. It is often seen as the most stationary and enduring part of the tree; it is considered older than the rest of the tree, the part from which everything else arises; and at the same time it is the most inaccessible part of the tree, connecting it to the ground and feeding its growth but all in a way that is invisible. As it happens the root is not older than the rest of the tree, and the comparison is misleading in other ways. Scholars have made various attempts to challenge the analogy, but it continues as one of the most productive metaphors for thought, structuring how scholars conceive of the relationships among species, languages, human populations, and much else, and it captures the subterranean character of origins that is our focus here: our sense of origin as something buried underground, something important for understanding what the tree has grown into but cannot be seen, and something that has to be dug out to be understood.

In the next two chapters I will focus on two of the methods scholars use to uncover the root of the Jews—genealogy and etymology. In both cases the Jews are conceived as an organic and interconnected whole, a tree with many proliferating branches and stems that grow in different directions but that all arise from a firmly situated root composed of the ancestors from which the Jews descend. The search for origin is the effort to follow the structure of the tree backward to this hidden root. Both genealogy and etymology are about establishing connections between then and now, but they are also about tracing the flow of something through these connections, something transmitted through the tree's invisible vascular structure, from the ancestors to their present-day descendants. In what follows I explore what scholars have been able to learn about the origin of the Jews in these ways but also think about the limits of this way of conceiving origin; why it is difficult from a practical, methodological perspective to establish the connections needed to relate Jews to their ancient ancestors; and why it is that, at a deeper, conceptual level, some scholars think it is never really possible to trace something back to its roots.

The Search for Ancestors

The present chapter begins this survey by focusing on genealogy, the study of family lineages. Genealogical inquiry is arguably the oldest of the approaches I examine in this book—it lies behind the Book of Genesis itself—but my focus is on its role as a modern form of origin research, a mode of critical historical inquiry marked by careful, skeptical approach to documents, and by increasingly sophisticated ways of collecting, searching, and analyzing data. Genealogical research in this sense might well be the most popular method by which Jews today investigate their origins. I once happened to stay in a Jerusalem hotel hosting a conference by the International Association of Jewish Genealogical Societies, which is an umbrella organization comprising more than seventy local and national organizations from fourteen different countries. It felt like a much more inclusive affair than the academic conferences I normally attend, involving not just professional scholars but hundreds of hobbyists and people on various kinds of personal quests to understand their family histories. There are recognized genealogical experts, but to an outsider at least there is not as sharp a line between professionals and amateurs as there is in other academic disciplines, which makes genealogy a less snooty field than others but also raises questions about who to believe and what counts as reliable research.

The difficulty of distinguishing the reliable from the unreliable in genealogical research is a challenge that we will have to struggle with as we consider what this kind of research might tell us about the origin of the Jews. For me, however, it is not a reason to simply dismiss this kind of research since, for better or worse, far more Jews use the methods of genealogical research to investigate their origins than any of the other methods described in this book, with the exception of the field of genetics (treated in chapter 8).

One thing that is clear is that we cannot simply rely on the genealogical information in the Bible as a starting point for our inquiry. The authors of the genealogies recorded in the Bible also seem to have worked from a careful examination of sources—oral traditions in some cases, written documents in others—but their genealogical claims have not held up very well under the lens of critical analysis.

Scholars in the twentieth century noted that the genealogies transmitted in other tribal societies are often quite fluid, undergoing changes to reflect evolving social and political relationships, and they believe the same is true of biblical genealogies as well—that much of their information was probably adapted to reflect changing social conditions in ancient Israel. (It is also possible that the authors of biblical narratives simply invented some of the genealogical information they report in order to advance their story in some way.) Here and there, in fact, we even have direct evidence of genealogical tampering.

An intriguing example—if one is reading the text in Hebrew—is the genealogy of a corrupt priest in Judges 18:30: "Jonathan, son of Gershom, son of Manasseh." The information seems straightforward enough, but in the Hebrew text of Judges there is something odd about how the name Manasseh is spelled: the letter *nun*, corresponding to our letter *n*, is strangely suspended above the line, as if someone had tried to stick it in after the fact without fitting it in completely (see Figure 1). Remove this suspended letter, as many modern commentators are inclined to do, and the remaining consonants spell out the name Moses. The corrupt priest described in this story appears to have been a descendant of the prophet, and it would seem that some later scribe, embarrassed by this fact, tried to protect Moses's reputation by changing his name to the name Manasseh through a belated insertion of the letter *nun*. This is a rare case where we can actually see genealogical tampering, but scholars suspect that much of the genealogical information we have recorded in the Bible may reflect similar revision or even outright fictionalization.

Modern genealogical research seeks to establish genealogies that hold up according to the standards of critical scholarship, crosschecking records and treating dubious sources with an appropriate level of skepticism in an effort to extract reliable information. As a result, genealogy has emerged as an increasingly respected mode of historical research, and many people, Jews and non-Jews, now turn to this kind of research to find out information about their ancestors—so many, in fact, that the endeavor has given rise to a lucrative genealogical industry led by companies with names like Ancestry.com, Geni.com, and Myheritage. (For a sense of how

FIGURE 1. Tampering with a biblical genealogy? The outlined letters betray an effort to wedge the Hebrew letter nun into the name "Moses" in Judges 18:30, evidently in order to conceal the prophet's role in the genealogy of a corrupt priest described in the chapter. The effort was not entirely successful, however, for the inserted nun remains partly suspended over the rest of the word. *Source*: Image reproduced from https://archive.org/details/Aleppo _Codex under Creative Commons Public Domain Mark 1.0 license.

lucrative, note that, according to the consulting firm Global Industry Analysts, it costs people between $1,000 and $18,000 to find out their roots, and that in 2012 Ancestry.com was sold for $1.6 billion.) But as popular as it is, can this kind of research connect a Jew alive today to ancestors living thousands of years ago? There are Jewish families that can trace their lineages hundreds of years, to the time of the expulsion from Spain in 1492 and earlier, but can genealogy go even further into the past? Can it reach all the way back to the beginning, to the earliest forebearers of the Jews?

There are certainly reasons to be dubious of such a possibility. Tracing the lineage of a person alive today all the way back to antiquity has been described as the ultimate challenge for genealogists. Many have tried to surmount the documentary challenges, but success remains elusive. Genealogists can trace certain individuals back to the Middle Ages; but the question I am broaching here is whether it is possible to follow a genealogical trail from the Middle Ages back to antiquity. Genealogists have not been able to do that even for the royal families of Europe, which have lineages that can be traced as far back as Charlemagne in the eighth century CE but not to the ancient Roman Empire. And yet despite the challenges, some now claim to be able to establish this kind of long-term genealogy, purporting to document a lineage for certain Jews that not only goes back to biblical times but traces a line of descent to a specific individual: King David.

This is the goal, for example, of the Shealtiel Family World Association, an organization whose efforts to reconnect the descendants of the Shealtiel family, now reaching some twenty-five hundred people, include annual reunions and the publication of a newsletter, the *Shealtiel Gazette*. After learning from his father that their family descended from King David, Moshe Shaltiel-Gracian, an Israeli-born member of the family who lives in the Chicago area, undertook a twenty-year quest to reconstruct his family's lineage. He claims to be able to prove a lineage for the Shealtiel family that runs through the Exilarchs, medieval leaders of the Babylonian Jewish community who claimed Davidic descent, back to the king himself. Another contemporary would-be Davidic descendent is Susan Roth, an actress, mystic, and founder of the organization Davidic Dynasty, which has sought to identify other descendants of David (such as the comedian Jerry Seinfeld according to Roth), and of the King David Private Museum and Research Center in Tel Aviv (the website of which, unfortunately, is now defunct). In the case of Roth and other Jews with Ashkenazic backgrounds, the link to David is not through the Babylonian Exilarchs but through the medieval French-Jewish commentator Rashi (Rabbi Shlomo Yitzhaki, 1040–1105) via the lineages of such famous rabbis from Central or Eastern Europe as the Maharal of Prague (ca. 1525–1609) and Nachman of Breslov (1772–1810). Many people have sought to trace themselves to King David—I have found a news report from the 1970s that suggests many Jews were interested in such a pursuit back then. What draws our attention to these two recent cases is not just their claim of Davidic descent but their use of the methods of modern genealogical research—the effort to find documentary support for their genealogical claims and even the use of DNA testing to confirm common ancestry among those who believe they descend from the king.

To scholars in other fields, this kind of research will seem preposterous, or at the very least, amateurish. It claims to be able to demonstrate what genealogists have failed to show for any other individual (with the possible exception of the pedigree of the Chinese philosopher Confucius, born in 551 BCE, whose descendants can be traced over some eighty generations into the present era). It is also at odds with biblical scholarship and its doubts about David as a historical figure. But even if we are inclined to dismiss claims of Davidic descent, we should not be too quick to dismiss genealogy as a way of seeking out the origin of the Jews, if only because it raises larger questions. The effort to trace individuals back to King David gives us an opportunity to explore what we know or can prove about the connection between present-day Jews and distant biblical ancestors, but even more importantly for our larger quest, it also gives us a way to reflect on the search for roots in a broader sense—the kind of insight that such research is capable of achieving, the challenges that it must overcome, and some of the hidden problems with conceptualizing the search for origin as a genealogical quest.

Genealogy, as Eviatar Zerubavel points out, is not just a particular method but "a way of thinking," a form of cognition that structures our experience of time, social relationships, and personal identity. We may think of genealogical research as a hobby, but genealogical thinking—the kind that classifies the present by tracing lines of descent back to common ancestors—is actually essential to many forms of scholarly thinking. Somewhere in the background of this way of thinking, as Mary Bouquet has shown, is the European scholarly tradition of using the image of a tree—initially as a way of representing family relationships and the earthly genealogy of Jesus and then, later, in a secular and abstracted form, as a convention of scholarly taxonomy. The root or trunk of the tree signifies the *ur*-form—the earliest form of life, for example, or the earliest proto-language—and the branching out from there signifies increasing diversification over time. The "tree model" or "cladistic" model (from the Greek for "branch") remains central to the scholarly search for origin. The theory of evolution is in part a genealogical inquiry that aims to uncover a common descent for human and nonhuman organisms. In the field of historical linguistics, genealogical thinking structures how scholars describe and explain the relations among languages, with related languages described as mother languages and daughter languages or put into other kind of kinship relations within a linguistic family tree that branches out from a trunk—a proto-language that plays the role of common ancestor. Text-critical scholars similarly organize variant manuscripts according to the tree model in an effort to reconstruct the *ur*-text from which all the texts descend. Although its origins go back to antiquity, genealogical thinking is at the heart of the modern search for origin.

Genealogy, not as a tracing of a family tree but as an underlying structure of thought, is also woven into some of the methods scholars use to investigate the origin of the Jews—the use of historical linguistics to trace the Israelites back to prebiblical ancestors and the use of genetics to trace a biological line of descent from present-day Jews to distant ancestors. If I begin with genealogy, it is not only because its history predates most of the other methods this book considers or because it is the most popular method by which Jews today investigate their ancestry, but also because it gives us a chance to reflect on the root as a metaphor that guides and sometimes misleads people in their search for their origins.

Genealogical Sleuthing

As we have noted, contemporary Jewish genealogical research has its own genealogy that goes back to the Book of Genesis, and it can be understood as a continuation of a kind of study that predates modern critical scholarship. Establishing a genealogical connection to King David was especially important because of the special status it conferred. In chapter 7 of 2 Samuel, God promises David that he and his descendants will form an enduring royal dynasty that will rule forever, and later Jews would come to believe that one of those descendants would be the Messiah, the savior figure who delivers Jews from their troubles. To be a descendant of such a line has always been a marker of high status within the Jewish

community. To cast Jesus as a descendant of David, as do the genealogies that appear in the gospels of Matthew and Luke, is to assert
that he is heir to the promises made to David—a direct successor—
and thus qualified to be the Messiah. In later history numerous rabbis, nobles, and a few would-be messiahs would also claim Davidic
ancestry, in some cases producing genealogical documents as proof.
Contemporary claims of Davidic descent build on this tradition,
and indeed they draw on some of the same genealogical information from the Bible, rabbinic literature, and medieval sources.

But alongside the continuity there are also some important
differences between contemporary claims of Davidic descent and
earlier genealogical practice. While Jews have been interested in
genealogy since antiquity, present-day interest in Jewish genealogy is of more recent origin. The two books said to have sparked
this interest, Dan Rottenberg's *Finding Our Fathers* and Arthur
Kurzweil's *From Generation to Generation*, were published in 1977
and 1980, respectively; *Avotaynu*, the leading journal of Jewish
genealogy that has now published some three thousand articles,
printed its first volume in 1985 (preceded by another publication,
Toledot: The Journal of Jewish Genealogy, published between 1977
and 1981); and the International Institute for Jewish Genealogy,
associated with Israel's National Library, was established in 2006.
None of this is a coincidence, as it reflects a broader interest in genealogy since the 1970s—many cite the television miniseries *Roots*
as a turning point. Genealogy seems to owe its increasing popularity in the following decades to the rise of the Internet, which has
made genealogical research accessible to a much broader public as
a do-it-yourself project, facilitated contact among people in different parts of the world, and drawn people's interest to the question of how we are all interconnected. Though interest in Davidic
ancestry has its roots in an earlier era, contemporary efforts to establish such a lineage are also a part of this recent wave of genealogical research.

How does this recent kind of genealogical research differ from
earlier genealogical inquiry? To begin with, as Eviatar Zerubavel
notes in his study of genealogy as a way of thinking and a form
of social practice, genealogical information plays a different role
in modern culture than it did in earlier periods of history. In the

society described by the Bible, a person's genealogical background determined his or her membership in the community—judging from the Bible, their ancestry determined who the Israelites were entitled to marry, which territory they could claim as a possession, who was a friend, and who was a foe. Compiling and preserving genealogical information was for this reason a communal effort; the effort to ascertain and confirm people's lineages defined the boundaries of the group, who was a member and who was an outsider. When the survivors of the Babylonian exile returned to the land of Judah, for example, they found themselves unable to confirm who descended from whom—oral tradition did not preserve all the genealogical information intact, and some written records had been lost, to the point that, as the Book of Ezra reports, many "could not tell the houses of their fathers or their seed, whether they were from Israel or not" (Ezra 2:59). In the case of one group of priests who could not find documentation for their lineage in the written records, they were expelled from the priesthood (Ezra 2:62). In that kind of social context, the ability to demonstrate one's ancestry, to trace it back to an ancestor like Aaron, determined who one was in the eyes of other members of one's community.

Genealogical information does not play this kind of role in contemporary Jewish culture outside certain Hasidic and ultra-Orthodox communities. Many Jews do not know much about their ancestry beyond their grandparents or great-grandparents, or if they can trace their lineage further back in time, it is because they have actively sought our such information at their own initiative—not because such information was of consequence for their social standing in the larger community but because they were curious about their family's history or wanted to honor the memory of relatives lost in the Holocaust. Genealogical research, in other words, represents a voluntary act of self-discovery, a way of learning about hidden or forgotten aspects of one's personal history. It can also serve a therapeutic role, guiding medical or reproductive decisions by revealing one's risk for inherited diseases or addressing people's questions about their identity and place in the world. In biblical times the community as a whole had a stake in determining a person's genealogy; in contemporary culture, such information is more personal and self-reflexive.

If the motives for seeking out genealogical information have changed, so too have the methods people use to establish such information. It is clear that people in the world described by the Bible engaged in some kind of genealogical research to address situations where a person wasn't sure about his or her ancestry or to sort out the difference between true and false genealogical claims. According to the historian Flavius Josephus (37– ca. 100 CE), for example, the priests took special care to guard the purity of their lineage by consulting genealogical records inscribed on "public tablets" in Jerusalem. While this constitutes a kind of research, however, it is very different from that practiced by genealogists today.

So far as we can tell, the documents ancient genealogists relied on were pretty much accepted at face value, never subject to what we might call critical examination. Indeed, there are many examples of garbled or dubious genealogical information to be found in biblical and Second Temple period sources. As the Gospel of Luke lists the ancestors of Jesus, for example, it claims that Shelah (a descendant of Noah through his son Shem) was the son of Cainan, and Cainan was the son of Arphaxad (Luke 3:36), but no Cainan appears in the genealogy in Genesis 10:24 from which the author of Luke otherwise drew his information—in the Hebrew text Arphaxad is the father of Shelah, not his grandfather. Another example comes from Josephus, who assures his readers that he has reported his own ancestry exactly as he found it in public records, but who nonetheless skipped over a generation or two according to modern scholars who have scrutinized his pedigree carefully. Ancient genealogists did not question their sources in the way modern professional genealogists do. Sometimes ancient authors recognized inconsistencies, as when Josephus noticed that the genealogy of King Herod reported by the historian Nicholas of Damascus did not match his own information, but they did not undertake a systematic comparison of their sources or try to corroborate them, and they were especially trusting of biblical sources without realizing that things get garbled in the Bible, too. Sometimes they even seem to have invented genealogical records when it served their purpose to do so. A text known as 1 Maccabees, an account of the Maccabean Revolt probably composed in the late second century BCE, refers to a document claiming that the Jews and the Spartans were both descended from Abraham (1 Maccabees 12:5–23). Although this document has not survived, scholars agree that it was a forgery, because the "discovery" of a kinship relationship between the Jews and the Spartans was so politically convenient for the Maccabees at that particular juncture of history, justifying exactly the kind of military alliance they were trying to forge with the Spartans in their war against Antiochus IV.

Something similar is true of Jewish genealogical documents from the Middle Ages: they too are unreliable and in some cases fictionalized. The Babylonian Talmud, probably finalized in the sixth century BCE, reflects a rabbinic culture that greatly esteemed lineage as a source of prestige (impugning another's pedigree was considered a great insult) and closely monitored pedigrees to prevent intermarriage. The importance ascribed to lineage in Babylonian Jewish culture—as opposed to Palestinian Jewish culture in the same period, which was not as concerned with problems of tainted genealogies or distinctions in the quality of lineages—may reflect the influence of the surrounding Persian culture, and the significance of lineage only increased in an Islamic age that assigned nobility to those who could trace their pedigree to the Prophet Muhammad. It is hard to gauge how much ordinary Jews in medieval Babylonia, North Africa, or Europe knew or cared about their genealogies, but we know from material found in the Cairo Genizah, a storehouse of hundreds of thousands of manuscript fragments found hidden away in a synagogue in Old Cairo, that the elite of medieval Jewish communities—rabbis and other community leaders—kept detailed genealogies that traced their ancestry all the way back to David or else to Aaron, Moses's brother and founder of the priestly line.

While Talmudic and medieval pedigrees were subject to close scrutiny, however, that does not mean their testimony is any more reliable than ancient genealogies. The first known Jewish attempt to trace the genealogy of David into the postbiblical period—if we do not count the Gospels of Matthew and Luke—is from the early ninth century CE, in a work known as *Seder Olam Zuta*, which traces an unbroken line of descent over roughly eighty-five generations, from Adam through David to the Babylonian Jewish communal leaders known as the Exilarchs. Filling in the genealogical gap between the biblical period and the rabbinic period, *Seder Olam Zuta* was a work on which later Jewish communal leaders in the tenth, eleventh, and twelfth centuries would draw to connect themselves to David. However, since the rise of critical scholarship in the nineteenth century, it has been recognized that its information is unreliable, even in some cases fabricated, as when *Seder Olam Zuta* takes members of David's family who are described as contemporaries in 1 Chronicles 3 and recasts them as successive generations. Probably composed to defend the Exilarchs against opponents who challenged their lineages, *Seder Olam Zuta* illustrates the gap filling that is common in royal genealogies: when a ruler's legitimacy depends on an unbroken line of succession from an illustrious ancestor, there is pressure to fill in the gaps of the genealogical record in any way possible, even if that means inventing ancestors.

All this stands in contrast to modern genealogical research and its aspiration to be critical and even scientific in its approach to the data. Medieval scholars sometime recognized mistakes and falsehoods in genealogical records, but they had a hard time recognizing forgeries, not having developed the kind of critical approach that has taken root in genealogical studies only in the past century or so. Modern genealogical research, aspiring to be accepted as a legitimate form of historical research, needs to answer a series of questions about its sources before its testimony will be accepted as evidence: Are the sources reliable, free of obvious error or fabrication? Can their claims be corroborated? Was the search for evidence thorough? Were the data assembled and described correctly? And can one overcome possible objections to the evidence, such as a contradictory claim found in another source? Only if the answer to all these questions is yes can a genealogical claim be considered proven—this according to the Board for Certification of Genealogists, an organization established in 1964 to promote public confidence in genealogical research.

To be sure, genealogical research is often undertaken by people who do not have formal academic training, a point of contrast with other, more established academic fields that draw a sharper boundary between professional scholars and hobbyists. But Jewish genealogical research has developed beyond the status of a hobby: "Step by step," wrote the Israeli scientist Daniel Wagner in

2006, "genealogy is mutating into a major academic discipline." There are now experts on the subject, including Orit Lavi, Alexander Beider, and Rose Lerer Cohen (to mention some of the experts featured in the 2015 conference on Jewish genealogy I stumbled on in my Jerusalem hotel), and peer-reviewed journals like *Avotaynu: The International Review of Jewish Genealogy* that suggest a field developing into a full-fledged area of research. Indeed in Wagner's view the field has matured to a point that it must now be divided into subfields: microgenealogy (the study of specific family lineages) and macrogenealogy (the study of the range of genealogical relationships within a community or region).

There are many challenges faced by such research. It is limited by its sources—most of the kinds of documents that genealogists rely on for their research (birth certificates, death records, immigration records) came into use only in the past few centuries, and even within this time frame, a lot of evidence was lost as the result of migration and the Holocaust. The search for ancestors is further obstructed by the fact that many Ashkenazic Jews took on surnames only in the eighteenth and nineteenth centuries, making it hard to trace connections to specific individuals in the record before then. Even for the period after the introduction of surnames in the modern era, it can be difficult to match names in different records since spelling was not uniform (e.g., Weitzman and Wajcman are both spellings of my family name). And yet despite such challenges, recent genealogists have been able to document lineages that go back centuries, sometimes all the way into the medieval period. The genealogist Maria Jose Surribas Camps, for example, has been able to identify very distant ancestors of present-day Sephardic Jews, members of medieval Spanish-Jewish communities who in some cases lived more than seven hundred years ago.

What is impressive about this research is not only its chronological and geographic reach but its power to discern the difference between true and fictional genealogical claims. A recent episode touted as a major triumph for Jewish genealogical research involved a Holocaust memoir published in 1997 by Misha Defonseca, a Belgian woman who had moved to the United States. According to her narrative, Misha was born to Jewish parents who were deported by the Nazis in 1941, but Misha was at school when they were arrested. She was rescued by being secreted to a Catholic family who gave her the name Monique de Wael. After her adoptive mother began to treat her cruelly, she escaped, setting off on a remarkable nineteen-hundred-mile journey in search of her parents that took her from Belgium to the Ukraine, including a period when she was saved from starvation by a pack of wolves and another episode where she stabbed a Nazi soldier to death with a pocket knife. Defonseca's memoir was so successful that it was translated into eighteen languages and was made into the French movie *Survivre avec les loups* ("Surviving with the Wolves," 2007).

A decade later, however, the episode became a case study in genealogical detective work. Although the story was incredible and even some of the author's childhood friends claimed that it was false, the accuracy of the story was never tested—not even during a lawsuit against the book's American publisher—until a forensic genealogist named Sharon Sergeant began to look into the documentation. Sergeant found inconsistencies in the timeline and other suspicious details that eventually led her to piece together Misha's true identity. Her real name was in fact Monique de Wael. As shown by a baptismal certificate, she was born a Catholic, and while her parents were indeed imprisoned and executed by the Nazis, this was not for being Jewish but for their participation in the Belgium resistance. Most damning of all, it was also possible to show that Misha/Monique was enrolled in grammar school at the time she was supposedly living with wolves. Sergeant's research was definitively vindicated when de Wael admitted in 2008 that her story was made up.

Writing about the episode in an article recently published in *Avotaynu*, Sergeant cited it as an example of the field's power to get to the bottom of things. Many people wanted to believe that such a remarkable survival story was true, and even those who had their doubts were reluctant to challenge the testimony of someone who claimed to be a Holocaust survivor; but Sergeant was able to prove the story false by painstakingly tracking down documents and correlating information from different sources. She describes the particular challenges that made ascertaining Misha's true origins seem impossible—the fact that most of what she claimed to have experienced would have been undocumented and unwitnessed, along with Misha's efforts to conceal information about who she really was—but perseverance and meticulousness prevailed in the end: "Researchers always fail when they believe proof is impossible or when difficulties dissuade them from persisting. In contrast, those refusing to accept a 'Myth of Impossible Proof' may succeed."

Turning back to recent efforts to establish a Davidic ancestry for Jews today, do they succeed in the way that Sergeant's research did? Do they adhere to the same standards of proof? Are they able to overcome the sort of evidentiary problems and doubts that undercut the reliability of ancient and medieval genealogical sources? The publications available on the Web suggest an effort to adhere to those standards. Let us consider the claims of the Shealtiel family first. The name Shealtiel itself is a connection to David—it was the name of the son of the last king of Judah, according to 1 Chronicles 3:17–18—and Shaltiel-Gracian accepts it as a given that there is a connection between that figure and the later Exilarchs to whom he traces his family's pedigree. The question for him is whether the Shealtiel family can be connected to the Exilarchs in a documentable way, and he argues for such a connection through the last of the Exilarchs: Hezekiah, who lived in the twelfth century. The precise genealogical link between the Shealtiels and the Exilarchs, according to Shaltiel-Gracian, is "Mar Saltel," a figure mentioned in a Hebrew document from 1061. "Saltel" here is understood as a variant spelling of Shealtiel, and "Mar" was a title reserved at that time for an Exilarch, as in the names Mar Zutra or Mar Ukba. Shaltiel-Gracian reasons that Mar Saltel, an ancestor of the Shealtiel family, was the grandson of the Exilarch Hezekiah through his son Isaac, who had fled with his brother to Spain after their father was executed. The Shealtiel website cites other evidence as well—a family coat of arms rediscovered in 1997 that features the Lion of Judah (a symbol of the Davidic dynasty), and a DNA study that tested men from the Shealtiel family and another family that claims Davidic descent, the Charlaps, to see if they share a common ancestor.

Susan Roth's research into her lineage began when she had an opportunity to see a chair that had belonged to Rebbe Nachman of Breslov, the founder of an important Hasidic movement, an experience that was important to her because the only thing she knew about her family history was that a distant ancestor had carved the chair. After discussing her background, the head of the Breslov synagogue in Jerusalem showed her a genealogical chart that he said demonstrated she was a descendant of Rebbe Nachman, who was supposed to have descended in turn from David. This is what led her to found the Davidic Dynasty project, with the goal of assisting others who think they are Davidic descendants—and ultimately to restore the Davidic dynasty on the model of England's monarchy.

To establish a connection with David, Roth has turned to both documentary and scientific evidence. In her case the link is not the Exilarchs but the commentator Rashi, supposedly an ancestor of Nachman; Rashi serves in turn as the link to a second-century sage named Yohanan Ha-Sandlar, a great-grandson of Gamaliel the Elder, known as a descendant of David. Roth's organization has also undertaken an effort to use DNA testing, enlisting the help of Dr. Chaim Luria, an administrator for the Luria DNA Research group on FamilytreeDNA.com.

How does this kind of research hold up when subjected to the kind of scrutiny that exposed Defonseca's claims as false? We have already seen reason to question *Seder Olam Zuta*, the earliest known source to detail the genealogy connecting the Exilarchs to David, and later lists of the Exilarchs exhibit similar problems and possible inventions—and do not agree with each other on the chronology and even the names of the Exilarchs. Shaltiel-Gracian does not reckon with the fact that, as a source of prestige, claims of Davidic descent were quite common in the Middle Ages, as was a preference for personal names associated with the Davidic family (Hezekiah, Shealtiel, etc.) and the use of the Lion of Judah as a personal symbol. Nor does he acknowledge that some Davidic genealogies from the period were fabricated. Thanks to a letter found in the Cairo Genizah, we know that in the very century when Mar Saltiel lived, an individual in Palestine used a forged genealogy to pass himself off as a Davidic descendant—a credential sufficiently impressive that the man was accepted as a leader of a community until doubts arose about his lineage.

I am not suggesting Mar Saltiel was another Davidic imposter, but what is germane is how common it was in this period for leaders to claim Davidic descent. In fact the Arabic term *al-dawudi* (the descendant of David) was itself a widely used political title,

not just an assertion of genealogy but a designation of office sometimes used in place of the title *nasi* (prince or patriarch). Even if
Shaltiel-Gracian is correct to trace the lineage of his family to a
person in the eleventh century who claimed a connection to the
Exilarch and to David, one must factor into the equation that this
was an age when many leaders were vying to link themselves to the
Davidic dynasty, when claims of a Davidic lineage were contested,
and when people had an incentive to fill in gaps in their lineage in
whatever way they could, even to the point of fabricating genealogical documents.

There is also reason to question the alternative pedigree that
runs through Rashi, another illustrious figure to whom later rabbis strained to connect themselves. The late David Einsiedler, a
cofounder of the Jewish Genealogical Society of Los Angeles, undertook an examination of this pedigree and found several problems: (1) the documents that supposedly connect Rashi to Yohanan
Ha-Sandler either are lost or do not account for all the generations
between the two figures; and (2) neither Rashi nor his immediate descendants are known to have made a claim of Davidic descent, and there are sources that list his ancestors without reference
to David. After examining other lineages that connect to David
through Judah Loew the Elder (great-grandfather of Maharal of
Prague), Einsiedler concludes, "There is no complete, reliable and
positive proof of claims of descent from David, whether via Rashi,
Judah Loew the Elder, or any of the other families claimed." Einsiedler shows that it is not possible to trace Rashi back to David,
nor is it any easier to trace modern-day people to Rashi (an ancestor claimed by the likes of Elie Wiesel, winner of the 1986 Nobel
Peace Prize); there are just too many gaps in the genealogical record to prove that any particular family descends from the illustrious scholar.

But aren't such doubts overcome by the DNA testing? It is true
that genealogical research has embraced genetics, the only way to
scientifically validate a shared ancestry and an exciting new possibility for overcoming the limits of the documentary evidence,
as part of the future of the field. If those who believed themselves
descendants of David truly shared a common ancestor on the paternal side, then in theory that genetic lineage might be reflected

in distinctive similarities in the male Y chromosome passed down from fathers to sons. It is hard to pin down the results of the DNA testing performed on members of the Shealtiel family, but a newsletter published by the Charlaps, a family that claims to share descent from David with the Shealtiels, cites a breakthrough study that seems to substantiate their professed ancestry. According to the newsletter (published in December 2000), Dr. Neil Bradman, a geneticist known for his work in identifying a common genetic ancestry for Cohanim (the priestly caste of Judaism), collected samples from male members of the family to see if they shared a common ancestry with the Shealtiels. The preliminary results, as reported in the newsletter, seem to confirm that the Charlaps also descend from David.

But is this what Bradman's test actually showed? I will be discussing genetics in chapter 8, and there I will address in more detail what it might reveal about the origin of the Jews, but suffice it to say for now that it does not prove a genetic connection between people today and David. The use of genetic testing to establish a link to a famous person is generally frowned on by genealogists and geneticists as unscientific, a kind of "genetic astrology" to be avoided, and the effort to establish Davidic ancestry for the Shealtiel clan illustrates the dubiousness of this kind of research. So far as I know, the results of Bradman's research have not been published—it does not appear among the refereed articles listed on his website—but the description of his research by other geneticists suggests that it did not in the end provide the kind of confirmation reported by the newsletter. According to the geneticist Harry Ostrer, Bradman acknowledged that while there may be people with a Davidic lineage, it is not possible to know who carries it on the basis of this research. Shaltiel-Gracian too seems to have eventually acknowledged the inconclusiveness of the research, though he tries to explain the lack of a genetically demonstrable connection between the Shealtiel and Charlap men by suggesting that somewhere along the way descent may have gone through a woman.

What difference does it make to our larger inquiry if it turns out that this kind of genealogical research is bogus? Even many of those who pursue it see it as a kind of hobby, a source of personal pride but not much more than that, and it has no real impact on how most Jews see themselves or their history. Jews to this day understand themselves as the descendants of common ancestors— Abraham, Isaac, and Jacob—but Jews have also long recognized that most cannot trace their descent back to particular Israelites mentioned in the Bible, and that fact does not affect their sense of identification with their forebears. What is at stake here is not whether Jews are wrong to see themselves as the descendants of biblical Israelites but whether the methods of critical scholarship can corroborate a genealogical connection, and the efforts to establish a link to King David can help us to see why they cannot. There is simply no way to establish a secure evidentiary chain to connect contemporary or recently living people with ancient ancestors. What documents exist, when judged by the standards of contemporary genealogical and historical research, raise too many doubts and contain too many gaps, and whatever potential genetics might hold as a way of overcoming the limits of the written evidence has yet to be realized.

Shaltiel-Gracian and Roth are hardly representative of the kind of scholarship I will be surveying in this book. They are amateur sleuths without the training in ancient languages, history, archaeology, or science that mainstream scholarship relies on to address the question of Jewish origin. If I have begun our quest with them, it is because their efforts can help us to understand why, despite the fact that Jews have often articulated their origins in genealogical terms, it won't work for us to take a genealogical approach to the question. Such an approach requires the ability to trace a line of descent, and we simply cannot draw that kind of line from Jews today to people in antiquity, not in a documentable way that would satisfy a professional genealogist. Yes, every once in a while, genealogists can break through beyond the modern period, tracking a line of descent into the Middle Ages, but there are simply too many gaps in the evidence, too many questions about the sources to extend the search beyond that. I want to repeat that this does not mean that Jews are wrong to see themselves as the descendants of ancient ancestors—when to place the origin of the Jews is still an open question as far as this investigation is concerned. My intent, rather, is to call attention to the limits of genealogical research as a way to address our question. Genealogists often speak of hitting a "brick wall," some barrier to their research that they hope to over-come by looking in another direction or finding some new sources. There is no way around the brick wall we are faced with here: we know enough about the unreliability of genealogical claims in an-cient and medieval periods to realize that there may be nothing beyond the brick wall to seek, that a breakthrough discovery is not possible in this context.

But while we have reached a dead end in our effort to trace the ancient ancestry of the Jews, we have not yet exhausted the lessons to be learned from genealogical evidence. For genealogists like Ser-geant and Einsiedler, the fact that some people misremember or make up stories about who their ancestors are is a challenge they seek to overcome by using rigorous historical study to distinguish between reliable genealogical information and false or fabricated claims that have to be discarded. For other scholars those fictitious genealogical claims are not obstacles that stand in the way of their inquiry but rather objects of study in their own right. Approaching the question of origin from the perspective of anthropology, one sees that the goal of such scholars is not to verify genealogical claims but to understand those claims as part of the process of social identity formation, an internal, subjective process by which people come to-gether as a group. In the past few decades, scholars have applied this perspective to Jewish genealogical claims, and I want to briefly look at this kind of research as a way to introduce another approach to origin that we will be considering over the course of the book—an alternative to genealogical thinking that traces the origin of collec-tive identity not to distant ancestors but to acts of self-invention.

The Genealogical Imagination

As I noted in the introduction, many scholars today believe there is no such thing as an origin, if by that we mean something that happened in the world external to how we understand and nar-rate it. From this perspective, even the most scientific origin ac-counts are like creation myths, to the extent that they impose on the past a coherence and comprehensibility—a beginning, middle, and end—that does not inhere in the evidence itself. How does one study an origin from this point of view? Not by looking for evidence of ancestry but by asking why people remember and narrate their origins as they do.

The originator of this approach, if we were to single out a founder, is the sociologist Max Weber (1864–1920), who defined ethnic groups as "human groups that entertain a subjective belief in their common descent" (this from his discussion of ethnic groups in his book *Economy and Society*, published posthumously in 1922). The key word here is "subjective"—it does not matter for people's sense of identification with each other whether they actually share a common ancestry, only that they see themselves as co-descendants from such an origin. Building on Weber's insights, scholars like the sociologist Maurice Halbwachs (1877–1945) and the anthropologist Fredrik Barth (1928–2016) developed a perspective often referred to as the constructivist approach, which explores how communities "construct" shared identities for themselves through stories they tell about themselves and their origins.

This kind of perspective takes a very different approach to genealogical claims. Kinship relations, it argues, are not determined by the biological facts of sexual reproduction: they can be modified, even invented, in ways that reflect a group's circumstances, needs, and relationships with other groups. It follows, as Eviatar Zerubavel has pointed out, that genealogies are not mere records of natural succession, passively documenting our ancestors: "They are narratives we construct to actually make them our ancestors." We have already seen an example of one of the techniques people use to construct ancestors for themselves, what Zerubavel refers to as "stretching"—the artificial extension of a genealogy back to a heroic ancestor. This is the very technique used by the author of *Seder Olam Zuta* and other medieval sources to connect modern rabbinic families to King David. Other techniques include the suppression of embarrassing or socially inconvenient genealogical information, as when an ancient scribe tried to protect Moses's reputation by suppressing the disclosure in Judges 18:30 that one of the prophet's descendants was a corrupt priest; and the lumping together of discrete genealogies to foster an alliance or merger between two groups, as when the early Jewish text 1 Maccabees makes Abraham a common ancestor for both the Jews and the Spartans.

To illustrate the difference between how anthropologists think about genealogical claims and the kind of genealogical research described in the last section, let us consider an example not from ancient times but from the past few decades—the belief among certain people today that they descend from Jews who had to convert to Catholicism during the period of the Spanish Inquisition in the fifteenth century but who preserved a "crypto"-Jewish identity they subsequently passed on to their descendants. There now exists a number of organizations whose purpose is to help those who believe they descend from these crypto-Jews to recover their lost ancestry, organizations like the Society of Crypto-Judaic Studies, established in 1991; the Sephardic Anousim Cultural Resource Center, established in El Paso, Texas, in 2013 ("Anousim" refers to Jews forced to convert against their will); and Sephardic Home International, which has partnered with a DNA testing company to encourage discovery of hidden Jewish lineage. In fact, interest in retrieving a lost Spanish heritage has become so widespread that the Spanish government has taken note of it, offering automatic citizenship to the descendants of Spanish Jews as a gesture of repair for their ancestors' expulsion in 1492. (The day after it established the law offering automatic citizenship to such Jews, Spain granted citizenship to 4,302 people.) Our focus here, however, is specifically on those who did not realize they were the descendants of expelled Spanish Jews until very recently—Latinos or Latinas living in the American Southwest who thought of themselves as Christians until they rediscovered their Jewish ancestry with some guidance from genealogical research.

According to this research, such crypto-Jews are the descendants of Jews who fled from Spain during the period of the Spanish Inquisition and expulsion to the territories in the New World under Spanish control at the time—what is now Mexico, New Mexico, and other Southwestern states. Although the people today who claim this identity are Catholic, they believe their ancestors were Jews who outwardly converted to Catholicism but continued to practice Judaism in secret. In some cases they remembered older relatives or neighbors practicing certain customs that seemed to be of Jewish origin—secretly lighting candles on Friday night, using six-pointed stars on tombstones, playing with toys that resembled the dreidels used during Hanukkah, and other practices that resembled Jewish ritual. It is not impossible that such practices were inherited from crypto-Jews. There were crypto-Jews in Mexico, after all—by the time the Inquisition in Mexico came to an end in 1821, about a hundred people accused of being crypto-Jews had been put to death there. It was thought that the crypto-Jewish culture that first developed in the fifteenth century disappeared by the end of the 1700s, but it appears that the descendants of crypto-Jews survived into the twentieth century. In 1917 a small community of such descendants, still practicing certain Jewish rituals, were discovered in the Portuguese town of Belmonte by a Polish-Jewish engineer named Samuel Schwartz. In the 1980s a number of Latinos and Latinas in New Mexico began to suspect that they too might be the descendants of crypto-Jews who had fled to the far reaches of the Spanish Empire.

These would-be descendants of crypto-Jews did not recover their ancestry on their own. They had help from Stanley Hordes, a historian working in the state of New Mexico at the time who also happened to be Jewish. Although there was little documentation to substantiate the claims of crypto-Jewish descent, Hordes believed the stories he was hearing could well be plausible, and he began to gather such stories, track down grave markings, and even research a disease supposedly common among both Latinos and Jews that pointed to a shared ancestry. Hordes was not the first person to entertain the idea that some Southwestern Latinos might descend from crypto-Jews, but his efforts drew the attention of the radio producers Ben Shapiro and Nan Rubin, and they produced a documentary that aired on National Public Radio in 1987, a broadcast that drew the largest volume of mail ever received by NPR up to that time. Thanks to this and other documentaries that followed in the 1990s, the crypto-Jews of New Mexico came to the attention of a larger public, which led scores of people from New Mexico and neighboring states, and eventually from farther afield, to begin to realize that they too may descend from crypto-Jews. In 1991 Hordes helped to found the Society for Crypto-Judaic Studies, which seems to be going strong twenty-five years later, and in 2005 he published his research as a book, *To the End of the Earth: A History of the Crypto-Jews of New Mexico*.

The Society for Crypto-Jewish Studies now runs an annual conference that includes academic sessions, the sharing of personal narratives, and workshops for those interested in using genealogy or genetics to pursue their heritage. For some people the effects of such scholarship have been transformational, moving them to convert to Judaism, and those effects now go beyond the Southwest and even beyond the United States, reaching people in the Caribbean and other Spanish-speaking regions. But for all the attention the crypto-Jews of New Mexico have garnered in the past three decades, there have also been skeptics who doubt the underlying research on which their genealogical identity depends.

After hearing about Hordes research from the NPR report, a folklorist named Judith Neulander began to pursue her own research into the crypto-Jews of New Mexico, hoping to use her skills as an ethnographer to give some substance to a topic that was mostly the subject of pseudoscientific research, rumors, and sensationalizing media reports. After doing some research, however, she began to develop doubts. She met with Hordes, who showed her pictures of the gravestones inscribed with a Star of David, but the pictures obscured last names and other information that might help her locate the graves herself. Observing Hordes's interviewing technique, she found that he asked leading questions that seemed to plant ideas in the minds of his informants. And after researching the crypto-Jewish customs noted by Hordes, she found that those were unlikely to have a Jewish origin, reflecting customs widespread in Latin America or traceable to non-Jewish sources. It is known that Muslims also fled from Spain to Mexico, for example, and it is possible that some of the practices Hordes identified as crypto-Jewish—such as the avoidance of pork—might be of Muslim origin. Other Jewish customs might have been picked up from German and East European Jews who have lived in Mexico and the Southwest for 150 years.

Neulander eventually developed her own origin account for the crypto-Jews of New Mexico, arguing that they were the descendants not of Spanish crypto-Jews but of more recent sectarian Protestants, a fundamentalist splinter group known as the Church of God Israelite that left Mexico City in the early twentieth century to proselytize in the American Southwest. Like certain other Protestant sects, the members of this community identified with

the people of the Old Testament and adopted certain Jewish practices, but in places like Santa Fe, they encountered a Catholic
hostility that eventually forced them to pull their ministers out
of New Mexico, leaving behind former members whose children
and grandchildren had forgotten the group's historical origins but
vaguely recalled a connection to the people of the Old Testament.
The descendants of this community amounted to a small group
of people, but Hordes's theory, which garnered the attention of
the media, helped to disseminate the idea to other Hispanic New
Mexicans after the 1980s. At a time when New Mexican society
was increasingly dominated by Anglos of European descent, the
claim of Spanish-Jewish descent gave some Latinos a way to re-
identify themselves as white Europeans and thereby to elevate
themselves above nonwhite neighbors—in other words, the assertion of a crypto-Jewish lineage was rooted in a kind of self-hating
racism.

In fairness to Hordes, we should note that he and other scholars
have sought to defend his argument against Neulander's critique,
countering that she was too quick to dismiss the signs of crypto-
Jewish culture that he discovered, and we are not going to be able
to resolve their debate here. If Neulander is right, the research into
crypto-Jews has permanently contaminated the ethnographic evidence, making it impossible to sort out what people would have
believed about themselves if they hadn't come into contact with
Hordes or his theory. My focus is on what this debate tells us about
the potential of genealogical research as a way of understanding the
origin of the Jews. While such research continues apace, growing
in popularity, there exists now a counter-scholarship: ethnographic
research that looks at the same evidence from the anthropological
perspective of constructivism. Hordes's approach is focused on recovering an origin that has been all but forgotten, and his research
has helped people to reconnect to an identity that he believes was
literally hidden from view. According to the sort of constructivist
perspective adopted by Neulander, genealogical research does not
reveal the true origin of crypto-Jewish identity. In contrast to Sergeant's effort to discredit Defonseca's story about her childhood, she
is not accusing those who claim a crypto-Jewish lineage of fraud,
but the thrust of her research is nonetheless to demonstrate that

crypto-Jewish identity is a collective fiction, and one that a scholar encouraged and perhaps helped to create.

It is one thing to be skeptical of a particular genealogical claim. It is another to call into question an entire field of scholarship. It is not my intention to do so here, nor do I want to slight the accomplishments of Jewish genealogical research over the past several decades. But Neulander's critique asks us to think about such research as a form of identity construction in its own right, and she is not the only scholar who views it from this perspective. Another scholar, Rachel Jablon, has shown how Jewish genealogical research, much of it happening online now, is giving rise to virtual communities drawn together by their shared genealogical interest and by the common ancestors they discover. (Jablon does not address the efforts of Shaltiel-Gracian and Roth, but her analysis probably applies in their case as well; their genealogical efforts have certainly created new worldwide networks of people drawn together by the connective powers of the Internet.) According to the kind of perspective Neulander represents, the personal motives at stake in this kind of research, and its implications for who people understand themselves to be, skew the results, revealing not the actual ancestors of living people but the kinds of ancestors from whom they would prefer to be descended—ancestors who are famous, heroic, or prestigious.

The relationship between anthropology and genealogical research need not be as antagonistic as it is in the case of Neulander and Hordes, but there is a built-in tension between them. Anthropologists are not interested in tracking down the ancestors of their subjects the way genealogists do; they tend to be interested in a group's "subjective belief" about its ancestry, a focus that predisposes them to treat a community's claims about its ancestry as a fiction, a construction, which does not correspond to the history of how the group actually came to be. Genealogists also recognize that people can invent genealogies for themselves, but in their case, the value of identifying genealogical fiction is that one can then separate it out from more reliable information as one seeks to reconstruct the actual ancestries of people. For constructivist anthropologists, genealogies are always in some sense a fiction, even when they involve real-life, confirmable people.

The orientation that we have referred to as constructivism has had a major impact on anthropology today, and its influence makes it all the more difficult to defend a genealogical quest for the origin of the Jews. At the same time, however, it should be noted that this kind of scholarship does involve its own kind of origin-related research—not as a central focus but to establish a kind of historical background for its inquiry. For Neulander to demonstrate that contemporary crypto-Jewish identity is a fiction, she has to demonstrate that the self-image of her subjects, their perception of their origin, is historically inaccurate, that their "real" origin is different from what they think it to be, and that part of her argument involves its own inquiry into the circumstances that produced crypto-Jewish identity, a search that takes her back to a midcentury Protestant missionary movement.

Neulander's account is actually the mirror image of the origin that her subjects imagine for themselves. Whereas they claim an exalted lineage for themselves, positing an origin that links them to an important and dramatic episode of Jewish history, her account of their origin ascribes to them an ancestry that is much less astonishing and heroic, much more localized, far more recent—and the ancestors it reconstructs aren't Jews. But even if it is not the kind of genealogy the crypto-Jews of New Mexico would prefer for themselves, Neulander's research does generate a genealogy, tracing them back to specific forebears. She does not like the kind of research Hordes practices, but she does share with him the belief that it is possible to reconstruct the origin of a group.

In this sense Neulander's research is itself subject to critique by those scholars who reject the very idea of searching for an origin. As I noted in the introduction, some scholars reject the premises built into genealogical research, the idea that one can grasp something that exists today by going back to its moment of origin or by tracing a line of descent from a beginning point into the present. We need to factor this perspective into our inquiry as well. The conventional notion of genealogy assumes a movement forward from a point of origin—a common ancestor—to the ancestor's descendants. While it eschews genealogical research in this sense, the constructivist approach also traces things back to ancestors and foundational moments. This third kind of research, closely associated with postmodernism, rejects both kinds of projects because it rejects any attempt to trace things back to an origin.

Our effort to explore this third approach will give us a chance to reflect on a strange twist in the history of genealogy: while it is very different from conventional genealogical research, this alternative approach casts itself as a genealogical inquiry in its own right. The term "genealogy" has several meanings in contemporary scholarship, and one of its more common meanings nowadays refers to a kind of research that critiques the search for origin as practiced in earlier generations of scholarship, and that aims to push history and philosophy beyond their reliance on foundational moments, roots, and clear-cut beginnings. This critique runs deeper than the kind of criticisms mounted by Neulander against Hordes because it does not seek merely to construct an alternative origin account but challenges how scholars think about origins, the underlying modes of reasoning that structure their thought. How did genealogy develop in this direction; what precisely is the nature of its critique; and what are its implications for the search for the origin of the Jews? We will try to address these questions as a way of introducing a third perspective on the search of origin that challenges the very premises on which such a search is built.

Genealogy as Antigenealogy

As I have noted, genealogical thinking is not limited to genealogists. Some would argue that it is essential to the structure of scholarly thinking itself and its penchant to trace things along vertical lines from a point of origin toward a pinnacle or conclusion. Over the past fifty years of so, that kind of thinking has been a major target of postmodern critique by thinkers like the French philosopher Gilles Deleuze (1925–1995) and his collaborator Félix Guattari (1930–1992). What we are referring to as genealogical thinking Deleuze and Guattari refer to as "arborescent thought," the kind of thinking reflected in genealogical trees that moves in one direction from an origin to a destination, from a trunk to branches. In their work *A Thousand Plateaus*, Deleuze and Guattari offer an alternative model for thought, the rhizome—a way of thinking that seeks to understand multiplicity without needing to sort everything hierarchically into roots and branches. A rhizome is a plant stem, usually horizontal rather than vertical in orientation, that sends out shoots above and roots below not from one place but from various nodes. For Deleuze and Guattari, it signifies a way of thinking that is nonlinear, nonbinary, nonhierarchical, and nonsequential, and that does not start from a clear point or move forward in a unilinear way. "There are no origins in a rhizome, no points of entrance or straight lines that lead from one point to another. . . . [A] rhizome has no beginning or end; it is always in the middle, between things, interbeing."

To explain the workings of the rhizome, Deleuze and Guattari offer several examples and analogies—the structure of the human brain, for example, or grass—but many people these days now compare the rhizome to the Internet, which also has numerous points of entrance and exit and features a multiplicity of websites that cannot be organized into any hierarchical structure. If you think about your own experience roaming across the web, you might see the limits of the tree or root metaphor as a way of comprehending the connection between things: it does not make much sense to think of the web as something with a clear beginning or end. There is no originating root or central trunk from which everything else emanates: there are a countless number of nodes from which an endless number of shoots can grow and connect to one another in an endless number of ways.

I mention the argument of Deleuze and Guattari because it illustrates why genealogical research does not fit well in a postmodern context. Such research depends on precisely the kind of arborescent thinking that postmodernism would seek to thwart. In fact Deleuze and Guattari themselves explicitly describe the rhizome as "antigenealogy." And yet from the same kind of suspicion of origin that produced the rhizome—indeed from the same specific intellectual subculture that produced Deleuze and Guattari themselves—there has emerged an alternative conception of genealogy that, paradoxically, incorporates the "antigenealogical" thinking they champion. How did that development happen, and how does such genealogical inquiry relate to the more conventional kind of genealogical inquiry we have been considering thus far?

The key figure in the development of this alternative form of genealogy is Michel Foucault, a friend of Deleuze's for a time, whose thinking moved along similar tracks. What Foucault has in mind by genealogy, a method he first deploys in a work called *Discipline and Punish* (1975), exhibits some of the characteristics of conventional genealogical research—Foucault describes it as "gray, meticulous, and patiently documentary"—but it is in fact quite a different project, developing out of Friedrich Nietzsche's conception of genealogy as a form of critique. Foucault's writing is difficult, and his conception of genealogy cannot be distilled into straightforward methodological principles, but for our purposes, I would emphasize three differences from conventional genealogical research:

1. Foucault's genealogical inquiries are focused not on people and their ancestors but on ways of thinking, knowing, and conceiving the self. Thus he was interested in the genealogy of subjectivity, the ancestry of the self as a thinking or conscious being, rather than the genealogy of particular individuals or groups.

2. Foucault was not seeking to reach some ultimate point of origin at the beginning of the genealogy, nor was his goal to trace a line of continuity or the transmission of an inheritance across time. He was interested in how things (e.g., knowledge and power) are interconnected, but he also used genealogy to break up the sense of continuity between present and past, and to puncture the illusion that certain truths are unchanging. Some have discerned something Darwinian in his conception of genealogy because of its focus on change and struggle, but Foucault also contrasts what he has in mind with an evolutionary narrative. Rather than trying to fit things into the unitary structure of the family tree model or a unitary narrative of progress or development, he sought to expose the clashes, ruptures, and randomness that produce the changes he discerned within the genealogy of the self.

3. The goal of Foucault's version of genealogy was a different kind of self-knowledge than that achieved by the other kinds of genealogical research we have reviewed. In all three kinds of inquiry, genealogy functions as a history of the self, how the self came to be, but beyond that, their objectives diverge. The goal of Hordes's research in this regard was to

help the New Mexicans he met to recover a lost part of their identity. The goal of Neulander's research was to nullify that identity by showing that it was rooted in a false origin story and faulty scholarship. Foucault's goal, one might say, was to reveal to the self that its origin was different from what it had assumed. Neulander's research has a similar effect. It too reveals that its subjects did not originate in the way they imagined themselves originating. But her focus is on debunking what other people believe about themselves, whereas Foucault's genealogy is self-reflexive: its intended effect is to change the self's relationship to itself by revealing that qualities that seemed timeless—sexuality, for example—have undergone many changes and have a rather troubling past.

Foucault's conception of genealogy is not just different from the conventional form of genealogical research published in *Avotaynu*; like the concept of the rhizome, it is a metaphor for antigenealogical thinking, rejecting the underlying structures of thought that genealogists (among other scholars) use to organize the information they uncover. But Foucault's use of the word "genealogy" has had an interesting if unintended effect, prompting certain scholars to try to integrate his perspective into the kind of genealogical research that looks for ancestors and kinship relations. The result is a kind of hybrid inquiry, a reconceptualization of genealogy that bridges between the questions posed by conventional genealogists and the anti-arborescent thinking of postmodern scholarship.

An example of the sort of scholarship I have in mind is the work of Catherine Nash, a cultural geographer whose recent work focuses on the search for Irish origins. Like the many Jews who belong to Jewish genealogical societies or pay for the services of a genealogy company, many people of Irish descent are also keen to find out about their ancestry, pursuing genealogical knowledge through the same kind of research used to pursue Jewish genealogy. Nash recognizes that this search for roots represents the arborescent thinking Deleuze and Guattari reject, but what is of interest for us is her contention that genealogical inquiry can also serve as a way to undercut such thinking. The search for one's ancestors need not reveal the origin that people are looking for, nor does it always satisfy the nostalgic feeling for a lost homeland. It can also show that people's ancestries are "wildly rhizomatic," going back not to a single source but to multiple points of origins—to Ireland but also to people from other places or to those thought to be foes, people on the other side of the political divides in Northern Ireland: "Here genealogy works in its radical mode, uncovering hidden histories that challenge narratives of neat identities and absolute loyalties." This is closer to Foucault's sense of genealogy, but she fuses this kind of genealogy with the kind that obsessively tracks down birth certificates and assembles family trees, arguing that such research can do similarly subversive work.

Can one envision a similar role for Jewish genealogical research? Two scholars have come close. In 1993 the Talmudist Daniel Boyarin and his brother Jonathan, an anthropologist, published an essay in which they tried to make what we might think of as a postmodern case for genealogy—the idea of the Jews as a people united by their descent from common ancestors—as a legitimate source of Jewish collective identity, even in a world suspicious of genealogically based identities as a form of ethnocentric or racist supremacism. Group identity, they note, is constructed in one of two ways, either figured as a product of a common genealogical origin or traced back to a common geographical origin. The latter idea is implicit in Zionism, which calls for Jews to return to their common point of origin. The Boyarins respect the feeling of attachment to the land that has long been a part of Jewish culture, comparing it to the feeling of attachment that binds other indigenous peoples to the land of their ancestors, but they nonetheless reject it as a source of contemporary Jewish identity: for them, Zionism and its territorial conception of origin, reflecting the influence of a European nationalism, is at odds with traditional Judaism as they see it, a culture formed in a diasporic condition of dispersion and powerlessness that required Jews to coexist with, intermingle with, and learn from others. A genealogically based identity, on the other hand, need not be problematic: critics are wrong to conflate it with racism because it is not restricted to those born Jewish, making room for converts to become a part of the family as it were, and it allows Jews to sustain a distinct identity, a sense of commonality, without requiring them to impose themselves on others in the ethically compromising ways that reclaiming the land of one's origin demands.

On the surface the Boyarins are referring to genealogy in its traditional sense, a line of descent that connects Jews to a common ancestor, but a closer look reveals that they also have in mind genealogy as a mode of "self-critique," as they put it. Genealogy provides Jews with a sense of rootedness, of coming from something, but it also functions in their argument as an alternative to Zionism; and Zionism as they describe it depends on a concept of origin very similar to the kind of origin Foucault opposed—a myth that traces Jews back to a fixed and static point of origin (the Jews all come from a single place and time) and that posits seamless continuity between present and past (the Jews have always lived in the land of Israel), a myth that represses and excludes alternative perspectives and that creates artificial boundaries and hierarchies. By contrast genealogy as envisioned by the Boyarins allows for a Jewish identity that can persist in the absence of a clear beginning point (their genealogy traces the Jews back to biblical ancestors but those ancestors were themselves unsettled wanderers from the very beginning), a Judaism that is heterogeneous and nonhegemonic and that allows for hybrid relationships with non-Jewish culture. The Boyarins associate this kind of Judaism with diaspora, a condition that has been a part of Jewish experience from the time of Abraham's wanderings, and they trace it back to the Bible and the Talmud. But their efforts to assert its antiquity mask its postmodern pedigree: a genealogically based Judaism as they envision it has all the qualities of the rhizome, an originless culture marked by diffusion and openness to multiplicity.

Given the opposition to origins characteristic of postmodern thought, one might have assumed that it would also oppose genealogical research and its quest for ancestors and clear lines of descent, but it turns out that it has generated a new rationale for genealogical inquiry. Genealogy, paradoxically, need not involve the sort of genealogical thinking that tries to trace everything back to an origin. As Foucault wrote, "The search for descent is not the erecting of foundations: on the contrary, it disturbs what was previously considered immobile; it fragments what was thought unified; it shows the heterogeneity of what was imagined consistent with itself." With this approach as a model one can imagine a kind of Jewish genealogical research that is not reaching back to a common point of origin but is focused instead on tracing the heterogeneous origins of the Jews or on identifying intersections with non-Jewish ancestors—questions that disrupt the effort to draw a straight line between Jews today and a single point of origin in the distant past.

But as one might expect, this is not the conception of genealogy that draws so many people to Jewish genealogical research today. Of all the methods we will be examining, with the exception of the related field of genetics, genealogical research has the broadest appeal, engaging not only academic experts but self-trained hobbyists and first-timers. Based on what we know about the motives of such people, they are looking not to disrupt or fragment their sense of origin but to connect to or reassemble it in order to understand who they are, where they come from, what they have inherited from the past. Postmodern genealogy does not address such curiosity—in fact, it thwarts it at every turn.

It is probably the case that many Jewish genealogy seekers have the kind of experience Nash describes, that their research ends up disturbing or confounding their sense of origin by revealing something they were not expecting about their past or by complicating their relationship to their ancestors. A sociologist named Arlene Stein undertook a study of post-Holocaust genealogists in the 1980s and 1990s—the children of survivors who were seeking information about ancestors lost during the Holocaust—and she observes that this kind of genealogical quest often ends in a way that challenges how people initially imagine their origins. But this is not the intended outcome of such research; as Stein concludes on the basis of interviews with post-Holocaust genealogists, their work is motivated by a desire to reconnect to a lost origin (a quest that is often, quite literally, a search for lost objects—lost photos, lost letters, lost names) and to reestablish a line of continuity disrupted by the Holocaust, motivations she compares to the intense desire felt by many adoptees to know their biological parentage. Notwithstanding Nash's argument, I myself find it hard to imagine how a Foucauldian conception of genealogy can ever be successfully integrated into mainstream genealogical research, because it does not address the yearning for connectedness and continuity that draws so many people to this kind of research. It offers self-insight, but not the kind of self-insight many genealogists are seeking. Though Foucault's influence has helped to spawn a new academic field of genealogy—genealogy as a self-reflexive way of interrogating the history of the subject—that kind of genealogy has little to do with the search we have been focused on: the search for common ancestors and clear lines of descent. The idea that it can be fused together with conventional genealogical research greatly understates the contradiction between two ways of thinking that are really at odds with each other.

A Fork in the Road

Our goal in this chapter has been to explore what genealogical research might tell us about the origin of the Jews. Such a method is relevant both because Jews have long traced their origin to common ancestors and because the modern field of genealogy has had a lot of success in recovering lost ancestors and tracing lineages over time. There have in fact been many advances in the field of Jewish genealogy over the past several decades—the development of new sources of evidence and new ways of managing and analyzing their testimony—and genealogists have been able to fill in many gaps and answer many questions as a result. But in terms of the goal we have set for ourselves in this book—to find the common origin of the Jews in general—genealogical research offers little help. The evidence by which we might reach beyond the past few centuries or connect a person alive today to an ancient ancestor—if we judge that evidence by the standards of professional genealogical research—is full of gaps and question marks that cannot be resolved. Anthropology gives us even more reason to doubt what we can learn from genealogy by calling attention to how communities, including Jewish communities, invent ancestors and pedigrees for themselves as part of the process of identity formation. Postmodern genealogy further frustrates the search for origin by arguing that there is something wrong with the genealogical thinking that underlies such a search. Genealogists pride themselves on being able to overcome dead ends, but this dead end seems insurmountable.

But even if it has not advanced our quest very much, our brief survey of genealogical research does carry important lessons as we move forward to other approaches. Beyond wanting to introduce genealogical research itself, I have had another goal in this chapter—to introduce three different approaches to the question of origin that we will encounter throughout our search: (1) a form of sleuthing that treats origin as a lost object to be sought out by methodically following a series of clues that lead from the present back to a hidden past; (2) a constructivist approach that treats origins as a work of imagination that can be understood only in the way one understands a fictional story; and (3) a postmodern approach critical of the thinking inherent in the search for origin. Scholars have used a wide range of methods to address the question of Jewish origin, drawn from a variety of fields—genealogy but also linguistics, history, archaeology, genetics, even psychology. As our survey moves from one field to the other, we will find that many are marked by a debate among different approaches to the question of Jewish origin that corresponds to the divergent kinds of genealogical research introduced here. If the scholarly search for the origin of the Jews has reached an impasse, it is in part because it has not been able to reconcile or overcome the differences among these three ways of conceiving origin.

If there were some way to show that one of these approaches was superior to the others, we would not have to vacillate among them as we will do in coming chapters. I am not the only one who struggles to relate them to each other; all three continue as rival paradigms for the understanding of origin. To search for the origin of the Jews as if that origin were something hidden in the distant past is to take it for granted that the first of these approaches is the best one, and there are many scholars who would contest such an assumption. To be faithful to scholarship in all its diversity, we can acknowledge only that there is no one way to address the question of Jewish origin and no one way of pursuing answers, which means that in moving forward with our search, we won't henceforth be able to follow a straight line. Like a good genealogist, we will need to be prepared to consider different starting points and to follow divergent pathways wherever they lead.

CHAPTER TWO

Roots and Rootlessness

PALEOLINGUISTICS AND THE
PREHISTORY OF THE JEWS

*Thanks to his retrospective method, the linguist can go back through the
centuries and reconstruct languages that were spoken by certain nations
long before their written history began. But might not reconstructions also
provide information about the nations themselves—their race, filiation,
social relations, customs, institutions, etc.? In short, does language
provide some answers to questions that arise in the study of anthropology,
ethnography, and prehistory?*

—FERDINAND DE SAUSSURE

"PREHISTORY" REFERS TO a span of time that unfolded thousands of years ago and does not have a clear beginning point, but a case can be made that its history actually begins much more recently—in 1851 to be exact. That was the year Scottish-born Canadian archaeologist Daniel Wilson introduced the word "prehistoric" into English in a study of Scottish archaeology, a coinage that crystalized a growing recognition among scholars in the initial decades of the nineteenth century that the beginning of humanity went much further back into the past than anyone had previously imagined. This prehistoric age had literally been hidden from view. There was no written evidence from this earlier age, since writing had not been invented yet, so in order to retrieve information about it, people had to learn how to identify other, less obvious clues that this age had left behind—to recognize, for example that strange triangular-shaped rocks previously assumed to have fallen out of the sky were the fossilized teeth of creatures that had lived long ago (the insight of the seventeenth-century Danish anatomist Niels Stensen). Eventually, the search to understand the prehistoric age developed into a scientific field, paleontology, which uses the study of fossils to acquire knowledge about the past before the past recorded in written sources; and its influence helped scholars to realize that maybe they should be seeking the origin of other things in the prehistoric past as well. Europeans had long turned to Genesis to understand the origins of language, religion, and other aspects of social life, but it became apparent that these too had originated in an age long before the Bible's composition, and scholars thus began to look for ways to retrieve their prehistory, modeling their approach on paleontological study.

The recognition that humans have a prehistory led scholars to think in new ways about the origin of the Jews: they too were ascribed a kind of prehistory. A key development in this regard was the rise of the category of the "Semite," a classification developed over the nineteenth century that included Jews, Arabs, and other speakers of languages common in the Middle East. To this day Jews are sometimes referred to as a Semitic people (the label is implicit in the term "anti-Semitic," for example, a nineteenth-century term for anti-Jewish prejudice), and in the background of this classification lies a certain theory of Jewish origin that emerged in the eighteenth century. Scholars had recognized the similarities between Hebrew and languages like Aramaic and Arabic since medieval times, but it was only in the eighteenth century that the German Orientalist August Ludwig von Schlözer (1735–1809) proposed the classification of these languages as "Semitic," deriving the name from his observation that many of the nations who used these languages were identified as descendants of Noah's son Shem according to Genesis 10:21–31. Later scholars came to believe that Semitic peoples shared more than language—they were also believed to share certain religious practices, cultural traits, and physical characteristics—and their explanation for the similarities combined genealogy and paleontology: Jews, Arabs, and other Semitic-speaking peoples were similar to one another because they were all the descendants of a people who lived thousands of years ago, a prehistoric Semitic people. Buried in the background of the term "Semite," in other words, is a model of origin similar to that which governs how paleontologists conceive the origin of humans. Along with other Semitic peoples, the Jews descend from a small group of people in very remote antiquity from whom they inherited their defining qualities. To understand them one has to travel back to this distant point of origin, just as paleontologists reach back hundreds of thousands of years to understand the origin of humans.

Some of this prehistory of the Jews was recorded in documents that came to light as European powers expanded into the Middle East, giving Western scholars access to ancient Near Eastern sources. After the decipherment of Phoenician (a Semitic language used by a maritime people based in what is now Lebanon and northern Israel) in 1759, scholars began to realize that many aspects of the culture recorded in the Hebrew Bible had precedents in earlier cultures, and subsequent breakthroughs—the decipherment of Akkadian over the first half of the nineteenth century, for example, and the later discovery of texts from the ancient Syrian city of Ugarit in 1929—confirmed that impression by showing that the culture and religious life recorded in the Hebrew Bible drew on ideas, terminology, and social conventions that originated in prebiblical Near Eastern culture. The discovery of such ancient texts, written in Semitic languages related to Hebrew, allowed scholars to trace the history of the Semites into the millennia before Moses, and in the process revealed what they took to be long-term continuities between present-day Jews and Middle Eastern peoples who lived in the age before biblical literature was composed.

But some scholars thought it was possible to go even further back into the past, taking their search for the Semitic ancestors of the Jews into prehistory, to the period that predated the invention of writing itself. The best evidence that the various Semitic-speaking peoples all descend from a common ancestry came from historical linguistics, the study of language change over time, which traces the various Semitic languages back to a single proto-language, what is now referred to as "proto-Semitic." Today scholars no longer conflate the history of a language family like Semitic with the history of those who speak those languages, but in the nineteenth century, many scholars did not make that distinction; they defined the term "Semite" not just as a linguistic category but as a distinct population, the literal descendants of a particular group of people who emerged in a specific time and place in prehistory. What they were seeking to understand by reconstructing those ancestors was not just the origin of Hebrew but the origin of Jewish culture, religion, and psychology, and even Jews' distinctive appearance and biological traits. Since their more immediate predecessors had lived in Europe for many centuries and had adjusted to those environs, present-day Jews might appear different from those early ancestors—imagined as a simple people shaped by life in the desert—but it was believed that they preserved characteristics transmitted to them from their earliest Semitic forebears. To reconstruct these ancestors was thus, in effect, to reconstruct the Jews in their original and essential form—and thus to be able to distinguish what in Jews today was an inheritance from their earliest ancestors and what was the result of later intermixing with non-Semites.

But since these very early Semites had not left any records behind, how was one supposed to learn anything about them? There was no kind of fossil record to work with, but scholars proved resourceful in their search for other kinds of evidence, working backward from what they took to be survivals of early Semitic culture that could be detected in the present. The French scholar Joseph-Ernest Renan (1823–1892) found such evidence in the grammatical structure of Hebrew and other Semitic languages. A philologist, philosopher, historian, and political thinker, Renan was famous for, among other reasons, his wide-ranging scholarship on Semitic languages; he is also infamous for championing a racialized anti-Semitism and a stereotyped view of other "Oriental" cultures. Renan, seeking to reconstruct the origin of Semitic languages in the way the German scholar Franz Bopp (1791–1867) had reconstructed the common origin of European languages, believed that such study could help reveal "the embryogeny of the human mind," the development of thought among primitive humans. For Renan, Semitic languages were distinguished by a grammatical system that had not changed over the course of the millennia. In contrast to European languages, they also did not conjugate for mood or tense in as nuanced a way, and their syntax seemed simpler than that of European languages as well: they did not order words in the complex arrangements found in Greek or German syntax. For Renan the supposed linguistic characteristics of Semitic languages were a reflection of the mental characteristics of the early Semites, a people he believed intolerant of change and incapable of registering complexity and abstraction. According to Renan the intellectual accomplishments of Greek and German cultures went back to the greater intellectual capacity of ancient Aryans, as facilitated by their language, whereas the cruder quality of Hebrew and other Semitic languages derived from the limited intellectual capacity of the Semites at the beginning of their history "ten or fifteen thousand years ago."

Another way of reaching this prehistoric age was developed by William Robertson Smith (1846–1894), a pioneer in the ethnographic and comparative study of religion. Smith began his career as a professor of Hebrew at the Aberdeen Free Church College in Scotland, but some of the ideas he championed there about the Old Testament proved so controversial that he was put on trial for heresy and fired from his position. The situation gave him time to travel to the Near East, where he acquired Arabic and even briefly lived under the alias Abdullah Effendi (see Figure 2). What is now his most famous work, *Lectures on the Religion of the Semites*, draws on his experience and research there to reconstruct the religious life of the early Semites before the emergence of Judaism, Christianity, and Islam. Like Renan, Smith believed that the various Semitic peoples—the Israelites, the Phoenicians, the Babylonians, the Arabs—were descended from a common ancestral group, probably a people that originated in the Arabian Peninsula, and their common inheritance included not only language but a shared kinship-based social structure, a moral code, religious institutions, and forms of worship. To reconstruct the early Semitic religion from which these similarities emerged, it was not sufficient to study the earliest documents of Mesopotamian civilization. The Semitic culture recorded in those texts was already well developed and reflected the influence of non-Semitic cultures. One had to go back further, to an even earlier and more pristine form of Semitic culture.

Smith felt he was able to do this by studying the nomadic Bedouin he encountered in Arabia, believing that their isolation had

FIGURE 2. William Robertson Smith dressed as "Abdullah Effendi,"
an alias he used while traveling in Arabia.
Source: Photo by A. Dew Smith, Esq., reproduced in Sutherland Black and George
Chrystal, *The Life of Robertson Smith* (London: Adam & Charles Black, 1880).

preserved Semitic religion in a primitive form. By comparing the
lifestyle of the Bedouin with that of the Israelites as described in
the Old Testament, Smith believed he was able to sort out what
was early and what was late in Semitic religion, what was inherited
from the distant past and what was borrowed from other cultures.
He published the results as a series of lectures delivered between

1888 and 1891, which laid out his reconstruction of the primitive religion from which the religion of Israel had developed.

Scholars today do not accept most of what Renan and Smith observed about ancient Semitic culture, and their notions of the Semite went the same way as the idea of the Aryan, losing credibility after World War II, when the world had reason to regret the racialized thinking that had fed Nazi ideology. But the basic method they deployed—a kind of genealogical-paleontological approach that traces similarities to a common ancestor—is still used to reconstruct the ancestral form of the language from which later Semitic languages like Hebrew and Arabic developed. Scholars no longer equate this language with a specific mind-set or distinctive behaviors, but they do trace it back to a specific group of language users in the Neolithic period. Some scholars still believe, as Smith did, that Semitic originated in Arabia, but many now think it originated from an offshoot of a still earlier language in North Africa, perhaps in the southeastern Sahara. Settlement was more widespread in this region before it became the desert that it is today. Indeed, it might have been the process of desertization that forced its inhabitants to migrate in the fourth millennium BCE, some southeast into what is now Ethiopia (Ethiopic is also a Semitic language); others northeast out of Africa, into Canaan, Syria, and the Mesopotamian valley. Languages remain a thread that connects people today to prehistoric ancestors, changing and ramifying all the time but also exhibiting enough continuity over the millennia that they can still be traced back to the homelands of their earliest speakers.

While the idea of proto-Semitic illumines the prehistory of Hebrew, however, scholars today do not enlist it to address the question of Jewish origin in any way that resembles the theories of Renan and Smith. The speakers of proto-Semitic are an entirely hypothetical reconstruction—even the theorizing about where the earliest group of such speakers came from is little more than informed speculation, and there is no way to document any kind of connection between this original population and later Semitic-speakers, other than to conjecture about where the former migrated after it left its homeland. Even if it was somehow possible to prove the existence of these early Semitic-speakers or track their movements, scholars today would not draw any conclusions from such evidence about those who speak Semitic languages today. Already in the early twentieth century, there were some who protested that it made no sense to conflate the history of Semitic language with the history of a specific race—as the scholar Hilary Richardson noted in an essay on the Semites published in 1924: "Two peoples living close together and speaking Semitic might be as different from each other racially . . . as the English speaking North American Indians and the whites living in the same community." While it took many decades and the discrediting of the concept of race after the Holocaust, the racialized concept of Semite has been discredited among scholars: the idea that all Semitic-speaking peoples share distinctive psychological and physical traits inherited from a common set of ancestors in prehistory is recognized as a myth and an expression of racism.

If scholarship has given up searching for the Semitic ancestors of the Jews, however, it has not quite abandoned the kind of reasoning that motivated that search—the use of language as a way of tracing a connection between the Jews and their ancestors. It proved fruitless to try to go all the way back to prehistory to understand the origin of the Jews, but the decipherment of ancient Near Eastern languages proved that ancient Israel did not emerge from a vacuum, showing a particularly strong connection to earlier Canaanite culture of the Late Bronze Age (ca. 1600–1200 BCE). Hebrew itself, in fact, was recognized as an offshoot of the indigenous language of Canaan, almost interchangeable with Phoenician, Moabite, and other languages in the Levant, and there emerged other lines of continuity as well, from one of the names used for God ("El") to the categories of sacrifice performed in the Temple, to the literary devices used in biblical poetry. But moving beyond general parallels, was it possible to tie the Israelites in a more direct way to what was going on in Late Bronze Age Canaan, to fill in their specific prehistory prior to the age recorded in the Bible? This is where linguistics still has a role to play in retrieving the Jews' prebiblical ancestors: its methods are used to this day to show continuity between the Israelites and an earlier Late Bronze people from whom they were thought to descend.

Our more specific focus in the rest of this chapter is the use of etymology, the study of the origin of words, as a way to penetrate the prehistory of the Israelites. Modern etymological research derives from the insight that words preserve within themselves a clue about their origin, the "root" of the word that refers to the core meaning of the word but that also often connects it to the earlier, more primitive word from which it descends. Roots are particularly easy to recognize in Hebrew and other Semitic languages because they usually take the form of three consonants that carry the basic semantic meaning of the word. Almost everything else about a given Hebrew word is mutable and temporary—vowels vary from one form to the other, individual letters can double or disappear, prefixes or suffixes come and go—but with some exceptions, the root remains more or less the same in all the possible permutations, the most enduring aspect of the word, the inner core most resistant to change. This is what makes etymology so valuable for the paleolinguistic endeavor we are contemplating here. Because roots seem more immutable than other parts of language, because they are seen as the most primitive and enduring part of the word, they have served linguists as a way to get back to very ancient times and distant ancestors.

Indeed, in the nineteenth century, as scholars set about trying to reconstruct the prehistoric age, the roots of words were recognized quite explicitly as linguistic fossils, evidence not just of a word's own origin but of prehistory in general. In 1859, the same year Darwin published *The Origin of Species*, the Swiss linguist Adolphe Pictet (1799–1875) established a field that he referred to as "linguistic paleontology" (the word "paleontology" itself having been coined just a few decades earlier, in 1822). Just as paleontologists used the fossilized remains of species to reconstruct their evolution from earlier forms, Pictet used etymology, the analysis of the roots of words, to reconstruct the prehistory of Europeans. His *Les origines indo-européennes, ou, Les Aryas primitifs: Essai de paléontologie linguistique*, published between 1859 and 1863, uses such analysis to reconstruct the life of "the primitive Aryans"—their tools, weapons, domesticated animals, social and economic life—and to trace them back to a homeland in Central Asia. Other scholars in this period used linguistics to reconstruct the religion and mythology of the Aryans—a "paleontology of the human mind," as the philologist Max Müller (1823–1900) referred to such work. The nineteenth-century idea that Europeans descend from primitive

Aryans is now recognized as a myth (and an extremely dangerous one), and already before the end of the nineteenth century, certain linguists had grown very skeptical of linguistic paleontology (as we will discuss in more detail later in the chapter). But what is now more commonly known as paleolinguistics still has practitioners—including Colin Renfrew, Mario Alinei, and John Bengtson, among many others—who study Indo-European and other proto-languages to glean insights into the history, society, and thought world of prehistoric peoples. There is even a journal devoted to the field, *Mother Tongue*, published by the Association for the Study of Language in Prehistory.

What makes such research relevant here is that a similar kind of etymological reasoning has also produced a prehistory for the Jews, not the kind that goes back tens of thousands of years but a prehistory in the sense that it predates the earliest written evidence for the ancient Israelites. In this instance we are dealing not with a hypothetical people like the early Semites, a people that was only ever known through inference and reconstruction, but with a group actually attested in ancient Near Eastern sources, and one that lived not in a remote era that preceded the invention of writing but in the age just before the appearance of the Israelites, the Late Bronze Age, which ended around 1200 BCE. For the purposes of understanding the origin of the Jews, however, the Late Bronze Age functions like the prehistoric age, an age prior to the emergence of the thing we are trying to understand. The group we focus on, known as the Habiru, plays the same basic role that proto-humans do in paleontological accounts, serving as a proto-people: an incipient population who are not yet Israelites and who represent a kind of missing link between them and the world that existed prior to the Bible. The Habiru will help us think about how the concept of prehistory reshaped the way scholars approached the question of Jewish origin, but what also makes them relevant here is that their connection to the Israelites depends on an etymological argument, the analysis of a linguistic root. Can linguistic paleontology help us to penetrate the prehistory of the Jews? The connection made to the Habiru is evidence that it can, but it also illustrates the challenges of reconstructing a prehistory for the Jews prior to and independent of the biblical account, and the problems with relying on etymology as a way to connect that prehistory to the Jews as they emerge in a later age.

Etymology and the Origin of Nations

Before we turn to the Habiru, however, it is worth learning a bit more about the method we will be employing. In a way etymology reflects a variant form of the genealogical thinking introduced in the last chapter—the family tree model of thinking that seeks to illumine a thing by seeking out its roots. It too involves the act of connecting ancestors and descendants (in this case archaic words and the more recent words that descend from them); and it too is an effort to trace continuity rather than to explain change. Some reflection on this connection between etymology and genealogy will help us to understand how scholars came to use this kind of method to illumine the origin of the Jews.

One of the great masters of etymology was the seventh-century bishop Isidore of Seville (560–636), author of the compendious *Etymologiarum Sive Originum* (known in some early printed editions simply as *Origins*), and his work illustrates how, in premodern times, etymology was essentially a genealogical undertaking. For Isidore all languages descended from a common ancestor, Hebrew, and thus all names can be placed into a kind of family tree in the way that all the peoples of the world can be traced back to the three sons of Noah. Isidore acknowledged that names can change over time, but he was nonetheless able to discern the ancestry of many names by noting resemblances with words in other languages, resemblances born of their common ancestry in distant antiquity.

But the relationship between etymology and genealogy goes beyond this general analogy: etymology could literally function as a tool of genealogical inquiry, as it does in the Book of Genesis, where genealogy and etymology are woven together into the narrative. The genealogy that spools out over the course of Genesis situates the Israelites within the larger family of humanity, positioning them within a hierarchical structure of ancestors and children, older siblings and younger siblings. The etymologies that are interspersed within this genealogical narrative call attention to important ancestors by revealing something special about their names, something that happens at the moment of birth or at the point where they change their names that signals their distinctive role in history. In the case of Jacob, for example, there are three such etymologies: one to explain the meaning of the name Jacob (Genesis 25:26), the other two to explain how he came to acquire the name Israel (Genesis 32:25–29; 35:10). And there are similar etymologies offered for other key ancestors in Israel's ancestry— Noah, Abraham, Isaac, and Jacob.

Most of these etymologies, it should be noted, have an ethnological focus: their purpose is not only to explain the name of a particular person but also to explain the name of a larger group that claims that person as their founding ancestor. An example is the narrative's etiology for the name of the Edomites, descendants of Jacob's brother, Esau. Some of the etiologies offered by Genesis are quite explicit, but its approach to the name Edom is more subtle, insinuating an explanation by repeatedly associating Esau with the color red, or 'adom, which sounds like Edom in Hebrew: "the first [baby] to come out [of Rebecca] was red" (Genesis 25:25); and a few verses later, "Esau said to Jacob, 'please let me eat from some of this red, red stew'" (25:30). It is possible that "Edom" did originate from the word red—some speculate that the name arises from the red sandstone that colors the terrain of the Edomites' territory south of the Dead Sea—but Genesis does not make the connection, instead deriving the name from Esau's biography because its approach to the origin of people's names is fundamentally genealogical rather than topographical. Genesis applies a similar kind of genealogical-etymological approach to other neighboring peoples— the Ishmaelites, Moabites, and Ammonites—along with the Twelve Tribes of Israel, deriving all their names from episodes associated with the birth of their eponymous ancestors.

In the centuries following the biblical age, scholars continued to use etymology to tease out information about the origins of various peoples, including the Jews. We noted in the introduction that the Roman historian Tacitus recorded half a dozen opinions about the origin of the Jews. Among these, at least two were derived through etymological reasoning: The tradition that they originated from Crete is based on the supposed derivation of *Iudaios* (Jew or Judean) from the name Ida, a mountain in Crete; while another tracing the Jews to the Solymi, a people mentioned in Homer's poetry, is based on the name's alleged etymological connection to "Jerusalem." This is the intellectual tradition from which Isidore, known as the last great scholar of antiquity, inherited his own use of etymology. Isidore used etymology to understand everything—he believed that, by understanding the origin of a word, one could understand the true essence or character of the thing it described—and he applied that approach to the names of various peoples as well, going through the dozens of peoples descendant from Noah's sons to explain how they got their names. It was not always easy to fit the various peoples of the world into the genealogy of Noah's sons as recorded in Genesis, because the names did not match up. Thus, for example, there was no way to connect the name "Egypt" to the Hebrew name for Egypt in Genesis—*Mesraim*, a son of Ham—and Isidore could explain the difference only by acknowledging that the names of many people had changed over time in ways that scholars could not fully understand. But in many cases the original names had been partially preserved, and Isidore was often able to glean information from them about the ancient origin or early history of the people in question—the name of its first ruler, its origin in a particular environment, or a physical or behavioral trait that distinguished it from others.

Jumping ahead in this brief history of etymology to the sixteenth century, one can find in scholars from this time the beginnings of a critical consciousness, a skepticism about what names could reveal about the peoples who bore them. This, after all, was the age of Erasmus (1466–1536), who ridiculed the absurd etymologies proposed by scholars, and of the skeptic Michel de Montaigne (1533–1592), who questioned the use of names to reveal the essence of the people and things to which they were arbitrarily connected. But it was also an age in which Isidore's etymologies were widely read, and scholars emulated his method to learn about the ancient history of the peoples of their day. Historians from the era like William Camden (1551–1623), celebrated for his efforts to recover the ancient history of Britain, were conscious of how difficult it was to penetrate the origin of modern peoples—"the first originals of nations are obscure by reason of their profound antiquitie"—but he saw in etymology a way to bridge the passage of time; in Camden's words, etymology was the "surest proofe of peoples original," which could work to reveal the derivations of people even in the absence of any other kind of documentation.

There was clearly a political, polemical, even incipiently nationalist dimension to such scholarship. Camden's scholarship revealed that the Britons descended from Gomer, a grandson of Noah through Japhet. For the poet and historian Jean Lemaire de Belges (1473–1525), etymology revealed that the French descended from Noah himself. (The linguistic connection was the word "Gaul," an ancient name for France that he derived from the Hebrew word *gal* (wave), supposedly a title born by the seafaring Noah.) Here etymology supplies the nation with a venerable pedigree; other scholars from the era used it to disparage nations to whom they were hostile, as did the poet Edmund Spenser (1552–1599), who enlisted etymology to show that unruliness had been an Irish trait from ancient times. All such scholars assumed, as Isidore had done, that names reflected the character of the person to whom they were originally attached, and that this essence was transmitted to all those descendants who inherited the name. They thus used etymology not just to provide the peoples of their day with an ancient genealogy but to reveal their defining traits and to situate them relative to each other within a political, spiritual, and moral hierarchy.

Modern etymological inquiry is supposed to be very different from all this—objective, nonpolemical, and grounded by the recognition that there is no inherent connection between names and what they represent. Its orientation developed in the nineteenth century in tandem with the study of natural sciences and the theory of evolution, and it was distinguished from earlier etymological scholarship by its own aspiration to become an empirical science. This new orientation is clearly reflected in the work of the philologist Friedrich Diez (1794–1876), who made an explicit distinction between what he referred to as "uncritical" and "critical" etymology. The former "derives its interpretation from a superficial similarity of forms or else it forces an interpretation if the similarity is only vague," a good description of the etymologies in Genesis. The latter "is subject to the principles and rules which have been discovered in phonetics" (the linguistic study of sounds), and its explanations had to conform with a scientific approach to language. Etymology thus became unshackled from Genesis and from the theory that Hebrew was the original language of humankind. Scholars stopped trying to relate the names of peoples to those found in the genealogy of Noah, and instead they sought to understand their origin in light of what was being learned about the evolution of language.

Despite this difference between premodern and modern etymology, however, scholars continued the practice of using etymology to reconstruct the origin of nations. Some of the assumptions that underlie Isidore or Camden's approach to etymology—their belief that words were resistant to the ravages of time, that they told the story of their origins, that the names of people could be used to discern their ancestry, geographic origin, and even their collective character—persisted into nineteenth-century linguistic study, which no longer used etymology to trace the peoples of the world back to the sons of Noah but did use it to reconstruct their origin in distant antiquity or prehistory. The French jurist Jean Bodin (1530–1596), another scholar who used etymology to reconstruct the origin of nations, described names as "clearly marked footprints for the everlasting record of posterity": something that could be followed from the present to the time and place where the nation had begun. The perception of names as "footprints" that one might use to track a history of a people to its point of origin remains a part of etymological inquiry to this day.

This brings us back to the word "Hebrew," which has been recognized by scholars as one of these linguistic traces, a vestige of a very early period in the Israelites' history. As we will see in what follows, the modern scholarly explanation for the name "Hebrew" is very different from the premodern etymology practiced by Isidore, who derived the name from Eber, a descendant of Noah's son Shem. But in a way its goal is the same: not just to understand the origin of the name itself but to reveal something about the origin of the people that bears the name. What scholars have learned about the origin of the Hebrews in this way is our subject in the next section. It is a story about how scholars have used the origin of a word to reconstruct a prehistory for the ancient Israelites, but it is also meant more broadly as a case study in the use of etymology as a form of genealogical inquiry—what this kind of study can and cannot reveal about the origin of people, and what has become

of this approach among those scholars who are opposed to genealogical thinking.

The Prehistory of the Hebrews

The meaning of the Hebrew word for "Hebrew" in the Bible is
very different from what it is today. In modern times it refers to
a language, and it overlaps with the word "Jew," referring to the
same people though carrying a different set of connotations. Over
the course of history, the word "Jew" developed derogatory connotations, especially among non-Jews but also among some Jews
themselves, evoking a variety of negative traits, from miserliness to
weakness. (The online *Oxford English Dictionary* still lists "Jew" as
a verb that means to cheat or haggle, documenting its usage with
this meaning into the 1970s. I once saw a news story about an Okla-
homa state representative publicly using the term in this way in
2013, without embarrassment or regret.) "Hebrew" offered a less
stigmatized self-designation, even functioning in some contexts as
a kind of antonym for "Jew," the former ascribed a positive value,
the latter assumed to have a negative connotation. When in 1925
its Zionist founders opened up a new university in Jerusalem, for
example, they called it "the Hebrew University" to *distinguish* it as
something different from, and by implication as something better
than, the Jewish seminaries of Europe.

The modern connotation of the word "Hebrew" obscures the
meaning of its biblical ancestor, *'ivri*. In the Bible the term never refers to the Israelites' language (known not as Hebrew but as *yehudit*,
the language spoken in the territory or kingdom of Judah), and it is
not implicitly contrasted with the word "Jew," since the latter word
did not exist yet with its present-day meaning. (The term *yehudi* in
the Bible refers to a member of the tribe of Judah or an inhabitant
of the territory of Judah.) It has been noted that the term "Hebrew"
is rarely used by the biblical Israelites as a self-designation, often
coming from the mouths of foreigners—especially more powerful
foreigners like the Egyptians and Philistines—in reference to the
Israelites; it is used by Israelites about themselves chiefly in their
interactions with those foreigners, as if referring to themselves from
the latter's point of view. It remains unclear how the term relates

to "Israel" and why the biblical authors sometimes used the one term, sometimes the other, but most scholars believe they are not completely synonymous—that "Hebrew" means something different from "Israel." In Genesis the term appears earlier than "Israel" does—Genesis 14 refers to Abraham as a "Hebrew" long before Jacob is even born, suggesting that its author believed that the term "Hebrew" emerged much earlier in history than "Israel" did. For reasons we will see shortly, modern scholars have also concluded that the term "Hebrew" originated before the Israelite people.

What might the etymology of the word "Hebrew" tell us about the prehistory of the Israelites/Hebrews? Since Genesis likes to trace the origins of groups and their names back to specific ancestors, it is possible, as Isidore suggested, that the word derived from the name of a specific ancestor, Eber, from whom Abraham descends. But Genesis also implies another possible origin for the word by insinuating a connection to Abraham's status as a wanderer, a person who crosses from one place to another. *'Ivri*, the Hebrew pronunciation of "Hebrew," sounds like the word *'avar*, to pass, a verb which is often used in connection to Abraham in particular. Perhaps the repetition of this verb in the story of Abraham is like the tacit puns that connect the Edomites to the story of Esau, an attempt to imply an etymology for "Hebrew" by suggesting that the name goes back not just to a particular ancestor in Abraham's lineage but to the crossing that brought him to the land of Canaan.

If we had only the biblical evidence to go on, we would not be able to make much more progress in our etymological quest. For modern scholars, however, the word "Hebrew" has taken on new significance in light of the discovery of the similar term "Habiru" in prebiblical sources. The most important of these sources for understanding the prehistory of the term were found in Egypt in 1887: 382 clay tablets discovered among ancient ruins on the east bank of the Nile, about 190 miles south of Cairo. The place of their discovery, El-Amarna, was the site of a capital city founded in the fourteenth century BCE by the reformer king Amenophis IV, better known as Akhenaten, to whom we will return later. The letters, written in the Mesopotamian language of Akkadian, record the correspondence between the Egyptian king and his vassals in Canaan, the kings of Jerusalem and other city-states, and they are fascinating, among other reasons, for the glimpses they offer of Canaan a few centuries before the Israelites emerged there. What makes the Amarna letters of interest for us is the references they make to a group known as "Habiru." The term's exact pronunciation is not quite clear, as we will see, but it bore enough of a resemblance to "Hebrew" that scholars immediately saw a connection between the names.

It should be noted that the Habiru cannot simply be identified as the Hebrews. The term "Habiru" refers not to some specific ethnic group—a group defined by descent from a set of common ancestors or by association with a particular piece of territory—but to a social class of some sort found throughout the ancient Near East, an underclass of people living on the fringes of society yet also often drawing the attention of the authorities as outsiders and troublemakers. The term appears in more than two hundred documents that span the period between the eighteenth century BCE and the eleventh century BCE. We have no way of knowing whether those called "Habiru" ever referred to themselves in this way, and as the term was used by others about the Habiru, it seems to have been an insult. Depending on how one understands its etymology, the term might be connected to a word for "dust," as if referring to someone covered with dust, but scholars have also associated it with a range of other words and phrases, including "to cross over," "companion," and "to kill." What appears to be an equivalent term in Sumerian, represented by the logogram SA.GAZ, is puzzling in its own right but may reflect the word *shagashu,* or "murderer." (A logogram is a sign that indicates a concept rather than a sound.) While such explanations suggest a people associated with violence and predation, the Habiru were not always troublemakers: there are sources that depict them working as mercenaries, manual laborers, even as singers. Some scholars believe the term referred not to the violent character of this group but to its outsider status, encompassing rebels and outlaws but also migrants, fugitives, and others on the margins of society.

For reasons that remain unclear, "Habiru" is not attested in any source from after the twelfth or eleventh centuries BCE, which means that it stopped being used at around the same time when we have our first datable reference to Israel (around 1207 BCE) in an inscription known as the Merneptah Stele, and before the period when biblical authors started using the term "Hebrew" as a reference to the Israelites. Is this because the term underwent a change of meaning in the Late Bronze Age, losing the general meaning that it had in earlier periods and surviving only in Canaan as a reference to the ancestors of the Israelites? We lack the sources to resolve this question, but the possibility that the term "Hebrew" emerged from "Habiru" has led scholars to propose that the earliest Hebrews originated not as a tribe defined by its ancestry or place of origin but as an offshoot of a broader class of semioutsiders defined by their marginality, by their uprootedness, or by their unruly, troublemaking propensities.

The identification of "Habiru" with "Hebrew" did more than reveal an origin for the latter word; it launched new theories about the origin of the Hebrews themselves by establishing a linguistic connection with an earlier group of people, not a tribe or ethnic group but a social class of outsiders and outlaws dispersed throughout the Near East. The Habiru mentioned in the Amarna letters were particularly important to these theories because they lived in Canaan just before the appearance of the Israelites and because they are often referred to by those who dispatched the letters as an aggressive enemy force, a rebellious group that was threatening the Canaanite rulers of cities like Jerusalem. Here, for example, is how the Habiru are described in a letter from a ruler named Mayarzana, from a town in what is now Lebanon (the material in brackets fills in broken or missing text):

> The Habiru captured Mahzibtu, a city of the ki[n]g, my lord, and plundered [it] and sen[t] it up in flames, and then the Habiru took refuge with Ama[nharp]e. And the Habiru captured Gilanu, the city of the king, my lord, plundered it, sent it up in flames, and hardly one family escaped from Gilanu. Then the Habiru t[o]ok refuge with Amanharpe. And the Habiru cap[tu]red [M]agd[a]lu, a [ci]ty of the king, my lord, my god, m[y] Sun, plundered it, se[n[t it up in flames, and h[a]rd[l]y [on]e family escaped. . . . We he[ar]d [tha]t the Habiru [w]ere with Amanhatpe, so [m]y broth[ers] and my so[ns], your servants, d[rov]e a chariot t[o] Amanhatpe. My brothers sa[id] to Amanhatpe, "Hand ov[er] the Habiru, traitors to the king, our lord. . . ." (From a letter numbered EA 185).

The term "Habiru" here and elsewhere is associated with havoc, plunder, and disloyalty—the letter refers to them as "traitors to the king"—and it was sometimes applied to fellow rulers who had abandoned their loyalty to the Egyptians. For the most part it seems to refer to bands of marauders. So far as we can tell, the Habiru do not seem to have been a major military threat to Egyptian rule over Canaan, but they were enough of a problem for some of its local rulers that they pleaded for help, and the Egyptians did intervene now and then.

The discovery of the Habiru/Hebrew connection allowed scholars to reconstruct a prehistory for the Hebrews very different from the one described in Genesis. The earliest Hebrews, or the people from whom the Hebrews descended, emerged from a class of bandits and fugitives, neither farmers nor city dwellers but roving, rapacious, and violent troublemakers prone to harass those who lived within the cities of Canaan. In the period recorded in the Amarna letters—the fourteenth century BCE—the Habiru posed a threat to city-states like Jerusalem, albeit one they could contain with support from the Egyptian king; but as Egypt's control over Canaan declined over the next two centuries, the Habiru were thought to have eventually overcome or absorbed the cities of Canaan, establishing the kingdom depicted in biblical narrative as the one established by Saul and David. (David, scholars have pointed out, bears a certain resemblance to a violent and rapacious Habiru outlaw, spending the early part of his life on the lam from Saul, conducting raids, and occasionally hiring himself out as a mercenary.) The Bible registers the end of this process, but the Habiru-Hebrew identification made for a different beginning to the Hebrews' story than that suggested in the Torah: their ancestors were not migrants from Mesopotamia or Egyptian ex-slaves but Canaanite brigands, vagabonds, and rebels.

Subsequent research would reveal other connections between the Hebrew Bible and Canaan of the Late Bronze Age, striking parallels among Israelite and Phoenician and Ugaritic cultures, and there is now something like a scholarly consensus that Israelite culture emerged out of earlier Canaanite culture. Beyond linking the Israelites to a specific population in prebiblical Canaan, however, the Habiru-Hebrew connection played another role in how scholars came to understand the origin of the Jews by suggesting what it was that had differentiated the Israelites from other Canaanite peoples: the prebiblical ancestors of the Israelites were not part of the settled population of Canaan; in fact, they were at odds with that population. The Amarna letters give no indication that the Habiru came from outside the land of Canaan, as Genesis reports about Abraham, but the letters clearly indicate that they came from the margins of Late Bronze Age society and represented a destabilizing presence from the perspective of those who lived within Canaan's cities. Even as it established a line of continuity with prebiblical Canaanite history, in other words, the Habiru-Hebrew connection also seemed to get to the bottom of what had made Jews different from other peoples, a sociological difference that made a marginal and lowly social status, unsettledness, and rapacity a part of their collective pedigree from the beginning, to the extent that such a beginning could be established by scholarship.

The identification of the Habiru with the Hebrews provided a kind of transition between earlier Semitic culture and the Jews. The Habiru were nomadic, restless, unruly, and prone to violence. As such they filled in a missing link between the Jews and the earliest Semites as they were conceived at that time; but there may have been another reason this theory resonated as true for scholars in the late nineteenth and early twentieth centuries. Long before the discovery of the Amarna letters, there had existed in Europe a stereotyped image of the Jews as a people never at home in any particular place, never able to settle down. Some of this stereotype is personified in the widely circulated story of the Wandering Jew, a legendary figure doomed to walk the earth for eternity, but it also surfaces in depictions of the Jews as an essentially nomadic people. In an 1887 book titled *The Law of the Nomads and the Contemporary Domination of the Jews*, for example, the Viennese Orientalist Adolf Wahrmund (1827–1913) argued that the nomadic and plunderous character of the Jews is manifest in the form of "wandering merchants and dealers who cross the land selling junk . . . [and] rob our peasants and return on the Sabbath with their plunder." In a similar vein the German Assyriologist Friedrich Delitzsch (1850–1922) depicted the Jews as a "homeless or international people" who were a perpetual menace to other people, and he traced this quality back to the Hebrew Bible, which he described as an attempt to pass off "wandering and murdering nomads" as a chosen people. The image even made its way into the scholarship of the great German economist Werner Sombart (1863–1941), who in his *The Jews and Modern Capitalism* attributes the alleged Jewish affinity for capitalism to nomadic instincts inherited from ancestors he describes as "restless, wandering Bedouins." The discovery that the Hebrews emerged from the Habiru seemed to corroborate this image of the Jew as innately rapacious and nomadic.

I do not mention this background to suggest that contemporary scholars who embrace the Habiru as the ancestors of the Hebrews are motivated by anti-Semitic prejudice. There are reasons to accept the connection that have nothing to do with one's understanding of later Jews: the resemblance between the two words is indeed very striking, as is the resemblance between the Habiru and early biblical figures like Abraham, Jacob, and David. Indeed, many Jewish biblical scholars have also accepted the Habiru as ancestors of the Hebrews, including the great Moshe Greenberg, a former incumbent of the professorship I now occupy at the University of Pennsylvania, who devoted a monograph to the Habiru and cautiously endorsed the idea that the Patriarchs of Genesis might have been Habiru. But I would argue that the stereotyped image of the Jew as a perpetual and plunderous nomad is not irrelevant for understanding how scholars initially interpreted the connection between the Habiru and the Hebrews, and that we have to factor in this background as we weigh what this discovery tells us about the prehistory of the Jews.

The connection between the Habiru and the Hebrews was first made by a German scholar named Hugo Winckler (1863–1913), a brilliant philologist and archaeologist known not only for his work with the Amarna letters but for his excavation of the Hittite capital of Boğazkale, in what is now Turkey, and his discovery of a royal archive there. One of Winckler's breakthrough discoveries was his realization that the term "Habiru" in the Amarna letters was synonymous with the Sumerian logogram SA.GAZ, a discovery that had the effect of significantly expanding the Habiru's presence in Canaan, because the term "Habiru" is used in only a few letters from the king of Jerusalem, while SA.GAZ shows up in letters from throughout Canaan. He is also known as one of the founders of the Pan-Babylonian School within the field of Assyriology (another member was Delitzsch), which argued that what was most morally and culturally advanced about the Hebrew Bible was due to the external influence of Babylonian-Assyrian civilization rather than an internal development from within the Bedouin-like culture native to the Hebrews.

Winckler's effort to connect the Hebrews to the Habiru can be seen as part of a broader trend among European scholars during the nineteenth century—the effort to find ancient ancestors for various modern people. The most notorious example is the philological reconstruction of the Aryans, a now discredited hypothesis that traced various European peoples to an ancestral population more or less contemporary with the Habiru. The hypothesis that the Greeks, Germans, Irish, and other modern nations descend from an ancient Aryan people goes back to the philological work of Sir William Jones (1746–1794) and his insight, in 1786, that Greek and Latin shared certain roots with Sanskrit and Persian. This observation laid the groundwork for the idea that European, Persian, and Indian languages descended from a common ancestor. Although Jones's focus was the history of European languages, other scholars—including Friedrich Schlegel (1772–1829), Renan, Pictet (who used the field of paleolinguistics, which he founded, to investigate Aryan origins), Jacob Grimm (1785–1863, of the Brothers Grimm), Max Müller, and many others—saw the Aryans as a discrete population, even as a racial group, of proto-Europeans who migrated from India or Persia, across the Near East and Asia Minor, to settle in Europe, where their descendants developed the cultures that defined European civilization—the Greeks, Celts, Germans, and others. Linguists now recognize that much of this reconstruction is baseless: the ancient Iranian *ariya*, from a Sanskrit term that meant "noble" or "of good family," did not originally refer to a discrete population with a distinctive culture or racial profile; to the extent that the term "Indo-Aryan" is still used today, it is only in reference to a family of languages. But from the nineteenth century into the first half of the twentieth century, many scholars saw the Aryans as the ancestors of Europeans, an ancient tribe or race that had migrated to Europe and planted there the culture that had made European civilization so culturally dynamic and politically dominant.

Winckler, it so happens, was one of those scholars, detecting the presence of the Aryans at Boğazkale by uncovering various Indo-Aryan names in the documents discovered there. Indeed Winckler thought he found the word "Aryan" reflected in the word "Huru"/"Harri," the name of a people who formed a large part of the population of the Hittite Kingdom in what is now Turkey and northern Syria and Iraq. The population of the Hittite Kingdom, it seemed, included a large number of Indo-European-speaking Aryans, and Winckler and those who followed him credited that part of the population with the success of the Mitanni Kingdom in southeastern Turkey. What were Aryans doing in the otherwise Semitic Near East? Their presence there was understood as a stage in their migration from Central Asia to Europe. They were understood to be a highly dynamic people who brought order and civilization wherever they traveled, including a Near East inhabited by more static Semitic peoples. It was Aryan influence that had made the Babylonians so successful: according to this school, the Babylonians were not 100 percent Semitic but had Aryan blood in them as well, thanks to their interaction with the Sumerians, and it was this partial Aryan inheritance that supposedly accounted for why they were more culturally creative, intellectually advanced, and militarily dominant than other full-blooded Semites like the Arabs. It was also the presence of Aryans in Anatolia (identified by some scholars as the homeland of the Aryans) that had allowed for the rise of the Mitanni Kingdom there, supposedly the first Aryan kingdom. This is what made Winckler's discovery of putatively Aryan words in texts from Boğazkale so significant from the vantage point of those wanting to understand the history of the Aryans: it seemed to corroborate the Aryans' emergence as a dominant political elite.

What is striking about the Aryan hypothesis for us is how similar it is to the Habiru-Hebrew hypothesis. It too depended on etymological reasoning, as when Max Müller drew a connection between "Aryan" and "Ireland" (through the word *Eire*) or when Winckler connected "Aryan" to the name of the Hurrians. But we are dealing with more than just a parallel here. By discerning an Indo-Aryan origin for divine names and other words that surfaced in ancient sources, Winckler and other scholars believed themselves able to follow the movement of the Aryans across the Near East in a way that allowed for their history to literally intersect with that of the Habiru in Canaan. One of the rulers mentioned in the Amarna letters was a king of Jerusalem named Abdi-heba: he is one of the most vocal complainants about the Habiru, and it is his letters that actually use the word "Habiru" (as opposed to the logogram SA.GAZ). Using etymological reasoning, it was possible to argue Abdi-heba was himself of Indo-Aryan descent, for the second part of his name seems related to the word "Hebat," the name of a deity worshipped in Mitanni. The effort to reconstruct the linguistic-geographic-racial roots of names seemed to reveal that, even as early as three thousand years ago, the unruly Habiru ancestors of the Jews posed a threat to the Aryan ancestors from whom Europeans in this period believed themselves descended.

The Habiru and the Aryan hypotheses have had very different fates. The idea that Europeans can trace their ancestry to a noble race of conquerors known as the Aryans, an idea discredited by its role in Nazi ideology, is now regarded as a myth—a myth plus footnotes, as one scholar puts it. The Habiru-Hebrew hypothesis has had much less of an impact on the broader culture, but, in contrast to the Aryan myth, it survives as a viable idea: not accepted as fact but a respected hypothesis that scholars continue to build on to reconstruct the origin of the Israelites. My point is not that the Habiru-Hebrew connection is erroneous in the same way the Aryan hypothesis is but that it developed in interaction with the Aryan myth in a way that should give us pause. Both ideas, emanating from overlapping networks of scholarship, started from a single word discovered in ancient sources (*ariya* in the case of the Aryans; *habiru* in the case of the Habiru), which was spun out into an ancient population through various kinds of philological dot connecting, as when scholars identified an Aryan ruler of Jerusalem by connecting his name with an Indo-Aryan name, or when they expanded the Habiru presence in Canaan by equating the word *habiru* with a Sumerian logogram. In both cases, moreover, the people reconstructed in this way bequeathed not only its name to a successor people (the Hurrians, the Irish, the Hebrews) but also its character: the Aryans transmitted their dynamism to Europeans, while the Habiru passed on their nomadism to the Jews. It is not too much of a stretch to propose that the image of the Habiru, like the related category of the Semite, of which it was a subcategory, developed as the inverted image of the Aryan, for while the Aryans embodied the qualities of an idealized European (high-minded nobility, a genius for order and stability, a penchant for creativity), the opposite qualities were ascribed to the Habiru (lowliness, unsettledness, unruliness, an association with destruction).

Should we then treat the Habiru-Hebrew connection as another myth plus footnotes? Not in the way the Aryan myth is. The Habiru (or the SA.GAZ) are attested in more than two hundred sources from the Near East, not just in the Amarna letters but in other texts from Egypt and Mesopotamia; they were a widely recognized class of person on the margins of ancient Near Eastern society. The question is not whether the Habiru existed but how to connect them to the Hebrews mentioned in the Bible, and this is where there is room to debate the straight line of succession that scholars draw between them. While many scholars continue to see a link between the Habiru and the Hebrews, a closer examination of the evidence shows that it is not quite so easy to make the connection.

To begin with there is a distinct possibility that the words "Hebrew" and "Habiru" are not actually related etymologically. They certainly look similar, especially given how "Habiru" is transliterated into English, but appearances can be deceiving. The first letter of "Hebrew" (ʿivri) in Hebrew is the letter ʿayin, a guttural sound that does not have an exact equivalent in English; whereas the first letter of "Habiru" seems to be a ch sound. That is the first difference, but it can be accounted for. In 1862, a few decades before the discovery of the Amarna letters, the Egyptologist Francois Chabas (1817–1882) uncovered references in Egyptian texts to groups called the ʿpr or ʿpr.w (the character ʿ signifies an ʿayin sound), which he equated with the Hebrews of the Exodus. Later scholars came to identify ʿpr as a variant spelling of Habiru—ʿApiru—which shares the initial ʿayin sound with the Hebrew ʿivri. It is possible, in other words, that the cuneiform writing system of the Amarna letters, which did not have a distinct sign to represent the guttural ʿayin, used another sign in its effort to approximate that sound, just as in English we sometimes use an h to approximate the ch sound of a Hebrew word. But while the connection of the Habiru with the ʿApiru of Egyptian texts helped scholars bridge between the *h* of "Habiru" and the ʿ*ayin* of ʿ*ivri*, that comparison also introduced another problem with the second consonant—the difference between the *p* of "ʿApiru" and the *b* in "Habiru." Scholars have offered explanations for how one sound could become the other, but those explanations are ad hoc, and no one knows for sure how to account for how one sound became the other. In short, despite the resemblance between "Habiru" and "Hebrew," it is possible that two of the three root consonants of "Habiru" do not match the root consonants of "Hebrew" (not to mention that scholars also haven't been able to account for the differing vowel patterns of the two words).

As pedantic as this difference might seem, it helps to explain why there have long been dissenters from the Habiru/Hebrew equation, though admittedly they are in the minority. Seemingly related words can be "false cognates," similar or even identical in form and sound but arising from different roots. An example comes from the similarity between the word *ur-*, a prefix meaning "original," and *Ur*, the name used in Genesis for the place from where Abraham originated. It is tempting to connect the two words—they look identical, and one can see semantic overlap as well—but they are unrelated: the former arises from a proto-Germanic word for "out," while the latter from the Semitic for "city." As similar as they seem, "Habiru" and "Hebrew" could likewise be false cognates.

Even if we are inclined to discount or explain away the phonetic differences between "Hebrew" and "Habiru," it is not so easy to account for another difference between the two words—their different meanings. The term "Habiru," as we have noted, describes not an ethnic or religious group but a class of outsiders, fugitives, outlaws, people on the margins of society. In some texts the Habiru seem to be Semites; in other texts they can bear non-Semitic names; and there is no indication that they shared an ancestry or came from a particular place. People even seem able to join the Habiru, as some of the people mentioned in the Amarna letters do by fleeing their city and joining the enemy. It describes a social position in society, not an ethnicity, tribal affiliation, or geographic origin.

By contrast, the word "Hebrew," as used in the Bible, is applied only to the Israelites and their ancestors and to no other group.

Though it sometimes appears in apposition to the word "slave," it clearly is not a synonym for "slave"—otherwise it would be redundant to refer to a "Hebrew slave." We have noted the possibility that whoever composed Genesis understood the word to derive from the name of "Eber," as if the name were understood to signify a certain ancestry (descent from line of Eber), and its form is consistent with such an understanding: the suffix -*i* at the end of the word gives it the form of a "gentilic," an adjective or noun used to describe affiliation with an ethnic, tribal, or religious group (e.g., "Israeli"). How did a label used throughout the Near East to refer to a whole class of people narrow down into a gentilic, a mode of self-identification limited to a specific community? Even if we accept the derivation of "Hebrew" from "Habiru," the connection does not account for the semantic transformation required for one word to become the other.

For scholars like the late Anson Rainey (1930–2011) of Tel Aviv University, an expert in the Amarna letters, these kinds of problems were enough to undermine the Habiru/Hebrew equation altogether: He rejected the attempt to connect the two people. From his perspective there is little difference between the Habiru/Hebrew hypothesis and the kind of premodern etymologizing we described in the preceding section: both involve an overinterpretation of a superficial linguistic resemblance. Many others aren't as bothered by the differences between the two words, or assume that there must be some explanation for the differences that we cannot recover from the evidence. We will not be able to resolve the debate here, but what is clear is that the connection to the Habiru does not reveal quite as much about the origin of the Hebrews as it might seem to at first blush: even assuming that there is a linguistic connection between the two terms, there is something about the form of the word "Hebrew"—and even more important about the meaning that it has in the Bible—that cannot be accounted for by investigating what the word descended out of, an unexplained break in the period between the Amarna letters and the Bible that detached "Hebrew" from the meaning of its ancestor "Habiru." There have been attempts to account for how one word became the other, but they are speculative, going beyond the evidence we have. The discovery of Habiru revealed a thread of continuity between the Israelites of the Bible and the Canaanite population of the

earlier Late Bronze Age, but in the process it has also revealed a
gap—a discontinuity between the two names and the two groups—
that we cannot bridge.

Beyond the particular problems with the Habiru-Hebrew comparison, there is one more reason to question what this connection might tell us about the origin of the Jews: not a problem of
evidence or how to interpret it, but a critique of the underlying
method we have been using—linguistic paleontology. While there
is still important work being done in paleolinguistics, many are
dismissive of efforts to use the history of words to reach a point of
origin—an attitude found among a number of twentieth-century
thinkers (Jean Paulhan, Derrida, Maurice Blanchot), as Christy
Wampole shows, but that ultimately goes back to the end of the
nineteenth century and Pictet's most famous student. As a young
man, Ferdinand de Saussure (1857–1913) was fascinated by Pictet's
linguistic-paleontological project: "The idea that with the help of
one or two Sanskrit syllables . . . one could reconstruct the life of
people who had disappeared, inflamed me with an enthusiasm un-
equalled in its naïveté," he would later observe. As suggested by
his use of the term "naïveté," however, Saussure had grown disenchanted with Pictet's approach, rejecting the search for prehistoric
mother tongues and the use of language to recover the lives of lost
people. If we are to understand why, according to some scholars,
we have been off track in our efforts to use the origin of the word
"Habiru" to reconstruct the prehistory of the Hebrews, we need to
understand why Saussure rejected the thinking of his own mentor.

The Turn from Linguistic Paleontology

Ferdinand de Saussure, who is sometimes described as a founding father of modern linguistics, was related to Adolphe Pictet not
just intellectually but personally, as a friend to Pictet and even a
member of his extended family through marriage. Saussure acknowledged Pictet's *Les origines indo-européennes, ou, Les Aryas
primitifs* as a major influence on him as a young man; and some
of his earliest scholarship continued his mentor's interests, treating various problems in Indo-European historical linguistics. Even
after Pictet's death in 1875, Saussure published several essays about

Pictet's scholarship, noting that his mentor's work took the reader "to the threshold of the origin of language."

But in retrospect it is clear that Saussure's own approach to language was premised on a rejection of linguistic paleontology. As his thought would develop, the questions that had engaged Pictet—the origin of language and the use of linguistic history to reconstruct national origins—lost their interest: "the question of the origins of language does not have the importance generally attributed to it," he wrote in his posthumously published *Course in General Linguistics*. "It is not even a relevant question as far as linguistics is concerned. The sole object of study in linguistics is the normal, regular existence of a language already established." Elsewhere in that work he asks, "Does language provide some answers to questions that arise in anthropology, ethnography and prehistory?" "Many people think so," he answers himself, "but I believe this is an illusion." Saussure was not completely opposed to drawing historical and anthropological conclusions from the linguistic evidence—he believed, for example, that language offered insights into the family structure of the prehistoric Indo-Europeans—but he questioned many of the basic premises and conclusions of linguistic paleontology of his day: the way it identified racial and linguistic groups, for example, and its effort to attribute the particularities of Semitic syntax to the nature of the Semitic mind. Saussure's dismissal of linguistic paleontology as largely illusory—and the corollary idea that the focus of linguistics should not be the origin of words but their meaning and use after they are already established—set a new direction for linguistics, encouraging a shift from origin-centered subfields like linguistic paleontology, to the synchronic study of language as a system of interlocking parts.

Among its many consequences, this reorientation has led to a marginalization of etymology as a branch of linguistic inquiry. Saussure himself acknowledged that language originated in the past, but its origin, the moment at which a word was attached to something in the world, was beyond empirical observation and was largely irrelevant in any case, for the meaning of such a word in his view was determined not by its ancestry but by its current usage: from how a word is used within a living language. Whereas etymology focused on continuity and genealogy, the tracing of words back to their roots, Saussure's approach emphasized difference—how words differed from other words within the same language system. His approach in this respect is an important precursor to the anti-genealogical orientation of thinkers like Foucault, Deleuze, and Guattari. The history of a word before it entered language in a particular moment—the fact that some earlier form of the word might have once had a certain meaning in Latin two thousand years ago—was of no value for understanding what it meant in the present context of actual language usage.

Saussure's approach helps to explain why we had such a difficult time bridging the semantic difference between "Habiru" and "Hebrew." Perhaps the word "Hebrew" descends from the word "Habiru" in a linguistic-genealogical sense, but from the perspective introduced by Saussure, we cannot understand what the word "Hebrew" signified by going back to some moment prior to the language in which this word was used; we can understand its meaning only from within that language, in relationship to other words used in that language at that particular point in time. To try to explain the meaning of "Hebrew" by deriving it from a linguistic ancestor is thus to conflate completely separate words, even if they happen to share a genealogical connection, for the meaning of a word is not predetermined by genetic transmission—by having inherited a root meaning from a linguistic ancestor—but is generated through its interactions with other words within the same linguistic system.

The influence of Saussure's approach has not put a stop to the effort to use "Habiru" to illumine the origin of "Hebrew," but it has introduced an alternative approach to the relationship between the two terms that stresses the *irrelevance* of "Habiru" for understanding the meaning of "Hebrew" within the Hebrew Bible. In 1999 the Israeli scholar Meir Sternberg published a study of the word "Hebrew" that perfectly captures the shift from linguistic paleontology to the Saussurean perspective we are describing here. Sternberg is a literary scholar whose approach to narrative, like that of many literary scholars active after the 1960s, reflects the influence of Saussure. His first major publication in biblical studies, *The Poetics of Biblical Narrative*, is premised on the Saussurean insight that linguistic signification (in this case, the stories that appear in Genesis and other biblical narratives) can be understood without needing to understand the origin of the biblical text or the narrative's relationship to a historical reality external to language. In his follow-up work, *Hebrews between Cultures*, Sternberg applies a similar approach to the word "Hebrew" as used in the Bible. I will not try to summarize his argument here—Sternberg's writing can be turgid and hard to follow—but its core argument is worth highlighting as an illustration of what a Saussurean approach would make of the Habiru-Hebrew connection.

Sternberg starts from the observation that "Hebrew" as it is used in the Hebrew Bible often appears in the mouths of foreigners, especially more powerful foreigners like the Egyptians and the Philistines, or else it is used by the Israelites but only when they are referring to themselves from the perspective of such foreigners. Its use seems tied to the power imbalance between those others and the Israelites: whenever it is used, it implicitly acknowledges a class difference between the foreigner and the Israelite, ascribing to the latter the status of a lowly and less powerful alien—this is true even when the Israelites apply the term to themselves. When Moses instructs the Israelites on how they are to treat the "Hebrew slave" in Exodus 21, his use of the term "Hebrew" as opposed to "Israelite" acknowledges that the enslavement of fellow Israelites involves a kind of self-estrangement, treating one's own people as they had been treated by the Egyptians, and his legislation is meant to curb the Israelites' tendency to think of themselves as slaves.

The association of "Hebrew" with outsider status recalls the connotation of "Habiru," but Sternberg scoffs at earlier scholars' use of "Habiru" to illumine the meaning of "Hebrew," ridiculing the "acrobatic circling and twisting" required to connect the biblical and extrabiblical evidence. His own approach is to explicate "Hebrew" as it is used within particular biblical stories, as a term whose significance can be understood not by tracing its roots into earlier prebiblical sources but only through the kind of synchronic literary analysis that Sternberg developed in *The Poetics of Biblical Narrative*, an analysis that focuses only on the meaning of the term "Hebrew" within the biblical corpus. Sternberg's analysis takes seven hundred pages to unfold, and I am not conveying some of the more farfetched parts of his argument, but the key point to grasp about it is its Saussurean approach to the meaning of "Hebrew." The word as used in the Bible should not be explained genealogically, as a descendent from an earlier term, but needs to be approached as a word whose meaning is generated by its participation in a self-enclosed linguistic network. Calling his approach Saussurean is not something I came up with myself; Sternberg himself compares it to Saussure's theory of the language system (p. 186).

Here then is an explanation for the semantic break that we came up against in the attempt to trace continuity from "Habiru" to "Hebrew." For a scholar like Sternberg, the semantic difference between "Habiru" and "Hebrew" cannot be overcome by learning more about the word "Habiru" as used in the Late Bronze Age or by filling in the documentary gap between that period and the age of the Hebrew Bible; for the etymology of a word, its genealogy, has no bearing on how it is used within language at a particular moment of its existence. What generates the word's meaning is its relationship to other words within the same language, and that can be investigated only synchronically, through the study of the rules and usage of a language at a specific point in time. Thus the meaning of the term "Habiru" in the Amarna letters has to be understood within the context of the Canaanite-influenced Akkadian used in the letters, while the different meaning of "Hebrew" in the Bible can be made sense of only in the context of its poetics, and there is no bridging between these different systems of meaning. Linguistic paleontology is not just tangential to the sort of Saussurean analysis that Sternberg practices but all but impossible, for in his view there is no connection that one can trace between "Habiru" and "Hebrew," no line of genetic transmission or evolutionary development. Each word is embedded within a self-enclosed language system and can be understood only within the borders of that system.

The conclusions Sternberg draws about the meaning of "Hebrew" are idiosyncratic, but his anti-paleontological bent is reflective of a broader turn in scholarship that makes it difficult to draw any kind of conclusion about the origin of the Jews from the terms they have used to describe themselves. As further evidence for this trend, consider recent efforts to illumine the origin of another name of relevance for understanding our topic—the word "Jew." A standard account of the history of this word will trace it back to ancient terms like *iudaios* in Greek, which goes back in turn to the earlier Hebrew word *Yehud*, or Judah. This appearance of a word evolving in a straight line from an ancient ancestor into the present is misleading, however. It is not that we cannot trace its history. The problem is that, from a Saussurean perspective, none of this historical background is especially relevant for understanding what the term "Jew" means now, for that meaning depends less on its derivation from an earlier ancestral term and more on what is happening in the language around it today. The mind derives the meaning of the word "Jew" not by delving into its etymology but by contrasting it with other terms as they are used within the speaker's language: in the case of "Jew," as it is used in American English today, its meaning is defined in opposition to terms like "Christian," "Arab," or "Hebrew," as these words are also used today. This emphasis on synchronic analysis, which focuses on language at a particular point in time without concerning itself with how it got to that state, makes it more difficult to trace continuity of meaning across historical periods. To compare words from two different historical periods is really to mix apples and oranges as far as this perspective is concerned, treating words that come from two unrelated linguistic systems as if they came from one system. The influence of this approach helps to explain why it is that when scholars today treat the history of the word "Jew," their impulse is often synchronic, to focus on its differences from other words at that same point in history, rather than genealogical, to reconstruct a relationship of descent from words in earlier languages.

The influence of this perspective can be illustrated by means of a recent debate that played out online in 2014, a debate triggered by the question of whether the term "Jew" is the appropriate translation for the Greek *iudaios* in ancient sources like the New Testament. Several scholars involved in the forum argued that the translation "Jew" does not capture the original meaning of the term *iudaios*, and that the difference was worth conveying to readers of English translations by using the less familiar term "Judean" to represent *iudaios* rather than "Jew." The other side in this debate argued that translating the term as "Judean" negates the evidence for historical continuity between the ancient *iudaioi* and later Jews.

The basic issue that divided the two sides was whether translators should emphasize discontinuity with later Jews by using

"Judean" to translate the term *iudaios*, or accentuate the continuity between them by translating it with the more familiar "Jew." There are powerful arguments in support of either position, etymological and also ethical. Advocates of the "Judean" translation point out that the use of the New Testament to justify Christian anti-Judaism is premised on the identification of ancient Judeans with present-day Jews. By calling attention to the historical difference between the two peoples, their translation is meant to discourage present and future readers of the New Testament from thinking that the text is talking about or meaning to condemn their own Jewish friends and neighbors. Opponents argue that by erasing the word "Jew" from antiquity, the translation "Judean" erases Jews themselves from antiquity, an act that, far from exhibiting sensitivity to the Jews, shows disrespect to them by nullifying their self-image as an ancient people. The biblical scholar Adele Reinhartz, raising the emotional stakes of the debate considerably, complained that the "Judean" translation reminded her of how pro-Nazi theologians used their scholarship as a pretext for purging the life of Jesus of any detail that suggested his Jewish origin.

Both sides of this argument agree that the word "Jew" derives from or shares a common ancestry with *iudaios*: the point of contention is what the relationship between these terms tells us about the relationship between Jews today and their ancient forebears. Does the etymological connection between them imply what philosophers refer to as "identity over time," the persistence of some essential trait from antiquity to the present? Are Jews today, in some collective sense, *the same people* as the Judeans described in the New Testament, or are they fundamentally different, transformed by the passage of time or by some intervening change into another people? A similar difference over continuity and discontinuity is also inherent in the debate about the relationship between the Habiru and the Hebrews, where one is also faced with two words from different periods that seem related to one another: Does their possible etymological connection imply continuity of identity, or are the differences between the terms evidence of an essential discontinuity?

No one in this recent debate endorses anti-Semitism (though some are critical of Israel), and no one draws from the linguistic evidence any kind of conclusion about the Semitic or nomadic character of the Jews. As much as things have changed since the days of Pictet, however, there is nonetheless a certain resemblance between their paleolinguistic project and the method of those who emphasize the continuity between *iudaios* and "Jew." In both cases etymology works to show the long-term continuity of a people by tracing their name back to an ancient origin. Contemporary scholars of course recognize that the form and meaning of the word "Jew" is different from that of its Hebrew, Aramaic, and Greek ancestors: the word no longer has the tribal resonance of the biblical Hebrew word *yehudi* or the geographic resonance of *iudaios*, and it seems to be only in a much later period that it began to acquire the religious connotation that now places it in the same semantic category as "Christian" or "Muslim." But even so, for scholars in this camp, something in the word "Jew" has nonetheless carried over from its ancient predecessors, just as there has persisted something in the Jews themselves that carries over from their Judean ancestors.

Our focus here, however, is the other side of this debate—those who argue for the discontinuity between *iudaios* and "Jew"—for it is their position that demonstrates the influence of the Saussurean perspective. None of those who argue for the "Judean" translation cites Saussure by name, but that is only because his influence has so deeply penetrated scholarly thinking that it does not have to be acknowledged. Thus, for example, the argument that one shouldn't mix up the meanings of the terms *iudaios* and "Jew" because they come from two different linguistic and historical contexts is indebted to the Saussurean distinction between the diachronic and the synchronic, a distinction that makes it anachronistic to pluck a word from one period in the history of a language and use it to interpret a word from another period. Behind the translation of *iudaios* as "Judean" is the assumption that the meaning of words is not an enduring essence registered in their root letters but rather that they can be understood only in relation to other terms used within the same language at the same point in history—a perspective scholars owe to Saussure.

To the extent that this perspective shapes current intellectual thinking about the meaning of terms like "Hebrew" and "Jew," it makes it all the more difficult to enlist linguistic paleontology to address the question of Jewish origin. It is one thing to account for phonetic differences. Although scholars' various attempts to account for the phonetic differences between "Habiru" and "Hebrew" are speculative and ad hoc, it is possible that they are on the right track, that the root letters of the two words are different because they evolved slightly different pronunciations over time or were written in one way in one language system and another way in another language system. But such explanations do not account for the semantic gap between "Habiru" and "Hebrew" or *iudaios* and "Jew." From a Saussurean perspective, such gaps open up in the space between different synchronic states of a language, in which what happens within one state cannot be understood in light of what happens prior to that state or used to explain what emerges within a later state: there is only what happens within language at a given point in its history, and etymological reasoning cannot bridge between one point and another.

The discovery that the Jews have a prehistory, that they have an ancestry that predates the biblical sources, transformed how scholars think about their origin, pushing their search into much earlier history. Later chapters will look at some of the other methods scholars use to illumine this prehistory, and it is not my intention to argue against this larger quest or to dismiss what scholars have learned from undertaking it about the connections between ancient Israel and earlier Near Eastern culture. The question we are seeking to address here is whether the study of linguistic roots can help us to penetrate this prehistory—whether etymology can function as a form of paleontology—and after several centuries of such scholarship, we must acknowledge that the results are rather mixed. Scholars have uncovered intriguing linguistic links between the Jews' Israelite ancestors and earlier people in Bronze Age Canaan, but there are also those who resist the effort to tie the Hebrews etymologically to the Habiru—indeed, some scholars reject the possibility of linguistic paleontology itself—and the reason for this skepticism isn't only that there is little evidence to work with: there are conceptual issues as well—concerns about the underlying ideology and biases at work in the scholarship, unresolved questions about how to trace continuity from ancient ancestors to later peoples, and a certain fuzziness in scholars' understanding of what is getting transmitted from one generation to the next.

We will be learning more about all these issues as our quest continues in subsequent chapters. All that I would note by way of a conclusion to this one is that the success of the Saussurean paradigm has implications for our inquiry that go beyond the way it complicates the search for the prehistory of the Jews. Saussure's rejection of linguistic paleontology reflects—and in fact helped to precipitate—a broader opposition to the search for origin that became increasingly influential over the course of the twentieth century. As Saussure himself put it, the scholar "who wishes to understand a state must discard all knowledge of everything that produced it." In the intellectual culture that took root in the twentieth century, that attitude would become widespread—and not just among scholars of language and literature but also among scholars of religion, ethnicity, and other subjects bearing on how the question of Jewish origin is pursued today. We cannot hope for scholarship to make much progress in addressing this question if scholars no longer believe the question is worth asking. This is why, for all the obstacles we face in our quest, one of the most formidable turns out to be the synchronic orientation that Saussure helped to make so influential, a perspective that makes the search for origin seem irrelevant for many scholars, a distraction from what they really want to understand.

CHAPTER THREE

Histories Natural and Unnatural

THE DOCUMENTARY HYPOTHESIS AND OTHER DEVELOPMENTAL THEORIES

All that we see are the mingled facts of persistence and change. We see migrations and wars, dynasties toppled, governments overthrown, economic systems made affluent or poor; revolutions in power, privilege and wealth. We see human beings born, mating, child-rearing, working, worshipping, playing, educating, writing, philosophizing, governing. We see generation succeeding generation, each new one accepting, modifying, rejecting in different proportions the works of preceding generations. . . . We see all of this and much more.

But we do not see "death," "decadence," "degeneration," or "sickness." We do not see "genesis," "growth," "unfolding," or "development." Not in cultures and societies. All of these words have immediate and unchallengeable relevance to the organic world, to the life-cycles of plants and organisms. There they are literal and empirical in meaning. But applied to social and cultural phenomena these words are not literal. They are metaphoric.

—ROBERT NISBET

FOR SOME SCHOLARS in the nineteenth century, the search for the origin of the Jews led them to prehistory, to the antecedent peoples from whom the Jews descended, early Semites and the Habiru.

For others, the search pointed them in a different direction, to a later historical period, and to a process of change rather than long-term continuity. The Jews of their own age, such scholars noted, could be distinguished from the people described in the Bible. They were called "Jews" and not "Israelites," after all, and their culture was different from the Israelite culture described in the Bible—they no longer worshipped in the Temple; study had replaced sacrifice as the central religious act; the central religious authority was not the priest but the rabbi, whose interpretation of the Five Books of Moses went well beyond anything explicitly recorded in its text. In the eighteenth century it began to strike scholars that the origin of the Jews involved some kind of transformation that took place in the period between the Israelites of the biblical age and the Jews of the present day. To understand the origin of the Jews, it was not enough to understand their Semitic ancestry or their roots in earlier Near Eastern culture: one had to grasp the developmental process that had turned the Israel of the Bible into present-day Judaism.

For many this turning point was registered in the Bible itself, in the biblical books of Ezra and Nehemiah. By this point, in the fifth century BCE, the kingdom of Judah had been devastated by the Babylonian Empire, which had conquered the city of Jerusalem, executed the king and his sons, destroyed the Temple, and sent the population into exile. What was left of the population, mostly the descendants of the tribe of Judah who lived in the kingdom of Judah but also survivors from the tribes of Levi and Benjamin, might well have disappeared altogether, as the other tribes of Israel had disappeared in the wake of their conquest by the Assyrians in the eighth century BCE, but they were spared by another act of military conquest. Within a few decades the Babylonians fell to another empire: the Persian Empire established by Cyrus the Great, who allowed the people of Judah to return home and rebuild the Temple in 539 BCE. The books of Ezra and Nehemiah, named for important leaders of the Judean community after its return to Jerusalem, depict the age of Persian rule as a period of restoration and rebuilding; but there was something different about the returnees, something that distinguished them from their Israelite ancestors, and the search for the origin of the Jews amounted to the quest to understand that difference.

The idea that the Jews, as distinct from the biblical Israelites, began in the "postexilic" age (roughly 539–400 BCE) goes back to the eighteenth century, and it continues to shape how many scholars think about the origin of the Jews to this day. In many standard reference books, this is where things start. In the multi-volume *Cambridge History of Judaism,* for example, the first volume focuses on the Persian period that began with Cyrus's return of the Jews to Jerusalem in 539 BCE and ended with Persia's defeat by Alexander the Great in the 330s BCE. This represents a variation on the idea that the Jews originated in the postexilic period, for the Persian period is more or less coterminous with the postexilic age. In some scholarly accounts the idea is reflected in the identification of the scribe Ezra, living in the midst of this period in the fifth century BCE, as the leader who created Judaism by codifying the laws of the Torah; in others, the honor of founding Judaism is conferred on Ezra's contemporary, the governor Nehemiah, who was appointed to his role by a Persian king named Artaxerxes. The books of Ezra and Nehemiah do not themselves report the emergence of anything new in this period—what they describe is a process of restoring what was lost during the exile. What I am describing is a modern narrative that begins the history of the Jews in this period based in the belief that their religion or culture was different in an essential way from that of the pre-exilic Israelites.

I can illustrate the impact of this view in light of my own scholarly formation. The department where I did my graduate training was Harvard's Near Eastern Languages and Civilizations department. It is located within a museum, the Semitic Museum, which is a monument to the continuity of Semitic culture from the ancient Near East into the modern day. But the organization of the NELC department also registered an important rupture, the break between biblical Israelites and postbiblical Jews, and the dividing line between them was the postexilic/Persian period. As a biblical scholar-in-training, I was required to learn about the prehistory of the Bible, to study ancient Near Eastern languages like Ugaritic, and to learn about proto-Semitic. I was also required to study the Aramaic used in the Persian period and to learn about Ezra and Nehemiah and other books from that age, such as 1–2 Chronicles and Esther, but that is where the requirements stopped; everything that happened after that was the purview of a separate program, Jewish Studies. There was nothing idiosyncratic about this division between biblical studies and Jewish studies—to this day, in my role as a biblical scholar, I feel a little out of place in Jewish studies conferences, and as a Jewish studies scholar, I feel a little out of place in biblical studies conferences because, surprisingly, there is so little overlap or mutual engagement between the fields: for the purposes of scholarly inquiry, biblical Israel and the Jews are two distinct entities. I did not realize until later that this intellectual and organizational distinction went back to a particular origin account, with the postexilic/Persian age as the point of demarcation between Jews and their biblical ancestors.

How then did the postexilic/Persian period come to play such a transitional role in the emergence of Judaism? The answer to this question begins in eighteenth- and nineteenth-century Europe and the emergence of biblical scholarship as represented by figures like Johann David Michaelis (1717–1791), Johann Gottfried Eichhorn (1752–1827), Wilhelm de Wette (1780–1849), and Abraham Kuenen (1828–1891), all scholars who made a sharp distinction between the age before and after the Babylonian exile. Thus, for example, De Wette—known for his pioneering effort to provide a historical explanation for the composition of the Five Books of Moses—asserted the following distinction:

> The sojourn in a foreign land under a foreign people of a completely different outlook and religion, in addition to the impact the destruction of the state had upon the people, must have been of decided influence upon their religion. This influence was so great that we must view the nation after the Exile as a different one, with a different worldview and religion. We call the people in this period *Jews*, and in the period before, Hebrews; and what belongs to the post-exilic culture is called *Judaism*, while in the pre-exilic culture, it is called *Hebraism*.

De Wette and other scholars of his era were not the first to distinguish between the biblical Hebrews and the Jews of their own day. It is not clear to me when Jews began to use the name "Jew" to refer to themselves. (In the Talmud for example, it is common to refer to an individual Jew as "Israel," and in the Middle Ages, Ashkenazic Jews, at least, used terms like "Israel" or "children of the covenant.") But they were routinely referred to as the *iudaioi* or its Latin equivalent in non-Jewish sources from antiquity, and already in the first century CE, the historian Josephus felt the need to explain the change in nomenclature, ascribing it to the period of the return from exile (*Antiquities* 11.173). This was a distinction picked up by later Christians, such as the historian Eusebius (ca. 260–340 CE), though he placed the terminological shift from "Israel" to "Jew" much earlier, at the time of Mount Sinai. What is new in the eighteenth century is the idea that the difference in name reflects a deeper change and one that can be explained historically— Jews were to be distinguished from the Israelites/Hebrews not just because those who returned from Babylonia were from the tribe of Judah, but because, as a result of their experiences during exile, they had developed—in De Wette's words—a "different outlook and religion."

The effort to distinguish early Hebrews and later Jews was part of a long tradition of Christian anti-Jewish polemic that sought to discredit the Jews as authentic heirs to biblical Israel, but what added a new dimension to it in modern times was the emergence of developmentalist thinking as a way to account for the difference between Israelites and Jews. The seventeenth and eighteenth centuries saw the rise in Europe of an age when scholars began reconceptualizing the origin of all sorts of things as an unfolding process or sequence of stages, an approach that motivated research into geology, embryology, the evolution of species, and human cultural and social history. The first person to propose that humans developed out of earlier apes, for example, was Jean-Baptiste Lamarck (1744–1829) in his book *Zoological Philosophy*, published in 1809, just four years before De Wette published the passage cited above in his *Biblical Dogmatic of the Old and New Testaments*. In the same period Georges-Louis Leclerc, Comte de Buffon (1707–1788) developed the idea of degeneration (from the Latin *degeneris*, "removed from one's origin"), a process whereby a species or race of man became smaller and weaker through the effects of climate, diet, and domestication. The naturalist Johann Friedrich Blumenbach (1752–1840), known as the "father" of physical anthropology, was among the first to apply such an approach to human development when he proposed that, after the Flood, nonwhites had degenerated into a more apelike form under the influence of the differing geographical conditions found in Africa, Asia, and the Americas.

Thus it was not a coincidence that De Wette understood the development of Judaism in a very similar way, referring to it as a "degenerate and petrified Hebraism." The Enlightenment offered more positive models of development as well, but whether things got better or worse in a given account of the origin of the Jews, what these theories shared was the framing of that origin as a process of gradually unfolding change—a process of maturation from an immature state into an adult form, degeneration into a weaker form, epigenesis in which a seed or egg develops along a series of stages, or petrification into a desiccated and deadened form—all ways of describing the origin of the Jews that took root in the eighteenth century under the influence of a developmental turn in scholarly thinking. To account for the origin of the Jews required identifying the causes and successive stages of development that led from the biblical Israelites to the Jews of the Talmudic age (and to Christianity), with the postexilic age serving as a crucial transition point in many accounts.

One of the most influential of these nineteenth-century developmental theories of Jewish origin—and our focus in this chapter—was one formulated near the end of the century by Julius Wellhausen (1844–1918), often described as the most important biblical scholar of the nineteenth century, though his contributions to Arabic and Islamic studies are equally significant. Wellhausen is famous for developing the Documentary Hypothesis, an attempt to account for the composition of the Five Books of Moses that built on the ideas of De Wette and other scholars. Wellhausen's work represents an example of "source criticism"—*Quellenkritik* in German—which in biblical studies refers to the attempt to distinguish the sources drawn on by an author or editor to compose a given biblical text and to understand those sources in relation to the context in which they were composed. (New Testament scholars apply the same technique to the Gospels.) In theory, a source can be any source of information in any medium, written or oral, but Wellhausen believed the sources of the Five Books of Moses were preexisting documents—differing accounts of Israel's history that existed prior to their fusion into a single narrative. Thus his theory of the Pentateuch's composition came to be known as the "Documentary Hypothesis."

More specifically Wellhausen's theory identified four discrete sources woven together into the Five Books of Moses: the Yahwist (or the *Jahwist*, in German, and hence now abbreviated as J), the Elohist (E), the Deuteronomic author (D), and the Priestly author (P). These were once-independent accounts that Wellhausen believed were written at different periods before they were woven together into the Torah. Building on earlier scholarship, Wellhausen was able to differentiate the sources from one another (except for J and E, which he believed were fused together very early on) because their literary styles and vocabulary were different from each other, and because they operated with different ideas about God and other religious matters. The authors of J and E, for example, believed the Israelites could sacrifice to God from any location, whereas the Deuteronomic and Priestly authors viewed sacrifice as an act that could be undertaken only at a specific location (never identified by these sources but probably understood by their authors as the Temple in Jerusalem).

What fascinates many people today when they learn about the Documentary Hypothesis is the way it challenges the traditional ascription of the Torah to Moses. But for Wellhausen the goal wasn't simply to explain the origin of the Five Books of Moses but to account for the origin of the Jews, their development out of the biblical Israelites. By using source criticism (the analysis of the sources used to produce the Torah), he was able to reconstruct the stages of the developmental process that transformed the Israelites into the Jews, beginning from an initial stage reflected in J and E; moving into a transitional stage reflected in D, which Wellhausen associated with the reign of King Josiah (641–609 BCE) and his effort to centralize worship in the Jerusalem Temple; and reaching the latest stage in P, which registered the beginnings of the kind of Judaism that crystalized in later rabbinic sources. The religion reflected in J and E was nature-based, originating from the rhythms of agricultural life and the spontaneous emotional needs of the people. It was then disrupted by a sequence of events that increasingly alienated it from this nature-based lifestyle, especially the Babylonian exile, which forcibly removed the people from its land; and the result, reflected in the Priestly source, was Judaism, the religion that would produce the Pharisees, the Mishnah, and the Talmud. The idea that biblical Israel had devolved into Judaism was fairly similar to what earlier scholars like De Wette had proposed. What distinguished Wellhausen's work was *how* he demonstrated his thesis: his use of source criticism to demonstrate a step-by-step development from Israel to Judaism.

The result of this analysis was a kind of evolutionary account of Jewish origin that spanned several hundred years. J and E preserved the earliest documentable stage of this development, reflecting an Israelite culture of the ninth and eighth centuries BCE that lived close to the land, had a simple lifestyle, and was not very sophisticated, but was in tune with nature and its own emotions. P, on the other hand, reflected the end of the process, a postexilic Judaism detached from its land and from nature, desperate to salvage its ancient traditions but disconnected from them—an "artificial Israel" whose only link to its pre-exilic Israelite ancestors was through the study of texts and the compulsive enactment of the laws and customs it had inherited from Israel. Under foreign rule the survivors of the exile had been exposed to the ideas of others, making them more cosmopolitan than the pre-exilic Israelites, but they overintellectualized their tradition, focusing on a knowledge of the law to the exclusion of emotion and spontaneity. Subjugation had made them clever and manipulative but also politically passive, and their effort to conserve every detail of their tradition had stifled their spiritual life, making them legalistic and ritualistic, obsessed with enacting every detail of the law at the expense of a genuinely felt connection with God.

This difference between pre-exilic Israel and postexilic Judaism was reflected, for example, in how J and P depicted the creation of the world—J's account reflected in the Garden of Eden story in Genesis 2-3, P's account found in Genesis 1. In what Wellhausen regarded as the earlier, more poetic, and more mythlike creation story of J, man is meant not to seek knowledge but to live in harmony with nature and God, and it is a tragedy when humans are exiled from the garden to a life of knowledge, guilt, civilization, and alienation from the world. The priestly account, by contrast, is more logical and abstract, and less imaginative. For Wellhausen this difference between the two creation stories amounted to a before and after picture: in J a glimpse of the childlike culture of the pre-exilic Hebrews who did not know much about the world but breathed its air directly; in P a picture of a people more worldly and knowledgeable than their Hebrew forebears but less spontaneous and creative. The difference reflected a change that had unfolded between the pre-exilic period and the postexilic age, a process of alienation from the land, denaturalization (in the literal sense of being detached from nature or made less natural), political disempowerment, overintellectualization, abstraction, and religious rigidification.

What is of interest here is not the nitty-gritty detail of Wellhausen's source-critical analysis but the underlying narrative of Jewish origin that such analysis was meant to demonstrate. We have seen that he was drawing on a well-established tradition of developmental thinking that went back to the eighteenth century, but those earlier accounts were drawing on cruder models of change that were based on analogies with developmental processes that could be directly observed because they unfolded within a relatively short amount of time—maturation to adulthood, for instance, or the process of ossification. By the second half of the nineteenth century, as we noted in the last chapter, scholars had gained a better understanding of temporal depth, of how much time the earth or life or the human species had taken to develop. They were better able to trace long-term developmental processes by having figured out how to place evidence like fossils into a relative chronological sequence; and they had formulated more sophisticated mechanisms of evolutionary change. I want to situate Wellhausen's theory within this later thinking to help us better understand what exactly he was arguing about the origin of the Jews.

The most famous of these later developmental theories is, of course, Darwin's theory of evolution, which became widely influential precisely in the period when Wellhausen developed the Documentary Hypothesis. It seems fairly clear that Wellhausen did not draw on Darwin in the direct way that, say, the German writer Wilhelm Bölsche (1861–1939) did, by reading the Bible as the story of evolutionary development. Wellhausen himself lists his influences—De Wette, Edward Reuss, Leopold George, Willhelm

Vatke, K. H. Graf—and Darwin is not among them. But Wellhausen wrote at a time when many German scholars were enamored of Darwinism. The first translation of *The Origin of Species* into any other language was in fact the German translation of 1860, and by the 1870s, the decade when Wellhausen published his hypothesis, evolutionary theory was prevailing in many German intellectual circles. Especially given this intellectual context, it was hard to miss the resemblance between the Documentary Hypothesis and Darwin's theory, and Wellhausen's contemporaries did not miss it, as when Franz Delitzsch, father of the Assyriologist Friedrich Delitzsch, described Wellhausen's theory as "merely applications of Darwinism to the sphere of theology and criticism." Delitzsch, a highly conservative Lutheran theologian, did not intend the comparison as a compliment, meaning to dismiss the Documentary Hypothesis, and he was simply wrong to describe it as "merely" an application of Darwinism. In Wellhausen's reconstruction of Israelite history, for example, there is no competition of species or process of natural selection, as Darwin argued for the origin of species; we could cite other developmental theories from the era that exerted a more direct influence on Wellhausen, such as the philosophy of Georg Wilhelm Friedrich Hegel (1770–1831), whose sense of the world as moving progressively forward in a dialectical process of reasoning colored the thinking of some of the scholars who influenced Wellhausen. And yet there is something to the comparison, and pursuing it can help us understand how Wellhausen reconceived the origin of the Jews.

The Descent of the Jew

If we were to attempt a history of the idea of origin, one of the most important turning points in that history would be 1859, the year Darwin published *The Origin of Species*. As the reader may have learned from a high school biology class, it introduced a radically new way of thinking about the origin of living beings, one which Darwin contrasted with what he referred to as the theory of special creation, the creation of species as described in the Book of Genesis. Darwin's theory undercut many of the tenets of creation as described in Genesis: the idea that one needed God to explain the creation of species, of course, but also other long-cherished assumptions. It undercut people's sense of their genealogy by expanding the ancestry of humanity not just beyond the three sons of Noah but beyond the human species altogether. No less important was Darwin's claim that one did not have to go back to some absolute beginning point to understand the origin of species. Different species could still be traced back to a common ancestor, as in Genesis—in theory, in fact, all life descended from a single ancestor—but understanding that originating moment was not the focus for Darwin. He was for the most part uninterested in efforts to understand how life first came into being—the original origin of life—seeing the matter not just as too speculative but as largely beside the point for understanding the evolutionary process he was seeking to delineate. For Darwin what was of interest was not how life first emerged but the "innumerable miraculous creations" since then—not a single moment of genesis but an ongoing, proliferating process of originating.

Darwin's theory had a direct impact on how people conceived the origin of the Jews—in fact, he himself touched on the question, noting very briefly in *The Descent of Man*, a follow-up to *The Origin of Species* published in 1871, that European Jews were probably the result of racial mixing between peoples of Semitic and European stock. Other scientists and anthropologists quickly developed his theory into full-fledged biological histories of the Jews, seeking to account for their physical and mental traits by placing them within an evolutionary framework of natural selection and competition among different races. We will return to those theories later in the book, but for our purposes in this chapter, we are interested in Darwin's theory not as a source of scholarly thinking about the origin of the Jews but as the focus of an analogy, a comparison between two things whose similarities to each other are *not* the result of a shared ancestry. Darwin himself famously relied on an analogy between natural and artificial selection in *The Origin of Species* as a way to explain the workings of his theory. An analogy with Darwin can help us to highlight some of the distinctive features of Wellhausen's approach to the question of Jewish origin—a part of his argument now overshadowed by his theory of the Torah's origin—and to draw connections with the developmental thinking of his day.

For his part Wellhausen did not apply a biological approach to the origin of the Jews. He was not interested in the effects of natural selection, nor did he seek to place the Jews within the larger family tree of humans. And yet his account of the origin of the Jews does exhibit some striking parallels with Darwinian theory. There is of course the fact that Wellhausen's theory also involves development over time. Indeed the words Wellhausen used to describe this process of development—including "transformation" (*Umbildung*), "metamorphosis" (*Umgestaltung*), and even "evolution" (*Entwicklung*)—are the same kinds of words Darwin used for his theory. (Or rather, that his German translators used; these are all words that appear in the first German translation of *The Origin of Species* from 1860.) But the parallels go beyond this general resemblance in ways that reveal that Wellhausen's and Darwin's thinking were more closely aligned, analogically speaking, than many of Wellhausen's commentators acknowledge. I want to note four of these parallels, again not to suggest that Wellhausen borrowed specific ideas from Darwin but to help the reader appreciate how thoroughly his approach to the question of Jewish origin was grounded in late nineteenth-century developmental thinking in a broader sense.

THE DISREGARD OF PRIMORDIAL BEGINNING

The first of these parallels pertains to how Darwin and Wellhausen conceived the act of originating. As we noted, what Darwin had in mind by the "origin" of species was not an event in the past but an ongoing process that continued into the present. He did believe in the existence of a common ancestor for living things—he even posited a common ancestor for humans originating from Africa, in opposition to theories that traced different races back to different species of ape; but what he was chiefly interested in was not *the* beginning, the very first appearance of life or the very first ancestor of all living beings, but the innumerable moments of beginning that have happened ever since. Darwin did not pursue the quest to understand the origin of life in primordial times—never offering an explanation for whatever process turned matter into life—not because he was completely uninterested in the question but because he concluded that such an inquiry was beyond the reach of science, and because there was more to learn about the evolutionary process that set in after this initial, unknowable event.

Wellhausen adopted an analogous approach to the origin of the Israelites. Like his friend William Robertson Smith, Wellhausen did show some interest in uncovering "the original form" of Hebrew culture by comparing it with Arab-Bedouin culture; and here and there in the *Prolegomena to the History of Israel*, the work in which he develops the Documentary Hypothesis, he draws parallels with Arab customs that point to the Jews' Semitic ancestry. Yet the focus in that work isn't on the earliest phase of Israelite religion but on a historical development that sets in after the Israelites have already come into being. Even the earliest of the four sources, J, is from an Israelite society that already exists, that is already settled in the land and under monarchic rule, and while Wellhausen may have been curious about the origin of the Hebrews, his commitment to a scientific approach required him to acknowledge that their very earliest history was beyond the scholar's reach: "It is true, we attain to no historical knowledge of the patriarchs [i.e., Abraham, Isaac, and Jacob], but only of the time when the stories about them arose in the Israelite people [i.e., in the monarchic period]." The Documentary Hypothesis, like Darwin's theory, was an attempt not to go back to the absolute beginning but to trace the changes that set in after that beginning; in fact, as Wellhausen was able to demonstrate, Genesis itself was a record of that ongoing change, revealing nothing about the age of Abraham and Moses but capturing different stages of Israel's development in the period after its settlement in the land of Canaan.

MALADAPTATION

One reason historians of biblical scholarship do not buy Darwinian influence on Wellhausen is that the latter posits a process of *decline* from Israel to Judaism, a narrative of decay and death, whereas a Darwinian perspective, they assume, implies progress, a movement from a simpler state to a higher and more superior form of life. It is true that Wellhausen plots his origin story as a story of decline: Judaism as he conceived it was on a downward trajectory toward extinction, and it was Christianity that represented the developmental advance. Where this argument goes wrong is in its claim that Darwinian evolution necessarily connotes progress toward a higher state of existence. It has to be acknowledged that Darwin himself contributed to this interpretation of his theory by using words like "improved" and "perfected" to describe the results of the evolutionary process—and that idea would have sunk in even deeper through the German translation, which renders *The Origin*'s subtitle, *The Preservation of Favoured Races*, as *Erhaltung der vervollkommneten Rassen—The Preservation of Perfected Species*. But the association of evolution with progress reflects a later spin on Darwin's thinking that obscures the fact that Darwin did not equate evolution with progress. He recognized that species could be maladapted—an animal could inherit traits from its ancestors that became useless for survival when the species moved to a new habitat or its environment changed in some way. Evolution did not always lead from a lower to a higher state: sometimes organisms could evolve in a way that was not conducive to their species' long-term survival, that could weaken the species, make it fit less well with its environment, or even doom it to extinction.

This observation leads to a second key point of correspondence between the two theories. The Jews, as Wellhausen saw them, were like a species cut off from the environment in which it had first developed. His account of Israelite history is a story of how the Jews were dislodged from their natural habitat—the agrarian culture of ancient Canaan—and then adapted in unhealthy ways to life in exile. This process of denaturalization began with Josiah's centralization of the cult, the stage of Israel's religious development reflected in D, the Deuteronomic source. By moving Israel's religious life from the shrines of the countryside into a single location within the city of Jerusalem, the king severed the religious practices of the Jews, their sacrifices and festivals, from the natural environment in which they had initially developed. The process was then completed by the Babylonian exile, which completely tore the nation away from its original habitat and agrarian lifestyle. Those scholars who claim that the Documentary Hypothesis is different from Darwinism because it does not posit a narrative of progress have been misled by the common conflation of evolution with progress: Wellhausen's conception of Judaism as a religion maladapted to its exilic circumstances exactly corresponds to what Darwin envisions as the fate of a species facing environmental change to which it is ill adapted.

THE NATURAL VERSUS THE ARTIFICIAL

The third parallel I want to touch on concerns the nature of that adaptation—how the Israelites responded to their new environs. To fend off the possibility of extinction, the postexilic Jews of Wellhausen's narrative tried to revive themselves by doing everything they could to revive the life their Israelite ancestors had led prior to the Babylonian exile. Thus they clung to what they had inherited from their pre-exilic forebears—their laws, customs, and rituals— essentially trying to freeze them in place by obsessively reenacting them and by canonizing them in a form, the Five Books of Moses, that was meant to be permanent and changeless. This, according to Wellhausen, is what accounts for the legalism and ritualism that he ascribed to Judaism, first attested in the Priestly source and passed on from there into Pharisaic and rabbinic Judaism, a fossilized religion that preserved a desiccated shell of Israelite spirituality in a static and lifeless form.

What had doomed Judaism to this fate, according to Wellhausen, was that it was now detached from nature: Jews had tried to sustain themselves by replicating qualities that pre-exilic Israelites had developed organically, as a natural response to their environment, and that effort had failed precisely because it was unnatural, disconnected from the flow of life. As he writes in the *Prolegomena,*

> [A] complete breaking off of the natural tradition of life, a total severance of all connection with inherited tradition . . . was accomplished by means of the Babylonian exile which violently tore the nation away from its native soil, and kept it apart for half a century,—a breach of historical continuity than which it is almost impossible to conceive a greater. *The new generation had no natural, but only an artificial relation to the times of old*; the firmly rooted growths of the old soil, regarded as thorns by the pious, were extirpated, and the freshly ploughed fallows ready for a new sowing. (italics mine)

In line with this view, Wellhausen repeatedly uses the word "artificial" (*künstliche*) to describe postexilic Jews—in fact he refers to them as a "new artificial Israel," by which he meant that they were the product of conscious fabrication rather than an outgrowth of a natural development. Thus, for example, for Wellhausen the outstanding characteristic of the books of 1–2 Chronicles—a retelling of the books of Samuel and Kings composed in the Persian period, which Wellhausen reads as a reflection of postexilic Judaism—is its artificiality, manifest in the Chronicler's "artificial style" and the "artificial genealogies" that he manufactured to connect the temple officials of his day to biblical ancestors, and Wellhausen finds a similar quality in the Priestly author. Wellhausen likewise describes the Torah itself as it took shape in the postexilic period—not the specific laws inherited from J, E, and D but their systematization, integration, and codification as a sacred constitution of Judaism under the scribe Ezra—as an "artificial product." Having lost their connection to the land, the Jews tried to conserve as much of their ancestors' religion as they could, but they proved unable to artificially reproduce the qualities that pre-exilic Israelite religion had acquired in the natural way that a plant grows roots and stems.

Darwin also made a distinction between the natural and the artificial—the contrast is at the heart of his analogy between natural and artificial selection—which isn't to say that the contrast functions in the same way in their respective arguments. Both scholars were drawing on an understanding of the difference between the natural and the artificial that can be traced back at least to eighteenth-century Romanticism, and which was commonplace by the second half of the nineteenth century, as in an infamous 1850 essay by Richard Wagner in which the composer contrasted the "artificial" music of Jewish composers with the "natural" (and therefore more genuine) music of Germans. But there is nonetheless something more precise which connects the role of the artificial in the Documentary Hypothesis and Darwinism. Artificial selection is a kind of imitation of natural selection—conscious and intentional—whereas natural selection unfolds of its own accord, naturally, without any kind of human intervention involved. Darwin does not suggest anything wrong with artificial selection—it is just a technique that shows some of the workings of natural selection on a quicker scale—but he does suggest that natural selection was more powerful than what humans could accomplish through artificial means. As he writes in *The Origin of Species,*

We have seen that man by [artificial] selection can certainly produce great results ... but Natural Selection ... is a power incessantly ready for action, and is as immeasurably superior to man's feeble efforts, as the works of Nature are to those of Art. (1860 edition, published by John Murray, p. 62)

Or later,

Slow though the process of [natural] selection may be, if feeble man can do much by his powers of artificial selection, I can see no limit to the amount of change, to the beauty and infinite complexity of the coadaptations between all organic beings, one with another and with their physical conditions of life, which may be effected in the long course of time by nature's power of selection. (ibid., p. 109)

The results of artificial selection, associated with the feeble power of man, are contrasted here with the limitless beauty and complexity that can be achieved through natural selection. Later interpreters of Darwin built on this idea to argue that natural selection was vastly superior to artificial selection. One example from the American context is that of the conservationist John Muir (1838–1914), a contemporary of Wellhausen who lamented how the wonderful achievements of natural selection were being replaced by the inferior works of artificial selection. A similar preference for natural over artificial selection might have influenced the 1860 translation of *The Origin of Species* by H. G. Bronn, who used the word "perfected" (*vervollkommnet*) to describe the effect of natural selection but avoided using that word for artificial selection, apparently believing that humans could not artificially reproduce nature's power to improve life.

Wellhausen's distinction between pre-exilic Israel and postexilic Judaism corresponds in a way to the distinction between natural selection and artificial selection. Disconnected from nature, the Jews have been seeking to preserve themselves by trying to replicate the qualities of nature—attempting to artificially revive ancient customs and simulating blood ties to their ancestor by fabricating "artificial genealogies." Their and their successors' efforts were quite elaborate; indeed, as Wellhausen puts it, Judaism as the Pharisees and rabbis practiced it developed into an "art" in the sense of a highly stylized and intricate practice. But such efforts could not replicate the power of nature, and the resulting culture, for all its elaborateness, was dried up, dying, or already ossified. In an article he wrote for the *Encyclopedia Britannica*, he describes Judaism as a "dead work" incapable of blossoming again, and he predicted that it would eventually go extinct, though he envisioned the process taking centuries. This was the fate that Jews were trying to avoid by using artificial means to preserve their culture, but just as Muir believed artifice could not reproduce the wonders of nature, Wellhausen believed it could not reproduce the natural vitality of Israel.

LIVING FOSSILS

Wellhausen recognized that the priestly/rabbinical response to exile had preserved their religion for thousands of years. Part of what made it such an unhealthy response, however—and what ultimately doomed Judaism to extinction—was that it was born of an effort to resist change. The Jews were certainly influenced by their exposure to foreign culture, becoming more "cosmopolitan" in Babylonia and absorbing influences from later Christian and Islamic cultures. Uprooted from their agrarian way of life, they began to engage in trade and acquiesced to foreign rule, but they did not fully adapt to or integrate into their new environment. To the contrary, in a religious and social sense, they withdrew from the world, isolating themselves from other peoples, turning inward and trying to fix their traditions in a static form. Though it also developed out of the Old Testament, Christianity knew how to keep things fresh by unleashing the creative qualities of the spirit: in the light of the Gospel, Wellhausen explains, "the will . . . makes an absolutely new beginning not conditioned by the past." The rabbis, following the Priestly author, had opted for the opposite strategy, storing up as much of the past as they could; such a tactic could never work in the long run precisely because it was defying the dynamism inherent in nature, the fact that the living always need to grow and adapt. As the history of ancient Israel demonstrated, life imposes change, sometimes violently so, and the Jews had made a self-destructive choice by freezing their culture in place rather than starting anew. For Wellhausen, Judaism was the opposite of a developmental approach in the sense that it was born of thinking that refused to acknowledge the necessity of change.

There is something in Darwin's account that corresponds to the survival of Judaism as Wellhausen represents it: the persistence of what he calls "living fossils"—fish and other species that seemed to have remained immutable since ancient times. Wellhausen did not treat the Jews as a "living fossil"—his argument was not that Judaism preserved a vestigial form of Semitic religion, although it bore traces of that background—but rather that it had acquired its ossified character over time and in response to the changes imposed by foreign conquest and exile. But from the developmentalist perspective he was operating within, the self-imposed stasis of Judaism posed a problem not unlike that posed by the living fossil—what to do with something that seemed stuck in the past, that resisted development? In both cases what seems to be an exception to the general rule of change requires a special explanation that reabsorbs it into an evolutionary framework. Thus for Darwin living fossils like the platypus and the lungfish were explained as the least modified descendants of remote ancestors that had been able to persist in a relatively unchanged form because they inhabited confined environments where they faced less severe competition from other species. For Wellhausen Judaism had preserved itself intact by concealing itself "in a narrow shell that stoutly resisted all foreign influence," that is, by enclosing itself within social and religious barriers that minimized contact with outsiders. The two explanations are different—Darwin explains living fossils as creatures spared from change by their environments; Wellhausen's Jews aren't so lucky: a hostile environment moves them to isolate themselves to protect against further change. And yet there is a common logic at work here that qualifies these explanations as a fourth point of affinity between the Documentary Hypothesis and Darwinism: in each case what appears to be an anomaly from a developmental perspective, a living entity resistant to change, is accounted for developmentally.

{⚜}

The comparison we have undertaken here needs to be balanced by a recognition of all the non-Darwinian elements of Wellhausen's argument—the mechanisms of natural selection are never evoked, and Darwin himself is never mentioned except when Wellhausen notes that some of his predecessors were wrongly accused of Darwinism. The affinities of his thinking with Hegelian developmentalism are better known (long before Darwin's use of the term "living fossil," Hegel described the Jews as a fossilized people), and the Documentary Hypothesis shares much in common with nineteenth-century degeneration theories, including the thinking of Zionist leaders like Max Nordau (1849–1923), which depicted the Jews as weakened by the conditions of exile. The Documentary Hypothesis and Darwinism are but two of many different developmental accounts from the nineteenth century, and we could thus have undertaken other comparisons that would have called attention to other aspects of the Documentary Hypothesis not noted here. We focused on Darwinism simply because it is the most successful all these theories—and thus the most familiar way into the nineteenth-century developmentalist thinking from which Wellhausen's explanation for the origin of Judaism emerged.

Along the way, however, we have learned something else that speaks to the shortcomings of this way of thinking. In Wellhausen's account, the Jews stand in a divergent relationship to the developmental narrative in which they are being framed: they were static as opposed to dynamic, maladapted as opposed to well adapted, and the result was a culture defined by an inability to change and grow that put the Jews out of sync with the normal flow of evolutionary change. Wellhausen was not the only scholar in this era to ascribe an evolutionary stuckness to the Jews. Johann Friedrich Blumenbach, whom we mentioned earlier for his theory of degeneration, believed that humans in general were highly mutable and responsive to their environs, but the exception was the Jews: among all human beings, they alone seemed resistant to adaptation, preserving the facial characteristics of their Near Eastern ancestors in a way that suggested they were at least partially impervious to the effects of their environment. Others described Judaism as an atavism, an evolutionary throwback to a more primitive state. In the words of Jakob Friedrich Fries (1773–1843), a German philosopher contemporary with Hegel, Judaism was "an atavism of an unenlightened prehistoric era, which one should not limit but exterminate."

Even a century later, in 1911, the Jewish physical anthropologist Maurice Fishberg (1872–1934) found it necessary to debunk the claim that the distinctive Jewish nose—a sign for many Europeans in this period of the immutability of Jewish physiology—was an atavism that went back to the ancient Hebrews and their marriage with the tribe of Cushites from Africa. Not every such theory cast the Jews as an exception to the developmental rule, but Wellhausen certainly was not unique in his belief that there was something about the Jews that obstructed the regular progression of evolutionary change. His contemporary, the ethnographer Richard Andree (1835–1912), was expressing a widely held view when he wrote that "no other race-type but the Jews . . . displays such a constancy of form, none resisted to such an extent the influence of time."

How do we account for the strange developmental divergence of the Jews? Scholars at the time offered various scientific and historical explanations to account for it. For Wellhausen the key was the Babylonian exile, which forced the Jews' ancestors out of their natural habitat in Canaan, created conditions of passivity and self-isolation, and prompted the Jews to try to sustain themselves through artificial measures that ended up obstructing their natural development. From the vantage point of 150 years later, we can see that the explanation lies not in the Jews' physiology or history but in the developmental schemes in which they were being placed. The scholars who devised these theories began from certain assumptions about the Jews (e.g., that Jewish religious behavior was static) that interacted with their assumptions about the workings of evolutionary change (that it was supposed to move in a certain direction or according to a certain sequence) in a way that made the Jews appear anomalous within the developmental paradigm from which they were operating. But both aspects of this way of thinking have been challenged—not only the anti-Semitic premises but also the developmentalist paradigm. Even Darwin's theory of evolution, the most enduring of these theories, is not applied to cultural evolution in the way that it was in the nineteenth and early twentieth centuries—the application of his concept of the "living fossil" to human groups has been discredited, for example. The question we need to address in the second half of this chapter, therefore, is whether in a twenty-first-century context a developmental approach can still help us to understand the origin of the Jews.

The Persian Age as Turning Point

Before we turn to that question, however, there is another aspect of Wellhausen's argument we need to address: his assertion that Judaism began in the postexilic/Persian period. This aspect of his argument is closely tied to his developmental scheme. A close reading of the *Prolegomena* shows that Wellhausen believed the decline of the Israelite religion into Judaism had already begun in the days of J and E, the earliest of the sources, but the institution of the monarchy, the successors of King David, had kept the theocratic impulses of the priestly class in check during the pre-exilic period. This background, and not just the destruction and dislocation caused by the Babylonian exile, is what made it such a turning point. As Wellhausen put it, foreign rule was the "necessary counterpart" for the appearance of the "Mosaic theocracy" that constituted Judaism. With the disappearance of the Davidic dynasty, terminated when the Babylonian Nebuchadnezzar executed the last king of the Davidic rulers and his sons, there was no longer a political check and balance within Israelite society to restrain the religious impulses of the priests in the same way; once these priestly leaders secured the support of the Persian rulers who replaced the Babylonians, they were even freer to impose the ritualistic and legalistic religiosity that distinguished Judaism from Israelite religion in Wellhausen's view, the religiosity institutionalized through the publication of the Torah in the time of Ezra in 444 BCE. Thus the importance of the Persian period as the beginning point for Judaism, a role it still plays in contemporary scholarly accounts, as we have noted. But does this way of dating the origin of Judaism hold up if we question the developmental approach to which it is tied?

Wellhausen did not introduce the idea of the postexilic/Persian period as the starting point of Judaism—the idea goes back to earlier scholars like Eichhorn and De Wette—but I want to suggest that its increasing influence as a way of dating the origin of Judaism is interconnected with the developmentalist thinking I have been describing. Earlier scholars focused on the impact of the Babylonian exile, but by Wellhausen's day, the Persian period was also garnering a lot of attention from scholars—and for reasons that had to do with the Persians' distinctive role in the development of European culture. To decide whether it still makes sense to situate the origin of the Jews in this period, we need to explore the role that Persia played in nineteenth-century developmentalist thinking.

Of course, part of what recommended the postexilic period for scholars as the point of transition between Israel and Judaism was the fact that it came at the very end of the historical period covered in the Hebrew Bible. The books in the Hebrew Bible that come from the Persian period, including Ezra and Nehemiah, all refer to the returnees from exile as the *yehudim* (or the *yehudaye* in the Aramaic of Ezra)—that is, the people from the tribe of Judah or the kingdom of Judah, who formed the majority of those deported by the Babylonians. Since these are words that modern translations often render as "the Jews," the books of Ezra and Nehemiah seem to justify the view of Eichhorn, De Wette, Wellhausen, and so many others who want to see in these sources the transition from Israel to the Jews.

This way of recounting the origin of Judaism seems very straightforward, and it is certainly very widespread—it is how I have always situated the beginning of Judaism in my own teaching—but there are at least three problems with it. The first is the issue of nomenclature that we discussed in the last chapter, the argument that "Jew" is the wrong translation for the word *yehudim/yehudaye* in Persian-period sources. For as far back as we can trace the Jews, the returnees described in Ezra and Nehemiah have been understood as their ancestors, but there is nothing in these sources that can resolve the question of whether they should themselves be regarded as "Jews" in the sense that scholars like De Wette and Wellhausen understood that category of identity or in the way that we might use that term today. We will see that more recent scholars place the origin of Judaism in later periods, treating the people of Ezra and Nehemiah not as Jews but as Judean predecessors of the Jews, and placing the transition to Judaism on the other side of the Persian period, in the Hellenistic age or later; there is nothing in the biblical sources that can rule out that way of seeing things. We might still want to distinguish the returnees from the "Judahites" of the pre-exilic age, the subjects of the kingdom of Judah ruled by David's heirs, but that does not mean the religious practices they engaged in should be called "Judaism" or that we have accounted for its difference from Israelite religion by placing its origin in this age.

The second problem is how little we know about this period of history. We know more about the period of Babylonian and Persian rule in Judah (or *Yehud*, as the Persian province of Judah was referred to in Aramaic sources) than was known in Wellhausen's day. Inscriptions and other textual sources that were only beginning to come to light in Wellhausen's time have filled in our understanding of the Judean community in Babylonia and the workings of the Achaemenid Empire founded by Cyrus the Great in 550 BCE, and archaeologists have gained some insight into social, economic, and religious life within Yehud itself. But all that still does not amount to very much, and it is certainly not enough to help us flesh out the period as a formative age in the development of Judaism. We still have to rely on the biblical books of Ezra and Nehemiah, narratives with their fair share of inconsistencies and dubious historical claims, as our principal sources for what happened in Yehud during this period. And while some scholars still accept Wellhausen's attribution of the Priestly source to the postexilic period, there have been so many challenges to his dating of P that we can no longer rely on it as another source of insight into this period.

Consider as an illustration of our ignorance of this period how little we know about the scribe Ezra, to whom Wellhausen and many subsequent scholars attributed the promulgation of the Torah. As the book's title suggests, Ezra plays an important role in the narrative of Ezra, a priest and scribe dispatched from Babylon by a Persian king named Artaxerxes to travel to Jerusalem to teach the laws of his god to those who did not know them and to appoint officials to judge people according to those laws. He may well have been a historical figure, but it is hard to pin down when he lived or what he did exactly. Wellhausen's assumption that he was active in 444 BCE assumes that the Persian king mentioned in the text was Artaxerxes I (r. 465– 424 BCE), but it is possible that the king involved was Artaxerxes II (r. 404 –358 BCE), placing Ezra about fifty years later than Wellhausen did. The biblical sources never claim that he compiled, edited, or codified the Torah—in fact, their references to the "law of Moses" may presuppose that the Torah already existed in some form by Ezra's day. It is hard to credit Ezra with the creation of Judaism, as some would do, when there are scholars who doubt whether he even existed.

During the 1980s and 1990s, a German scholar named Peter Frei offered evidence that would seem to support Ezra's role as a catalytic figure in the creation of Judaism. Wellhausen had argued that Ezra, acting in concert with the governor Nehemiah, came to Jerusalem at the mandate of the Persian king to introduce the laws of God there, a mission that culminated with Ezra's role in editing and publishing the Torah as a kind of constitution or charter for the postexilic community, the act that inaugurated Judaism. Frei pointed to other sources—a Demotic chronicle from Egypt, an Aramaic letter sent to a garrison of Judean mercenaries stationed in southern Egypt, a trilingual inscription from the ancient city of Xanthus in present-day Turkey—that seemed to corroborate Wellhausen's reconstruction by showing that, throughout its empire, the Achaemenid government commissioned local scribes to codify their communities' legal traditions and used its authority to imbue the resulting law codes with the force of imperial law. For a time Frei's theory convinced scholars that Ezra may indeed have played an imperially sanctioned role in promulgating the Torah, but in the past few years, there have emerged skeptics who counter that a more careful examination of the sources Frei cited to support his theory show that none actually refers to the imperial authorization or codification of local laws. This does not mean that the account in Ezra and Nehemiah is a complete fiction, but it undercuts the external support that had made it seem much more plausible. The debate has reopened the question of whether Ezra or the Persian Empire had any role in the production, publication, or codification of the Five Books of Moses—and hence, whether they had a role in the creation of Judaism as Wellhausen claimed—and there is no reason to think that it will be resolved anytime soon.

Far from confirming the Persian period as the origin of Judaism, the study of this period in the past century actually complicates one's sense of how it developed. One of the few sources we have for Persian-era Judean culture comes not from Judea but from Egypt, from an assortment of Aramaic papyri discovered on the island of Elephantine in the Nile River that first came to light in the 1890s. The papyri, consisting of both private and official documents, come from a community of Judeans from the fifth century BCE, who settled in the southern border of Egypt as mercenaries for the Persian government in control of Egypt at the time. Scholars today often refer to the members of this community as "Judeans" rather than "Jews," since their culture was different from later Jewish culture in a number of important ways: They worshipped a god called "Yahu," a variant of the name "Yahweh," but also revered a goddess named "Anat-Bethel." They knew about the Temple in Jerusalem but offered their own sacrifices at a temple located at Elephantine. They observed holidays like the Sabbath and Passover but do not seem to have known about the Bible or biblical law. The Elephantine papyri reveal a Persian-era Judean culture very different from the Jerusalem-based community depicted in the books of Ezra and Nehemiah.

As the Elephantine papyri were initially published between 1906 and 1911, Wellhausen was in a position to learn from them (a study of the Elephantine papyri was included in a volume published in honor of his seventieth birthday), but they did not affect his thinking about the origin of Judaism. In fact the Persian-period Judean community they reveal, though coming from the same period as the Priestly source in Wellhausen's dating and in touch with religious authorities in Jerusalem, exhibits very few of the characteristics Wellhausen ascribed to postexilic Judaism—no legalism, no sly cosmopolitanism, no efforts to construct an artificial connection to biblical Israel. The papyri include legal documents, but their authors were hardly obsessed with Mosaic law—in fact, no copies of the Torah were even found at Elephantine, nor is it cited. Rather than modifying his hypothesis, however, Wellhausen absorbed the Elephantine community into his developmental scheme by describing it in a later account of Israelite history as "a strange vestige of pre-legal Hebraism" and as a "fossil remnant of a not yet reformed Judaism." In other words he interpreted it as something like a living fossil, a survival from the earlier pre-exilic era of Israelite religion.

Is this the right way to interpret the Elephantine papyri? If one really wants to, one can make Elephantine papyri fit into

Wellhausen's scheme by arguing that it reflects a now-extinct form of Judean religion unaffected by the Babylonian exile, but one needn't interpret it in this way. In fact it raises a pertinent methodological question: Should our understanding of this period start from a reconstruction that involves hypothetical documents of unknown date (i.e., J and P), incorporating new evidence into that framework, or is it better to start from actual documents like the Elephantine papyri, material that can be clearly contextualized within the Persian period? If we go with the latter option, it is not so easy to fit what we know about Judean religious and social life in the Persian period into a straightforward evolutionary account. Scholars today are wary of imposing anachronistic categories onto the Elephantine community, including the term "Jew"; and from that perspective it feels historically wrongheaded to describe its religious life as a "strange vestige" of an earlier form of religion, since such a description involves a retroactive judgment that measures it by what Judaism became—or what scholars assume it became—in a later period. It seems truer to the evidence to recognize that it simply does not fit into a Wellhausean narrative that traces a single line of development out of pre-exilic Israelite religion into postexilic Judaism. It is not that the Elephantine evidence disproves Wellhausen's hypothesis; it is that it reveals how much he left out by focusing only on the postexilic period as known from the Bible and discounting what was coming to light from the Elephantine documents about the development of Judean culture in this period.

The third problem with the postexilic period as a starting point has less to do with the evidence itself and more to do with the biases of the scholars interpreting the evidence. As we have been noting, the postexilic period overlaps with the period when Yehud was ruled by the Achaemenid Empire, and for European scholars in the late nineteenth century, the Achaemenid Empire was not simply another ancient empire—the ancient Persians, identified with the Aryans, were seen as the ancestors of Europeans. The word "Aryan" derives from the Old Persian word *ariya*, and it was a title that the Persian King Darius applied to himself in the "Behistun" inscription, an inscription from sometime around 500 BCE found carved on the side of a cliff in Western Iran: "I am Darius the Great King, King of Kings . . . an Aryan having Aryan lineage" (see Figure 3).

FIGURE 3. The trilingual Behistun Inscription, found engraved on a cliff that overlooks a road that connected the capitals of Babylonia and Media, accompanies a bas-relief that depicts the Persian king Darius stepping victoriously on a supine foe. For scholars inclined to identify the Persians with the Aryans, the inscription seemed to offer corroboration, referring to the "Aryan" language and the god of the Aryans. *Source*: Image by Ziegler175, reproduced under Creative Commons Attribution-Share Alike 4.0 International license.

The word "Aryan" here may refer to the royal family or the Persian elite, a select group of nobles or aristocrats, rather than to Persians in general, but in the nineteenth century, the inscription and other uses of the term in Greek sources were understood to mean that the Persians were Aryans in a racial sense and cited as evidence that Persia was the homeland of the Aryans or a place where they had developed their culture before spreading into other parts of the world. The success of the Persian Empire, its conquest of the Babylonian Empire, its expansion into Egypt, its near conquest of the Greeks, was credited to the dynamism and organizational ability of the Persians, traits they inherited from their Aryan ancestors. While European study of the Persian language went back to the sixteenth century, the nineteenth century saw a sharp increase in scholarly interest in Persia, not only because of the successful decipherment of old Persian but because of this connection between the Persians and the Aryans, which tied the Persians in turn to Europe. That connection then became part of the background of Ezra-Nehemiah for many scholars, turning it into an encounter between Semites and Aryans.

A bit earlier in the nineteenth century, when many scholars saw India and not Persia as a homeland for the Aryans, there was a corresponding effort among at least a few scholars to demonstrate an Indian origin for the Jews. As it happens, there is one ancient source, a text attributed to a disciple of Aristotle named Clearchus, that suggests that the Jews descended from a race of Indian philosophers known as the *Kalanoi*, a theory that may have been suggested by a false etymological connection between the names *iudaioi* and *Indoi*, and by a conflation of the Jews with the Greek philosophical school known as Cynicism, which was also sometimes traced to India. But in modern times the idea that the Jews originated in India emerged only in the wake of scholarship that focused on India as an origin for European culture. European fascination with India has been traced back to Johann Gottfried Herder (1744 –1803), the poet and philosopher who attributed to India an important role in the development of civilization, and India later aroused the interest of philologists who posited a common origin for European languages and Sanskrit. It is precisely in this period that there were scholarly efforts to trace connections between the Jews and India, such as the study *Braminen und Rabbinen, oder Indien das Stammland der Hebräer und ihrer Fabeln* ("Brahmins and Rabbis, or India as the Homeland of the Hebrews and Their Fables"), published in 1836 by a mythologist named Friedrich Nork (the pseudonym for a Polish Jew named Selig Korn). Such efforts seem to be imitating non-Jewish scholarship that looked to India to understand the origin of European language and culture.

By the final decades of the nineteenth century, however, India had lost its appeal as the homeland of the Aryans, and scholars turned instead to Persia. That's not to say that European study of Persia began in this period. In 1765 the German explorer Carsten Niebuhr (1733–1815) reached the ancient sites of Persepolis and came across the Behistun Inscription, which included a section in Old Persian that was finally deciphered in the 1830s by the young

British army officer Henry Rawlinson. By the end of the nineteenth century, however, scholarly interest in Persia had greatly intensified, both because many German scholars had come to see Persia as the homeland of the Aryans and because by this point Germany was developing strong diplomatic ties to Persia. Thus, for example, the writer Joseph Arthur de Gobineau (1816–1882), infamous for developing the idea of the Aryans as a master race, closely identified them with the Persians, giving the latter a central role in the development of European civilization (Gobineau worked in the French embassy in Tehran). The perceived connection between the Aryans and Persia is reflected to this day in the name "Iran," as in "the land of the Aryans," officially adopted as the name of the country in 1935—an initiative that originated from the Persian embassy in Berlin in part as a way to demonstrate to the Germans that Persia was the birthplace of the Aryans.

What made the postexilic period of interest from this perspective is that it was the first moment when biblical Israelites and Aryan Persians came into direct contact with each other, where there was the possibility of interaction and influence. More recent scholars have noted that the biblical authors do not seem to have known very much about the Persians. They were certainly aware of Persia as a ruling empire, acknowledging the patronage of rulers like Cyrus and Darius, and as illustrated by the Book of Esther, they told stories about life in the Persian court; but nowhere do they show any familiarity with the religious beliefs of the Persian kings, for example, and the narrow range of Persian loanwords in biblical Hebrew suggests that direct contact with the Persians was fairly restricted. But none of this impressed itself on scholars who believed that the Persians, as the more creative of the two peoples, had a profound impact on the Israelites. Thus arose various attempts to show that certain aspects of Christian belief—the dualistic conception of the devil as a rival of God or the expectation of an apocalyptic age at the end of time—could be traced back to Persian-Zoroastrian influence on the Judaism from which Christianity arose. But of even more relevance is the argument that Judaism itself was the result of Persian influence.

The most famous advocate of this view in Wellhausen's day was the renowned German historian Eduard Meyer (1855–1930), one of the last historians to try to develop a comprehensive history of the ancient world, and who stressed the interconnections among Greece, Rome, Judea, Persia, and other civilizations of the era. In a book called *Die Entstehung des Judentums* ("The Emergence of Judaism"), published in 1896, Meyer undertook an analysis of the royal documents cited in the books of Ezra in light of other documentary evidence from the Persian Empire and concluded that they were a reflection of an authentic Persian imperial policy that had shaped its treatment of various subject peoples. Not only did Judaism develop in the Persian period, according to Meyer, but it was the direct result of Persian intervention, coming about through the interaction with its policies and officials. It so happens that Meyer's view of Semites and Aryans was fairly typical of German scholarship in that era. He saw the Semites as stagnant, inert, and thus dependent for their accomplishments on the influence of more creative non-Semitic peoples, a view that also led him, like many of the Assyriologists he read, to attribute the accomplishments of Babylonian civilization to the non-Semitic influence of the Sumerians. It is hard to measure the impact of such views on his theory of Judaism as the creation of the Persians, but he did identify the Persians with the Aryans through their connection to the rulers of Media. The kingdom of the Medes, located in what is now northwestern Iran, was the first kingdom absorbed into the Persian Empire by Cyrus; Cyrus was personally connected to its rulers as the son of a Median princess, and according to Meyer, these rulers were of Aryan descent. Giving the Persians the initiative in the creation of Judaism was consistent with Meyer's view of the Aryans as inherently more creative than Semites and his predisposition to give them the credit for the more developed aspects of Semitic culture.

I would not suggest that this identification of Persia with the Aryans was what led Wellhausen to focus on the postexilic period—in fact, in a notorious review of Meyer's book, he was quite dismissive of the historian's scholarship. While he did teach Persian himself, developed a close relationship with a Persianist colleague Ferdinand Justi at the University of Marburg, and accepted the equation of the Persians with the Aryans, his account scarcely mentions Persian rule as a factor in the development of Judaism, focusing instead on the experience of exile and the self-isolation the

Jews imposed on themselves there. To recognize that Wellhausen did not fully buy into the Aryan myth is not to acquit him of anti-Jewish prejudice—opposed to Judaism on religious rather than racial grounds, he wrote an article for the *Encyclopedia Britannica* in which he envisioned the eventual extinction of Judaism as a religious system. But his account of the origin of Judaism did not make its development dependent on foreigners but rather depicted it as an internally driven evolutionary process, thus giving the Persians a very small role in his narrative.

While the association of the Persians with the Aryans does not explain the role of the postexilic period in Wellhausen's argument, however, it might help to account for why this dating for the origin of Judaism "clicked" for so many scholars at that time. As we have seen, Wellhausen's hypothesis was not Darwinian in a strict sense, but it tapped into enough of the same ideas that it was easily conflated with Darwinism, an association that may have contributed to the success of the Documentary Hypothesis by associating it with a theory that, by the 1870s, was having an immense impact on scientific thinking in Germany. By the same token Wellhausen's arguments for a postexilic dating took on new resonance in light of contemporary views of the Aryans. The theory of Judaism as a creation of Persia was not consistent with Wellhausen's view. Meyer's theory, as the sociologist Max Weber noted, was "epigenetic," stressing the impact of forces outside Israelite culture, while Wellhausen's was "immanent-evolutionary," emphasizing the changes coming from within the culture; but they nonetheless worked together to reinforce one another, as unfortunately illustrated by how they commingle in a book like *The Foundations of the Nineteenth Century*, by Houston Stewart Chamberlain (1855–1927), the self-proclaimed "evangelist of race" who drew on both Wellhausen's account of the postexilic age and Meyer's account of the Persian age in his perverse attempt to describe the development of Judaism. Read by the likes of Adolf Hitler, this work represents the most pernicious kind of racial history, and it drew on Wellhausen's scholarship to situate the origin of Judaism in the Persian period and thereby tie it directly to the history of the Aryans.

To connect the dots in this way is by no means to suggest that contemporary scholars who place the origin of Judaism in the Persian period—the editors of the *Cambridge History of Judaism* or the scholars who designed my own graduate program—were motivated by anti-Semitic prejudice or the scholars' sense of identification with ancient Aryans. The theory of a postexilic/Persian origin for Judaism has long outlived the ideological motives that helped to give rise to it. But those motives are part of the history of such a view, and they reveal a sinister dimension to it that gives one pause about the Persian period as a starting point for Judaism. We cannot prove that it is wrong to begin the history of Judaism in the Persian period; we cannot rule out a role for the Achaemenid Empire in the development of Israelite religion into Judaism; and it remains possible that Cyrus, Darius, and other Persian rulers played the catalytic role this approach assigns to them. But it is important to acknowledge that scholars have had reasons to look to the Persian period to understand the origin of Judaism and its relationship to German culture that go beyond the evidence we actually have from this very poorly understood age.

Evolving beyond Evolutionism

If we look back on Wellhausen's *Prolegomena* 140 years after its publication in 1878, how much of this argument about the origin of the Jews still holds up today? No credible scholar would defend Wellhausen's hostile caricature of Judaism, but what of the method that led him to the Documentary Hypothesis—source criticism, the effort to distinguish the underlying sources of the Torah and to place them in a historical sequence? Can a refined version of such a method still work to illumine the emergence of Judaism from ancient Israel? We have reason to at least be skeptical of the effort to situate the transition from one to the other in the Persian period, but that by itself does not discredit a developmental approach. Is such an approach the right way to understand the origin of Judaism, and if so, how does one trace the development involved?

We might begin to address such questions by noting that the method of source criticism is still in use today among many critical biblical scholars—in fact, it has undergone something of a resurgence among a younger generation of scholars in the United States, Israel, and Europe. To be sure, every aspect of the Documentary Hypothesis has been subject to critique, and there is not one element of it that is accepted today without question and debate. Not only do many scholars reject the dating of J to the pre-exilic period or P to the postexilic period, but it is no longer clear that the Five Books of Moses can be broken down into discrete "documents," with many arguing that it arose as an assemblage of many smaller traditions (the Fragmentary Hypothesis) or that it developed through a series of additions to an initial core of material (the Supplementary Hypothesis). While there is no longer any consensus on how the Five Books of Moses were composed, however, scholars still agree that this work *developed* into its present form in a way that can be reconstructed by breaking the Torah down into its constituent parts. Even the Documentary Hypothesis in its classic form has many adherents among scholars today.

But using source criticism to understand the composition of the Bible is one thing; enlisting it to illumine the origin of the Jews is another. While the contemporary scholars alluded to earlier retain their optimism about their ability to reconstruct the compositional history of the biblical text, the field of biblical studies now shies away from the use of source criticism as a historical tool that can help reconstruct the origin of Judaism. An example is the Israeli scholar Yehezkiel Kaufmann (1889–1963), a professor at the Hebrew University in Jerusalem who founded a distinctively Israeli school of biblical scholarship. Not only did Kaufman reject Wellhausen's dating of the sources, but his alternative reconstruction of the Torah's composition was really a rejection of an evolutionary approach altogether. For him the religion of ancient Israel began with a conceptual revolution, not evolution: it did not develop out of earlier Canaanite religion, as Wellhausen implies, and while Israelite religion does undergo an internal evolution in his reconstruction, there are no stages of religious development to be discerned between J and P. Coming from a different tradition of biblical scholarship, the German scholar Rolf Rendtorff (1925–2014) questioned source criticism's ability to date biblical sources to specific periods, including the postexilic/Persian period, which he acknowledged as a dark age that scholars know very little about. More recent source critics, like Joel Baden from Yale University, are similarly reluctant to connect specific sources to specific historical periods. Without the ability to assign specific sources to specific periods, or to place them in chronological order, source criticism loses its value as a way of supporting developmental narratives of how ancient Israelite religion gave rise to Judaism.

There are many reasons that source criticism no longer works in the way that it used to in Wellhausen's day. Scholars have become more sophisticated in their understanding of what it takes to assign a specific source or tradition to a specific historical period; they recognize how entangled the sources are in one another, and that it is not so easy to reconstruct their prehistory or place them in succession. Apart from challenging Wellhausen's specific observations, scholars are also now cognizant of how those observations were shaped by assumptions and biases that Wellhausen shared with other scholars of his era. Thus it has been argued that Wellhausen's portrait of J reflects the influence of Romanticism, and more specifically the influence of Johann Gottfried Herder and his description of the Hebrews as a simple and spontaneous people. Others have noted that his portrait of D bears the imprint of the liberalism of his day and its opposition to the centralization and urbanization under way in a newly united Germany; and that his portrait of P reflects not only the anti-Semitism of Germany in this period but its anti-Catholicism as well. (Wellhausen, the son of a Protestant pastor, described the Catholic Church as a "child" of Mosaic theology.) The effect of such scholarship is to discredit the Documentary Hypothesis, to undercut its claim to objectivity by revealing how it was skewed by the prejudices of its era, in contrast to Darwin's theory, which, of course, holds up even though it too bears the influence of the context in which it was initially formulated.

All this makes it practically impossible to use the Documentary Hypothesis to reconstruct the origin of Judaism in the way Wellhausen did, but there may be an even more basic reason that the source-critical study of the Hebrew Bible has lost its methodological power in this regard. The use of source criticism in this way, as we have noted, was closely tied to the developmental approach to origin that took root in the nineteenth century, and that kind of thinking has fallen out of favor with many scholars. Darwin's theory of evolution retains its intellectual stature, of course, but already by the early twentieth century, scholars were looking for alternatives to the evolutionary narratives so popular in the nineteenth century. Some scholars, like Robert Nisbet (1913–1996), in a work called *Metaphor and History* quoted at the beginning of the chapter, argue that, when applied to the history of societies, evolution is just another long list of metaphors that scholars have used to make sense of "the mingled facts of persistence and change," and it does not correspond to anything that can be established empirically. Evolutionary approaches to social and cultural development continued throughout the past century, but scholars grew dissatisfied with evolutionary accounts that unfolded in a predetermined direction or progressed from one stage to another along a neatly linear track. Even a true heir to Darwin, the biologist Stephen Jay Gould (1941–2002), resisted such linear thinking: for him, evolution is not one continuous story of unfolding change but a punctuated narrative marked by immense gaps in the fossil record and long periods without change; and is a process that, at any point, can lead out in multiple directions rather than simply moving along in a single, straight path.

Turning back to biblical studies, we can see this antidevelopmentalist trend reflected in how scholars today describe the relationship between ancient Israel and postbiblical Judaism. In the 1980s and 1990s, there emerged a school of thought in European biblical studies that came to be known by its opponents as "biblical minimalism." To generalize a bit, the proponents of this approach— Thomas Thompson, Niels Peter Lemche, Keith Whitelam, and Philip Davies—argued that the depiction of Israel in the Hebrew Bible was largely a fiction, bearing little resemblance to the historical Israel in the First Temple period as known from a handful of inscriptions. Most of the Hebrew Bible—not just Chronicles, Ezra, or P but narratives like those in Samuel and Kings—was composed in the Persian period or in the later Hellenistic age by authors who had little information about the pre-exilic community, and were projecting their own religious and political perspectives onto the past. As argued by Philip Davies, for example, the literary depiction of the Israelites in the Hebrew Bible—the stories of Abraham and Moses, the conquest of Canaan, and the kingdom of David and Solomon—is not a record of the real experiences of a real people from before the Babylonian exile; it is the past as imagined by immigrants newly settled in the Persian province of Yehud. There did exist a historical Israel—the Israel mentioned in the Merneptah

Stele and other extrabiblical sources from the Iron Age. But the Persian-era community of Yehud did not directly develop out of that Israel, inventing its memories of the pre-exilic period—even perhaps inventing its memory of the Babylonian exile itself—to lay claim to the territory in which it was now settling.

Biblical minimalism, as some of its own practitioners acknowledge, shares much in common with Wellhausen's approach. Like Wellhausen, it too is highly skeptical of biblical texts as a historical source, especially their testimony about the origin of Israel. Another parallel with Wellhausen is the fact that Davies and other scholars want to see the Persian period as a critical era in the formation of biblical literature. By treating biblical Israel as a figment of Persian-era imaginations, their thesis even calls to mind Wellhausen's description of postexilic Jews as a people that has fabricated its connection to the past, though they apply such an idea not only to the books of Chronicles but also to Joshua and Samuel. Describing biblical Israel as an "invention" and the biblical account of Abraham, Moses, and other early figures as a "myth," the so-called minimalist school has essentially revived Wellhausen's description of Judaism as an "artificial Israel."

But what such a comparison also reveals is that, for all they have in common with Wellhausen in other respects, the minimalists no longer operate according to the kind of evolutionary framework that governed his approach. They do not seek to trace an evolution from ancient Israel to Judaism or in fact recognize much of any kind of continuity between the pre-exilic and postexilic periods: they treat the Judeans of the Persian period as a distinct population that only claims succession from the Israelites of the biblical age without having actually developed out of it. I cannot think of a better way to illustrate the decline of a developmental approach to the origin of the Jews than the fact that even in a modern-day revival of Wellhausen that reproduces many parts of his argument, the evolutionary structure that held things together in the Documentary Hypothesis is missing.

If source criticism of the Bible no longer works as a way of understanding the origin of the Jews, it is not because scholars have abandoned source criticism itself but because they no longer believe it has the power to construct developmental narratives that bridge between the biblical Israelites and later Jews. In Wellhausen's day the method meshed perfectly with the unilinear evolutionary thinking so prevalent in the period: the sources Wellhausen uncovered offered glimpses of different moments of time, and in a late nineteenth-century context dominated by Darwinism, the concept of degeneration, and other developmental theories and narratives, it made perfect sense to plot these moments as different points in an evolutionary trajectory. If the Documentary Hypothesis has splintered into much less linear accounts of the Torah's composition, and if it no longer works as a way to document the transition from biblical Israel to Judaism, it is not just because the hypothesis itself has shortcomings but because a critical mass of scholars no longer thinks in terms of the developmental framework on which this kind of explanation depends.

As we have noted, many contemporary scholars of the subject make a distinction among the "Israelites" of the pre-exilic period, the "Judeans" of the Persian, Hellenistic, and Roman ages, and the "Jews" of later periods. Scholars argue over how to use these terms, but many agree that there is a distinction to be made between the people described in the Bible and the Jews as they are known from later sources, and that agreement is rooted in turn in the shared presumption that the Jews (or Judaism) resulted from a process of historical change and development. But that does not mean that we understand the nature of the development involved or that it can be tracked in the way Wellhausen believed it could. At what point did the "Israelites" become the "Jews," and how did the transformation come about? Can the change be broken down into stages or even plotted along a single line? Was the transition in the Persian period or in a later age, or was it so gradual that it cannot be confined to a specific period? Even a century after Wellhausen's death, none of these questions have been resolved, and there is reason to think that they remain unanswered not because the changes involved are hard to prove but because there is something insufficient about the developmental perspective from which they arise. Hence the emergence of approaches that account for the origin of the Jews in ways that do not entail following a development from one stage to another. I will be telling the story of how evolutionism gave way to one of those alternative approaches in the next chapter.

CHAPTER FOUR

A Thrice-Told Tel

THE ARCHAEOLOGY OF ETHNOGENESIS

*Long practice in excavation had taught me that one condition—indeed
the most important condition—of success was that the person responsible
for any piece of digging, however small and however large, should know
exactly what he wants to find out, and then decide what kind of digging
will show it to him.*

—R. G. COLLINGWOOD

NOT LONG AFTER Wellhausen published the results of his source-
critical investigation, an archaeologist named Sir William Matthew Flinders Petrie (1853–1942) initiated the first major scientific
excavation in Palestine in 1890, at Tel el-Hesi, in what was then
Ottoman-controlled Palestine. Petrie was renowned for his work
as an Egyptologist. Among his contributions was the discovery of
the Merneptah Stele, taken to be the earliest known text to refer
to "Israel," and by the end of his life, he had undertaken more than
fifty excavations in Egypt and Palestine. At Tel el-Hesi he believed
he was excavating a city mentioned in the Bible, the Amorite city of
Lachish, which according to the Book of Joshua had tried unsuc-
cessfully to repel the invasion of the Israelites before its king fled to
a cave, where he has tracked down by Joshua and executed (Joshua
10:5–27). Petrie found evidence of what he took to be the city's destruction in that period, a layer of ash from around 1200 BCE that
in his judgment marked "a great break in the history of Palestine

between the destruction of the Amorite civilization and the establishment of Jewish civilization under the Kings."

Petrie's interpretation turned out to be wrong—the actual Lachish would be found elsewhere, and the identification of Tel el-Hesi remains unclear to this day—but his work there had a lasting impact on Near Eastern archaeological methodology: he helped to illumine the *tel* (a mount formed by the human occupation and abandonment of a site over many centuries) as a succession of phases of habitation and destruction, and he pioneered the use of pottery as evidence for the dating of those phases to different periods. Of particular interest for this chapter is his belief that archaeology could illumine the break between Jewish and earlier civilizations, the moment of the Hebrews' arrival to the land. Over the next century archaeologists would build on, refine, criticize, and eventually abandon many of the methods Petrie introduced; they would no longer conflate "Israelite" and "Jewish" in the way he did as a scholar who bought into a nineteenth-century conception of the Jews as an enduring racial type; they would even question the idea of an Israelite invasion of Canaan. But to this day Petrie's successors continue to use archaeology to illumine the earliest history of the Israelites—and many continue to believe that something transformative happened around 1200 BCE, something that introduced a "great break" between earlier Canaanite culture and the Israelite culture from which the Jews originate.

The research of these archaeologists takes us back to a period long before the Persian age, and moves us from the question of how Israel became Judaism after the Babylonian exile to the preliminary question of how the Israelites themselves came into being; but it does not take us backward in a methodological or conceptual sense. Though Petrie and other early archaeologists also worked within an evolutionary framework (Petrie himself worked directly with the eugenicist Francis Galton, Darwin's cousin), more recent archaeologists have been looking beyond that kind of developmental framework to understand the origin of the Israelites, and it is this effort, and not just the discoveries of archaeology (as intriguing as they are), that is of interest to us in this chapter. How do we account for the emergence of the ancient Israelites from whom the Jews descend? If they did not "develop" in a straight line out of an earlier people, if they are not a product of a maturation process, or degeneration, or evolutionary change, how did they come into being? Archaeologists have been wrestling with these questions in a way that gives us an opportunity to explore alternative, non-evolutionary approaches to the question of Israelite origin from the past half century.

But a challenge for us is that biblical archaeology is not an easy field to summarize because of how dynamic and contentious it is. Continuing and new excavations make discoveries every season, and archaeologists struggle to make sense of and publish all the data their work has brought to light, never mind reading everyone else's publications. The field is riven by sharp differences over method, over whether to redate finds attributed to the eleventh century to the tenth century or to recontextualize finds from the tenth century in the ninth century; and even more contentious is the question of how or whether to incorporate the testimony of the Bible into the interpretation of the material evidence. What Petrie assumed to be the sequence of history as it actually happened—the Israelites' conquest of Canaan under Joshua, followed by the establishment of a kingdom in Israel—is not clearly historical according to many archaeologists today who doubt whether such events happened in the way the Bible describes or question whether they happened at all. There are too many digs, too much data, and too many unresolved debates to distill it all into a single chapter.

To focus this survey, therefore, we zero in on a single archaeological expedition now going on at the site of Tel Beth Shemesh, next to the modern-day city of Beth Shemesh. Beth Shemesh, a midsized city located in the kingdom of Judah, is not the most famous excavation in Israel today—the excavations of Megiddo, Lachish, and of course the City of David in Jerusalem have gotten more public attention—but it makes for an excellent case study for three reasons: (1) the history of its excavation spans almost the entire history of biblical archaeology, from 1911 to the present, which means that it can help us understand how the field has changed over the years; (2) the current expedition at the site, which was first inhabited during the Middle Bronze Age, has uncovered the period that spans between the Late Bronze Age and an early period of Israelite society in the Iron Age in a way that illumines the Israelites' connection

with earlier Canaanite culture; and (3) the archaeologists in charge
of the current expedition have drawn on what they have learned
from the site to support a new theory of Israelite origin that aims
to revise our understanding of the "break" that divides Israelites
from earlier Canaanites. Archaeology has perfected the art of sampling, working by subdividing a large terrain into more manageable
subsections and probing under the surface only in a percentage of
these subsections on the assumption that they reveal something
about the whole. That is the inspiration for the approach I take
here, using Tel Beth Shemesh to probe a much larger field and what
it has to say about the origin of the people from whom the Jews
emerged.

Ethnogenetic Excavations

My own introduction to archaeology came through my close friendship with an Israeli archaeologist named Zvi Lederman, a veteran
archaeologist who after many years of fieldwork went back to
school, enrolling at Harvard when I was a graduate student there,
in order to develop a deeper understanding of how to interpret the
evidence. In 1990, a few years before I met him, Lederman and his
colleague Shlomo Bunimovitz had begun to excavate at Tel Beth
Shemesh, and after we got to know each other, Zvi invited me to
join them as a kind of participant-observer. (They knew I wasn't
very good with a shovel, and my main role was to bring some funding and a group of students to work on the site.) Thus it was that in
the summer of 1995, together with a group of twenty students from
Indiana University, where I had gotten my first academic position,
I began learning firsthand about what they were discovering about
the site during the Iron Age phase of its settlement.

The ancient site of Beth Shemesh is only about a half-hour bus
ride from Jerusalem, located right outside the modern city of Beth
Shemesh, but looking out from the site itself, it feels very remote—
the only thing one can see from the site is a kibbutz on the other
side of a road. Just beneath one's feet, however, is a long history
of habitation that begins somewhere in the period between 2000
and 1500 BCE, stretches through the Late Bronze Age, continues
through the period of the kingdom of Judah, and ends with its

destruction during the Assyrian invasion of Judah at the end of the eighth century BCE. Among the many recent finds that make Tel Beth Shemesh so interesting is the discovery there of the only known palace from Amarna-age Canaan, and the emergence of circumstantial evidence that the city was once ruled by a queen mentioned in the Amarna letters.

Beth Shemesh is not nearly as prominent in the Bible as Jerusalem is, mentioned only a few times, but it does surface in some memorable stories, including one about the legendary Ark of the Covenant in 1 Samuel 6, which must have been the inspiration for the climactic scene of the Indiana Jones film *Raiders of the Lost Ark*. The name "Beth Shemesh" is related to Samson, the powerful and impulsive judge known for killing a lion, posing an impossible riddle, and killing lots of Philistines, and he was said to have been born exactly at the site of Beth Shemesh. (His story is told in Judges 13–16.) A small seal discovered at the site, from the eleventh century BCE, pictures a man fighting a lion, a scene that calls to mind Samson's fight with a lion in Judges 14. Both "Beth Shemesh" and "Samson" derive from the Hebrew word *shemesh*, or "sun"; the city's name, which probably goes back to the Canaanite name for the city in the Bronze Age, may have referred to a temple of the solar deity Shamash that once stood in the city.

From the point of view of critical biblical scholars, the stories told of Samson are certainly not the most credible part of the Hebrew Bible (Wellhausen refers to them as "legends"), but their author got at least a few details correct in terms of the topography and demography of the area. Whether there was a Samson or not, for example, the biblical author correctly understood that Beth Shemesh lay in the border zone between the kingdom of Judah and Philistine territory, just a few kilometers away from the Philistine town of Ekron. The region is known as the Shephelah ("lowlands")—foothills that roll down between the Judean mountains and the coast—and the rich agricultural land to be found there, especially the area's olive trees, is what drew both Israelites and Philistines to the region, where they bumped up against each other and had to vie for control of the land and its resources. It is also interesting that the only biblical stories told of Beth Shemesh are set fairly early in the history of the Israelites, in the time of the judges who ruled the Israelites before the kingdom of David and Solomon. The year before I joined the Beth Shemesh excavation for the first time, Lederman and Bunimovitz had uncovered evidence of the city's violent destruction by the Assyrians in the eighth century BCE, an event that may explain why there are no biblical stories about the city set after the eighth century—there were no more people in the city to serve as the subjects of such stories. But the city was inhabited in the preceding centuries, including just before and during the age when Israelite society itself was believed to have taken shape, roughly 1200 to 1000 BCE. That is what makes its excavation so potentially illuminating for understanding the origin of that society.

In the days of the kingdom of Judah, as we noted, the Shephelah was in a political and cultural intermediate zone between the Israelites and the Philistines, and that intermediate location was what drew my friends' attention to Beth Shemesh. There was a lot of debate at the time about the origin and history of the Israelite state, when it first arose and why, but that debate focused on major urban centers like Jerusalem, Samaria, and Megiddo. Reading up on anthropology about the importance of borders and boundary making in the process of state formation, Lederman and Bunimovitz reasoned that they might learn something about the social and political development of the ancient Israelite state by shifting from the center to the periphery, by looking at what was happening along the edges of Israelite society. States are defined by their borders, by their ability to protect themselves and to control what passes in and out of their territory, which is why, apart from their capitals, states are most often active along their perimeter. Perhaps, then, there was insight to be gleaned about the rise of the Israelite state by exploring what happened in settlements located along its border: how it established its boundaries, what it did to defend itself, and how it interacted with its neighbors. Tel Beth Shemesh made sense as a focus of this kind of study because of its location in the frontier zone between the Israelites and Philistines, and their work there has borne out that hunch, uncovering evidence that, during the tenth century BCE, the town of Beth Shemesh, probably because it was now on the border between Philistia and a young kingdom of Judah, was transformed into a well-planned, well-defended administrative center for the region. Lederman and Bunimovitz even found an inscription, the corner of a game board incised with the family name Hanan (which may have been a well-to-do family in the city), which recalls the name of a royal official placed in charge of the trees of the region in the time of David, according to 1 Chronicles 27:28—Baal Hanan.

But beyond their interest in the formation of the Israelite state, Lederman and Bunimovitz were also hoping to shed light on another question even more directly related to our own quest—the origin of the Israelites themselves. In earlier scholarship, that question came down to determining whether the Israelites had entered Canaan as invading attackers, as described in the Book of Joshua, or had migrated into the land in a more gradual and less violent way. Lederman and Bunimovitz, following in the footsteps of William Dever of the University of Arizona, were looking for a way to understand the emergence of the Israelites from within the indigenous population of Canaan, the result not of invasion or migration but of a process internal to Late Bronze Age Canaanite society.

To develop this explanation, they drew on the kind of anthropological theory that informs the work of Judith Neulander, which we described in chapter 2: a "constructivist" approach that makes a distinction between the historical origin of a people and how they understand their origin. Knowing that a certain group of people first came together in a particular place or time does not necessarily tell us much about the formation of their identity—how they see themselves in relation to other people. The "proto-Israelites," Dever had argued, were originally a Canaanite people or an amalgamation of different Canaanite peoples. The language they spoke and the pottery they produced revealed their roots in the indigenous culture of Canaan, but at some point in the period between 1300 and 1000 BCE, they came to see themselves as different from Canaanites, enforcing the difference through endogamy, dietary taboos, the worship of a particular deity, and other religious and social practices registered in the biblical description of the Israelites. Archaeologists had a name for the process involved—"ethnogenesis," the process by which a distinct ethnic group emerges with a common consciousness of belonging—but this process is much easier to label than to explain. In the case of the Israelites, it was not clear what had led a population of Canaanites to recategorize themselves as a people distinct from the Canaanites. Was there some environmental change during the early Iron Age, or some event or some encounter with others, that triggered the transformation? This was another of the questions Lederman and Bunimovitz were hoping to address, and they felt that Tel-Beth Shemesh was a good place to look for answers, because the anthropology they were following indicated that the frontier zones where groups encounter each other in a kind of liminal space are often the settings for the formation of sharply differentiated ethnic identities.

Before we get to their answer to that question, however, we need to tell another kind of story about Tel Beth Shemesh. Beyond exploring what archaeology tells us about the origin of the Israelites, another goal of this chapter is to nudge forward our understanding of how scholars think about questions of origin, and more specifically, to illumine the shift, over the twentieth century, away from the sort of developmental thinking described in the previous chapter. Lederman and Bunimovitz describe the origin of the Israelites as a process of "ethnogenesis." The term, a compound of the Greek words for "tribe" or "nation" and "birth," surfaces in the nineteenth century. (The first known person to employ the term was the French scientist André-Marie Ampère in 1834.) In that context it reflected the developmentalist thinking typical of the era, referring to the emergence of a race or nation through degeneration, evolution, or some other slowly unfolding process. As the term is used by contemporary archaeologists like Lederman and Bunimovitz, however, it has a very different meaning, one detached from a developmental framework.

Ethnogenesis in its nineteenth-century context basically involved variations of what Darwin referred to as "descent with modification": humans were originally divided into a much smaller number of races or primitive social groups that over a long period of time developed into a larger number of races or nations as their descendants migrated to new environments or interbred with each other. To understand the formation of an ethnic group according to this perspective was to trace some ancient core of identity over time and space—a Roman core, an Aryan core, a Celtic core—as it branched out and diversified into new forms of ethnic identity, understood as diluted or adapted versions of the core. As ethnogenesis is understood today, ethnic groups do not evolve out of a preexisting group in this way. Their ancestry is not determinative in any way of their sense of commonality—they might even emerge from a hodgepodge of different groups with distinct ancestries or backgrounds, as Dever imagines was the case for the early Israelites—because their sense of collective belonging comes about not diachronically but synchronically, through a process of differentiating themselves from other groups in their environs. The difference between the two conceptions of ethnogenesis corresponds to the difference between an etymological and a Saussurean approach to a word; just as, according to the latter perspective, one understands the meaning of a word not by tracing its root to an earlier ancestral word but by framing it as part of a broader system of differences with other words in the same language, one can understand the formation and content of ethnic identity only as part of a broader system of contrasts with other groups in the same environment.

The history of the term "ethnogenesis" reflects a broader shift in the scholarly conception of origin that we have been tracing in earlier chapters, and the excavation of Tel Beth Shemesh gives us an opportunity to explore the transition between perspectives—not because of anything discovered at the site but because of the history of the excavation itself. Lederman and Bunimovitz were not the first archaeologists to dig at Beth Shemesh. There were two earlier expeditions there: a British expedition led by a Scotsman named Duncan Mackenzie between 1911 and 1912; and a second, American, expedition led by the American Elihu Grant from 1928 to 1933. Each excavator interpreted the evidence he found at the site in light of the reigning intellectual paradigms of his day. Before we look at what the current excavation tells about the ethnogenesis of the Israelites, I want to recount the history of this dig, to learn about how archaeology came to be used to illumine the origin of the Israelites but also, more broadly, to track the shift from a developmentalist paradigm of ethnic formation to postevolutionist approaches.

To help make this history a little easier to follow, I have divided it into three stages, organized according to the three attempts to excavate Beth Shemesh over the past century.

THE FIRST EXPEDITION: ETHNOGENESIS
AS RACIAL EVOLUTION

When the Scotsman Duncan Mackenzie (1861–1934) began his work at Tel Beth Shemesh in April 1911, he was not there to investigate the Israelites—in fact, he did not want to be there at all. He was a specialist in the archaeology of the prehistoric Greek world, known for his work on the islands of Melos and especially Crete. He came to Palestine to work not on the Israelites but on the Philistines, a people suspected to have originated in the Greek part of the Mediterranean known from the poetry of Homer. Had it been up to him, he might have chosen to work at Ashkelon, a major Philistine city on the southern coast of Palestine; but the Palestine Exploration Fund, a British academic society established in 1865 to promote the scientific study of the Holy Land, was more interested in sending him to Beth Shemesh, because it was suspected, on the basis of biblical references, that it might throw some light on the Philistines. As it turns out, his expertise in preclassical Greek archaeology did prove crucial for Mackenzie's work at Beth Shemesh, enabling him to recognize that the Philistine pottery discovered at the site was related to Greek pottery. However, Mackenzie was able to work at Beth Shemesh for only three short seasons before funding ran out in 1912, at which point he returned to the excavation at Knossos where he worked until he was fired in 1929 for excessive drinking.

To understand the earliest excavation at Beth Shemesh, it is helpful to frame it in connection to the work of Sir Arthur Evans (1851–1941), the famed English archaeologist for whom Mackenzie worked at Knossos. Evans and Mackenzie worked together for thirty years, and their thinking is closely intertwined. In the very period when Mackenzie was working at Beth Shemesh, his boss at Knossos, Evans, delivered an address in which he explained that his goal as an archaeologist was "embryological": one cannot understand the fruits of Greek civilization, he explained, without understanding its roots, the prehistoric culture that eventually developed into Hellenic culture. For him that earlier culture was to be found in Crete. Evans's work in recovering Minoan civilization, which he began after Crete won its independence from the Ottoman Empire in 1898, was thus born of the same thinking reflected in the paleolinguistic effort to reconstruct Indo-European: it too was an attempt to reconstruct the prehistoric people from whom Europeans had inherited their culture.

Mackenzie's work at Beth Shemesh, while motivated in part by the references to the town in the Bible, was thus part of a larger effort to understand the early history and diffusion of a prehistoric Greek culture, and the city of Beth Shemesh offered an opportunity to explore its diffusion into Canaan. While Mackenzie did not find evidence of the prehistoric Megalithic people at Beth Shemesh, his experience at Knossos and his expertise in Greek pottery allowed him to make a highly significant contribution to the understanding of the Philistines, a people who migrated to the coast of Palestine from the Aegean world during the transitional period between the Late Bronze and Early Iron ages. Looking back on Mackenzie's work from the vantage point of a century later, the contemporary excavators of Tel Beth Shemesh admire his accomplishments, finding him to be ahead of his time. As one of the first truly professional and scientifically minded archaeologists to work in Palestine, he introduced innovative methodologies that were far more sophisticated than those being used elsewhere in Palestine at the time, and in this way he was able to work out an accurate picture of the site's features, stratigraphy, and chronology (see Figure 4).

But it is also clear in retrospect that Mackenzie's interpretation of the evidence was colored by scholarly thinking typical of his era, including its notions of the Semites and other races (he refers to the Israelites as "the Hebrew race") and its developmental approach to ethnogenesis. The work he and Evans did in Crete helped other scholars, such as the Italian anthropologist Giuseppe Sergi (1841–1936), to work out an alternative to Aryan racial history, a racial history that traced the great civilizations of Egypt, Greece, and Rome, not to the Aryans but to a prehistoric "Mediterranean race" that originated in Africa. While this theory challenged some of the racial assumptions built into the Aryan theory, however, it was based on the same underlying conception of ethnogenesis: some populations (in this case peoples settled around the Mediterranean and in Southern Europe, like Sergi's own nation, the Italians) preserved the physical and mental traits of their ancient forebears in a pure form, while for others farther away (the Nordic peoples),

FIGURE 4. Duncan Mackenzie, leader of the first archaeological expedition to
Tel Beth Shemesh from 1911 to 1912, inspecting the efforts of Arab laborers
as they remove material from the site. Wearing a white hat, Mackenzie is the
second figure from the right among the figures looking down at the site.
Source: Reproduced from Nicoletta Momigliano, *Duncan Mackenzie: A Cautious
Canny Highlander and the Palace of Minos at Knossos* (London: Institute of Classical
Studies, University of London, 1999), courtesy of the Palestine Exploration Fund.

that racial inheritance had been diluted over time by a move to a
different environment and by interbreeding.

The question of ethnogenesis scarcely comes up in what Mackenzie writes about Beth Shemesh, but his interest in the topic comes
through more clearly in his publications about Aegean civilization,
where it is clear that he too believed in the existence of a prehistoric race—neither Aryans nor Semites but a "Mediterranean race"
that could be identified by distinctive pottery, dress, architecture,
and a certain type of cranium. Like Evans, Mackenzie envisioned
this race as a seafaring people that had hopped from one island to
the next until it reached the European mainland and Asia Minor
and intermixed with the populations there, producing modified or
hybrid versions of the culture that Mackenzie and Evans believed
went back to Crete and, beyond that, to Northern Africa.

There are hints here and there that incline one to believe that this conception of ethnogenesis also influenced Mackenzie's understanding of what he found at Beth Shemesh, or would have had he been able to continue his work there beyond a few short seasons. According to his boss, Arthur Evans, most of the Semites who inhabited the Near East were not pure Semites in a racial sense. He understood the ancient inhabitants of northern Syria to be an assimilated people of "South Anatolian stock." The inhabitants of other parts of Syria were the descendants of Semites who had imposed their language on a race related to speakers of "Caucasian" languages. The Phoenicians were Semites who had inherited their entrepreneurial maritime spirit from the Aegean side of their ancestry, and likewise the Philistines were descendant from "colonizing Aegean peoples" who had merged with the Semitic masses they encountered on the coast of southern Palestine. This last claim is noteworthy because of the proximity to Beth Shemesh; for Evans the Philistines were Semiticized variants of the Minoans he and Mackenzie had found on Crete. Did Mackenzie see this kind of racial-mixing process at work in Beth Shemesh as well, a place where Semitic Canaanites and Aegean Philistines also came into contact? He never makes such a claim explicitly, but it is certainly possible that he saw things in this way, given what he and Evans argue elsewhere about the evolution of the Mediterranean race once it spread to Canaan.

Be that as it may, what is significant for our story about this earliest attempt to excavate Beth Shemesh is what it tells us about ethnogenesis as this phenomenon was understood in this period. For archaeologists at the time, ethnogenesis was an essentially developmental process, a process of evolutionary ramification that created new ethnic-racial groups through the effects of migration, adaptation to new environments, interbreeding, and racial dilution over time. Ethnic diversification was an essentially biological process. In the beginning there were a small number of geographically disparate races—the Semites, the Mediterranean Race, and a few other groups who passed on their physical and mental traits to their descendants, and these evolved into a greater variety of ethnic groups by fusing their qualities with those of other races. Archaeology, working in tandem with paleolinguistics, illumined this process by tracing the movement of peoples from one part of the Mediterranean to another and by uncovering material evidence of the racial-cultural intermixing that supposedly took place when different groups encountered each other.

In 1992 a scholar named Nicoletta Momigliano found Mackenzie's unpublished report of his last season at Beth Shemesh in the possession of the archaeologist's nephew. She shared it with Lederman and Bunimovitz, and together they published it in 2016, along with a commentary, producing a document that offers a fascinating glimpse of the differences between Mackenzie's approach to Beth Shemesh and their own. They admire the ahead-of-its-time sophistication and the meticulousness of his methodology, but looking at things from a much later intellectual perspective, they interpret the evidence very differently. Gone from their thinking is the concept of Mediterranean and Semitic races, along with the related conception of ethnogenesis that ascribes the similarities and differences among ethnic groups to a process of racial-cultural descent with modification.

How did they come to view the phenomenon of ethnogenesis so differently? To help answer that question, we need to turn to the second expedition that began at Tel Beth Shemesh in 1928, under the directorship of the American scholar Elihu Grant. In contrast to Mackenzie, Grant was not an experienced or particularly competent archaeologist, but he was connected to another archaeologist, William Foxwell Albright (1891–1971), who in the period between the 1920s and 1970s reshaped the study of what came to be known as biblical archaeology. Albright's approach to archaeology, spanning much of the interval between the first and third expeditions to Beth Shemesh, can help us understand how it is that the phenomenon of ethnogenesis as conceived in the age of Mackenzie gave way to the very different, nonevolutionist understanding of ethnogenesis among archaeologists today.

THE SECOND EXPEDITION: THE DECLINE
OF RACIAL ETHNOGENESIS

By the time of the second expedition to Beth Shemesh, there had been a major change in the field of archaeology: there now existed a subfield of archaeology focused on the Bible. By the end of the nineteenth century, scholars like the British Assyriologist Archibald Sayce (1845–1933) and the German archaeologist Ernst

Sellin (1867–1946) were arguing that theories about biblical history based on literary interpretation needed to be integrated with the scientific findings of archaeology. Mackenzie himself showed very little interest in the Bible, but the Bible-centered approach to the archaeology of Palestine would prevail after World War I precisely as the field was becoming more academic, with the most important excavations now happening under the auspices of universities rather than as the private initiatives of individuals. Paradoxically, after the 1920s the archaeology of Palestine became more religious even as it was becoming more scientific, and the second expedition to Beth Shemesh, which lasted from 1928 to 1933, was a part of this trend, with a director, Elihu Grant, who was both a professor at Haverford and a Methodist minister.

In contrast to Mackenzie, Grant came to Beth Shemesh with practically no fieldwork experience, and the reports he left behind do not hold up the way the Scotsman's reports do, though they make for an engaging read, mixing a description of the archaeological data with anecdotes about the challenges of running the camp and the mounting violence between Jews and Palestinians. (The late 1920s and early 1930s, the period of the British Mandate in Palestine, saw rising tensions between Jews and Arabs in Palestine as Jewish immigration to the area increased.) Grant lived at a time when many archaeologists, identifying their work as a scientific endeavor, focused on the presentation of facts, but his description of his finds at Beth Shemesh are arguably more self-revealing than scientific, including his occasional observations about the conflict between Jews and Palestinians then unfolding in mandate Palestine. Grant published three accounts about Palestinian life, and he took such an interest in the Arab cause that at the time of his death he was serving as president of the American Friends of the Arabs. That empathy spills over into his description of Beth Shemesh; its native Canaanite inhabitants seem modeled on the Palestinian villagers of his own day, just as he seems to have had the Zionists in mind when describing the Hebrew invaders who take over the city. While all this makes his account of his work fascinating for the glimpses it offers of Palestine in the late 1920s and 1930s, his publications are frustrating from an archaeological perspective because they are so impressionistic and imprecise. Lederman and

Bunimovitz have much more respect for Mackenzie than they do for Grant, criticizing the latter for not knowing what he was doing.

With little archaeological experience, Grant needed help analyzing and publishing his fields, and this is what led him to Albright, a figure who would come to personify the field of biblical archaeology. Born in 1891, Albright himself was still fairly young, only recently taking his position as a professor at Johns Hopkins University in 1927; but he was already a major leader in the field, having become director of the American Schools of Oriental Research in Jerusalem in 1922. He played only a peripheral role at Beth Shemesh, visiting the site, publishing a study of an inscription that was discovered there, and recommending his student George Ernest Wright (who would go on to become a major figure in biblical archaeology) to help Grant analyze and publish about the pottery from Beth Shemesh. But he exerted an enormous influence behind the scenes, not just on the thinking of Grant and Wright but on the field in general: Wright was just one of fifty-seven scholars trained by Albright during his thirty years at Johns Hopkins. Albright's contributions to archaeology were considered so significant that in 1970 the American Schools of Oriental Research in Jerusalem was renamed the Albright Institute of Archaeological Research.

Albright's research exemplifies the paradoxical mix of religion and science that defines the field of biblical archaeology. Raised by Methodist missionaries, Albright had a lifelong interest in the Bible as a living religious document. He has often been criticized for having a fundamentalist agenda, aiming to counter the historical skepticism of Wellhausen and other German scholars who treated the biblical stories of Abraham and Moses as legends by using archaeology to argue that such figures had really existed. He acknowledged his belief that there was "an Intelligence and a Will" guiding human history, that God had some role in how things would turn out. But on the other hand, Albright was deeply committed to scientific empiricism. While he did not conceal his religious beliefs, his faith in science was arguably as great, if not greater, and he saw what he was doing as a scientific endeavor, rejecting any essential distinction between the hard sciences and the kind of historical research in which he was engaged. In fact he once declared that, of all the sciences, the two making the most progress at the time were nuclear physics and Palestinian archaeology. He encouraged all his students to think of themselves as scientists—"Don't try to master science, but let the science master you," he told one student—and he even envisioned establishing an academy of scientific humanism.

Thus it was that while Albright affirmed the basic historicity of the Hebrew Bible, arguing for Abraham and Moses as real historical figures, he also understood these figures as part of a larger evolutionary process that began in the prehistoric period, as illustrated by the title of one of his most famous books, *From the Stone Age to Christianity* from 1940. Albright is sometimes said to have opposed an evolutionist approach to history, but in fact he adhered to a variation of what he refers to as an "organismic" approach to history, an approach that combined two different developmental narratives. On the one hand, he treated culture as an organism that is born at a certain moment, matures, and then dies in a life span that takes centuries to unfold, a pattern that simply repeats itself again and again over the course of history in a way that argues against the view that life is getting steadily better. On the other hand, there is a kind of progress that can be discerned over the millennia of human history, a progress that can come about only through catastrophe and upheaval as one culture is replaced by another. This process sometimes slows down to a centuries-long crawl, or it can even devolve into more primitive forms of thinking, but it is nonetheless lurching forward in a long-term sense. Earlier scholars like Mackenzie also plotted the history of peoples and cultures according to a model of birth, growth, and decline. Albright framed such a view within a much bigger evolutionary account of the entire species in which the rise and fall of particular cultures contributed to the intellectual and spiritual progress of all humanity.

In *From the Stone Age to Christianity*, Albright fleshed out his understanding of how the ancient Israelites fit into this larger narrative of progress. All of human history from prehistoric times until the present could be divided into epochs that Albright distinguished as different stages of expanding mental achievement. The beginning occurred sometime in the prehistoric period with the emergence of "prelogical, corporative thinking." The "logical age" of man, continuing into the present, begins around the time of the Greek philosophers of the fifth century BCE, and Albright's own specialty, the textual and archaeological study of the ancient Near East between the third millennium BCE and the first millennium BCE, revealed the transition from one level of thinking to another.

This transitional epoch is where the Hebrew Bible/Old Testament fit into the picture—its account of Abraham, Moses, and prophets like Isaiah registered important moments of "evolutionary mutation": a sudden, disruptive, and transformative change when human thought abruptly shifted to a higher level. For most of the transitional period between the prelogical and logical periods of human development, the Near East was dominated by the two great civilizations of Mesopotamia and Egypt, but a new era began to take shape between 1900 and 1750 BCE: the Middle Bronze Age, when Egypt's dynasty was displaced by Semitic invaders from Syria, and Mesopotamia was overrun by barbarian mountaineers, the Amorites, who introduced a dark age that lasted until around 1500 BCE. This was the age reflected in Genesis and its account of Abraham, according to Albright—in fact, Abraham was one of these Amorite nomads, he argued.

Out of this period of turbulent change there emerged a new cultural era marked by incipient monotheistic tendencies and a greater emphasis on the individual and ethics, trends evident elsewhere in the Near East (especially with the monotheistic Egyptian king Amenophis IV, also known as Akhenaten, from the age of the Amarna letters) but that reached full fruition only with ancient Israel and the religion of Moses. For Albright monotheism was not just a religious advance but an intellectual one, a break from mythological and corporate thinking, and he associates it with empiricism, a greater capacity for abstraction and universalism, ethical reflection, and greater respect for the individual. In his historical reconstruction, it was Moses—for Albright not a legendary figure imagined in a later period by J, E, and P, but a historical figure living around 1200 BCE—who initiated this new phase of human thought by completing the break from earlier religion and introducing full-fledged monotheism.

This view of history, and not just Albright's inclination to accept the historicity of the Bible, helps to explain why he emphasized *discontinuity* between the ancient Israelites and the earlier peoples of Late Bronze Age Canaan. The early Israelites as he describes their history fused very quickly with the Hebrews (whom he took to be an originally separate people, acknowledging a possible link to the Habiru), but they did not do so with the Canaanites, instead exterminating them or driving them from the land as the Book of Joshua reports (an event Albright believed had been recently proven by archaeological evidence showing the destruction of Canaanite towns in the thirteenth century BCE). Whereas Grant empathized with the Canaanites conquered by the Israelites, Albright, if not completely unsympathetic to the Canaanites, was not inclined to condemn their conquerors, cautioning his American readers not to judge the Israelites too harshly given America's own history of exterminating those already living in the land it conquered. Indeed he even suggests the elimination of the Canaanites was necessary for the spiritual progress he was tracing, to the extent that it cleared a space for the emergence of a new way of thinking:

> It is fortunate for the future of monotheism that the Israelites of the Conquest were a wild folk, endowed with primitive energy and ruthless will to exist, since the resulting decimation of the Canaanites prevented the complete fusion of the two kindred folk which would almost inevitably have depressed Yahwistic standards to a point where recovery was impossible. Thus the Canaanites, with their orgiastic nature-worship, their cult of fertility in the form of serpent symbols and sensuous nudity, and their gross mythology, were replaced by Israel, with its nomadic simplicity and purity of life, its lofty monotheism and its severe code of ethics.

Elsewhere in the book, Albright acknowledges important parallels between Israelite and earlier Canaanite religion, but he found it remarkable that there were so few such parallels. For him the Exodus, Moses, and the conquest of Canaan introduced a radical break between Israelite religion and what preceded it in Canaan: "there is no clear trace of any West Semitic influence of characteristically Canaanite type on the earliest religion of Israel," he writes. The survival of Canaanite elements can be detected here and there in the Bible, he concedes, but usually in texts from a later period of history, after the seventh century BCE; and Canaanite culture plays hardly any role in the initial formation of Israelite religion, since there is such a sharp divide between the two.

It has been suggested recently that Albright's representation of the Canaanites reflects the religious biases he absorbed from his Methodist evangelical upbringing—he identified the Israelites with his own Protestant community and the Canaanites with Catholics against whom he was opposed. There may be something to that explanation, but Albright's depiction of the Canaanites and their relation to the Israelites also reflects his particular view of human cultural evolution: there could be no direct development of one people or culture into another, no transitional, intermediate, or mixed stage of the sort that Evans and Mackenzie imagined for the Mediterranean race as it interbred with various local populations, because for Albright Mosaic religion represented one of those abrupt "mutations" that introduces a distinctly new phase in human development, a sudden alteration of thought that makes everything after it different from what went before.

Albright had an indirect influence on Grant's expedition to Beth Shemesh—not only did he recommend Wright to help analyze the finds from the site, but their analysis relied on the pottery typology and chronology that Albright had worked out from his excavation of Tel Bet Mirsim. But neither Grant nor Albright ever fit Beth Shemesh into the evolutionary scheme he lays out in *From the Stone Age to Christianity*. (Albright does include Beth Shemesh in a list of significant excavations from the 1920s and 1930s, but that is almost the only time he mentions the city in the book.) Albright's relevance to the larger story we are telling is what he reveals about the fate of the nineteenth-century conception of ethnogenesis in the altered intellectual terrain of biblical archaeology as it formed under American influence in the 1930s. Albright still thought within an evolutionary framework, but he also expressed strong discontent with the approach, spending forty pages of *From the Stone Age to Christianity* criticizing various evolutionary theories from the likes of Hegel, Oswald Spengler, and Arnold Toynbee.

One can also detect in *From the Stone Age* Albright's reservations about another premise of nineteenth-century ethnogenesis—the concept of race and racial mixture. Such ideas, of course, were alive and well in the 1930s. Grant uses the language of race to describe the Philistines, Canaanites, and Hebrews at Beth Shemesh—he even mentions approvingly the theory that the Phoenicians were an offshoot of the race that once inhabited Crete—and Albright thought in similar terms as well, approvingly citing the idea that the population of Canaan descended from a mixture of Semitic and non-Semitic peoples in Palestine in the course of the eighteenth century BCE. But what is striking about Albright's references to race is his dissatisfaction with how the concept was being used to explain cultural history—not that he questioned the basic category, but he was openly critical of the effort to equate a given culture with a physically defined race, precisely the kind of equation that Mackenzie had relied on for his history of the Mediterranean race. Partly this reflects Albright's intellectual opposition to any kind of determinism, biological, environmental, or economic, and one guesses that it was also a response to Nazism and its use of race science to justify its policies against the Jews. (Albright completed *From the Stone Age* in 1940 and was aware of and opposed to the racial theories circulating in Germany at that time.) Although Albright does not challenge the underlying idea of race in the way the anthropologist Franz Boas did earlier in the twentieth century, his effort to play down the role of race as an explanation for Israel's cultural and mental traits is part of the turn against race scholarship that set in more broadly after World War II.

Albright thus represents a dividing point between the ethnogenetic project of Mackenzie and that of Lederman and Bunimovitz. He is still tethered to the thinking that produced the race-based accounts of ethnogenesis of the early twentieth century, but he also personifies the changes that reshaped archaeological work in Palestine after the 1920s, as Americans began to exert influence over the field—not just the increased emphasis on the Bible and the scientification of archaeology but also the discontentedness with evolutionary accounts and a detaching of race from material culture. Albright's own account of the origin of Israel eschews a unilinear evolutionary narrative (though the alternative he proposes turns out to be such a narrative), and it scarcely invokes race, instead attributing the emergence of Israel to a mental leap that could not be explained by the descent-through-modification paradigm that governed earlier studies of ethnogenesis.

But Albright's approach is nonetheless very different from that proposed by Lederman and Bunimovitz. Although he rejects a

racialized approach, his account is still steeped in an evolutionary perspective (albeit one that, under the influence of genetics research, posited descent with sudden mutation rather than
gradual modification). For Lederman and Bunimovitz, by contrast, ethnogenesis is not an evolutionary process in any sense;
they simply do not try to explain it on a biological model. Nor do
they accept Albright's contention that Israelite identity was fundamentally discontinuous with earlier Canaanite culture. Picking
up on something Mackenzie observed, they note the cultural continuity between the Canaanites of Late Bronze Age Beth Shemesh
and its presumably Israelite inhabitants during the Iron Age, and
they reject Albright's idea of a violent Israelite conquest as a dividing line between the two periods. The difference between their
perspective and Albright's is arguably much greater than the difference between Albright's and Mackenzie's. To explain the change,
we need to fill in some of what happened to biblical archaeology in
the fifty-seven years between the end of Grant's expedition to Beth
Shemesh in 1933 and the beginning of the third expedition in 1990,
including the end of the use of evolution as an explanatory model
for the origin of the Israelites and the rise of a new paradigm of
ethnogenesis much closer to the thinking of Saussure in a way than
to that of Darwin.

THE THIRD EXPEDITION: THE NEW ETHNOGENESIS

Zvi Lederman and Shlomo Bunimovitz, the directors of the current
excavation at Beth Shemesh, are both Israeli archaeologists who
were exposed to the work of Albright and other giants from the
golden age of biblical archaeology but whose perspective is in part a
reaction against their influence. Israeli archaeology, emerging after
the establishment of the state in 1948, was similar in many respects
to the kind of archaeology practiced by Albright. As led by figures
like Yigael Yadin (1917–1984), Israeli archaeology, too, was initially
focused on major urban centers and momentous events, especially
conquests and destructions, and it too read the archaeological evidence in light of the Bible. But it had a different cultural orientation,
more secular than American biblical archaeology, despite a similar
attachment to the Bible, and it had its own internal divisions, such

as a rivalry between a Jerusalem school, led by Yadin, and a Tel
Aviv school, led by Yohanan Aharoni (1919–1976). Free from the
influence of Yadin, who was based at the Hebrew University in Jerusalem, archaeologists trained at Tel Aviv were willing to challenge
his views, to consider more rural kinds of archaeological sites, and
to be open to other theoretical approaches that were at odds with
the thinking characteristic of biblical archaeology in that period.
This is the environment in which Bunimovitz and Lederman were
educated in the 1970s and 1980s, and their work can be seen as a
continuation of the effort to develop an alternative to the kind of
biblical archaeology practiced by Yadin.

Of interest here is how Bunimovitz and Lederman came to see
the process of ethnogenesis so differently than Evans and Mackenzie did. I would emphasize three key developments. The first is
the demise of the Albrightean paradigm and its particular account
of Israel's emergence. Albright had helped to diminish the role of
race as an explanation for the rise of the Israelites, but his own approach to biblical archaeology had begun to break down by the
1960s, as new evidence emerged that challenged his interpretation.
A classic example is the city of Jericho, one of the cities destroyed
by the Israelites during their conquest of Canaan, according to the
Book of Joshua. An excavation conducted during the 1930s by the
British archaeologist John Garstang (1876–1956) found evidence of
destruction during the Late Bronze Age, seeming to confirm the
biblical account from Albright's perspective; but renewed excavation during the 1950s, under the leadership of Kathleen Kenyon,
showed that Garstang had misdated that level of settlement and
that Jericho during the Late Bronze Age was not a formidable
city but rather a small settlement without walls to come tumbling
down. To discover that there might have been no conquest, that the
Israelites might not have been the invaders described in Joshua,
not only challenged the Bible's historicity; it also undermined Albright's evolutionary scheme by nullifying the role he had ascribed
to the conquest as an explanation for the break between Canaanite
and Israelite culture. After Albright's death in 1971, archaeologists
like William Dever began to openly challenge his approach, and
by the time Bunimovitz and Lederman came on the scene, scholars thought in completely different ways about how to connect the

Bible and archaeology and how to understand the relation between Israelite and Canaanite culture.

A second development was the emergence of nonevolutionary explanations for the origin of the Israelites. The first such theory that I know of came from one of Albright's own students, George Mendenhall, who recently passed away about a week before his one hundredth birthday. In an argument first published in 1962, Mendenhall introduced an alternative to the two theories that at that point represented the only options for understanding how the Israelites appeared in the land of Canaan: the idea of George Ernest Wright, building on Albright's view, that the Israelites were invaders who overtook the land in a dramatic act of conquest; and the hypothesis of the German scholars Albrecht Alt (1883–1956) and Martin Noth (1902–1968) that the Israelites were nomads who peacefully infiltrated the land and gradually settled down into a more sedentary existence. Mendenhall proposed instead that the Israelites originated not from outside Canaan but from within it as a group of Habiru (here understood as Canaanite peasants) who decided to break free from the city-states that had exploited their labor. Before they were the tribes of Israel, in other words, the earliest Hebrews were originally the underclass of Canaanite society, and what drew them together was shared economic and political grievances—and the leadership of a small group of fugitives who had managed to escape slavery in Egypt. In Mendenhall's reconstruction, the Hebrews do not begin as invaders; there was no conquest of Canaan, and there was no genocidal war waged against its inhabitants. The Israelites emerged from within Canaanite society through what Mendenhall calls a "peasant's revolt," an uprising among the lower classes of Canaan against their oppressors.

Mendenhall's theory was an attempt to overcome a number of established ideas in biblical scholarship. One of his goals was to refute the long-established image of the early Israelites as nomads, the stereotype that had shaped earlier understandings of the Habiru. Citing a recent anthropological study of the Bedouin of Saudi Arabia, Mendenhall noted that the nomadic lifestyle was really an extension of settled village life, a temporary migration into the fringes undertaken during certain seasons of the year, and that people living this sort of life always represented only a small part of the population. The idea that the early Israelites were nomads was thus based on a romanticized conception of the nomad as a perpetual wanderer, and there is no reason to think that the mass of them trotted into Canaan as desert-dwelling nomads or that a group of nomads could have been large enough to overtake the people settled in the land.

He also challenges what was left of the racialized conception of the Israelites. In his view they were not the lineal descendants of a single already cohesive kin group but arose instead from a hodgepodge of separate clans and a group of Egyptian fugitives without any original connection to each other. Originally, they did not even speak the same dialect of Northwest Semitic, and their sense of solidarity was not based on any actual biological connection. Their perception of themselves as what we might call an ethnic group, a super tribe united by common ancestry, was a byproduct of class consciousness. The Israelites were unified by religion, not by genealogy, and the tradition that they descended from common ancestors arose later as an attempt to express the solidarity created by a common experience of oppression.

What is most noteworthy in this context, however, is Mendenhall's effort to develop a nonevolutionary explanation for the Israelites' origin. Wright's theory of a rapid conquest might seem to be antievolutionary—indeed, he explicitly rejected the idea that the Israelites evolved out of earlier Canaanite polytheism—but we have noted that it originated from Albright's evolutionary approach, and he clearly thought in evolutionist terms, referring to Israelite religion as a "mutation" and situating it as part of the "evolution" of human faith. The gradual settlement theory reflected another strain of evolutionary thought, positing a slow transition from a less civilized mode of nomadic existence to a more civilized one. In contrast Mendenhall's theory—formulated at a time when communist insurgencies were on the ascendency and when increasing numbers of academics were being drawn to visions of radical change—was based not on evolution but on revolution, an intentional rejection of the status quo. The crucial difference between the two models is not the violence of revolution (Wright's Rapid Revolt theory involved a far more violent scenario) but the fact that revolutionary change involves a willful and disruptive act of self-transformation, a decision to refuse a situation and to create a different kind of society. Though the Israel of Mendenhall's account emerges from the population of Canaan, it does not evolve out of that population. It erupts into existence, willing itself into being *as Israel* in conscious opposition to Canaanite culture.

The third development came in the 1970s and 1980s, when the perspective of Saussure began to penetrate archaeological thinking through a movement known as postprocessualism. Processual archaeology, associated with a neoevolutionary approach to social change, refers to a form of archaeological theory dominant in the 1960s that set out to think more carefully about the *process* of social change, to move beyond the kinds of explanation that earlier scholars had used to explain such change—migration, invasion, diffusion—to more complex models that factored in people's relationship to the ecology of their local environment, their economic circumstances, and other variables that required adaptation. Postprocessual archaeology was born of discontent with this approach: it rejects the scientificism of processualist archaeology, its pretension to be objective and rigidly empirical and aims to be more self-reflexive, seeking to illumine and critique its own assumptions and pretensions. It also rejects much of the evolutionist thinking of earlier archaeology, voicing skepticism of the ways in which earlier archaeologists embraced various theories of cultural evolution as an explanation for their material finds. Bunimovitz and Lederman explicitly acknowledge the influence of this challenge to processualism on their own thinking—in fact, their recent publication of the finds from Beth Shemesh is an experiment in postprocessual archaeology, fusing the content of a traditional processual field report together with self-reflexive interest in their own thinking and practice.

Saussure's approach to language entered the field through the intercession of postprocessualists who saw in it a new model for archaeological interpretation, a kind of alternative to evolutionism. Under his influence, postprocessual archaeologists treated artifacts as if they were signs in a linguistic system. The things uncovered in an excavation once had a meaning for the people who used them, a meaning constituted by their place in a semiotic system; the goal of postprocessual interpretation was to resituate them as a part of that system, to read artifacts and features as if they were words in a language, and thereby to understand their significance (and not just their function) within the context in which they were used. Thanks to Saussure's influence, in other words, some archaeologists moved in the same way linguistics did, turning from diachronic questions of transmission and change to synchronic questions of what objects signified for those who used them.

The breakdown of Albright's approach paved the way for the downfall of evolutionism in biblical archaeology, but it didn't quite kill it. Mendenhall's revolution-based account of Israel's origin had a connection to nineteenth-century developmentalist thinking in the sense that it arose out of a Marxist view of history as a development from elite-dominated societies to a more communal and egalitarian society. Postprocessualism went much further in its rejection of developmentalist thinking, not just disavowing an evolutionary approach but turning from diachronic analysis altogether to a focus on interactions within cultures or between cultures. To explain the objects they uncovered, postprocessual archaeologists did not appeal to evolutionary explanations or try to reconstruct long-term developmental schemes; they situated their finds synchronically and relationally, and they especially emphasized the role of *oppositional* relationships in the creation of material culture—competition among neighboring groups or the struggle between a community and the conquerors who ruled it—just as Saussure's approach had focused on the oppositional relationship between signs within a linguistic system.

Against all this background, we are in a position to better understand what is postevolutionist about the concept of ethnogenesis deployed by Bunimovitz and Lederman. Although its roots went back to nineteenth-century developmental thinking, the term "ethnogenesis" began to take on a completely different meaning in the 1960s that mirrors the trajectory we have been describing here. The turning point, if we can point to a single turning point, was an essay published in 1962 by the American sociologist Lester Singer titled "Ethnogenesis and Negro-Americans Today." Prior to the experience of slavery and segregation, Singer argued, Negro-Americans did not see themselves as a single group of people— that is, they were not yet a distinct "social entity" connected by distinct networks and patterns of social relationships and by self-recognition. What had transformed them into such an entity was a sociological process that began when slavery cut Africans off from their original social identities and that was continuing into the present through segregational policies that treated blacks as a single group and encouraged the development of a common consciousness. Singer does not refer to Saussure, but his approach was congruent with the latter's approach to language: the social identity of African Americans was determined not by their roots, which had been effaced by slavery, but by differentiation from another group in the same society. Singer's approach to ethnogenesis would undergo much refinement as it made its way into anthropology and archaeology, but it remains intact, fusing with a Saussurean perspective, and the theory developed by Bunimovitz and Lederman is basically a twenty-first-century variant of the same idea.

Because of the self-reflexive character of this scholarship, Bunimovitz and Lederman acknowledge that their approach to the evidence reflects assumptions specific to their era, and their conception of ethnogenesis is a perfect example of the thesis that archaeological interpretation changes over time. Before it was possible to conceive their theory of the Israelites' origin, the field of biblical archaeology had to undergo certain changes, coming to recognize that the archaeological evidence diverges from history as known from the Hebrew Bible, shifting its focus from major urban centers to the periphery, and—most significant for our purposes—turning from one paradigm of origin to another. The racialized evolutionary thinking so influential in Mackenzie's day had to be overcome, a change we can glimpse in the writing of Albright; so too, in turn, did his version of evolutionism and the sharp break it introduced between the Canaanites and the Israelites. The field finally moved beyond evolutionism altogether by embracing a synchronic and relational model for ethnogenesis in which the explanatory mechanisms of the past—gradualism, racial persistence, intermixing, migration, mutation—no longer had a role.

But all this amounts to an intellectual prehistory of the current excavation at Tel Beth Shemesh, and we have not yet considered what exactly has been discovered there. The time has come to turn back to the question that inspired this chapter: What does archaeology tell us about the origin of the Israelites? But our inquiry, I hope, feels a little different now, for what our excavation of ethnogenesis has confirmed is that the question itself is not a static thing but instead has evolved or mutated or been reconceived in several different ways in the period between the first expedition to Tel Beth Shemesh and the current one. Bunimovitz and Lederman offer a new answer to the question of Israelite origin, but as they themselves acknowledge in their self-reflexive model, it is an answer that makes sense *now*, in light of how the process of ethnogenesis is understood today.

Border Narratives

At its core, the new conception of Israelite ethnogenesis proposed by Lederman and Bunimovitz is an attempt to solve a conundrum posed by the evidence found at Beth Shemesh. As we have noted, Albright and other scholars from the "golden age" of biblical archaeology saw discontinuity between Late Bronze Age Canaan and Early Iron Age Israel. Albright described this break as a "mutation," an abrupt and abiding change that he attributed to the Israelites' conquest of the land, but sites like Beth Shemesh posed a problem for such a view: the material culture of the city's Iron Age inhabitants showed not discontinuity but continuity with earlier Canaanite culture across the supposed divide between the Bronze Age and the Iron Age, following the same traditions of pottery making and metal working and building houses in the same architectural style. This in contrast to nearby Philistine cities where one can see archaeologically that the city's Philistine occupants brought with them their own distinctive pottery and architectural traditions, different from those of earlier Canaanite inhabitants. Indeed, there was so little in the material evidence at Beth Shemesh to suggest that its Iron Age inhabitants were foreign invaders that Grant believed the city continued to be inhabited by Canaanites even after the Hebrews invaded the land—this despite the Bible's testimony that the city was already inhabited by Israelites in the period before the kingdom of David and Solomon.

By the time the third expedition began in 1990, as we noted, many scholars had come to believe that the Israelites had originated from within Canaan—that they did not come in as conquerors or nomadic settlers but emerged from the local population—and the finds at Beth Shemesh were consistent with that conclusion. The puzzle then was this: Were the inhabitants of Beth Shemesh in the Early Iron Age Canaanites or Israelites? If Canaanite, how did the city become Israelite if there was no evidence of an invasion or peasants' revolt in the transition period between the Late Bronze Age and Early Iron Age to account for the change? And if the city's inhabitants were already Israelite in this period, why were they indistinguishable from Canaanites from the perspective of their material culture?

To solve this puzzle, Bunimovitz and Lederman turned to the concept of ethnogenesis in its postevolutionary, postracial form. Ethnic identity was a subjective category, not a biologically predetermined one, and it depended on the perception of difference, a contrast between an "us" and a "them." The process of ethnogenesis was thus in part a process of self-differentiation and boundary construction, the drawing of a line between insiders and outsiders. Historians had shown such a process at work for modern ethnic groups, especially those who lived in frontier regions—liminal, anarchic, or contested zones where the boundaries between different groups were confused or fluid. When an intruder entered the region and threatened to overwhelm or absorb its inhabitants, a frequent response from those already living there, if they were able to resist, was to band together, laying aside whatever kinship affiliations, cultural differences, and political squabbles might have previously fractured them to form a united front against the enemy, unified by a newfound recognition of themselves as a distinct group vis-à-vis their common foe. Ethnogenesis, according to this view, is a form of self-defense, a way for the people of a region imperiled by an external enemy to strengthen itself by pulling together what had been a heterogeneous population under the banner of a single cohesive identity.

By drawing on this model of ethnogenesis, Bunimovitz and Lederman have been able to propose an explanation for how the Canaanites of Beth Shemesh became the Israelites, or the people who would become the Israelites. The catalyst was the arrival of the Philistines, a group who traveled via the Mediterranean Sea to the southern coast of Canaan from Cyprus or from the southern coast of Anatolia as part of a larger migration wave of Aegean peoples known in Egyptian sources as the Sea Peoples. In the same period that other Sea Peoples were settling on the coast of northern Canaan, Lebanon, and Syria, the Philistines settled on the southern coast of Palestine, sometime around 1150 BCE, where they founded the city-states of Ashdod, Ashkelon, and Gaza. From there they moved inward into the interior of Canaan, setting up additional cities at Tel-Miqne (biblical Ekron) and Tel es-Safi (probably biblical Gath). Reaching into the Shephelah, they made it to the area around Tel-Batash (biblical Timnah), about seven kilometers from Beth Shemesh, but, significantly, they did not take over Beth Shemesh itself. Contrary to what Mackenzie and Grant believed, Bunimovitz and Lederman have found that it was never inhabited or controlled by the Philistines: Beth Shemesh remained in territory beyond Philistine control.

It is not clear what stopped the Philistines from penetrating all the way to Beth Shemesh, but it seems to be around that area, the vicinity of the Sorek Valley, where the region's inhabitants were able to put up an effective line of resistance, establishing a well-defended border region in the Shephelah that protected against further Philistine conquests. Part of this process of self-defense, it seems, was the creation of a kind of social boundary with the Philistines. Within a few generations of their arrival, judging from the fact that both Philistine and Canaanite cooking vessels and pottery styles are found in practically every single home in twelfth-century Philistia, the Philistines began trading, collaborating, and intermingling with the local Canaanite population living in the regions under their control, resulting in a process of two-way cultural hybridization that is common in frontier regions where different populations live in close proximity. The Bible itself registers this process of coalescence in the story of Samson, who found himself attracted to a Philistine woman from nearby Timnah and decided to marry her (Judges 14), but this story also suggests that not everyone in Samson's community was so accepting of this kind of cross-group mixing: his own parents warn him against the marriage, encouraging him to find a wife from among his own kin. While the Samson story contains many legendary elements, it may in this regard at least reflect how people in the border region of the Shephelah in the Early Iron Age actually responded to the Philistines' presence nearby: some were drawn into relationships with them, while others sought to preserve the difference between them by avoiding interaction. It was to protect against a merger between the two groups, Bunimovitz and Lederman believe, that the Canaanites developed certain practices meant to accentuate the difference between the two groups, creating an invisible social barrier meant to keep the two populations apart.

It is possible that a number of practices were developed in this period to serve this function. There is reason to think, for example, that the inhabitants of Beth Shemesh avoided the bichrome pottery produced by the Philistines; and it is even conceivable that circumcision, the rite of marking the body of male infants in a way that signifies their membership in the community, arose in this period for similar reasons, since it makes for a sharp contrast with the Philistines who did not practice circumcision. But the best example of such a practice, one supported by evidence uncovered at Beth Shemesh, is the emergence of a food taboo: the avoidance of pork.

With help from the late zooarchaeologist Brian Hesse, Lederman and Bunimovitz found that almost no pork was consumed at Beth Shemesh—there were virtually no pig bones found there—a telling contrast with nearby Philistine sites where such bones were common. The Philistines, like their distant Greek cousins, had a taste for pork, as reflected in the fact that at nearby Philistine centers like Ashkelon and Ekron, pork accounted for 20 to 25 percent of the animals consumed. At Beth Shemesh, on the other hand, pork was completely avoided. The explanation for this difference is not likely to have been ecological—there is no apparent environmental reason for why the Philistines would consume pork while their nearby non-Philistine neighbors would avoid it. The people of Beth Shemesh *chose* to shun a kind of food that the Philistines loved to eat, a taboo that would have probably impeded other forms of interaction between the two peoples since feasting together was such an important way for strangers to get to know one another in ancient Mediterranean culture.

The evidence from Beth Shemesh does not tell us at what point the Canaanites came to see themselves as Israelites or illumine how that part of the process worked, but other archaeologists believe that what happened in the region may have triggered a broader change throughout Canaan. While some Canaanites acquiesced to Philistine rule and others stood their ground against it, still others appear to have fled from the coastal region into the hilly interior of the country, which would help to account for the proliferation of small settlements in this region during this period—from 47 during the Late Bronze Age to 219 known sites during the Early Iron Age— and perhaps that massive migration seeded the growth of ethnic consciousness there as well. Israel Finkelstein believes the inhabitants of these villages and hamlets—presumably the early Israelites or proto-Israelites but in any case a population that also avoided the consumption of pig—were former nomads who settled down in the region after the fall of the Canaanite city-state system at the end of the Bronze Age. But more recently Assaf Yasur-Landau has suggested that they included refugees driven inland by the Philistines, which would explain their connection to what was happening in the area of Beth Shemesh. It is possible, in short, that Tel Beth Shemesh and its vicinity was the place where the Canaanites first became conscious of themselves as a people defined by its difference from another group, and that it was from there that this new collective self-consciousness radiated to other Canaanites throughout the country.

Is this then the very earliest chapter of the origin of the Jews? It remains to be seen what kind of impact Lederman and Bunimovitz's theory will have, but it fits what evidence there is, and it overcomes some of the objections that beset earlier theories. Thus, for example, in contrast to the Peasant Revolt theory that asserts a massive Cuban Revolution–style uprising for which there is little evidence, this theory relies on a catalytic event, the Philistines' incursion into the Shephelah, which has left a major imprint on the archaeological record. Bunimovitz's own students—most prominently, Avraham Faust of Bar-Ilan University, who worked at Beth Shemesh as a graduate student—have become scholars in their own right, and through their work ethnogenesis has emerged as the prevailing model for understanding the rise of a distinctive Israelite identity in the Early Iron Age, even if not every scholar ties it so closely to Tel Beth Shemesh in particular.

It is important to acknowledge that this theory is vulnerable to its own share of criticisms. Its interpretation of the evidence is in line with recent anthropological theory, but a lot of that evidence comes down to pig bones—or the absence thereof—and not every scholar buys the excavators' attempt to locate the origin of the Israelite pig taboo in the Shephelah since such a practice has been detected elsewhere in Canaan. In the end, there is no way to fully reconstruct the process of identity formation that may have been at work in early Iron Age Beth Shemesh because such a process unfolded internally, within the minds of the Israelites as they formed a certain kind of self-perception, and such a process is far less accessible to archaeological retrieval than the military conquests and migrations posited by earlier theories of Israelite origin, events that leave a clearer archaeological trail. And one should note one other challenge for their theory, a potential objection posed by the post-processualism to which both Lederman and Bunimovitz adhere. Postprocessualism underscored the importance of trying to understand artifacts and features from the inside out, from the subjective experience of those who created and used them, but by acknowledging that archaeological interpretation is itself inherently subjective, it also calls into question the field's capacity to describe the past as it actually happened.

Whatever Tel Beth Shemesh might tell us about the ancient Israelites and the origin of their identity, it has proven revealing in another way. Thanks to the century-long history of excavation that has happened there, we have been able to sketch a history of evolutionism as a way of understanding the origin of the Israelites, beginning with early twentieth-century theories of racialized ethnogenesis, moving to the midcentury version of cultural evolution championed by Albright that rejected the racialism and determinism of earlier theories, and finally progressing beyond evolutionism altogether as it was supplanted by other ways of accounting for the origin of ethnic groups. Though not every scholar interested in the origin of social groups has abandoned an evolutionary perspective—and now and then, there are attempts to revive it—it has become rare for that kind of approach to be applied to questions of ethnogenesis, a trend that is reflected in how archaeologists account for the origin of the ancient Israelites. Many scholars of the subject agree that the ancient Israelites emerged out of earlier Canaanite culture, but that process is no longer conceived as a straightforward evolutionary one, and many contemporary archaeologists instead emphasize the agency of the Israelites, their shaping of their own identity through acts of resistance to others and through practices of self-definition. For them, as for scholars in other fields today, the question of origin has been denaturalized—detached from naturally occurring evolutionary processes—and is now conceived on the model of intentional, self-determining human endeavor, as an act of self-construction.

The eclipse of evolutionism has also had another kind of impact on how scholars account for the origin of the Jews. The sort of evolutionary perspective embraced by someone like Albright produced an origin story that moves in a straight line from a before to an after: the task of explaining the origin of the people was one of describing successive stages, transitions or jumps along that straight line. The decline of the evolutionary perspective in the study of ethnogenesis has made more room for other kinds of stories— stories, for example, where the originating people's perception of its origin is an important part of the plot. In the next chapter, I turn to one of those alternative origin accounts, a theory for the origin of the Jews introduced by Sigmund Freud. Freud was a contemporary of Albright, and they shared a scientific orientation, but his theory begins from different premises about what constitutes an origin and leads to a very different conclusion. It has not proven the most persuasive of theories, but it is worth exploring nonetheless because it represents another memorable example of how many different stories modern scholars have told about the origin of the Jews, stories that include evolutionary narratives, tales of migration and revolution, and, thanks to Freud's detective skills, even a murder mystery.

CHAPTER FIVE

Thought Fossils

PSYCHOANALYTIC APPROACHES

We wish to maintain the idea that there may be other types of fossils to be studied than those derived from plants and animals, namely, thought fossils, and that to paleobotany and to paleozoology, we may add a science of paleopsychology.

—SMITH ELY JELLIFFE AND ELIDA EVANS

IT MAY SURPRISE some readers that I have included psychoanalysis among the methods I am using to investigate the origin of the Jews. Psychoanalysis as understood by many people today is a theory of the mind, a therapeutic practice, or a set of techniques used to diagnose and treat mental illness, not a way of investigating questions of ethnogenesis. From its inception, however, psychoanalysis was a mode of etiological inquiry, used not just to investigate the origin of mental illness but to delve into the origin of religion, art, and civilization. Many scholars today would dismiss it as a form of historical or paleontological inquiry, but the field of "psychohistory" still has its advocates, and its core premise—that the mind bears traces of its origin—is too intriguing to simply ignore. The question we pursue in this chapter is whether there is anything to learn about the origin of the Jews from a psychohistorical approach as practiced today.

Sigmund Freud himself famously used his method to excavate the origin of the Jews in his final book, *Moses and Monotheism,* published a few months before his death in September of 1939. The true origin of the Jews, he argued, was very different from the biblical account. Moses was a historical figure, according to Freud, but he was not an Israelite; instead he was a native Egyptian who left his homeland to become a leader of a band of Semites he encountered in the Sinai desert. Not long after he became their leader, however, the Israelites rose up against Moses and murdered him, and that triggered in the Israelites a complex psychological response that Freud aims to illumine in *Moses and Monotheism*. Judaism is the result of this psychological process, and the secret of its genesis, hidden deep in the collective unconscious of the Jews, is one that Freud aims to recover by applying a psychoanalytic approach to the biblical account.

Although there are a good number of Jewish studies scholars today who are fascinated by Freud, it is hard to find one who takes *Moses and Monotheism* seriously as a historical account of the origin of the Jews. The idea that Moses was originally Egyptian is based on very slim evidence—the resemblance between the name Moses and the Egyptian word for "son of," which appears as an element in names like Thutmose (son of the god Thoth) and Ramses (son of Ra)—and all the rest is an elaborate conjecture, as Freud himself acknowledged. Some of his own disciples were troubled by the book. Even his friend Ernest Jones (1879–1958) reports begging him to omit a passage in *Moses and Monotheism* he found particularly objectionable from a scientific perspective, and many of the reviews from the time are far more skeptical. Typical, for example, is the reaction of the great Jewish historian Salo Baron (1895–1989), who pronounced the book a "magnificent castle in the air," and Albright responded similarly, dismissing Freud's work as "totally devoid of serious historical method." Some seventy-five years later, scholars of biblical and Jewish history remain just as dismissive of *Moses and Monotheism* as a historical account of the origin of Judaism—as the Jewish studies scholar Peter Schäfer has put it, "Today, having entered the 21st century, we can look back at this reconstruction of the Jewish religion, developed in the 1930s, and dispassionately state that it contains virtually nothing that is true from a religious-historical standpoint."

What is of interest to me here, however, is not the details of Freud's reconstruction but the method that led him to that reconstruction, the method he himself pioneered—psychoanalysis. From very early on in his career, Freud conceived of psychoanalysis as a kind of archaeology, as in his address "The Aetiology of Hysteria," the first major paper that he presented in 1896 (the same year he coined the term "psychoanalysis"). In a well-known passage, he likened the psychoanalyst to an explorer arriving at an expanse of ruins. On the surface one could see the remains of a great civilization buried underneath—the remains of walls, broken columns, and "tablets with half-effaced and unreadable inscriptions." The explorer could have contented himself with asking natives about the history of the place, but he had come equipped to go deeper—to penetrate beneath the surface and to decipher the mysterious inscriptions discovered amid the ruins. Psychoanalysis, in other words, was a kind of archaeology of the soul. Freud also believed that the mind unconsciously registered experiences inherited from earlier generations, bearing traces of primal impulses and traumas. Someone who knew how to interpret the unconscious could retrieve and use this evidence to go back well beyond childhood to a much earlier prehistoric age when humanity's collective psyche was taking shape.

Using this technique in a work titled *Totem and Taboo* (1913), Freud was able to go all the way back to prehistory and propose an explanation for the origin of religion, and it was by means of the same method that he sought to illumine the origin of Judaism. Drawing on concepts and insights developed from his clinical work with his patients—his observation that sons want to murder their fathers, the hypothesis of a latency period in which children repress their sexual and aggressive impulses, and the concept of "the return of the repressed" in which those desires find ways to reassert themselves indirectly—Freud uncovered an unwritten history of the Jews that the biblical account had sought to repress.

In the 1980s and 1990s, scholars developed a newfound appreciation for *Moses and Monotheism*, but that appreciation was for the biographical insights this work offered into Freud and his Jewish identity, not for its theory of Jewish origin. Indeed, many of these scholars regard Freud's arguments as so farfetched that they treat *Moses and Monotheism* as if it were a work of fiction or autobiography, not a work intended to be taken literally as an attempt to answer the question of Jewish origin. If we are willing to entertain Freud's theory here, it is not because I am ignoring what is now so objectionable about it but because *Moses and Monotheism* gives us an opportunity to explore another way to address the question of Jewish origin that is simply too intriguing to ignore. We have found our search for the origin of the Jews stymied by the limits of the written and archaeological sources. Through psychoanalysis Freud developed an alternative to both philology and archaeology, a kind of "paleopsychology" (to use a term coined by the neurologists Smith Ely Jelliffe and Elida Evans in 1916) that could take the search for the origin of the Jews beyond the documentary sources and beyond the material ruins into a prehistory preserved only as "thought fossils" buried deep in the most primal parts of the human mind.

It is this method that interests us in this chapter, not the particular hypothesis that Freud develops in *Moses and Monotheism*, and what we seek to understand about it is whether there is any way to salvage it, to adapt it in a way that scholars today would find credible. As it happens, there has been an attempt in recent years to update Freud's approach to Moses. Understanding that effort, by an Egyptologist named Jan Assmann, is our ultimate goal in this chapter, but before we turn to him, it will help us to learn more about Freud's theory itself. His answer to the question of Jewish origin cannot simply be transferred from his age to our own—it reflects assumptions and ideas from another era that in some cases are highly suspect or objectionable from the perspective of present-day psychology, biblical studies, or history. By looking a bit more carefully at Freud's theory, I want to try to distinguish between those aspects of it that no longer strike scholars as true and those that might retain credibility, as a way of gaining the background we need to judge whether Assmann has succeeded in reviving a psychoanalytic approach to Moses.

From Moses to Masochism

Moses and Monotheism actually reconstructs two kinds of historical accounts. The first loosely corresponds to history in the usual sense, involving events that happened in the real world of ancient Egypt and the Sinai wilderness. I say "loosely" because, as Freud acknowledged, his reconstruction of these events had little evidence to support it and was largely conjectural. The other kind of history was an internal, psychological history, a series of unconscious events that took place within the minds of Moses's followers and their Jewish descendants—impulses, feelings, reactions, and repressed memories that operated according to principles that Freud had worked out through psychoanalysis. Freud reconstructed the first kind of history as he did because he believed it corresponded to the second kind of history—in other words, he discerned an analogy between the development of the Jews and the development of the psyche. Grasping this analogy hardly proves the more farfetched aspects of Freud's theory—his argument that Moses was really an Egyptian or his proposal that the Bible covers up his murder. But it reveals the logic at work in what might otherwise seem a preposterous reconstruction, and it helps to explain why our true task in this section is not so much to assess Freud's claims about Moses as a real-life figure but to understand the unconscious mental processes to which he ascribed the origin of the Jews as a people constituted by a shared traumatic experience deep in its past.

This psychological history of the Jews, Freud argued, followed a pattern in human history that he had worked out in *Totem and Taboo* twenty-five years earlier, so it is important to begin by laying out that pattern. This earlier work argues that, in prehistoric times (Freud does not know when but probably sometime before humans had developed language), there had existed a clan of humans dominated by a tyrannical father. Freud speaks as if he is referring to a particular group of people, but he admits it is possible the situation he is describing was a recurrent one that repeated itself over and over again, probably in real life, though Freud acknowledges that it might have played out only in the unacknowledged fantasies of prehistoric minds. In any case, the book is about events, historical and psychological, that occurred in an age before civilization, before there was a society or a sense of a moral code to constrain the father from acting on his every impulse.

Embodying Freud's notion of the id (the most primal part of the mind that seeks instant gratification for its every want), this original father took every female in the group for himself despite the fact that many were his own daughters; and he killed off, drove off, or castrated all the young males who might threaten his position, despite the fact that they were his sons. But those sons eventually struck back. Although they were terrified of their father and awed by his power, they felt the same impulses and desires—in effect, each wanted to take the place of the father, to be the father—and finally decided to band together to defeat him, killing him and eating his body so as to partake of some of the power they coveted for themselves. A period of fratricide followed as each son tried to take the place of the father, but that endangered the existence of the horde; when it became clear to all that no son could finally overcome the others, they came to an arrangement that would allow them to cooperate while still acting on their desires in a less destructive way.

This stage corresponds to the development of the superego, the part of the psyche that tries to reign in the id, and it was during the analogous period of primeval human history that religion developed as a way to restrain the destructive impulses that had nearly destroyed the horde. The concept of the protective spirit (the totem), the earliest form of what would later become the gods people worshipped, arose as a sublimated form of the slain father, a way for the mind to manage its conflicting feelings of aggression, awe of the father, and guilt for his murder. A prohibition of incest, the first taboo, was instituted to redirect the desires of the sons beyond the women within the horde, and sacrifice and other rituals were developed as a way for the sons to safely act on homicidal (and cannibalistic) impulses that could not be expressed more directly without annihilating each other.

For those who might find such a scenario overly fanciful, Freud points to echoes of this primeval family drama in contemporary religious behavior, what he too describes as a kind of fossilized preservation of primeval thoughts. One example is the Christian communion, where the believer symbolically incorporates the blood and flesh of a murdered god; but a more pertinent example for our purposes, mentioned briefly in *Totem and Taboo* and at greater length in *Moses and Monotheism*, is the practice of circumcision as an initiation rite. In the latter work, Freud points to circumcision as evidence that the religion of Moses was originally a form of Egyptian religion, since the Egyptians were known for their practice of circumcision, but it also represented a fossilized form of a prehistoric trauma—the father's effort to castrate his sons to prevent them from copulating with his wives. Circumcision was a "symbolic substitute" for that act, a ritualized reenactment, and this is why it provoked such a negative response: it recalled "the dreaded castration and along with it a portion of the primaeval past which is gladly forgotten."

The origin of the Jews as Freud describes it in *Moses and Monotheism* follows this prehistoric pattern. In the beginning, as it were, there is an act of rebellion against an overpowering father figure—in this case the Egyptian king Akhenaten, who established his capital at Amarna (where the Amarna letters were found) and was known for introducing the earliest known version of monotheism—a monotheistic and iconoclastic spin on Egyptian religion focused on the sun god Aten. Akhenaten had staged his own patricidal rebellion by revolting against the traditional gods but then became an overbearing father figure in his own right against whom the next generation of Egyptians rebelled, and it was during this period of backlash that Moses, a follower of Akhenaten, decided to leave Egypt.

Freud's idea that Moses was originally an Egyptian was not based on very much—his most solid piece of evidence is the similarity between the name Moses and Egyptian names like Amen-mose. (Like earlier scholars, Freud derived the name Moses from the Egyptian term meaning "born of," as in royal names like Thutmose, "born of the god Thoth.") But this was just enough evidence to allow Freud to fit Moses into the same father-son dynamic that he described in *Totem and Taboo*. Moses was himself part of a rebellion against an earlier patriarchal religion, the Akhenaten revolution, and like the king he admired, he would become a domineering father figure against whom others would rebel. Freud speculates that he may have been the governor of a border province where certain Semitic tribes had settled, and it was these Semites who became Moses's earliest supporters, following him out of Egypt as he sought to reestablish the cult of Akhenaten beyond its borders. Moses was a far more enlightened figure than the primeval father was, but he fell into the same pattern, becoming overbearing and tyrannical, and this is what eventually led his followers to rise up against him, killing him early on during their trek through the wilderness. Moses's followers don't eat him, but they do repress the memory of having murdered him, triggering the same process of repression, guilt, and sublimation that had followed from the murder of the primeval father. Judaism, in other words, is the result of the same kind of process Freud describes in *Totem and Taboo*—the idealization of the murdered father figure as a powerful and punitive deity; taboos to reign in the people's impulses; and the use of ritual as an outlet for suppressed desires and aggression.

The Torah itself reports several rebellions against Moses, but those familiar with its contents will know that it never claims the prophet was murdered, reporting that he died of old age, alone, just before the Israelites crossed over into the land of Canaan. According to Freud, however, there was a reason the Bible did not report events as they actually happened. When the mind is faced with a traumatic experience, Freud explained, it is often torn between two responses—drawn to reliving the trauma but also seeking to extinguish its memory—and it usually finds its way to some kind of compromise, healthy or unhealthy, in which it preserves the memory of the trauma in disguised form. This is the process the Israelites undergo in the wake of Moses's murder. Sometime after his death—Freud guesses two generations or maybe a century later—Moses's Semitic followers came to an oasis of Qadesh, where they encountered an Arabic tribe of Midianites. By this point they were being led by the Levites—in Freud's view, the descendants of Moses' inner circle of followers and servants—but they were still in need of a strong father figure, and they found such a leader in the priestly leader of the Midianites, an unnamed figure who worshipped a demonic volcano god named Yahweh. They embraced some of the beliefs and practices of the Midianites, adopting Yahweh as their god while retaining elements of the cult of the Egyptian Moses— circumcision, the restriction on the use of the divine name, and a memory of having come from Egypt—and embraced the Midianite priest himself as their new leader. They did not forget about Moses, but they wanted to forget that they had murdered him, and as that part of their history was repressed, his memory became fused with the unnamed Midianite, producing the portrait of Moses in the

Bible that obscures his Egyptian origin, idealizes him, and tries to erase his guilt-inducing demise.

Here too there is little evidence to support Freud's hypothetical scenario. About the best that can be said about it from a historiographical perspective is that it reconciles two hypotheses that have merits in their own right—the theory of an Egyptian origin for monotheism, an idea supported by the discovery of Akhenaten and his monotheistic religious reforms, and another hypothesis, championed by the historian Eduard Meyer (the same Eduard Meyer disparaged by Wellhausen), that traced the worship of Yahweh back to the religion of Midianites settled in the Sinai desert and southern Canaan. Neither idea is beyond the realm of the possible—variations of each hypothesis persist to this day—but there is certainly no evidence to support Freud's particular way of combining them.

Again, however, what leads Freud to propose this reconstructed scenario is not the historical evidence but his understanding of psychological development and, more specifically, what happens to the mind during the latency stage of development, which occurs between the ages of three and fifteen. The compromise at Qadesh resembled the psychic compromise that forms the personality of the neurotic as he or she is growing up: just as maturing children repress the unruly sexual feelings and aggressiveness of their first few years of life, entering a seemingly stable period when these impulses seem to have been completely curbed, the Jews' merger with the Midianites likewise allowed them to enter a stable period that lasted for several centuries, as they went on to invade the land of Canaan, joined with the Habiru they encountered there (and thus acquired the name Hebrew), and settled down.

But this situation, though it lasted for centuries, was inherently unstable. While one response of the mind is to try to forget the traumatic experience of childhood, another is an impulsion to repeat the experience, to revisit it and to relive it. The struggle between these responses eventually results in a return of the repressed, a resurfacing of the repressed experience in a disguised form that makes it difficult to recognize as a repetition. This too is what happens to Moses's followers, according to Freud. They carried their new Yahweh religion with them into Canaan, a religion that probably was not very different from the religions of the various peoples they encountered there, but the impulses that had led them to murder Moses had never really been lost; they had merely been pushed underground, becoming stronger by virtue of the act of repression, like water pressure building up behind a dam. The latency period comes to an end, Freud explains, when puberty strengthens the sexual and aggressive instincts to the point that they can overcome the mind's defense mechanisms. For the Jews the latency stage ended many centuries after Moses, when their ancestor's repressed experiences and feelings came back in the form of an idealized but terrifying father figure, a benevolent but highly demanding God. The feelings that had impelled the Israelites to slay Moses had not gone away: they had been hidden in the unconscious all along and were now turned against the self in the form of a masochistic theology in which one always deserves to be punished.

Freud recognized that much time had passed between the days of Akhenaten and the finalization of Mosaic religion after the Babylonian exile, and that the laws of the Torah had been expanded over time, but for him there was an enduring psychic core to Judaism that was crystallized at this moment of the return of the repressed. The experience of killing Moses and the intense feelings and psychic struggles that followed in the wake of that act—all protected from the erosion of time and true forgetfulness by having been buried within the unconscious—were preserved intact over the centuries and were now manifest in psychological propensities he believed common to Jews of his own day, including their perpetual consciousness of guilt. For Freud Judaism was not so much a religion as a kind of collective personality, a neurotic personality, that surfaced in Jews by virtue of their having inherited the unconscious trauma of their ancestors. Whatever his shortcomings as a historian, Freud believed that the psychoanalytic method gave him a way to identify and understand the nature of this trauma, and that was why, in his mind at least, he was positioned to understand the origin of the Jews in the way previous scholars could not.

Psychoanalysis and Its Discontents

How much of Freud's argument, if any, can we believe? There is (I will admit, despite my skepticism) something strangely compelling about it, and the way I account for that is to attribute it to Freud's ability to construct a perfect correspondence between the internal realm of the unconscious and the external realm of history. In the end, however, Freud's theory was only as strong as the parts from which it was constructed, and almost every one of those parts has been criticized or debunked by later scholarship—not just his claims about the real Moses but the underlying theory of psychological development. This is what makes it such a huge challenge to rehabilitate Freud's approach: there is hardly anything in what he argues in *Moses and Monotheism* that is not considered dubious or refutable.

To start with the historical part of his argument, first let us focus on his claim that Moses was originally an Egyptian, and that the religion he developed was a version of Egyptian religion. The idea that early Israelite culture was influenced in some formative way by Egyptian culture is certainly possible. Scholars have long sought to identify the ancestors of the Israelites with the Hyksos, a dynasty of foreign rulers in Egypt who entered the country as part of a larger migration from Canaan or Syria in the eighteenth century BCE and were later expelled by the native Egyptian ruler Ahmose I. Some see Hyksos rule as the historical background for the biblical story of Joseph, who rises to a position of leadership in Egypt, and the expulsion of the Hyksos as the historical kernel of the Exodus story. However that may be, we also know that Canaan in the Late Bronze Age was under Egyptian control, that there was contact between the rulers of Canaan's cities and the court of Amarna, and that Egyptian culture almost certainly had direct influence on ancient Israelite culture and literature. (Some scholars believe, for example, that Psalm 104 might be a kind of Hebrew translation of a hymn to the god Aten composed by Akhenaten, because their content is so similar.) The idea that Moses was an Egyptian or that he borrowed from Egyptian religion is not as farfetched as it might seem at first.

In Freud's defense, moreover, one might also note that he wrote *Moses and Monotheism* in the wake of what was probably the most exciting period of Egyptology, the age of its rediscovery of Akhenaten and his family. Akhenaten, also known by his earlier name Amenhotep (IV) before he took on a new name in honor of the god Aten, was not a well-known figure prior to the end of the nineteenth century. The ancient accounts scholars relied on for their understanding of Egyptian history knew nothing about the king, nor was he known to the Orientalist Jean-François Champollion (1790–1832) at the time he unlocked the secrets of hieroglyphics by deciphering the Rosetta Stone. The extraordinary character of his seventeen-year reign became clear only following the excavation of Amarna in 1891–1892 by Flinders Petrie; the discovery in 1912 of the bust of Akhenaten's beautiful wife, Nefertiti; and the most sensational development of them all, Howard Carter's discovery of the tomb of Akhenaten's son Tutankhamun in 1922. The excitement caused by these discoveries had not abated by the time Freud was writing *Moses and Monotheism* in the 1930s. The king and his family were such celebrities during this period that Herbert Hoover, US president from 1929 to 1933, was inspired by them to name his dog King Tut, and Hitler was so enamored of Nefertiti that he refused to hand her bust back when the Egyptians asked for its return. As a scholar fascinated by ancient civilization, reflected in a lifelong obsession with collecting antiquities, Freud can be forgiven for trying to draw on these discoveries to illumine the origin of the Jews (see Figure 5).

As tempting as it is to associate Moses with the illustrious Akhenaten, however, there is no real basis for connecting them as directly as Freud does. Even at the time when Freud published *Moses and Monotheism*, there were skeptics like the previously mentioned Salo Baron who noted that the supposed Egyptian etymology for the name Moses no more proved an Egyptian origin for Moses than the use of a Babylonian name for postexilic biblical figures like Zerubavel proved that they were Babylonian. It is also now clear, moreover, that Akhenaten is not the figure Freud assumed him to be. He relied in part for his understanding of the Egyptian king on the work of James Henry Breasted (1865–1935), the renowned Egyptologist who described Akhenaten not just as a fully realized human being but as the first real individual in history. In today's scholarship, the king's reputation as a monotheist is intact, but he is now recognized as a much less accessible figure who represented himself in different ways to different audiences in a way that obscures what he was like in person. Freud understood him as a rebellious son and overbearing father figure, focusing so much on the oedipal father-son struggle that he scarcely takes note of the women in Akhenaten's court—his wife Nefertiti or his

FIGURE 5. Stela from El-Amarna depicting Akhenaten
in the act of worshipping the sun god Aten.
Source: Image #175960. Reproduced courtesy of the University
of Pennsylvania Museum of Archaeology and Anthropology.

mother Tiye. But Freud's disciple Karl Abraham (1877–1925), in an earlier study, saw a different Akhenaten, a figure greatly influenced by his mother, and other scholars describe him in yet other ways: as a prig, a progressive, a fascist, a black nationalist, and a transgender pioneer. Somewhere behind all these accounts is the historical Akhenaten, but at present at least, there is no way to get to the bottom of what he was like, much less to demonstrate his influence over Moses.

Freud's reconstruction of Moses's life is no less questionable. Most critical biblical scholars today would agree that Moses, if such a figure existed at all, is beyond the historian's reach, but even if we posit that he really lived, and place him in the time of Akhenaten, and make him an Egyptian, there is still the problem of how to demonstrate that he was murdered. Freud got that idea from the biblical scholar Ernst Sellin (1867–1946), who had discerned what he construed to be allusions to the murder in the books of Numbers, Hosea, and Isaiah. But a reader of the relevant passages will not find any reference there to Moses's murder. Sellin was able to uncover the crime only by reading the names Zimri and Cosbi, an Israelite man and Midianite woman slain by the priest Phineas according to Numbers 25, as pseudonyms for Moses and his Midianite wife, Zipporah, an idea so implausible that Sellin eventually renounced his own theory.

As easy as it is to poke holes in the historical side of Freud's argument, however, none of that is fatal to his argument, for as we have noted, its real force comes from his psychoanalytic method and its ability to penetrate the prehistory of the unconscious; but in that respect, too, his argument has not held up well. Freud certainly has his fair share of present-day advocates, of course, but it is harder to find defenders in the field of academic psychology. Within the field of psychoanalysis as it developed after Freud, some of the key concepts essential to Freud's argument in *Moses and Monotheism* were challenged: Melanie Klein (1882–1960) rejected the male-centeredness of his theory of psychological development, while Franz Maciejewski (b. 1946) reads Freud's work as a projection of his own unconscious struggle between a desire for the death of his younger brother Julius (who died as an infant) and the guilt arising from such a feeling. Beyond psychoanalysis, even more fundamental concepts, like Freud's theory of repression, have been criticized or dismissed for having no scientific support. According to one recent study, only 30 percent of the research-oriented psychologists surveyed agreed to some extent that traumatic memories are often repressed and can be retrieved through therapy, and organizations like the American Medical Association have concluded that repressed memories are of "uncertain authenticity." This is not the place, and I am not the person, to undertake a critique of Freud's theory of psychological development, but there is one idea that he introduces in *Moses and Monotheism* that scholars have found particularly objectionable, and it is worth mentioning because his argument depends on it—the idea that Jews are defined as a group by a collective psychology inherited from their ancestors.

In a sense Freud's project in *Moses and Monotheism* was similar to the racialized study of ethnogenesis that we discussed in the previous chapter, the kind of scholarship that sought to account for the cultural characteristics of different ethnic groups by tracing their racial-biological history. It is true that race scientists were often focused on physiological traits (a certain shape of the head or a distinctive size and shape of the nose), but they were also sometimes interested in psychological traits, believing that they too had been inherited from their ancestors (as in Arthur Evans's idea that the Phoenicians inherited the "spirit of maritime enterprise" from the Mediterranean race). Freud's project was a similar effort to account for the distinctive personality traits of the Jews as he perceived them—their proclivity toward intellectual pursuits, their high opinion of themselves as a people chosen for a special purpose, and their "interminable" feelings of guilt—and he did so in a similar way, by treating them as phylogenetic traits. It is true that the origin of these traits resulted not from the racial characteristics the Jews shared with other Semites but from a traumatic experience suffered by their ancestors at a particular moment in history, but once this experience was inscribed into the unconscious of these ancestors, it was passed down in the same way that racial traits were, from parents to children. (Freud does not explain why these traits did not get watered down over time, as supposedly did the racial characteristics of so many people, but one guesses that he would have explained it in light of the Mosaic law against mixed marriages, which prevented

the Jews from interbreeding with other groups and thus from dilut-
ing the traits inherited from their biblical ancestors.)

Freud's conception of Judaism as a phylogenetic inheritance
is objectionable on many different grounds. To begin with, there
is Freud's generalizations about the character traits of the Jews—
their supposed affinity for intellectual and spiritual pursuits and
their perpetual consciousness of guilt—which have to be tossed into
the same trash can of discredited scientific generalizations already
overflowing with the piles of cranial measurements and noseo-
logical comparisons produced by nineteenth-century race science.
Freud was certainly not meaning to endorse prejudice against his
own people—he was its victim, after all, and one motive for writing
Moses and Monotheism was to counter anti-Semitism by diagnosing its cause—but one of the more disturbing aspects of *Moses and
Monotheism* is how it puts the blame on Jews for their own persecution by treating anti-Semitic caricature not as prejudice but as an
accurate reflection of inherent Jewish traits.

Equally objectionable is Freud's description of these traits as an
inheritance, passed down generationally on the model of racial or
genetic transmission as understood in that period. Some traits are
inherited directly from the personality of Moses himself; others
are generated as a reaction to the traumatic way in which Moses
died; and somehow everything sticks, forming a psychological
core of memory traces, feelings, and psychological characteristics
passed down not through a consciously communicated tradition
or an educational process but through unconscious transmission
from one generation to the next. Freud does not offer a clear explanation for how traits like an acute consciousness of guilt can
be passed down phylogenetically in this way, but he suggests the
process is biological, describing it as Lamarckian (a reference to
an evolutionary theory in which animals pass down traits acquired
during their lifetime) and comparing it to how an animal inherits
instincts that allow it to act as if born with a memory of its ancestors' experiences.

In fairness to Freud, he was only one of many scholars at the
time who argued that memory could be inherited. But he also knew
that there were serious objections to the sort of Lamarckian view he
was arguing. At least one of Freud's own disciples tried to talk him

out of this part of his argument—this was what Ernest Jones was trying to expunge from *Moses and Monotheism* by imploring Freud to remove a certain passage from it. If he stuck to his guns, perhaps it is in part because he realized that without some idea of biological transmission, his whole theory falls apart. If Jews were not conscious of the trauma Freud describes, if they did not write it down or transmit it through oral instruction (a possibility Freud considers but rejects), there was no way to account for how it had been passed down to present-day Jews without positing unconscious biological transmission. Even if there had been some way to address all the other problems with Freud's argument, the Lamarckian process it required would have doomed it in the end since, in general, theories that purported to explain the mental habits and character traits of people as a biologically transmitted inheritance were discredited after World War II.

If Freud's approach to the origin of the Jews is to be salvaged, therefore, it will have to be detached both from the stereotyped traits he ascribed to the Jews and from the implausible conception of heredity used to explain their presence in an entire population. The question we now face is whether it is possible to purge Freud's approach of these shortcomings and apply it in some modified form to our question. As we have noted, there continue to be advocates for the field known as psychohistory, the study of the psychological unconscious motivations at work in historical events, and Freudian ideas, his notion of trauma and repression, continue to play an important role in such scholarship. Can an updated version of Freud's approach still work to retrieve the origin of the Jews?

This brings us to the work of the Egyptologist Jan Assmann, an exceptionally wide-ranging scholar known not only for his studies of ancient Egyptian texts but also for influential studies of collective memory. Assmann, who has published highly respected scholarship on the historical Akhenaten, has developed a modified version of Freud's thesis about the Egyptian origin of monotheism, and that research can serve us as a case study in the salvageability of psychohistory. If a scholar with his Egyptological erudition and sophisticated understanding of memory cannot overcome the shortcomings of Freud's approach, it may well be best to look elsewhere to understand the origin of the Jews.

The Return of the Repressed

Freud's reconstruction of the origin of Judaism might be farfetched as a description of historical events, but he himself suggested a way to overcome this problem that later scholars would seize on as a way to rehabilitate his approach. Toward the end of *Totem and Taboo*, Freud considers the possibility that the primordial events he had reconstructed did not really happen and that what he was detecting in the unconscious was not a historical reality but a psychical one—murderous fantasies never acted out in reality, though they nonetheless left an imprint on the unconscious and its development. In the end he rejects this possibility, concluding *Totem and Taboo* with the words, "In the beginning was the deed," by which he meant that primitive man probably acted on his impulses. But his consideration of the question suggested a distinction between what the philosopher Richard Bernstein calls "material truth" and "historical truth," between the truth of what happened in the external world and the truth of what happens in the unconscious. The two can converge but need not be the same, allowing one to adopt a Freudian approach to the origin of the Jews without having to buy into the idea that Moses was actually murdered.

This is the approach that Assmann has adopted in a number of books where he develops a modified version of Freud's thesis. For Assmann, Moses is not a historical figure. It is not clear that he ever actually existed; we have no knowledge of him apart from the legendary traditions preserved in the Bible; and Assmann believes that the stories told about him represent a distorted memory of the reign of Akhenaten and his attempt to introduce a monotheistic version of Egyptian religion. What Assmann is seeking to understand is the role of Moses in religious and cultural memory—a clear point of difference from Freud's approach; but despite making this distinction, Assmann nonetheless develops an origin narrative for Judaism that is essentially an updated version of Freud's thesis. For us his argument offers a chance to explore whether it is possible to update *Moses and Monotheism* in a way that overcomes the many problems with it.

Assmann's objective, it should be noted, is not to reconstruct the origin of the Jews per se: what he seeks to understand is the origin of monotheism, by which he means not just the belief in one god but the impulse to distinguish between good and bad religion, to define one's own religion as right and other people's religion as wrong, the kind of outlook that produces the persecution of heresy, sectarianism, and religious violence. Polytheism as Assmann conceives it is an essentially tolerant form of religiosity—ancient polytheists accepted other people's beliefs and emphasized the compatibility or mutual translatability of different religious cultures, equating the gods of one people with the gods of another. Monotheism, imposing a sharp distinction between true and false religion, is inherently intolerant of the other, dividing the world into incompatible opposites—true believers and idolaters. As an exponent of religious tolerance, and as a German scholar living in the shadow of the Holocaust, Assmann has been clear that he is referring not to Judaism per se but to all monotheistic faiths, and in his reconstruction of history, it is not the Jews who create this kind of religiosity but the Egyptian Akhenaten. But critics have noted that he seems to have the Jews in mind: Akhenaten might have been the first to conceive monotheism, but it is the Jews who introduce this kind of religiosity to the world. The personification of its intolerance is the prophet Moses as he is described in the Bible—hence Assmann refers to this kind of religious attitude as the "Mosaic distinction," and he associates it with the Five Books of Moses and their condemnation of idolatry. For all intents and purposes, Assmann is seeking to account for the origin of Judaism's essential quality as he sees it—its perception of itself as a true religion, its condemnation of other religions as idolatrous, its compulsion to make distinctions and impose sharp boundaries.

On the surface, Assmann employs a very different kind of method than the kind Freud practiced: not a psychoanalytic study of what people have forgotten about Moses but a "mnemohistorical" study of how the prophet has been remembered over the course of cultural history. *Moses and Monotheism* posited the existence of repressed "memory traces," memories that might now appear in distorted form but registered real experiences from the primordial past, whether we mean by that the individual's primordial experiences during childhood or those of humanity in general in ancient times. Assmann's approach is born of a different theory of memory associated with the sociologist Maurice Halbwachs (1877–1945) and the art historian Aby Warburg (1866–1929), a sociological or "constructivist" approach that sees memory as something continuously built anew by social groups in response to and in light of their present circumstances and relationships. As he writes in an essay titled "Collective Memory and Cultural Identity," Assmann notes that "no memory can preserve the past. What remains is only that 'which society in each era can reconstruct within its contemporary frame of reference'" (Assmann is quoting Halbwachs here). Whereas Freud's approach can be seen as a kind of archaeological endeavor, a search for "thought fossils" from the primordial past, Assmann's study of Moses rejects archaeology as its model, focusing instead on the plasticity of memory as a vehicle of self- and social construction. In line with this view, much of his work is a charting of how the memories of Moses and Egypt have changed over the course of history, from the Bible to Freud, in ways that mirror the history of monotheism and its discontents.

For all the differences between their approaches, however, Freud's approach to memory makes a kind of return through Assmann. In a part of his argument that is at odds with his constructivist approach to memory, Assmann sometimes speaks as if memory can survive unchanged for long periods of times. In the decades following his death, there was a backlash against Akhenaten and the monotheistic cult he tried to introduce, and the traditionalists were able to erase Akhenaten from collective memory so successfully that no one knew about his religious revolution until the rediscovery of the court of Amarna in the nineteenth century. And yet, Assmann argues, there endured under the surface of culture a memory of Akhenaten and his iconoclastic actions, a memory nowhere written down or even consciously remembered but somehow persisting throughout the rest of ancient Egyptian history, penetrating the imaginations of those who wrote the Exodus story, shaping the biblical representation of Moses, and thus exerting an influence over the development of Judaism and other monotheistic faiths. One of the most questionable aspects of *Moses and Monotheism*—Freud's idea that traces of real experiences have been transmitted unconsciously across the generations—makes an unexpected comeback through Assmann, and it is this part of his argument that I focus on here to see if he has found some way to overcome the kinds of objections we noted in the last section.

Assmann finds evidence of this memory's persistence in a story recorded by an Egyptian priest named Manetho, who lived in the third century BCE, a thousand years after Akhenaten. Manetho's account of Egyptian history is an important source for Egyptologists, helping them to establish the sequence of the different dynasties that ruled Egypt in the age of the pharaohs, but it also tells us something about how Egyptians in the Hellenistic period (i.e., after Egypt's conquest by Alexander the Great) perceived the Jews. By that point there were Jews resettled in Egypt, especially in the city of Alexandria, and Manetho's account reflects his resentment of their presence; he saw them as foreign invaders and xenophobes hostile to the gods of Egypt. In the part of his narrative we know about only from a citation in Josephus (in his work *Against Apion* 1.232–250), Manetho recounts the origin of the Jews in a way that clearly reflects this hostility, and it so happens that this part of his story—as Assmann reads it—also reflects a dim memory of Akhenaten.

The story in question begins when an Egyptian king named Amenophis undertakes to see the gods for himself. To do so, as he learns from a seer, he must first cleanse the land by ridding it of the lepers who live in its midst, and he does so by sending them to work in the stone quarries of the eastern desert—a detail that calls to mind the Egyptians' enslavement of the Israelites. But then the seer has second thoughts, coming to realize not only that the king will suffer divine punishment for treating the lepers in this way but that the lepers will one day strike back, foreseeing that they will take over Egypt for thirteen years. Afraid to deliver this news to the king, the seer kills himself, but before doing so, he writes the prophecy down. When Amenophis learns of it, he relents, allowing the lepers to settle in Avaris, the ancient capital of the Hyksos. By then, however, it is too late to avoid his fate: the lepers join with the Hyksos and launch a war against Amenophis.

The lepers choose as a leader a priest from the city of Heliopolis named Osarsiph, who prohibits his followers from worshipping the gods of the Egyptians. Together with his Hyksos allies, he sets out against the Egyptians, driving the king from Egypt, setting fire to its cities, pillaging its temples, and mutilating the images of its gods in a reign of terror that lasts for thirteen years, as the seer had predicted. The story then ends with something of a twist that explains why Josephus, a Jew, would take an interest in the story. At some point, the renegade Osarsiph changes his name; he is none other than Moses. Manetho's narrative is an origin story for the Fifteenth Dynasty, the reign of the Hyksos rulers who controlled Egypt until they were driven from Egypt, but here it has been reinterpreted as an origin story for the Jews, with Manetho suggesting that they and their laws went back to the sacrilegious followers of Osarsiph, a marauding force of lepers and their Hyksos allies.

Though clearly distorted by its author's hostility to the Jews, Manetho's account draws together several different historical memories, not only preserving a garbled account of the Hyksos period but also probably drawing directly on the Exodus story, which by that point was accessible to Hellenized Egyptians like Manetho through a Greek translation of the Pentateuch. (Osarsiph might be a garbled version of the name Joseph, conflating his story with that of Moses, and many of the other details of the story can be understood as an effort to parody the Exodus.) For Assmann, however, the story also preserves a memory of the Amarna revolution, with Akhenaten himself making a return in the guise of Osarsiph/Moses. One connection to the era of Akhenaten is the name of Amenophis, Greek for Amenhotep, the name of Akhenaten's father and Akhenaten's own name before he changed it to honor the sun god Aten. But an even more striking parallel is Osarsiph's call for his followers to shun the gods of Egypt and destroy the statues of the gods, actions that recall Akhenaten's iconoclastic campaign to mutilate or remove the names and images of the gods. The echoes of events from the fourteenth century BCE in an Egyptian writer from a millennium later suggest that, despite the fact that no known source from all the intervening centuries records Akhenaten's reform or even takes notice of his reign—despite the fact that Akhenaten's opponents suppressed the memory of what he did shortly after his death—that memory survived underground and resurfaced after a millennium of latency.

If the memory of Akhenaten's reign was deliberately and completely suppressed, how and why did it resurface a thousand years later during the Hellenistic period? Assmann argues that the Jews were the catalyst. During the Hellenistic period, large numbers of

Jews settled in Egypt, and their rejection of the gods of Egypt triggered the very distant memory of Akhenaten's religious reform. This explains why Manetho's account conflates Akhenaten's figure with that of Moses. The two experiences—Akhenaten's violent elimination of the gods of Egypt and the arrival of iconoclastic Jews—were unconsciously associated in the minds of native Egyptians, reviving the traumatic memory of the king's actions but confusing it with what Egyptians knew about the Jews and the Exodus in a way that transferred Akhenaten's role to Moses. According to Freud, Moses was an actual follower of Akhenaten, and his departure from Egypt, the historical event behind the Exodus, was a direct response to the backlash triggered by the king's reforms. According to Assmann, the connection between the historical Akhenaten and Moses is unclear, but over time their memory became intertwined in a way that allowed one figure to be reimagined as the other, for the memory of Akhenaten to come back in the form of Moses.

Although Assmann's approach to memory normally follows the sociological approach of Halbwachs, here he momentarily veers back to a Freudian mode. True, there is no Moses or murder or Midianite compromise, but Assmann's narrative follows the same basic sequence of events. First there is a traumatic experience—not the murder of Moses but the religious revolt of Akhenaten, which according to Assmann was imposed in such a violent and shocking way that it left a permanent imprint on the collective unconscious of ancient Egyptians. Then comes an act of repression, a traditionalist backlash against Akhenaten that erased his memory from consciousness. And finally the repressed experience reasserts itself after a long dormancy, resurfacing in the much later Hellenistic period in a highly distorted form but still attached to the same disturbing emotions that the original event generated. There are lots of differences from *Moses and Monotheism*—Moses, the follower of Akhenaten, is replaced by Akhenaten himself; the hypothetical murder of Moses has been replaced by a real, historically confirmable religious crisis in Egyptian history; and Assmann casts his narrative not as a psychoanalytic investigation but as a Halbwachs-style study of collective memory. But the basic components of Freud's narrative are still there in a distorted form: trauma, repression, the return of the repressed.

The question I consider here is whether Assmann has found some way to overcome the shortcomings of *Moses and Monotheism* that we noted earlier. It is hard to imagine a scholar in a better position to do so. As a leading Egyptologist, Assmann is able to correct for the historical shortcomings of Freud's narrative, aligning his theory with what scholars actually know about the historical Akhenaten and Moses. As an expert in collective memory (and as the husband of one of Germany's leading experts on this subject, Aleida Assmann), he is also able to correct for the problems in the psychological narrative that Freud constructs. Assmann knows better than to embrace Freud's biological-Lamarckian explanation for the transmission of unconscious memories, and he detaches his reconstruction from other questionable aspects of Freud's theory of the mind as well—the id's father-slaying impulse, the compromises of the ego, and the unconscious as a shelter for unwanted memories. If anyone is in a position to save Freud's approach to the origin of the Jews from the problems that beset *Moses and Monotheism*, Assmann is the scholar to do it.

As a way to test for whether Assmann has succeeded in this regard, let us consider how he accounts for the long-term transmission of Akhenaten's heresy. How does the memory of an event that was deliberately expunged from collective memory survive for such a long period of time without people consciously preserving and transmitting it? One can understand how the memory of Hyksos rule survived despite the fact that it predates Akhenaten's reign by several centuries—it is mentioned in royal inscriptions and king lists—but there is no evidence that Akhenaten's reign was recorded in this way. To the contrary, in the decades following the end of Akhenaten's reign, there was a systematic effort to erase his name from the record and to undo his reforms. If the memory of these events was not preserved in writing, how does one account for the long-term preservation of its memory in a form that could be reactivated by Egyptians a thousand years later?

Since Assmann rejects Freud's biological/phylogenetic explanation for the transmission of unconscious memory, there would seem to be only one other possible explanation: oral tradition, the telling of stories by one generation to the next. Ernst Sellin invoked that kind of explanation when he proposed that the memory of

Moses's murder had been preserved by a small group of priests who mostly kept the story to themselves. But Freud himself pointed out the problems with this kind of explanation: as anyone familiar with the transmission of folk stories or gossip can probably confirm from their own experience, consciously communicated memories are highly vulnerable to change and distortion as they are passed from one generation to the next. From his studies of collective memory, Assmann certainly knows full well that such memory is constantly changing as it is communicated by one generation to the next, even claiming at one point that it does not remain intact beyond a horizon of from eighty to at most a hundred years.

There is another problem with the oral tradition explanation as well: it does not address the emotional force and psychological impact this kind of memory is supposed to have carried with it, its power to induce people to mentally relive the original trauma, to respond to it as if they themselves had experienced it. Assmann seems to believe that the memory of Akhenaten carried with it that kind of emotional force—its attachment to a certain kind of anxiety or fear is what brought it back to mind during the Hellenistic age, when Egyptians were growing fearful of the Jews and their iconoclastic religion. But it is hard to see how that emotion gets transmitted over such a long period, whether in written or in oral form, given the inherent mutability of consciously transmitted memory, how it is constantly being reshaped in light of what people are thinking and feeling in the present.

For Freud only unconscious transmission could account for the survival of a repressed memory like the murder of Moses. Buried deep within the unconscious, such a memory would be protected from the changes that inevitably snuck in through oral transmission, and the accompanying experience of trauma—the repressed feelings of aggression and guilt—would persist as well or even intensify in the absence of a way to discharge itself. But Assmann, knowing that many psychologists are skeptical of the Freudian concept of repression and that Freud's theory requires some kind of biological transmission to move from parents to children, does not accept this explanation and seeks an alternative way to account for the unconscious persistence of Akhenaten's memory. He argues that Freud misunderstood how cultural transmission works, erring by restricting it to consciously transmitted messages, and he points to other unconscious ways in which cultures preserve and transmit collective memories. As an example, he points to how Akhenaten's opponents etched out his name from inscriptions. The act erased the king's name, but the erasure was still visible in its own right and thus preserved a partial memory of what it was trying to blot out. Cultures have many ways to store information in a latent form without people making a deliberate effort to transmit the information, and in such ways, Assmann proposes, the memory of Akhenaten's heresy was able to survive unconsciously but without the active and ongoing repression that Freud's theory required.

Such a view is consistent with a revamped version of the unconscious that has arisen in the new field of neuropsychoanalysis, which detaches it from Freudian repression, but it clearly has problems of its own. So far as I can tell, it does not really account for how a memory remains in a fixed form for so long, nor does it account for the emotional resonance that Assmann ascribes to the memory of Akhenaten, its attachment to certain disturbing feelings. This is where Assmann's argument has to turn back to Freud: the only way he can account for the persistence and emotional force of Akhenaten's memory is to dust off Freud's notion of trauma as a uniquely fixed and static kind of memory, an experience that sears itself into the unconscious, that persists there unchanged, that is impossible to dislodge, and that insists that the mind return to it again and again. According to Assmann, what made the memory of Akhenaten's revolution so indelible, and what gave it the power to tap into the anxieties of people many centuries later, was its traumatic character, something he emphasizes in his description of the event: "The monotheistic revolution of Akhenaten was not only the first *but also the most radical and violent eruption* of a counter-religion in the history of human-kind" (italics mine). The destruction of divine images, the closing of temples, and the erasure of names must have been a terrible shock for the Egyptians, he surmises, and the terror it inspired was compounded by a catastrophe at the end of the Amarna age, a terrible epidemic that raged throughout the Near East for twenty years. Assmann finds a way to detach the process of unconscious transmission from Freud's notion of repression, but for his alternative theory to work, it does not suffice to show that a memory of the experience could have been transmitted without people realizing they were doing so; he has to revive a Freudian-like concept of trauma by describing Akhenaten's reform as a shocking experience that overcame the mutability of memory by leaving a permanent scar on people's minds.

Is this explanation for the survival of traumatic memory that much more plausible than the explanation Freud proposed? Is it that different? Not that Assmann cites it, but there is research to suggest that traumatic experience and the stress it creates have long-term repercussions for individuals (think posttraumatic stress disorder); there is even a recent experimental study that purports to show how the brain hides from itself memories that it finds fearful or painful. But none of that is the same as saying that such a memory can be unconsciously transmitted intact for centuries. Other scientists have noted that the children of Holocaust survivors, veterans, and others who have suffered trauma can absorb the psychological effects of their parents' experience, and even more remarkably, that they can pass those effects on in turn to their children. But there are questions about such research, especially beyond the second generation, and in any case, there is a long way to go between that possibility and Assmann's claim that such memory can survive for a millennium within an entire population. It is very hard to believe that the inheritance of trauma, if such a process actually happens, works the way genetic inheritance does.

The truth is that we do not even know for certain that the memory of Akhenaten did survive in the way in which Assmann claims. His argument depends on his reading of the Osarsiph episode as a distorted memory of Akhenaten's iconoclastic reform, but that is not the only way to explain the similarity between the story and Akhenaten's actions. The act of violently disrupting religious tradition—destroying temples and the mistreatment of divine statues—was ascribed to many rulers in the ancient Near East, not just to Akhenaten. In royal inscriptions from the ancient Near East, a good ruler was conventionally described as a protector of religious tradition, building and restoring temples, maintaining and safeguarding the statues of the gods, and seeing to their restoration if they were ever captured or destroyed. The flip side of this motif was the description of enemy kings as violators of religious tradition—rulers who damaged the temples and mistreated the gods—a motif that also appears throughout the Near East, including in texts about Egyptian rulers, and which continued into the Persian and Hellenistic periods. What is to say that this standard rhetorical motif of the sacrilegious ruler is not also being applied to Osarsiph in his role as an enemy leader? Akhenaten was not the only ruler of Egypt remembered for committing offenses against the gods of Egypt; there were more recent rulers described in this way as well such as Cambyses, a Persian king who invaded Egypt in 525 BCE and was accused of violating Egyptian religious tradition, killing the Apis bull, a sacred animal, scourging its priests, and mocking the statues of Egyptian gods (these offenses are catalogued by the Greek Historian Herodotus in book 3 of his *Histories*). It is even possible that Manetho's account of Osarsiph might be conflating the biblical story of the Exodus with the memory of Cambyses's sacrileges. This idea may not be as tantalizing as the possibility that Manetho tapped into the far more distant memory of Akhenaten's heresy, but until it can be excluded, there is no clear evidence that the memory of Akhenaten, however traumatic his acts might have been for Egyptians at the time, resurfaced in any form prior to his rediscovery in the nineteenth century.

But even if we accept the possibility that the memory of Akhenaten did survive in some subterranean way, Assmann's explanation for that survival cannot be considered an improvement over Freud's. In fact I am arguing that it is a disguised version of the same explanation, reassigning some of the roles, imagining a different set of historical events, and recasting its argument in light of Halbwachs's notion of collective memory, but still following the basic outline of *Moses and Monotheism*. The problem with Assmann's argument is not just that it, too, entails a conjectural and contestable reconstruction of what Freud referred to as a "primal scene," an initial traumatic experience that permanently affects the consciousness of the person who suffers it. It also fails to establish the transmission of this traumatic experience to later people. Perhaps scholars will one day work out how trauma is transmitted intergenerationally, but they have yet to do so, still debating whether there is unconscious transmission of trauma over a single generation or two, never mind following it for the scores of generations that Assmann's theory requires.

Assmann is by no means the only contemporary scholar to try to rehabilitate *Moses and Monotheism*, but most others who write about it are focused on what it reveals about Freud himself, and Assmann is the only major scholar I know of who has tried to revive it as a way of understanding the origin of Judaism and its defining characteristics. The fact that he does not succeed in overcoming the shortcomings of Freud's approach is not meant to detract from the value of his work as a whole or its fascinating account of why Moses was remembered by Freud and other scholars as an Egyptian, but it does suggest that "paleopsychology" may not be salvageable as a way of addressing the question of Jewish origin, at least not given what we know now or can expect to know. If the Jews have a collective unconscious of the sort Freud imagined, and if that collective unconscious somehow registers the circumstances of their origin, its secrets remain beyond our reach.

Slayers of Moses

Even though many historians would dismiss psychohistory, it might still be premature to give up on it as a way to explore the origin of the Jews. Since science is open-ended, there is always the chance that the recent effort to integrate psychoanalysis with neuroscience will lead to an advance we cannot anticipate right now. Indeed, recent research has managed to give the seemingly preposterous idea of "psycho-Lamarckism" a second life through the "new epigenetics," a kind of research that explores the impact of the environment and other nongenetic factors on what offspring inherit biologically from their parents. Such research has even suggested that Freud might not have been completely off base in his idea that the effects of trauma can be transmitted to children biologically.

Rachel Yehuda, a psychiatrist and neuroscientist at the Icahn School of Medicine at Mount Sinai Hospital in New York, is one of the scholars at the forefront of his kind of research, and in one of her best-known studies, she and her colleagues have offered evidence that traumatic stress may have altered the physiology and emotional response of survivors of the Holocaust in a way that was passed on to their descendants. To be more specific, Yehuda and her colleagues found that the children of Holocaust survivors, having inherited an altered way of circulating stress hormones from their parents, were more likely to respond differently to a car accident than the children of those who did not suffer through the Holocaust. The new epigenetics cannot take us back to primordial events: it can study the effects of only recent traumatic events like the Holocaust and 9/11. But as Yehuda acknowledges, it does represent a revival of a Lamarckian perspective by showing that the effects of trauma can be inherited in a biological way not that different from what Freud intuited but was not able to demonstrate.

But since it seems unlikely that research will speak to our question anytime soon, there is in the meantime another way that the afterlife of Freud's theory can help us to advance our quest. After reviewing the many efforts to integrate history and psychology, the historian Joan Scott has recently concluded that the two fields are incommensurate, that her fellow historians had never really figured out how to use psychology as a historical tool in a way that bridges between the two kinds of research. From her vantage point, however, the discovery that psychology does not work in the way historians want it to can be productive in another way: engaging psychology gives historians a chance to think about how they themselves think. If we engage Freud from this angle, perhaps there is something to glean not about the origin of the Jews but about how scholars think about that origin.

One aspect of Freud I find especially intriguing is the way his account of the origin of the Jews brings together different approaches toward origin. In the chapter on genealogy, I introduced three distinct approaches to origin that coexist uneasily in scholarship today; Freud, it has been noted, shares qualities with the first and the third—the search for origin as a hidden object to be sought out by following a series of clues from the present into the distant past, and the postmodern critique that treats origin as an illusion, as a form of thought to be shaken free of, opposed, or countered. The two approaches are antithetical, and yet Freud shares an affinity with both in ways that can help us to take stock of where we have gone in our quest thus far and to figure out how to proceed from here.

Freud's connection to the first approach to origin is easier to explain. Like Adolphe Pictet, Robertson Smith, Arthur Evans, and other scholars we have considered, Freud believed that origins were hidden but real and retrievable. As we have noted, in fact, he described his research as a kind of archaeology and drew on the methods and findings of other origin-centered fields like etymology and paleontology. This aspect of Freud's thinking is not surprising given the intellectual context in which he operated, but interestingly enough, a number of commentators detect in his writing another, more ambivalent relationship to origin. It would be anachronistic to treat Freud as if he were a postmodern thinker, and no less a figure than Derrida associated him with a kind of thinking opposed to his own approach to origin, diagnosing him with a case of what Derrida referred to as "archive fever" (punning on the Greek work *arche*, meaning beginning or origin): "the irrepressible desire to return to the origin, a homesickness, a nostalgia for the return to the most archaic place of absolute commencement." But other thinkers associated with postmodernism have found in Freud a kind of precursor.

In a lecture on *Moses and Monotheism* given at the Freud Museum in London, for example, Edward Said imagined Freud as a political and intellectual ally who, like Said himself, was an "overturner and remapper of settled geographies and genealogies." Others note how Freud called his own origin narratives into question by highlighting their constructedness and by often revising or supplementing the primal scenes that he postulated in ways that undid them or suggested their insufficiency. Thus in an essay published in 1975, the literary scholar David Carroll suggested that, while Freud never stopped pursuing origins, he came to recognize that their defining trait was elusiveness, even absence, that they were never where they were supposed to be, never to be pinned down. According to Carroll, Freud even came close to denying the very reality of origin in the way that someone like Derrida did: "it is consistent with Freud's work . . . [to say] that the origin is always in the process of being displaced by another, and that it is never present in itself as a reality but has the status of a myth."

Since Freud was so clearly interested in finding hidden origins, what is it about his thinking that makes him appear to postmodern readers as a deconstructor of origin? There are many affinities between psychoanalysis and postmodernism that emerge when the former is read in light of the latter, but what strikes me is the way his writing puts into narrative form the very act of challenging origin. What, after all, is the paradigmatic Freudian narrative, the tale that he tells again and again in *Totem and Taboo, Moses and Monotheism*, and other works? All these texts revolve around people who slay the fathers who begot them and who then fantasize other origins for themselves. There are two kinds of father figures at the center of these narratives: (1) figures like Akhenaten and the Egyptian Moses, who personify origin in its most authoritative and domineering mode and who inevitably provoke a violent backlash, the destruction and erasure of the father; and (2) fictitious and idealized fathers, like the Moses of the Bible, who personify origin as a fantasy arising from the mind's unconscious effort to fill in for an absent father, and whose unreality must be exposed if the mind is to truly shake free from the grip of its past. Both scenarios anticipate moves typical of postmodernism: the erasure of origin and the falsification of origin as a myth. For Freud the patricidal primal scene was the origin he was seeking to uncover, the secret buried at the base of the mind that explained civilization, religion, and Judaism. But it is not hard to grasp how, from a postmodern perspective, it might seem as if his intention was not to find a hidden origin but to expose its absence, to free the mind from its control or dispel it as a debilitating illusion.

Is Freud a seeker of origins or a slayer of them? The answer depends in part on one's own stance as an interpreter, whether one is drawn to reading Freud within his own context or in relation to intellectual trends that develop later in the century. But I think there is something to both ways of reading him, seeing in his work a clash between two approaches to origin that we have been wrestling with over the course of this book—the search for origin and the effort to negate its existence or dispel it as a myth. Freud does not offer a way to reconcile these two approaches to origin. To the contrary, the mind as he conceived it seems unable to work its way past its conflicting relationship to origin, consigned to an ongoing struggle between its need to relate itself to a point of origin and its need to efface that origin. What Freud also suggests, however, is that there is something important to be understood by examining the conflict between these two ways of relating to origin and their endless tug-of-war. This is where I see in his work a pointer for what direction to take as our search continues: if we cannot reconcile the conflicting impulses that shape the scholarship of Jewish origin today, perhaps we can at least gain some insight into how these impulses interact and what emerges from their struggle with each other.

CHAPTER SIX

Hellenism and Hybridity

DID THE JEWS LEARN HOW TO BE
JEWISH FROM THE GREEKS?

*The Greeks thought that man comes into the world as a sort of embryo
at birth, and that it had to develop into a man.*

—CHRISTOPH MARTIN WIELAND

SEVERAL OF THE THEORIES we have looked at thus far purport
to discover strangers hidden somewhere in the prehistory of the
Jews. In Freud's case, as we noted in the last chapter, the foreigner
in the background was an Egyptian, Akhenaten, who transferred
certain elements of his religious reform to the Jews through the
medium of his follower Moses. Others ascribed a seminal role to
the Babylonian or Persian culture that the Jews encountered at the
end of the biblical period or during their exile. What connects all
these theories is their conception of the Jews or Judaism as a hybrid
that can be traced back not just to the Israelites of the biblical era
but also to another people, religion, or culture.

The mechanism of transfer posited by these different theories,
the process by which the Jews acquired the qualities of others,
has been understood in a number of different ways, but basically the possibilities fall into two categories. In an earlier era, a
scholar might attribute this transfer to racial mixing, the infusion
of non-Semitic qualities through interbreeding and inheritance.
More recent theories, by contrast, attribute it to what is referred

to as "acculturation," with an emphasis on the word's connection to culture as the means by which Jews internalized the qualities of others—the act of learning from another people by imitating its ways or by remodeling oneself under its influence. While scholarship no longer accepts biological explanations for the affinities between Jews and other peoples, the cultural practices that it sees at work—imitation, borrowing, the psychological internationalization of another culture's ethos or values—still do a similar kind of explanatory work; they too attribute the emergence of the Jews to a process of absorption by which the qualities of another people penetrated the culture of the Jews' ancestors and produced a hybrid that exhibits the qualities of both parent cultures.

In the present chapter I focus on a recent theory that ascribes a role to the Greeks in the formation of Judaism, understood as a hybrid culture. Developed by the American scholar Shaye Cohen in a book called *The Beginnings of Jewishness* published in 1999, this theory argues that Judaism is the result of contact with the Greeks who conquered the Near East under the leadership of Alexander the Great in the period around 330 BCE. Before this period, there was a people in Jerusalem and its vicinity known as the Judeans, the *yehudim* of biblical books like Ezra and Esther, but this people is not yet what Cohen would refer to as "the Jews" (he calls them "Judeans"), for there was something missing from their culture and from their thinking that is constitutive of Judaism in his view, a key difference from Jews as they would develop in the rabbinic period that began with the formulation of the Mishnah around 200 CE. To explain the transition from one people to another, he turned to the Greeks, suggesting that it was the Judeans' imitation of Greek culture during the Hellenistic age (the era between Alexander and the fall of the last Hellenistic kingdom to the Romans in 31 BCE) that transformed their culture into Judaism.

In what follows I examine this theory as another option for understanding the origin of the Jews, but I have another objective in mind as well—to better understand the role of the foreigner in the origin stories that scholars tell about the Jews. Why do some scholars focus on the Egyptians, others on the Persians, and still others on the Greeks? The answer, I suggest, goes beyond anything to be found in the evidence itself and has to do instead with the symbolic associations attached to these peoples. To argue that the Jews arose in some way from these other peoples was not just to make a historical claim; it was also to fit them into a symbolic universe whose inhabitants all signified different things: the Egyptians, buried or cryptic memory; the Persians, Aryan dynamism and nobility; the Greeks, freedom and the perfection of the individual. The Greeks are an excellent case study in this regard because their symbolic resonance is so closely bound up with what the Jews came to represent. Over the nineteenth century, the two peoples came to signify not just different but opposing sets of values: The Jews were associated with faith, tradition, and obedience to authority, while the Greeks embodied rationality, inventiveness, and democracy. Whatever the role of the historical Greeks in the actual origin of the Jews, in their respective roles as signifiers of contrasting values or mind-sets, the two peoples helped to constitute each other within the divided consciousness of European and American thinkers torn between secularism and religion, or tradition and modernity.

The contrasts drawn between "Hebraism" and "Hellenism" by thinkers like the poet Heinrich Heine (1797–1856), the critic Matthew Arnold (1822–1888), and other intellectuals in the nineteenth and twentieth centuries were not based on what is now known about ancient Jews and Greeks as real-life peoples. The study of the Hellenistic period in particular not only helped to dismantle each stereotype but also challenged their description as opposites by revealing a period of intermixing between the two cultures. Cohen's argument is part of that corrective scholarship, and the work that he and his predecessors in the study of Jewish Hellenistic culture have produced in the past fifty or so years represents a genuine advance over earlier accounts that relegated the Jews to serving as a foil for Western secularism. What they propose as an alternative, however—Judaism as a Hellenized hybrid—is nonetheless also a part of the history of the Hebraic-Hellenic opposition, or so I argue by showing that we need to look at Cohen's theory not just in light of who the Greeks were historically but also in light of what they are symbolically, if we are to understand their role in his account as the cocreators of Judaism.

Hellenization as Cross-Fertilization

Before turning to Cohen's theory, I begin by thinking a bit more carefully about the Hellenistic period—what we know about this period, how the Jews fit into it, and, at a meta level, where the idea of the Hellenistic period comes from. Like other concepts that structure how scholars think about the origin of the Jews—the Semite or the postexilic period—the idea of the Hellenistic age has a history going back to the first half of the nineteenth century, and some reflection on that history helps to illumine why this age, as opposed to the biblical or the Persian period, appealed to scholars as a context for the origin of Judaism.

Essential to the idea of the Hellenistic age as conceived by scholars is the notion of hybridity, symbiosis, or melting together. From the time that it was first identified as a discrete period of cultural history, the Hellenistic age was perceived as a period of cultural fusion between the peoples of ancient Greece and the Near East, and that perception remains central to how scholars think about the period. In 331 BCE, the Persian King Darius III was defeated for a third and final time by the forces of Alexander the Great, leaving the young Macedonian to declare himself "the lord of Asia." The vast amount of territory Alexander passed on to the control of the generals who succeeded him after his death in 323 BCE, stretching from Greece to India, soon fractured into several kingdoms, including the Ptolemaic Kingdom based in Egypt and the Seleucid Kingdom based in Syria. The influence of the Greek culture these rulers brought with them transcended political boundaries, however. Greek became the language of the educated classes throughout the Near East, and its influence permeated indigenous languages like Aramaic and Egyptian as well. Cities were reorganized on the model of the Greek *polis*; local architecture and art emulated Greek models; and Greek philosophy, science, and literature reshaped thought, imagination, and self-expression. What emerged from this process of cultural fusion or synthesis were people who brought together Greek and Near Eastern cultures in various ways—Manetho, the Egyptian writer mentioned in the last chapter, who wrote in Greek; the Babylonian-born Berossus, who wrote a Greek history of Babylonia; the satirist Menippus, born in

Syria; the mathematician and astronomer Erotasthenes, born in what is now Libya; and Cleopatra VII, the last ruler of the Ptolemaic Kingdom, heir to the ancient pharaohs and to a Macedonian Greek family at the same time. These kinds of hybrid figures typify the Hellenistic age in general, an age that is supposed to have combined the qualities of West and East—classical Greek and ancient Near Eastern culture.

For their part, the Judeans might at first seem to have been resistant to this process, but they too were subject to the cultural hybridization characteristic of the age. Readers who know something about the Maccabean Revolt, the war commemorated during the holiday of Hanukkah, might recall that this was a war against a Greek force and their Judean allies, priestly leaders who introduced Greek practices and institutions into Jerusalem. That event, a Judean rebellion against the Seleucid Kingdom that lasted from 167 BCE to a formal declaration of Judea's independence in 141 BCE, has helped cement the idea that the Jews were deeply opposed to Greek culture. But historians have come to realize that Judean culture in this period developed in much the same way that other Hellenized Near Eastern cultures did: there were Judeans resistant to the culture of their Greek rulers, especially when it conflicted with their religious traditions, but Judeans also learned to speak and write in Greek (hence the Torah was translated into Greek in the third century BCE); their intellectuals absorbed ideas from Greek philosophy and literature; and they emulated the practices and institutions of the Greeks. Even the descendants of the Maccabees who went on to rule Judea (known as the Hasmonean dynasty) reflect this trend, using Greek in the coins they minted, emulating Greek models in the monumental tombs they built for themselves, and adopting Greek names and epithets like Aristobulus the Philhellene—"lover of the Greeks."

The word "Judaism," appearing for the first time in the second century BCE, is an example of this fusion of Judean and Greek culture. The word is a hybrid in its own right, a coinage that merges the Greek spelling of *Yehuda* (Judah) with the Greek suffix -*ismos*, which was used in words like *medismos* (from the name "Media," a part of Persia, and referring to the act of aligning oneself with the Persians) and *hellenismos* (from "Hellene," and referring to the act of following a Greek way of life). Like these other words, *iudaismos* probably originally referred to a Judean way of life or to the act of aligning oneself with the Judeans. Its first known appearance is in a text written in Greek known as 2 Maccabees (4:13), an account of the Maccabean Revolt, and there it is placed in contrast to the word *hellenismos* in a way that suggests that the Judean and Greek ways of life were mutually exclusive opposites. But while the author of this work clearly objected to Greek customs that he considered at odds with the laws of Moses and ancestral tradition, the very use of this term illustrates the Hellenization of Judean culture under way in this period, since it is itself a compound of a Judean name and a Greek ending.

The historical picture I have sketched here is one that goes back in its basic outlines to the German historian J. G. Droysen (1808–1884), who was the first to formulate the concept of the Hellenistic age. Droysen did not invent the words "Hellenism" and "Hellenistic"—these were terms he inherited from earlier scholarship, which used them to refer to the way of thinking of Jews under the influence of Greek language and thought—but he gave them new meaning by extending them beyond Jews, to the culture and thought of all the populations conquered by Alexander the Great and subjected to Greek influence. In work published in the 1830s and 1840s, Droysen's approach to the period was typically developmentalist. Previous scholars had treated this period as an age of decay after the golden age of Athens, associating it with cultural sterility and languor. Droysen saw in it a step forward in humanity's development from paganism to Christianity, and the catalyst for the change in his view was what he referred to as the "cross-fertilization" of different peoples, not in the biological sense that a race scientist might intend but referring to a cultural process by which non-Greeks became Hellenized and Greeks became Orientalized. As he writes in the first volume of his history of Hellenism, "East and West were ripe for fusion, and cross-fertilization and metamorphosis quickly took place on both sides." For Droysen this cross-fertilization was a consciously undertaken process introduced by Alexander as a way to unify his empire, and it produced a hybrid Hellenistic culture that overcame the difference between West and

East, Greek and barbarian. Scholarship has since developed more complex understandings of the Hellenistic age, criticizing Droysen's conception of Hellenization as a deliberate policy introduced by Alexander, noting that it was not the mutual process that he imagined, and abandoning the thesis-antithesis-synthesis approach to history he learned from attending the lectures of Hegel. But for all the ways that scholars have moved beyond Droysen, his notion of Hellenization as "cross-fertilization" still shapes how the Hellenistic age is understood.

One difference between Droysen's conception of the Hellenistic age and more recent descriptions is that the Jews play almost no role in how he understood the period. The development he traced moved in a straight line from the pagan Greeks to Christianity, and the peoples involved in the intervening synthesis of Greek and Oriental culture were Egyptians, Syrians, and other pagans, not the Hebrews or the Jews. That omission might have been deliberate. Arnaldo Momigliano (1908–1987), the Jewish Italian historian of antiquity, noted that many of Droysen's closest associates were Jewish converts to Protestantism or the descendants of converts. This included his wife, Marie Mendheim, daughter of a Jewish bookseller who had changed his name from Mendel to Mendheim probably at the time of his conversion. While some of these associates—the theologian and scholar August Neander (1789–1850), for example, born David Mendel—continued to address Judaism in their scholarly work or remained devoted to their Jewish ancestors, they were expected to behave publicly as if they had no Jewish past, to remain silent about it, and Droysen abided by this expectation, never bringing up the Jewish past of his friends when writing to them. Momigliano speculates that the sensitivity of this issue lies behind Droysen's reluctance to include the Jews in his account of the Hellenistic age: he avoided the subject for the same reason he seems not to have brought up his wife's Jewish origin even within his family.

Whatever Droysen's reasons for excluding them, the Jews soon became a part of the story of the Hellenistic age. At the time Droysen was publishing his work, other scholars like Neander were taking interest in the writing of Philo and the Jewish background of the New Testament, helping to bring the Jews into the picture; and by around 1838 Droysen himself was showing some slight interest in incorporating the Jews into his narrative, though he believed that the deepest elements of Jewish and Greek culture did not fully converge until the rise of Christianity, and he never really pursued the Jewish side of its origin. In the twentieth century there emerged a new generation of scholars who could address the topic in a more direct way, and it was they who helped to illumine ancient Judaism as a kind of Hellenistic culture, a variant of the same melting together or cultural hybridization evident elsewhere in the Hellenistic world. Many of these scholars were Jewish—the Talmudist Saul Lieberman (1898–1983), the classicist Elias Bickerman (1897–1981), and Momigliano himself (1908–1987), among several others. I had the pleasure of knowing one of these scholars personally in the final years of his life—Henry Fischel, who was born in Germany in 1913 and produced many studies of Jewish-Hellenistic culture before passing away in 2008—and his research is typical of this scholarship. Drawing on a knowledge of classical and early Jewish sources acquired at the University of Bonn and the Hochschule für Wissenschaft des Judentums in Berlin, he added to the evidence showing that the thinking of the rabbis was as steeped in Hellenism as Christianity was.

This is the scholarly legacy to which Shaye Cohen was heir, and his own scholarship continues it. Some of his earlier work was devoted to finding even more parallels between Greek and Jewish culture in the Hellenistic-Roman period, showing how early rabbinic culture was modeled on the social structure of Greek philosophical schools, for example, but Cohen took things a step further. Judaism, he argued, was not merely reshaped by Greek culture; it was itself the result of Hellenization. It did not exist prior to the second century BCE, and it emerged only through the sort of fusion process that defines the Hellenistic age. In what follows, I look at this argument in more detail. There is a lot of evidence to recommend it; but as we consider its pros and cons as a theory, it will be important to keep in mind some of what we have seen here, including the ways in which scholars' understanding of how Jews and Greeks interacted in a hybridized Hellenistic world, mirrors the relationship between Jews and non-Jews in their own world.

Judaism as an Acquired Trait

The process that created the Jews according to Cohen—the process by which the Judean culture of the Persian period became Judaism—is Hellenization. Prior to the second century BCE, the *iudaioi*—a word Cohen would translate as "Judeans"—were what we would call an ethnic group. To be a Judean was to be born into a certain identity defined by a combination of ancestry and geography: one was considered Judean if one was born in Judea to the native inhabitants of the land or was a descendant of its habitants. Judeanness never lost its association with ancestry and geography, but after the second century BCE, it acquired the characteristics of a religion, a form of *voluntary* identity grounded in a choice to embrace God and adhere to the laws of Moses. To be sure, Judeans prior to this period believed in the God described in the Hebrew Bible and followed the laws of Moses—this we can infer from Ezra and Nehemiah from the Persian period—but that is not what made them Judean, an identity conferred on them by their genealogy and birthplace. Over the second century BCE, people began to *choose* to be Judean. It became a way of life that one could decide to embrace and that even those born into it had to work to sustain. To put things in sociological terms, Jewishness morphed in this period from an "ascribed" status, a fixed status assigned at birth, to an "achieved status," a position that one acquires or earns through one's own choices and actions. This difference, Cohen argues, marks the start of Judaism or what he prefers to refer to as "Jewishness," the transition of an ethnicity to the ethno-religion that exists today; and what caused it was an act of hybridization, the fusing of Judean identity with a new conception of identity introduced by the Greeks.

One sign of this transformation noted by Cohen is the appearance in the second century BCE of conversion stories, stories about foreigners choosing to embrace a Judean identity. When we think about conversions, familiar as many of us are with a Protestant conception of conversion, we often focus on the inner-psychological dimension of the experience—to convert to a new religion is to embrace a new view of reality—but it also has a sociological dimension: to convert is to take on a new identity, to affiliate as a member of a new community. We do not think of ethnicity as capable of that kind of change. One cannot convert from being Italian to being Irish, for these are identities inherited from one's parents: one can play them down as a part of one's identity, but one cannot change one's ancestry. The emergence of conversion supports the idea that Judean identity was reconceived in this period as an "achieved status," becoming a more voluntary and self-defining form of identity rather than an identity one is simply born into or inherits.

Jewish identity, Cohen argues, did not always have this mutable, acquirable quality—it absorbed it at a specific point in time. The Hebrew Bible includes what seems like a conversion story, that of how the Moabite Ruth joined the people of her mother-in-law, Naomi, but this episode ties the change to marriage: a foreign woman who married a Judean would typically embrace the god of the family she was marrying into, and Ruth is exceptional only because she sustains her loyalty to her new family and its god after her husband's death, when the family is only she and Naomi. By contrast, in the second century BCE, there appear stories about foreigners impelled not by marriage but by some religious experience or change of heart to adopt a new identity and way of life. At the end of Judith, for example—a book from this period included in Catholic and Orthodox canons but excluded from the Jewish and Protestant canons—an Ammonite named Achior is so awestruck by the power of Judith's god that he chooses to become circumcised and to join the Israelites. Similarly, in 2 Maccabees, a work probably composed in the same period as Judith, a Greek official named Heliodorus becomes a believer in God after three angelic beings stop him from entering the Temple. Even Antiochus IV, the Seleucid king who ignited the Maccabean Revolt, would have converted had he lived long enough, according to 2 Maccabees, vowing to become a Judean at the time of his death. Becoming a Judean in these cases has no connection to marriage; it is the result of witnessing or feeling the power of God. Such stories appear only in texts from the second century BCE and thereafter, and according to Cohen, the timing is not a coincidence: they reflect the shift to a new conception of identity introduced by the Hellenization of Judea during that century.

In truth there may have been a number of factors that contributed to this change as Cohen recognizes—the breakdown of Israel's tribal system may have diminished the significance of ancestry, and the dispersion of the population beyond Judea probably weakened the significance of geographic origin in Judea as a source of identity. The factor that Cohen zeroes in on, however, is Greek influence, and more specifically the influence of a Greek conception of Greekness itself. He cites a passage from Herodotus (*The Histories* 8.144.2) that identifies four qualities that held the Greeks together as kin—"blood" (i.e., physical descent from shared ancestors) but also a common language, common modes of worship, and a common way of life. What these last three elements all share is that they are all qualities someone can acquire by speaking, believing, and acting in a certain way. Greekness, in other words, was conceived as something that could be learned, a point registered by the orator Isocrates a few decades before the conquests of Alexander:

> Our city [Athens] has so much surpassed other men in thought and speech that her students have become the teachers of others, and she has made the name of the Greeks to seem to be no more of race/birth [*genos*] but of thought, *so that those who share our education* more than those who share a common nature, are to be called Hellenes. (*Panegyricus* 50; italics mine)

What makes a Greek Greek, Isocrates is saying here, is not "birth," or having been born to Greek parents, but an educational process that instills a certain way of thinking and speaking, and that educational process allows Greekness to be transferred to others—for Isocrates, non-Athenians but for later Hellenistic thinkers, non-Greeks as well. Cohen is able to show that this idea penetrated the self-image of Jews, as in a passage from the historian Josephus: "To those *who wish* to come and live under the same laws as us, [Moses] gives a friendly welcome, reckoning that affinity is not only a matter of birth [*genei*] but also a choice in lifestyle" (*Against Apion* 2.210). In Cohen's view, it is the importation of this idea into Judea that transforms Judean identity into Jewishness, and he attributes the change, ironically, to the Hasmoneans who ruled Judea in the latter part of the second century BCE. Given that they descended from the Maccabees, the rebels who opposed the Hellenizing reforms of Antiochus IV, one might think that the Hasmoneans would have resisted Greek influence, and in some ways they did; but we have seen that they too were subject to a Hellenization process, imitating the Greeks in many ways, and Cohen proposes that it was they who introduced the Greek conception of identity as an acquirable status to justify the absorption of local non-Jews into their kingdom.

Here then is an alternative to Wellhausen's explanation for the origin of Judaism, which places its emergence in the Persian period. For Wellhausen Judaism emerged from the religion of ancient Israel through a developmental process gone awry, or as I have argued, from an attempt to resist development, from a priestly effort to freeze the religion in place. Cohen describes the shift from Judean culture to Jewishness or Judaism as a partial absorption of a Greek conception of identity. The two theories not only date the relevant transition to different periods but also ascribe it to different kinds of processes, evolution versus hybridization that comes about through emulating the Greeks.

We have seen that Wellhausen's approach reflects the limits of the explanatory paradigm it was operating within, and that it is not possible to document the kind of sequential development he postulated. But the weakness of Wellhausen's theory is not enough to embrace Cohen's explanation. What reasons are there to accept it, and is there any reason to be skeptical?

On the positive side of the ledger, we can cite two kinds of evidence. The first is literary evidence that goes beyond what Cohen mentions. Other authors from the Hellenistic period attest to the same change, figures like Philo of Alexandria (ca. 20 BCE–50 CE), whose description of his biblical ancestors mirrors the Greek conception of Greekness as an achievable identity. A telling passage appears in his treatise *On Abraham*, where Philo explains why the Book of Genesis does not relate the genealogy of Noah:

> So highly does Moses extol the lover of virtue that when he gives his genealogy he does not, as he usually does in other cases, make a list of grandfathers, great-grandfathers and ancestors in the male and female line but of certain virtues, and this is little less than a direct assertion that a sage has no house or kinsfolk or country save virtues and virtuous actions. (*On Abraham* 31)

Here too is the idea that ancestry need not define one's identity: Noah's virtuousness renders his genealogy so irrelevant for who he is that Moses, when later recounting Noah's story in the Five Books of Moses, does not even bother to list his ancestors. It is clear from his other writings that Philo understands other biblical ancestors— and the Judeans of his own day—in a similar way: what defines his people as a people is their commitment to the laws of Moses, equated by Philo with what the Greeks referred to as a *proairesis*, a voluntary course of action or way of life undertaken in pursuit of a certain end. It is not that ancestry or inheritance are unimportant to Philo by any means, but they are not sufficient. There is an intentional, self-determining quality to being a Judean that requires schooling and ongoing focus to sustain: "having been trained in this doctrine [the idea that the laws of Moses are God's oracles], they carry the likenesses of their commandments enshrined in their souls" (from Philo's treatise *Embassy to Gaius* 210).

Alongside the literary testimony, there is also archaeological evidence that, while not confirming Cohen's account, is at least consistent with his claim that Judeanness shifted from an ethnicity to an ethno-religion over the second century BCE in tandem with Hellenization. Archaeological finds from Judea and elsewhere in Palestine from the late Hasmonean period reveal a shift in religious practice, the emergence of new forms of piety that involve ritualized self-monitoring, mental preparation, or self-discipline. One example is the appearance of the *mikveh* or ritual bath (plural *mikva'ot*) in Judea and elsewhere in Palestine at the end of the Hasmonean period, which people would have used to cleanse themselves of impurity through the act of immersion following a requisite preparatory process. The earliest known mikveh was found under a Hasmonean palace in Jericho, dated to 125–115 BCE, and they become more common after that. Another example is the wearing of *tefillin*, small boxes containing biblical texts worn by Jewish men during prayer; they are first attested by tefillin parchments and the pouches in which they were kept that were found among the Dead Sea Scrolls from the second or first century BCE.

It is possible that these practices arose much earlier—both are understood as ways of fulfilling scriptural commandments. But archaeologically speaking, the use of the mikveh and the wearing of tefillin do not surface prior to the Hasmonean period, and one of the reasons to place their origin in this time frame is the way they

parallel Greek practices. The mikveh resembles the Greek baths introduced to Judea in the Hellenistic period. The tefillin is harder to
relate to a specific Hellenistic practice—it is compared to the use
of amulets among other peoples, a ubiquitous practice in antiquity, but it is worth mentioning a more specific parallel from the
Hellenistic-Roman world which suggests it originated in that context: the fastening of the text of Homer to oneself as a talisman or
resting one's head on a Homeric text as a medical cure.

If we are dealing here with innovations from the Hellenistic
period, what is it about this period that encouraged Judeans to
behave in these ways? One way of answering that question is to
explain them from the perspective of Cohen's theory as an indirect
consequence of Judea's Hellenization in the late second century
BCE. The mikveh, found in places well beyond Jerusalem, suggests
that Judeans at this time felt they had to monitor their purity status
even when they were far removed from the Temple. In the same
period, some Jewish men were undertaking the discipline of putting on the tefillin as a reminder to themselves of their obligation
to follow God's commandments. Both behaviors can be understood
as different ways of monitoring, preparing, or focusing oneself, putting oneself in the right physical state or the right frame of mind
to sustain one's relationship with God. One way to understand why
such behavior suddenly seemed necessary is to connect it to the
new conception of identity that set in more broadly during the Hasmonean period, the perception of Judeanness as an achieved status
that takes resolve and effort to attain.

Clearly the process of Hellenization introduced many major
changes in Judean society, but before we embrace Cohen's account as an explanation for the origin of Jewishness, we need to
consider some of the ways in which it can be challenged. To begin
with, it does not represent the only way in which the evidence can
be understood. We do not know very much about what happened
in the centuries between the postexilic period described by Ezra
and Nehemiah and the Hellenized Judea described by books like
1 and 2 Maccabees, but there is just enough evidence to at least
call into question some of what Cohen understands to be an innovation of the Hellenistic age. The best example is the phenomenon of conversion, which Cohen treats as evidence of the change

he is charting. As he acknowledges, there are cases in the Hebrew Bible that seem to anticipate the act of conversion. We have already mentioned Ruth, but there is also Isaiah 56, a part of the Book of Isaiah that is clearly datable to the Persian period, which refers to foreigners "who have attached themselves to the Lord to minister to him." And there is a reference in the Book of Esther that notes that, in the aftermath of Haman's failure to exterminate the Jews, "many of the people of the country became Judeans, because the fear of the Judeans/Jews had fallen on them" (8:17). There are only a few such references, but they are potentially significant. For his overall narrative of the beginning of Jewishness to work, Cohen has to *impose* a distinction between pre-Hellenistic Judean culture and post-Hellenistic Jewishness, and that requires doing what he can to dispense of evidence that blurs that distinction. He must acknowledge that there are possible precedents for conversion that predate the Hellenistic period, but he minimizes their significance: if they happened earlier, he concedes, it was "not by very much, if at all" or else it should be considered a "harbinger" of what happens later, not qualifying as actual conversions but somehow anticipating a phenomenon that truly develops only in the Hellenistic period. Cohen's narrative requires a break between the pre-Hellenistic and the Hellenistic period, and any evidence that undercuts that distinction must therefore be explained away or minimized.

This is a minor objection to Cohen's larger argument, but it exposes a key premise of that argument. Why is it so important that the transformation he observes begin in the Hellenistic period as opposed to emerging from the earlier Persian period? The answer, I am inclined to think, is that the Hellenistic age is not just a historical period for Cohen; it is also the mechanism: it has built into it a way to understand the difference between Jews of a later period and their Judean ancestors. From its inception, as we have noted, the Hellenistic period was closely associated with hybridity, the act of cultural cross-fertilization, and that image of it persists into the present, even though scholars have challenged many aspects of Droysen's original account and have updated its concept of hybridity or cultural mixture. It is this association of the Hellenistic world with hybridity that provides Cohen with not just a context for the origin of Judaism but also a model for how to account for the change—Judeans became Jews because they, too, formed a hybrid-izing relationship with the Greeks.

One problem for such a view is that, in recent years, scholars have begun to express some discontent with hybridity as a model for understanding the Hellenistic world. To cite a recent example, in a 2014 study Rachel Mairs rejects the notion of hybridity as a model for understanding the mélange of cultural elements found in Hellenistic Afghanistan and India. In another recent study of Helle-nistic Babylonia, the art historian Stephanie Langin-Hooper argues for replacing the concept of hybridity with the idea of "entangle-ment" as a more multidirectional and complex way of understand-ing intercultural interaction; and in a similar vein, the historian Andrew Wallace-Hadrill proposes the metaphor of "bilingualism," by which he means to refocus scholarship on the question of how people in antiquity switched between identities and cultural codes. In some corners of classical scholarship, the language of hybridity came back into vogue after the term was used by Homi Bhabha, the dean of postcolonialist studies, to refer to what happens in the cul-tural space between colonizers and the colonized, and the ambiva-lence their interactions create; but he does not have in mind the kind of cross-fertilizing hybridity that Droysen was talking about, rejecting the idea of the hybrid as a bringing together of separate cultures in a way that resolves their difference. The more recent re-jection of the language of hybridity by scholars focused on the Hel-lenistic world suggests that the concept is in the process of breaking down as a model for understanding the process of Hellenization.

We can relate this change to developments noted earlier in the book and especially to the rejection of genealogical thinking by some scholars. The anthropologist Peter Wade has made the con-nection explicit: he rejects what he refers to as "roots hybridity," a kind of genealogical thinking that conceives of the origin of people as a syncretism of two anterior wholes into a third new whole, and notes the emergence in scholarship of a "rhizomatic" or "diasporic" hybridity that crisscrosses in multiple directions as opposed to mov-ing in a straight line from two parents to an offspring that combines their qualities. I will not be applying a "rhizomatic" approach to Jewish Hellenistic culture—I do not believe the evidence supports such an approach *over* the hybridity model of Hellenization—but the recent turn away from hybridity raises the question of whether we need to rethink the paradigm of origin implicit in Cohen's approach. Is the Hellenistic age the right period in which to place the beginning of Jewishness? The answer is tied to the question of whether hybridization is the right model for understanding the process of origination involved.

Learning from the Greeks

Critics of the concept of hybridity often object to its embrace of a biological model, the way it analogizes the intermixing of peoples and cultures with the crossing and grafting of species. But in truth the kind of hybridity at work in Hellenization is decidedly nonbiological, even in a way antibiological. It is not that sexual relations did not occur between Greek settlers and the populations they encountered—this was happening already in the time of Alexander—but sexual intermingling is not the kind of explanation scholars have in mind when they speak of Hellenization as a hybridizing process. Hellenization is usually understood as a metaphorical process of "cross-fertilization," a cultural process in which Near Eastern peoples absorbed the qualities of the Greeks not by mating with them, though they may have done that, but by learning to speak in Greek, reading Greek literature, and imitating Greek customs. Hellenistic culture, as noted by the historian Henri-Irénée Marrou, was a culture of *paideia*, of education, and its dissemination occurred not through interbreeding and sexual reproduction but through learning and emulation.

The importance of education to the process of Hellenization explains why one of the most vital institutions in this period was the gymnasium, a place for physical training and sport but also functioning as a place for young men to train their minds: we know of gymnasia that had libraries attached to them, where there were guest lecturers, where students engaged in literary and musical contests—hence the use of the term "gymnasium" in modern Europe to refer to a high school. Gymnasia in the Hellenistic world were not open to everyone—they were chiefly for the male citizens of the city—but they were open to distinguished foreigners who would come to the gymnasium to become educated gentlemen. It was in this setting that young men from the Egyptian, Syrian, Babylonian, and North African elite learned to think like Greeks and to be counted as Greeks socially and culturally. The building of the gymnasium was itself a way for a city to become Greek, marking its transformation into a *polis*, a proper city by Greek standards.

Greek influence may have reached Judea later than other regions, but by the second century BCE, it too was moving in this direction. In 175 BCE, the high priest Jason, like the nobles of other cities in the Hellenistic world, decided to build a gymnasium in the city—one of the events that precipitated the Maccabean Revolt, according to 2 Maccabees:

> [The high priest Jason] took delight in establishing a gymnasium right under the citadel, and he induced the noblest of the young men to wear a Greek hat. There was such an extreme of Hellenization and increase in the adoption of foreign ways because of the surpassing wickedness of Jason, who was ungodly and no true high priest, that the priests were no longer intent upon their service at the altar. Despising the sanctuary and neglecting the sacrifices, they hurried to take part in the unlawful proceedings in the wrestling arena after the signal for the disc-throwing, disdaining the honors prized by their ancestors and putting the highest value upon Greek forms of prestige. For this reason heavy disaster overtook them, and those whose ways of living they admired and wished to imitate completely became their enemies and punished them. (2 Maccabees 4:12–16)

If we overlook the author's hostility to the effort, we can see here how the process of Hellenization might have taken place in many cities throughout the Hellenistic world; a leader or noble within the community's power structure took the initiative to construct a gymnasium or some other educational institution that drew the young men of the city's elite to its sporting activities and competitions. They in turn began to imitate the Greek way of life, dressing in a Greek style, emulating Greek customs, and internalizing Greek values, and their influence transmitted Greek culture throughout the rest of society, from the top down.

It was through gymnasia, libraries, and other educational institutions, scholars believe, that Greek culture spread from those born Greek to the non-Greek elites of the Near East, including Judeans like Philo, who may have studied in a gymnasium in Alexandria; though it is possible, given the prosperity of his family, that he was able to study with his own Greek tutors as he imagines Moses doing in his biography of the prophet (*Life of Moses* 1.21–24). Even the author of 2 Maccabees, despite his hostility to the gymnasium in Jerusalem, may have learned his Greek in a similar way. The prologue to the work tells us that it is an abridgment of a five-volume work written by a Jason of Cyrene, in present-day Libya, and we know that there was a gymnasium in Cyrene to which some Jews were admitted.

As we try to think anew about the concept of hybridity at work in Cohen's theory, the key is this idea that Hellenization unfolded as a kind of educational process. We are not going to be able to resolve how exactly the Jews learned from the Greeks. As Cohen has pointed out in a study of the rabbinic educational system, while there are many parallels between the educational cultures of Jews and Greeks in the Hellenistic-Roman period, we do not know very much about schooling in this period, and we know far less about how Judeans in Judea or elsewhere learned the Greek language or absorbed Greek thought and culture, apart from glimpses here and there in sources like 2 Maccabees, Philo, and Josephus. What interests me here, however, is not the details of how Jews learned Greek but the underlying association of Hellenization with education. Why does education play such a central role in how scholars understand the process of Hellenization? It is not simply the sources themselves that generate this association, I propose, but something in the background of the scholars who constructed our image of the Hellenistic age, an aspect of their own educations. Probing that background is my way of questioning the implicit model of hybridity that underlies Cohen's account of the origin of the Jews.

Lest my argument in what follows be misunderstood, I want to be clear from the beginning that there is plenty of evidence to suggest that the educational culture introduced by the Greeks did have a significant impact on Jewish culture. Most of our principal sources from this period, including the books of the Maccabees and the writings of Philo and Josephus, were composed or translated into Greek. We have reason to think as well that Jewish education in Palestine throughout the Hellenistic and Roman period, even when conducted in Hebrew or Aramaic, was probably patterned on Greek models, something Cohen himself has proven for rabbinic education after the end of the Second Temple by showing parallels between the academies where the rabbis studied and the Greco-Roman philosophical schools.

But Jews have always learned from and emulated the non-Jews among whom they have lived. There is nothing unique about the Hellenistic period in that regard. What distinguishes the educational process we are focused on is the role it plays as an origin account, as an explanation for how one people became another people, related and yet different. It plays that role in Droysen's account of the Hellenistic age, where the fusion of Greek and foreigner leads to Christianity, and the precedent set by that work carries through into Cohen's use of the Hellenistic age to explain how the Judeans became Jews. To understand why it is that education came to play this transformative role, I do not think it is sufficient to look only at the ancient sources; we also have to learn a bit more about the scholars who formulated this image of the Hellenistic age and the educational culture from which they emerged—a culture that, as it happens, generated its own kind of hybrid Jew.

What lies in the background of this way of representing the Hellenistic period, I would argue, is the concept of *Bildung*, an idea that shaped the educational experience of the German or German-trained scholars to whom we owe our understanding of this period. An offshoot of the developmentalist thinking that set in during the eighteenth century, *Bildung* referred to the development of the individual, the unfolding of a person's inherent potential. It was associated with the liberation of the self from the constraints of tradition and ignorance, the kind of progression recorded in the *Bildungsroman*, the genre of coming-of-age story popular in this period that began with a hero's liberation from the home and a journey toward greater maturity. The concept had a major impact on the German educational system. As the historian David Sorkin has explained, when the Prussian educational reformer Wilhelm von Humboldt (1767–1835) envisioned what would become one of the earliest modern research universities—the University of Berlin, now Humboldt University—he was acting on his understanding of *Bildung* as the pursuit of freedom through inward and holistic self-development.

Though the university he actually implemented was designed to serve the state, his commitment to *Bildung* as an educational ideal is why he planned its curriculum to emphasize a general education beyond what was required to be a citizen or to serve as a government functionary, and why it was designed to allow for increasing independence as the student climbed the educational ladder.

The connection to the Hellenistic period springs from the fact that Humboldt and other exponents of *Bildung* looked to classical Greece as an exemplum of the educational ideal they were trying to achieve. From the days of the Enlightenment, German scholars had closely identified with the Greeks, so much so that the English scholar Eliza Butler (1885–1959), in a book that was banned in Germany when it was published in the 1930s, was moved to speak of the "the tyranny of Greece over Germany"—the way in which the ancient Greeks loomed over the thinking and self-perception of German intellectuals. The ancient Athenians had seemed to realize the ideals they were striving to achieve—the freedom, the rationalism, the perfection of the individual's abilities—and Germans saw in *paideia* a method, a curriculum, by which Germans might achieve these ideals. Thus, for example, in his inaugural address as the headmaster of the Ägidien-Gymnasium, Hegel advocated for the study of Greek literature as the foundation of higher education, a "secular baptism that first and indelibly attunes and tinctures the soul in respect of taste and knowledge," as he remarked in a speech delivered as rector of a Gymnasium in Nuremberg in 1809. And Humboldt went on to institutionalize such ideas through his educational reforms, including encouraging the study of the Greek language not as a rote linguistic exercise but as a way to infuse students with the creativity of the Greeks (see Figure 6).

These ideas certainly had an impact on scholars like Droysen—a student of Hegel's, a master at the most prestigious gymnasium in Berlin, and then a professor at the university Humboldt had established—and he developed his own view of *Bildung* that gave the study of history a central role in the process. For Droysen the development of the individual mirrored the history of humanity in general—which was, as he interpreted it, a process that moved the consciousness of freedom beyond its origin in ancient Greece into the broader world—and to study this history was to abet one's own

FIGURE 6. Wilhelm von Humboldt (1767–1835) surrounded
by Greek images in his study at the Tegel Castle, ca. 1830.
Source: Courtesy of the Bildarchiv Preussischer Kulturbesitz.
©Bildarchiv Preussischer Kulturbesitz.

formation, to break free from tradition just as the Greeks had done
by first developing historical consciousness. This sheds light on why
Droysen took such an interest in the Hellenistic age. Whereas previous scholars had treated it as the downfall of Greek freedom, he
saw in Alexander's conquest an explanation for how the ideal of
freedom had reached the rest of humanity.

We have noted that Droysen did not have much to say about the role of the Jews in the Hellenistic age, but other scholars, including Jewish scholars, would, and there is reason to think that the latter's interest had something to do with the concept of *Bildung* as well. From the time the eighteenth-century German-Jewish philosopher Moses Mendelssohn (1729–1786) used the language of *Bildung* to describe the Enlightenment, German Jews associated *Bildung* with emancipation, upward mobility, and integration, embracing it as a way for the community to overcome its perceived weakness and for individual Jews to gain acceptance into German society. The ideal toward which *Bildung* was aimed was one that was accessible to people regardless of their background or parentage, a secular and universalized conception of human potential achievable, in theory, by any individual who invested the effort to attain it: not just men but women too (*Bildung* was important to the German women's movement), not just Germans but people from other nations and religions. As a result *Bildung* was seen by Jews as a ticket into German society.

One of the results of this educational culture were people like my friend Henry Fischel, a committed Jew—a rabbi in fact—but also a lifelong lover of German culture who remained committed to it half a century after he had been driven from his homeland by his fellow Germans. As I recall, the two aspects of his life in Germany that Fischel was most proud of were the facts that he was from the hometown of Beethoven and that he had won awards as a gymnast, and he was not atypical in having found a way to integrate the Jewish and German parts of his identity. For some Jews *Bildung* was a way to assimilate, but for others like Fischel, it offered a way to fuse the Jewish and German parts of their identities.

But there were limits to the integrative power of *Bildung*—the anti-Semitism that was so deeply rooted in German culture, and the nationalism that became increasingly potent as the nineteenth century unfolded. *Bildung* was supposed to be open to all, but Germans were suspicious of those who did not live up to the ideal appearance, manner, or accent—and this meant the Jews whose attempts to come across as German were frequently described as overdone, improper, or fraudulent. Not even the mastery of Greek could overcome what many regarded as the Jews' inherent and immutable un-Germanness. A good number of Jews who sought to become classicists in the late nineteenth and early twentieth centuries, prior to the Nazi period, succeeded in finding positions, but they also faced suspicion and sometimes resistance from faculty who believed that Greek was too closely tied to German identity to be taught by Jews. Even a Jewish classicist of the intellectual stature of Jacob Bernays (1824–1881)—the uncle of Freud's wife, incidentally—had a hard time finding a position at a German university because he refused to be baptized. Learning Greek as a way into Germanness did not work as well in practice as it did in theory, as was true of writing great poetry in German or even being baptized.

Given these circumstances, it is understandable that many Jewish classicists would avoid even broaching the topic of how Jews and Greeks related to each other in antiquity—writing about the Jews might only call attention to one's own Jewishness. But some scholars did anyways, and we are in a better position to understand what they found of interest about the Hellenistic period in particular. The era as Droysen had defined it, an era when Greeks and Orientals had overcome their differences and merged into a single universal culture, was historical proof that Greek culture—that is, German culture—need not be restricted to a particular people but could be internalized by foreigners. It suggested as well that the Jews need not fully abandon their culture in order to integrate into German society. Germans could even benefit from absorbing some of the qualities of the Jews, just as the Greeks had benefitted from adopting customs from the Egyptians and the Persians. If Hellenism symbolized the German identity that Jewish scholars were hoping to fuse into, the Hellenistic age illustrated the possibility and path of fusion, a precedent for the symbiosis with German culture that they were striving to achieve in their own lives.

I cannot prove that their own experiences as hybrid German-Jews is what led these scholars to find a similar process at work in the Hellenistic period, but we can point to at least one case where a scholar's effort to relate the Jewish and German sides of his identity is clearly mirrored by his description of the Jewish-Greek relationship. Elias Bickerman, the subject of a recent biography by Albert Baumgarten, was a major scholar of the Jewish-Hellenistic period who in 1942 migrated from Nazi-occupied France to the United

States, where after a decade of uncertain employment he took up a position at Columbia University. Bickerman was born in the Ukraine and began his studies of antiquity with the Russian historian Michael Rostovtzeff (1870–1952), but he fled to Germany in the wake of the Russian Revolution and went on to do his graduate studies in Berlin, where he came into contact with the German scholars he admired. Although he embraced German culture, he struggled to be accepted as a German and was eventually driven from Germany by the Nazis in 1933. As Baumgarten notes, Bickerman's life is a case where *Bildung* failed; he never fully integrated into German culture, and his ambivalence toward Germanness—and to *Bildung*—comes through in his treatment of the Hellenistic period.

Among Bickerman's best-known works are *The God of the Maccabees*, first published in 1937 in German in Berlin (where it was still possible at that point for a Jewish scholar to publish a book provided the publisher was Jewish), and *From Ezra to the Last of the Maccabees*, published after his move to the United States. Part of what made these works controversial among scholars was their thesis that the Maccabean Revolt was not primarily a rebellion against Antiochus IV, as scholars had always understood, but a civil war among Jews—between reformers and an orthodox or traditionalist camp. What was it that led Antiochus IV to try to abolish the religious practices of the Jews? According to Bickerman, the idea came not from the Greek king but from a Jewish faction of "extreme Hellenizers," the high priest Jason and others, who were motivated to assimilate to the surrounding Hellenistic world by a universalism and skepticism they had learned from the Greeks. The revolt led by the Maccabees was targeted at them more than at Antiochus, a rejection by Jews of other Jews' turning themselves into Greeks.

As Baumgarten notes, the evidence in support of this theory is not very strong, and he believes that Bickerman really has in mind the situation in his own day. His description of the "extreme Hellenizers" seems modeled on a number of Jewish reform movements that in Bickerman's view had harmed Judaism from within. He is actually explicit in comparing them with the Jewish Reform movement that arose in Germany during the 1840s and its effort to do away with Jewish ritual in favor of a Judaism based on moral precepts—in fact, Bickerman suggests that, like the German reformers, the extreme Hellenizers even went so far as to accept a critical approach to the Bible. But Baumgarten believes that he may also have had in mind groups from Russian history, such as the Jewish modernizers who sought an alliance with Tsar Nicholas I (r. 1822–1855) to reform Jewish education and communal life and minimize the influence of Hasidic rabbis. It is impossible to know for certain what was going on in Bickerman's mind, but Baumgarten catches an outright anachronism in his account that gives away his conflation of the ancient and the modern. According to Bickerman, the Hellenizers sought to remove everything that smacked of the "ghetto"—that is, every aspect of Jewish tradition that separated the Jews from non-Jews—and that included a prohibition of beards, which they persuaded Antiochus to outlaw alongside circumcision, the Sabbath, and other practices. The problem is that a prohibition of beards is nowhere mentioned in the ancient sources among the practices banned by Antiochus IV. Why then did Bickerman imagine such a prohibition? According to Baumgarten he was projecting onto the Hellenizers another trait of Jewish modernizers, who were known for shunning the beards worn by traditional Eastern European Jews.

I would like to pursue a somewhat different reading of Bickerman's narrative, building on Baumgarten's suggestion but adding to it the idea that, like so many others in his day, Bickerman consciously or unconsciously conflated Greek with German culture, and in that light, his narrative makes sense not only as a response to modernizing Jewish reformers but as a reaction against *Bildung* in particular. What the extreme Hellenizers are calling for, in Bickerman's reading, is a new kind of education that would allow them to adopt Greek ways. As he would write in *From Ezra to the Last of the Maccabees*, "Greek culture, *like modern European culture*, was based upon education" (italics mine). This was what the Hellenizers understood, that education was the ticket into the larger world, and they hoped to merge their people into it by creating a new educational system modeled on that of the Greeks. Hellenic culture (as Bickerman represents it) was rationalistic, based on a universalizing conception of humankind. It transcended differences of ethnicity and religion, and it was something that anyone could participate in: "in the polytheistic world of Hellenism . . . all beliefs were admitted as refractions of the same eternal light"; "it was open to all." In other words, Hellenism had all the essential qualities of *Bildung*, and it seemed to offer to ancient Jews the same kinds of opportunities that the German educational system, with its focus on learning Greek, offered to Jews like Bickerman himself.

There are other similarities between the Hellenizers and the advocates of Jewish *Bildung* as well. To implement their plans, the Hellenizers turned to Antiochus IV for help, asking him to intervene to help impose the changes they wanted to make. The move calls to mind a debate over the role of the state in supporting *Bildung*. German education, as it developed over the course of the nineteenth century, became dependent on state support, which provoked differences among scholars and educators over whether and how the state should be involved in the *Bildung* process. There were intellectuals on both sides of this issue, and there were voices in the middle, like that of Humboldt, who sought to limit the state's role but also concluded that some intervention was required at least temporarily to establish the proper framework for *Bildung*. The Hellenizers, as understood by Bickerman, reflect the position of those who believed in state intervention. More specifically, their effort to enlist the support of Antiochus IV bears a striking resemblance to the efforts of Moses Mendelssohn, the archetypical Enlightened German Jew, who had suggested the state was essential to the "*Bildung* of Men." Mendelssohn drew the state into his effort to reform Jewish education when his ideas were embraced by the Prussian bureaucrat Christian Wilhelm von Dohm (1751–1820), whose position was then incorporated into the Edicts of Toleration issued in 1781–1782 by the Emperor Joseph II. In an effort to improve the education (*Bildung*) of the Jews, Joseph required that they be enrolled in state-sponsored German-language schools where they would receive a secular education, an effort mirrored in Bickerman's description of the role King Antiochus played in imposing the educational reform of the Hellenizers.

Even the imagined prohibition of beards can be understood in this context. The transforming effects of *Bildung* were not just internal but external: it was supposed to result in an improved physique and appearance, which was one reason Jews were thought by some to be incapable of full-fledged *Bildung*—they did not accord with the physical ideal associated with it. But others did believe it was possible for Jews to conform to the physical ideal of *Bildung*, and part of that ideal for men was clean-shavenness, a trait associated not just with modernization in general but with Germanness in particular, as when the *Maskilim* (those who advocated for reforming Judaism in light of the principles of the Enlightenment) were described by their traditionalist opponents as Germans who shaved their beards and sidecurls. In fact, to push beyond Baumgarten's explanation, Bickerman may have lifted the beard prohibition from a specific episode in German history: the reforms of Joseph II, who not only required Jews to take on German names and cease printing books in Hebrew but ordered them to shave their beards.

Bickerman's description of the extreme Hellenizers implies his rejection of the educational philosophy they represent, but that does not mean he rejected *Bildung* as an ideal. In *From Ezra to the Last of the Maccabees*, he notes that it was ultimately self-destructive to completely refuse the benefits of a Greek education:

> Other peoples shut themselves off from Hellenism, and its effects upon them were therefore only negative: the native cultures were disintegrated and enfeebled. They lost their upper class, whose connection with the people had been ruptured by the process of Hellenization. The Egyptians, for example, deprived of their upper class, their intellectual elite, for centuries lagged behind the inexorable march of history, and so suffered the fate of enslavement to foreign conquerors.

While he rejects the Hellenizers' elitist conception of education as a policy of "rationalistic assimilation," Bickerman suggests here that there was a reason for Jews to embrace *Bildung*—it could help foster an indigenous intellectual elite able to keep their people in step with the "march of history" and protect them from foreign oppressors. It is just that Jews would have to find a way to do so that accommodated and protected their native tradition. It so happens that this alternative conception of *Bildung* is embodied by none other than the Maccabees themselves, who represent not a complete rejection of Greek (that is, German) culture but a selective embrace of it that made sure that what was borrowed was subordinated to the Torah. The same approach was adopted by the Pharisees, the party of scribes and sages that emerges in the Hasmonean period and thought to be the predecessors of the rabbis of the Talmud; in fact, they developed this approach into an educational system that bears its own striking resemblance to *Bildung:*

> [For the Pharisees,] piety was teachable, and to be attained only through teaching. . . . But this is a Hellenic, one might say, a Platonic notion, that education could so transform the individual and the entire people that the nation would be capable of fulfilling the divine task set for it. . . . The Pharisees adopted these ideas and tendencies of the Hellenistic world, in that they associated the public sermons that had been customary since the time of Ezra with the teaching of the Torah. But it was not their ideal to fashion a Greek *kalos kai agathos,* or "gentleman," but to fulfill the precept which introduces the revelation on Sinai: "Ye shall be unto Me a kingdom of priests, and a holy nation."

We can see now that Bickerman is really talking about *Bildung,* or a modified version of it, imagining Pharisaic education as a vehicle of personal and collective self-transformation modeled on Greek *paideia*; the main difference is that the process has been repurposed for Jewish purposes, to strengthen Jews' sense of divine mission and their connection to their ancient traditions.

Bickerman's account of the Maccabees and the Pharisees mirrors his own biography as a Jewish semi-outsider who never fully fit into the German academic system that would eventually have no place for him, but it also shows how steeped he was in the culture of *Bildung* even after he moved to the United States. By the time he was writing these words, he had been betrayed by the German culture that had educated him, and yet that education still loomed so large in his understanding that he could conceive the Judaism of the rabbis—the Judaism that developed out of the Pharisees' efforts—as its cousin, descending from the same Greek educational ethos that had produced *Bildung.*

I have gone on at such length about *Bildung* because I believe it can help us to understand the concept of hybridity at work in scholarship of the Jewish-Hellenistic age. The underlying model for the process of Hellenization, the fusing of Greek and Near Eastern culture, is not biological but cultural: Hellenization was understood as the result of an educational process introduced by the Greeks after

Alexander the Great conquered the Near East, a kind of historicized *Bildung* stretched out over centuries and continents. There is perhaps no better example of this process than the Hellenization of Jewish culture, which unfolded through the construction of gymnasia and has resulted in a rabbinic culture organized around the act of education that is itself a hybrid of Greek and indigenous Jewish culture. This narrative can marshal plenty of evidence to support it, and might well approximate what really happened in antiquity, but what I am trying to account for is the modern idea that such a process happened, and the explanation I am proposing is that it is the result of viewing the ancient evidence in light of the idea of *Bildung*. That is to say, it represents a subtle form of anachronism that, by slightly reconfiguring and supplementing the evidence, produces a narrative that overlaps with historical reality to a large degree but not completely so, as we can glimpse in the case of Antiochus's imagined decree against Jewish beards, a reflection not of what really happened during the period of the Maccabean Revolt but of Bickerman's experience and memories as a hybridized Russian-German-Jew.

If there is something to what I am arguing here, what are the implications for Cohen's theory for the origin of Jewishness? He was writing sixty years after Bickerman published *The God of the Maccabees*, long after the devastation of German-Jewish culture during the Holocaust, and there is nothing in his narrative to suggest the direct influence of the concept or culture of *Bildung*; in fact, he operates with a very different conception of identity formation. But that said, Cohen's understanding of the Hellenistic period is not unconnected to Bickerman's. He knew Bickerman personally from his time as a graduate student at Columbia, describes him as an intellectual hero, and cites his scholarship approvingly. Against the backdrop of this connection, I conclude this chapter by broaching the possibility that Cohen's account reflects some of what was passed on to him from Bickerman and the thought world he helped to bring to American scholarship; that it too can be understood as a variation of the Hellenization as *Bildung* idea, albeit in a form adapted to contemporary intellectual culture. If there is such a connection, that does not mean Cohen is wrong, but it does raise the possibility that his thesis unconsciously perpetuates some of the anachronism we have detected in Bickerman's approach.

Graduating from Hellenism

Cohen's *Beginnings of Jewishness* was written in a different intellectual universe from Bickerman's *God of the Maccabees*, and that difference extends to how Cohen understands the process of identity formation. *Bildung* was born of developmentalist thinking. It assumed that human beings (or at least Germans) were born with certain inherent abilities that existed in a potential form, and education was a process of cultivating that potential, actualizing it or perfecting it. Cohen's approach is constructivist. He assumes that the self is plastic, malleable, and capable of molding itself. Bickerman came of age in a more essentialist intellectual context that treated identity as an ingrained, enduring, and indelible trait. I have not found him to make any racializing comments; but there are indications that biological determinism did shape his thinking at least in one respect. Baumgarten recalls an incident when Bickerman announced in class that he would never support female students for fellowships since he believed their scholarly careers would always be thwarted by their biology, by motherhood. For Bickerman, it seems, there were constraints on human potential that not even education could overcome, in contrast to Cohen, who asserts the absence of any inherent or inflexible difference among people, including the differences between men and women.

These differences are reflected in how Cohen and Bickerman describe the Hellenistic period. In keeping with the constructivist perspective that he embraces, Cohen believes that the one enduring quality of Jewish identity is its mutability, the fact that its boundaries have never been stable, that it has always been in a process of redefinition. If his argument can be distilled to a single point, it is that this mutability is something that goes back to the beginning, to the Hellenistic period, when the Judeans realized under the influence of the Greeks that identity was not fixed by birth, that one could *make oneself* into a Jew through conversion. Whereas Bickerman imagined the extreme Hellenizers, the Maccabees and the Pharisees, as advocates for various kinds of *Bildung*, Cohen projects his conceptual universe onto the period; Jewishness emerges in the history he describes at the moment when the Judeans shift in their understanding of their identity to what we might think of as an ambivalently constructivist perspective, not giving up on descent as the basis of identity but now recognizing that it has a variable and self-determining dimension.

For all his differences from Bickerman's perspective, however, Cohen's account of the Hellenistic period does retain certain elements of his teacher's account of the Hasmonean period, and this includes his understanding of the transition between Judean culture and Jewishness. The reader may recall that the key difference between Judeans and Jews in Cohen's account involves the source of identity. Judean identity was fixed at birth, determined in advance by a person's descent from certain ancestors. Jewishness is a voluntary identity, or a semivoluntary identity: People are still born into the status, but one can also now choose to become a Jew because it has been reconceived, under the influence of Greek culture, as a way of life, a voluntarily undertaken pursuit or affiliation closer to what we think of as a religion rather than an ethnicity. The seed of that narrative, I would argue, is already to be found in Bickerman's *From Ezra to the Last of the Maccabees*, in a section published in 1947, a year before Cohen's birth. We have already quoted the beginning of this story:

> Greek culture, like modern European culture, was based upon education. A man became a Hellene without at the same time forsaking his gods but merely by adopting Hellenic culture.

This is Hellenization as *Bildung*, an educational process; but the passage continues,

> During the three centuries which we call Hellenistic, that is, the period between Alexander the Great and Emperor Augustus (330 to 30 B.C.E.), the notion of the "Hellene," like the modern notion of the "European," *grew into a concept independent of descent.* (italics mine)

One can glimpse in this brief passage how the concept of *Bildung* gave rise to the kind of narrative Cohen develops in *The Beginnings of Jewishness*. Here too there is a transition in the Hellenistic age from a descent-based identity to one that was more self-forming; here too the catalyst is a concept introduced by the Greeks, but it is clearer that the model for this transformative process is *Bildung*, the educational process that helped "modern Europeans" (like Bickerman himself) transcend the circumstances of their birth and assert control over their identity. I would not know if Cohen was conscious of this precedent, and the connections to Bickerman's thinking are concealed by the constructivist framework that he deploys, but there is a line of connection that suggests *The Beginnings of Jewishness* is ultimately an offshoot of the Hellenization-as-*Bildung* thesis.

To point out this affinity is not to criticize any specific claim that Cohen makes. What I bring to light here is the paradigm of origin from which his argument emerged—*Bildung* as a way of fusing Jewish identity into Germanness—and it is that paradigm that I am questioning. Scholarship has been trying for decades now to undo the conception of the Hellenistic age introduced by Droysen, and it has been successful in many respects, managing for example to overcome the once-standard account of Hellenization as a process of spreading freedom to the world by recasting it as a phenomenon much closer to modern colonialism or the destructive dimension of globalization than to a benign educational process. But the influence of that original model persists in ways that have proven hard to completely shake—Cohen is no exception in that regard. As we have noted, scholars have been trying to break out of the description of the Hellenistic period as a *Mischkultur*, a culture formed by mixing, merging, or cross-fertilization, but the fact that they are still struggling against Droysen's thinking is itself evidence of how resilient certain ways of conceiving the past can be. It is similarly difficult to shake the analogy with *Bildung*, perhaps because the analogy was wired into the very concept of the Hellenistic age from the beginning. Tracing Cohen's narrative back to the *Bildung* analogy is not to discredit his account but rather to historicize it, to tie it to a specific way of thinking that emerged in a specific intellectual context in a specific period—and thereby acknowledge that there may be other ways to think about things.

But if we question the analogy between Hellenization and *Bildung*, does it make as much sense to place the beginnings of Jewishness in the Hellenistic period? There is certainly evidence to support such an account, but that evidence does not tell this story by itself: one has to overlook biblical sources from the Persian period that suggest the change may have been under way prior to Alexander's conquests, and there are some scholars today who argue conversely that Judaism jelled only after the Hellenistic period, arising much later under the influence of Christianity. What recommends the Hellenistic age as the *formative* age of Judaism, the age that reshaped the Judeans into the Jews, is not just the testimony of the sources but the perceived correspondence between Hellenization and *Bildung*, transforming a person into a new human being through education. Without that analogy to structure the narrative, it is far less clear that the beginning of Jewishness should even be placed in the Hellenistic age, much less that it is the outcome of what the Jews learned from the Greeks.

What of the larger idea that we have been exploring in this chapter—the notion of hybridity as a model for understanding the origin of the Jews? I must admit that the word "hybrid" still strikes me as a serviceable description of Jewish-Hellenistic culture, but we have also noted that some scholars have grown discontent with the notion of hybridity, both as a way to account for the origin of ethnic identity and as a description of Hellenistic culture, and those doubts should give us pause. Jewish culture in any period can be described as a hybrid—as we noted in the introduction, scholars like Amos Funkenstein contest that it ever existed in a pure or undiluted form—but the process of Hellenization has been singled out as generative in an essential way, giving rise to Judaism itself. What I have been arguing is that there is reason to rethink such a claim: it might tell us more about the scholars to whom we owe our understanding of the Hellenistic age, how their hybrid identity developed, than about the origin of Judaism. There is no doubt that Judean culture changed profoundly as the result of its interaction with Greek culture, but does this interaction mark the "beginning of Jewishness"? I mean to raise doubts by suggesting the Hellenistic age plays the role it does for Cohen because he was heir to a tradition of using Greek learning as a hybridization technique, a way to Germanize Jews. There is evidence to place the beginning of Judaism in the Hellenistic age, but there is also reason to be suspicious of an idea so reflective of how modern scholars used the Greeks to overcome their own ethnicity.

Hybrid Alternatives

Our treatment of Cohen's argument would not be complete if I failed to note that it now faces competition from another more recent effort to account for the origin of Judaism. Cohen's focus was not the origin of the Jews as a population but the beginning of Jewishness, a certain kind of identity that falls somewhere in between ethnicity and voluntary religious affiliation. In the past decade, Daniel Boyarin, a Talmudic scholar mentioned in our discussion of genealogy, has argued that this transition from ethnicity to ethno-religion occurred in a later historical period, the late antique age that saw the Christianization of the Roman Empire after the fourth century CE, and he assigns the role of catalyst not to Hellenization but to that process of Christianization. A comparison of his theory with Cohen's illustrates the ongoing debate over the origin of Jewishness/Judaism among contemporary scholars. It also reveals that there is more than one way to enlist the concept of hybridity as a part of this explanation.

Boyarin's argument, in brief, is that Judaism developed into an ethno-religion under the influence of Christianity, which in his view introduced religion as a category of identity detached from geography or genealogy. He draws inspiration for his theory from the work of recent scholars who have argued that even Hellenism itself as perceived by a late antique pagan like Emperor Julian the Apostate was reconceived on the model of Christianity as a kind of religion, a belief-based identity that constituted one's core identity in a deeper way than birthplace, ancestry, or language. The same process of recategorization led to the "invention" of Judaism, Boyarin argues. What was originally an ethnic identity was recategorized by Christians as a religion opposed to but also implicitly modeled on their own religious identity, and that change was then internalized by Jews, albeit only partially, through the efforts of the rabbis who produced the Talmud.

According to Boyarin's reconstruction, Judaism is a category that originates outside Judean culture, the invention of late antique Christianity inasmuch as the latter introduced religion as the core of identity and then imposed that conception onto the Jews. The rabbis abetted that change, internalizing the Christian conception of who the Jews were, though they also refused to completely embrace it by sustaining a genealogically defined conception of Jewishness as an identity determined by birth rather than by belief. The result was the kind of hybrid ethno-religious identity that, in Boyarin's account, characterizes the identity of many Jews to this day. "For the Church, Judaism is a religion, but for the Jews, only occasionally, ambivalently, and strategically is it so."

Cohen and Boyarin seem to agree in characterizing Jewishness/ Judaism as a hybrid—a fusion of an ethnic identity inherited from earlier Judeans with a more voluntary mode of religious identity absorbed from outside influence—but they place the origin of this new kind of identity in different historical periods and account for it in different ways. One reason for this difference has to do with how they understand the origin of the category of religion—Cohen sees it as an operative category in the Hellenistic period, suggesting the notion of Jewishness as a voluntaristic religious identity arose from the Greek conception of citizenship; Boyarin believes it was invented by Christians—but it also arises from two different conceptions of hybridity. We have traced Cohen's perspective to the nineteenth-century conception of Hellenization conceived as a process of cultural cross-fertilization. Boyarin's argument arises from the more recent conceptualization of hybridity introduced by postcolonialism.

One of the most important figures for understanding the postcolonial conception of hybridity is the aforementioned literary scholar Homi Bhabha, now at Harvard University. Bhabha is famous for studies that examine the often ambivalent interactions between colonized peoples and their rulers, how the colonized imitate the colonizer and resist him at the same time. Like other recent thinkers we have encountered, Bhabha does not pursue questions of origin, disavowing an interest in what the subjects of colonial ruler were like "originally"—that is, in what they were like before they were subjects of colonization. His focus is on what happens *through* the encounter between subjects and rulers. The identity of the colonized—how they see themselves, their interests and values—is not a continuation of what their ancestors were like before colonization, or an erasure of that identity for that matter: it is produced through an interaction in which the ruled internalize the ruler's perspective while also differentiating themselves.

As we have noted, the influence of postcolonialism has triggered a reassessment of the Hellenistic age. Increasing numbers of scholars have become resistant to understanding this age as a period of synthesis or merging, looking for other ways to describe the interactions between Greek and Near Eastern peoples, and Bhabha's notion of hybridity has offered an appealing alternative model because of the way it captures the political and cultural ambiguities inherent in the relationship between subject peoples and their rulers. In this model, the peoples conquered by the Greeks are not treated as passive subjects of Greek rule but are recognized as having their own agency, and scholars likewise recognize something more agentive in their embrace of Greek culture, treating it not just as slavish imitation or a synthesis of opposites but as an effort to negotiate between conflicting allegiances or as a mode of self-differentiation, self-assertion, or partial resistance.

Boyarin acknowledges the influence of Bhabha on his argument that Judaism originated through an interaction with Christianity, which in the context of the late antique Roman Empire was aligned with imperial power and hence had many of the qualities of colonial rule. His description of how Jewish identity was produced through an ambivalent relationship to a much more powerful Christianity—a narrative of an identity imposed by an imperial power that the rabbis internalized but also refused—builds on a plot line taken from Bhabha. More specifically, it emulates his notion of the "mimic man," the colonial subject who becomes like his white master but "not quite," imitating the ruler in ways that seem docile and derivative but are also dissonant and subversive.

One can challenge Boyarin's thesis on historical grounds by arguing that the shift from Judaism as an ethnicity to an ethnoreligion began earlier. It is also not clear that he is right to make Christianity the key protagonist in his narrative. The rabbinic composition at the center of his argument, the Babylonian Talmud, was produced in another milieu beyond the Christian Roman Empire, the Sasanian Empire, which ruled Mesopotamia from 224 CE to the rise of Islam in the seventh century, and that poses a problem for his effort to make Christianity the catalyst in his account: the complicated interaction between Christians and Jews in the Roman Empire may be the wrong or an incomplete context for understanding why the rabbis of the Talmud do not fully adhere to the Christian construction of Judaism as a religion. Boyarin has not explained how his argument might be impacted by recent scholarship that emphasizes the importance of reading the Talmud within the Persian/Sasanian context in which it was produced.

Whatever its shortcomings, Boyarin's argument helps us to see that the differences in how contemporary scholars account for the origin of Judaism arise not only from the ambiguities of the evidence but also from their different theoretical backgrounds. As we have noted, Cohen's effort to locate the origin of Jewishness in the Hellenistic age has a pedigree that fuses Bickerman with the constructivism that was so pervasive in anthropology and ethnic studies of the 1980s and 1990s. Boyarin's reconstruction emerges from the postcolonial perspective absorbed from the intellectual culture he encountered at Berkeley, where he teaches. There are many reasons for their different reconstructions—Cohen is trained to give more attention to the age of the Maccabees and Josephus, while Boyarin's work focuses on rabbinic literature and its intersections with Christianity; they understand the history of the category of religion differently; and one suspects their different understandings of contemporary Jewish identity are a factor as well—but one of the most important is that they are coming at the question of Judaism's origin from two different intellectual traditions, Droysenian hybridity versus the postcolonialist.

But there is overlap between their two theories. They both describe the origin of Judaism as a transition from an ethnicity to an ethno-religion, and they both attribute the change to hybridization, to a process by which the ancient Judeans absorbed or internalized the qualities of another people. As long as Judaism or Jewishness is conceived as a hybrid—whether that means the attribution of its qualities to racial mixing, schooling in a foreign educational system, or an ambivalent mimicry of a ruling power—the search for its origin will involve the effort to identify a coancestor, the other forebearer from which Judaism received its qualities alongside what it inherited from ancient Judean culture. That pursuit of the other within the self is ultimately what unites the efforts of Cohen and Boyarin across all their intellectual differences, the quest to reveal a second, non-Jewish lineage for Judaism.

CHAPTER SEVEN

Disruptive Innovation

THE JEWISH PEOPLE AS A MODERN INVENTION

The beginning of Nations, those excepted of whom sacred Books have spok'n, is to this day unknown.

—JOHN MILTON

IN AN ESSAY published in 1952, the previously mentioned Elias Bickerman floated an idea that has since become central to how scholars think about the origin of people. The essay in question, titled "Origines Gentium" ("Origin of Peoples"), was a study of ancient ethnogenesis, how Greek and Roman historians accounted for the origin of various peoples. The subject seems to have provoked much debate. Dionysius of Halicarnassus recounts twenty-five theories for the origin of the Romans alone; Tacitus mentions six theories for the *iudaioi*; and many other peoples, Greek and barbarian, attracted different theories about where they came from or who their founders were. None of these theories passes muster by modern historiographical standards, and yet, Bickerman suggests, they are not so different from modern accounts, the result of what he refers to as a "methodical science." It was not uncommon for such scholars to reject or ignore how the people in question accounted for their own origin, deeming their account implausible or self-serving, and they asked some of the same questions that modern scholars do: Are the sources reliable? Is there corroboration? Does the story in question fit one's sense of the probable?

Bickerman was trying to instill an appreciation for the intellectual accomplishments of ancient historians, but his argument was also meant to suggest something about modern scholarship—and it is on this point that it can be considered ahead of its time. The modern search for the origin of peoples is not that different from the ancient theories that the Romans descended from the Trojans or that the Jews originated as Egyptian lepers. Their use of linguistics and archaeology notwithstanding, modern scholars do not have that much more evidence to work with, and what they do with that evidence is very similar: they too fill in the gaps based only on their standards of what seems probable; they too are prone to stretch comparisons too far; they too interpret the past from an ethnocentric perspective. In fact, Bickerman suggests throughout this essay that ancient Greek scholars were better at ascertaining the origin of peoples than their modern counterparts in certain respects. Yes, the Greeks failed in their quest to pinpoint the origin of peoples, but "are modern theories much better? The 'Cro-Magnon' race of our textbooks or the 'Semites' as the substratum of 'Semitic' languages are fictions of a different kind but hardly of a higher value than the Trojan origin of Rome."

Bickerman was responding to the scholarship of his day, but his argument anticipates a position that has since become very influential: the various scholarly theories developed to account for the origin of the Jews have been recognized as a kind of mythmaking, "fictions of a different kind." Scholars have certainly overcome many of the problems that beset earlier theories. They have abandoned some of the problematic ideas that one senses perturbed Bickerman—the "Aryan myth" or the use of migration to explain how one people became another—and the category of race itself has been discredited, though scholars still use the term "Semite" as a linguistic category. But to the extent that it still tries to address the question of the origin of the Jews, scholarship has not yet overcome the kind of objections that Bickerman raised more than sixty years ago. For all the new evidence brought to bear, the methodological improvements, the importation of new models, and the increased theoretical literacy, scholars today must still rely on conjecture if they are to answer the question at all; they can still be criticized for credulousness; their theories can still be fairly described as "fictions of a different kind."

In the decades since Bickerman, the idea that scholarly origin accounts represent another form of mythmaking has developed into a full-fledged critique of the search for the origin of the Jews, one that argues that the very idea that they have an origin in antiquity is a scholarly invention foisted on the public by an intellectual elite and the educational system they controlled. In a work titled *The Invention of the Jewish People*, first published in Hebrew in 2008, the Israeli historian Shlomo Sand argues that much of what people think they know about the Jewish people goes back to historians in the nineteenth century and first part of the twentieth, and that their representation of the Jews was a fiction that they contrived. What we have been assuming about the Jewish people— that the Jews share a common origin that goes back to antiquity—is not born out by the evidence, Sand argues, and he introduces an alternative account that traces the origin of the Jews to more recent times. In what follows, I explore the arguments for and against this theory and try to probe the distinctive conception of origin on which it depends.

The Invention of the Jewish People created quite a stir when the original Hebrew version was first published in 2008. As the book's title suggests, it operates with a particular model of origin, "invention," which implies that the Jewish people came about as the result of conscious effort. The act of invention as we usually employ the term is often treated as a very positive thing, the beneficial result of human beings mastering their natural environment and asserting control over their destiny. Inventors are often seen as heroic, and the act of invention, as an advance, a leap forward from a dark age to a more enlightened time, as when we imagine that it was the invention of fire or the invention of writing that brought an end to the prehistoric age. But invention can also have a negative valence, referring to something fictional, made up, a figment of imagination, and that is its connotation for Sand: his title means to assert that the Jewish people is a contrivance—something that did not come into being naturally, that is false, and that need not or should not exist. Sand was not the first historian to argue that the Jews were an artificial people—we have seen a similar idea in Wellhausen—but Sand's use of the term "invention" ties his argument to a contemporary model of origin that is embraced by many social scientists, and that underlying model is part of what I consider here.

A Self-Inventing People

The response to Shlomo Sand's *Invention of the Jewish People* shows that there are many people in the world today receptive to scholarly narratives that challenge traditional or conventional thinking on the question of Jewish origin. First published in Hebrew, the book spent nineteen weeks on the best-seller list in Israel, and as it was translated into twenty languages over the next few years, it drew an even larger audience. In France it attracted twenty-five thousand readers in just six months and won the prestigious Prix Aujourd'hui (the "Today Prize") from the French press. In the United States it garnered many prominent reviews, including one in the *New York Times* that was ranked at the time as one of the most emailed articles in the world. It has had far less impact on how Jewish studies scholars understand the origin of the Jews—we will get to why scholars of Jewish history are so dismissive later—but there is no denying that the book has appealed to many readers, and this includes prominent scholars beyond the field of Jewish history.

Given that the Jews have long traced their history back to biblical times, how could Sand seriously maintain that the Jewish people was a modern invention? The key is the word "people" ('*am* in Hebrew), which Sand equates with the terms "ethnos," "nation," and even "race," modern terms that refer to a group defined by a common culture, language, and origin. He does not deny the existence of a religious community in antiquity whose members identified with the Israelites and tried to follow the laws of Moses, but this community cannot be described as a "people"—that is, the Jews were not a nation like the Germans or the French. They were adherents of a religion, like Christians or Buddhists—they shared beliefs and rituals—but they did not share common ancestors or come from the same place, and there was nothing to unite them as a kinship group or political entity: most were proselytes or the descendants of proselytes who inherited very different cultural traditions. The idea that the Jews constituted a "people," a race, a nation, or an ethnic group, did not arise until the nineteenth century, he argues,

and became a reality only as the result of a social-engineering process initiated by Zionist leaders and intellectuals.

Since Sand has complained of being misrepresented by critics,
here is his description of that process as he sums it up himself:

> To promote a homogenous collective in modern times, it was necessary
> to provide, among other things, a long narrative suggesting a connec-
> tion in time and space between the fathers and "the forefathers" of all
> the members of the present community. Since such a close connection,
> supposedly pulsing within the body of the nation, has never actually
> existed in any society, the agents of memory worked hard to invent it.
> With the help of archaeologists, historians, and anthropologists, a vari-
> ety of findings were collected. These were subjected to major cosmetic
> improvements carried out by essayists, journalists, and the authors
> of historical novels. From this surgically improved past emerged the
> proud and handsome portrait of the nation. (15)

Here we can see clearly the role of scholars in the process of inventing the Jewish people: the historians, archaeologists, and anthropologists who helped to create the narrative that supposedly connected Jews to their ancient ancestors in the biblical land of Israel.
A good portion of Sand's book is a survey of the intellectuals who
he says invented the Jewish people—the historians Heinrich Graetz,
Simon Dubnow, and Yitzhak Baer along with archaeologists like
Yigael Yadin and Yohanan Aharoni—scholars who assembled bits
and pieces from the past into a falsely unified and continuous account that stretched from antiquity to modern times. The problem
for these "agents of memory" is that history was different from the
narrative of continuity that they needed it to be for their political
aims. Present-day Jews were too fragmented and dispersed, coming
from too many different starting points and sharing too little in common physically and culturally to all come from the same ancestors or
homeland. Scholars overcame this problem by—there is no more accurate word for Sand's position—fabricating history, minimizing the
heterogeneity of the Jews by playing down the role of conversion as
an engine of Jewish demographic growth, and exaggerating the unifying experiences of Jewish history: the biblical age, the exile from
their homeland that followed the destruction of the Second Temple,
and other historical experiences that Jews supposedly shared.

This is why, from Sand's perspective, there is so much at stake in his own historiographical efforts; if the Jewish people was called into being through scholarship, it can be dispelled through such scholarship as well, and this is Sand's ultimate goal in *The Invention of the Jewish People*. His objective, in effect, is to uninvent the Jewish people by exposing the real history he accuses earlier historians of having suppressed, a step he believes is necessary if Israel is to become open to all of its citizens regardless of their ethnic or religious background.

We will address some of Sand's specific claims a bit later in the chapter, but one point should be acknowledged up front: much of his argument is a variation of how many contemporary scholars account for the origin of modern nations in general. A nation, as defined by the philosopher Ernest Gellner (1925–1995), is held together by two things—a common culture and an acknowledgment that the other is a fellow national with whom one shares certain mutual duties and rights as members of the same nation. This particular kind of self-perception, Gellner and other scholars argue, is a modern development. Gellner himself compared the nation to a navel-less Adam, by which he meant that there was nothing, or at least nothing essential, tying the nation to some premodern people or community; national identity emerged anew in the seventeenth and eighteenth centuries as a result of Europe's transition from an agrarian to an industrialized economy and the introduction of a standardized educational system. Benedict Anderson (1936–2015) explained the rise of nationalism somewhat differently, but he too saw it as a consequence of modernity, describing the nation as an "imagined community" that emerged as a consequence of capitalism, increased literacy, and modern technology. An actual community, he argued, is a small community held together by face-to-face encounters and personal relationships. A grouping like a nation is too large for this kind of interaction: most of its members will never meet each other; and their sense of themselves as part of a single community bound together by blood, common culture, and mutual obligation is perceptual, an act of collective self-imagining that became possible only when the invention of the printing press allowed for the dissemination of this collective self-image among a large and dispersed population.

This way of conceiving the history of the nation is related to another idea—the concept of the "invented tradition," a term coined by Eric Hobsbawm (1917–2012, one of Anderson's teachers) and Terence Ranger (1929–2015) to describe seemingly old but recently innovated customs and symbols that reinforce the nation's consciousness of unity and feeling of continuity with a distant and idealized past. The most oft-cited example from the book that introduces this idea, *The Invention of Tradition*—from an essay by the British historian Hugh Trevor-Roper—is the Scottish kilt woven in a tartan whose color and pattern signifies the wearer's clan. Its use as a symbol of Scottish national pride is only a few centuries old, Trevor-Roper shows, and its origin was entirely different from what people imagined, arising not from an ancient native Scottish population but from the clothing traditions of the Highlanders, a part of the population with Irish roots, and designed in the 1720s by an English Quaker, Thomas Rawlinson, who seems to have been the first one to actually use the term "kilt." How then did it become a symbol of a proudly native Scottishness? It was only in the nineteenth century, under the influence of nationalism, that it came to play this role. Thanks to the dubious history books of the brothers John Sobieski Stuart and Charles Edward Stewart (whose names were themselves a fiction), along with the efforts of writers like Sir Walter Scott, the kilt was given an ancient pedigree and spread to other parts of Scotland, where it was embraced as an expression of Scottish identity. This sort of invented tradition, the theory goes, is what allows a nation to conceal its novelty from itself.

Sand's argument is a variation of this theory of the nation's origin, which is probably why it garnered the endorsement of none other than Hobsbawm himself, the inventor of the invented tradition concept who welcomed Sand's book as a "much needed exercise in the dismantling of nationalist historical myth." But of course, to challenge a nation's sense of itself in this way is bound to trigger a strong reaction. Trevor-Roper's argument provoked a backlash from critics who accused the Englishman of "Scotophobia," a hatred of things Scottish, and the reaction to Sand's claims, lobbed into the midst of the ongoing Israeli-Palestinian conflict and sharp debates over the Jewish character of the state of Israel, was all the more intense. A number of Sand's fellow historians, though not always disagreeing with Sand's political vision of a secular and postethnic Israel, ridiculed the book for its sloppy and tendentious scholarship. As an example, Israel Bartal, a preeminent historian at the Hebrew University in Jerusalem, wrote in a review that he found the book embarrassing in its treatment of the historical sources, and he counseled critical readers not to overlook "the twisting of the rules governing the work of professional historians that result when ideology and methodology are mixed."

Sand's book created a significant stir, but the controversy it provoked needs to be placed in context. By the time of its publication, Israeli academia and the Israeli public had grown somewhat habituated to scholarship aiming to debunk the central foundation narratives of Jewish and Israeli society. For more than two decades, Israeli archaeologists had been challenging the historicity of biblical events like the Exodus and the kingdom of David. Hitting even closer to home was the work of the "New Historians." Israeli scholars like Benny Morris and Tom Segev published work in the 1980s and 1990s that challenged how Israelis remembered the war that established the state in 1948. Sand's argument went further than previous research in challenging Jewish identity itself, but it had to garner attention in a society already accustomed to having its identity challenged by revisionist scholarship. Certainly, the scholarly critics do not seem particularly scandalized by the book's thesis, just unpersuaded by it. The problem for them is that Sand seriously misrepresents the scholarship he claims to be reacting against, casting himself as a daring iconoclast for challenging positions that had never been argued by scholars to begin with or that, conversely, had long been broadly acknowledged. To quote Bartal again as an example, "no historian of the Jewish national movement has ever really believed that the origins of the Jews are ethnically and biologically 'pure'"—which runs contrary to Sand's suggestion that such a position was common among Zionist historians.

An example of the book's shortcomings is Sand's treatment of conversion. Sand's larger argument is basically equivalent to what is known in biology and linguistics as "polygenesis," the idea that a species or a language descends from multiple lineages or points of origin. There was a time when some scholars applied a polygenetic approach to the human species itself, explaining the

difference between white Europeans and black Africans by tracing them to different species of ape, an approach that was sometimes also applied to the Jews. Sand's approach does not involve
polygenetic thinking in a biological sense, but its embrace of the
"imagined community" model does commit it to another kind of
polygenetic understanding of the Jews. The Jewish people does not
descend from a small number of ancestors who have branched off
into different populations now spread across the globe: it began as
a heterogeneous population that was artificially re-formed as a single community under the influence of nationalism. To demonstrate
this point, Sand devotes a sizeable portion of *The Invention of the
Jewish People* to showing that Jews originated not from common
ancestors in the Middle East, from the Israelites of the Bible or
from the people of Judea in the Roman period, but from different,
dispersed, and genealogically unrelated communities whose only
connections to one another were the religious beliefs and practices
they shared. Stressing conversion as the major source of the Jewish
population is important to this part of Sand's argument as a way
to show that Jews do not share a common genealogy or come from
the same place.

In my own view, this part of Sand's argument is misconceived.
If what counts for a sense of ethnicity, peoplehood, or nationhood
is not actual descent but a group's subjective belief in a common
origin, I cannot see why it is germane to Sand's argument whether
or not Jews actually descend from common ancestors in a genetic
sense. What does seem relevant is the history of the *idea* of Jewish
peoplehood—where does this idea come from, and does it predate
the rise of nationalism or not? It seems to me that Sand should have
been thinking about these questions more carefully, and that what
he does instead—marshaling evidence to show that the majority of
Jews descend from various non-Jewish populations in North Africa, Arabia, and the Russian steppe—is at the very best beside the
point. Indeed, worse than that, it can be read as an endorsement of
a racialist conception of Jewishness, in the sense that it implies that
a Jewish population that does not all descend from ancestors who
were Jews does not thereby qualify as a genuine people or nation.

But for the sake of argument, let us accept Sand's logic and assume that it would undercut the concept of Jewish peoplehood

to show that, genealogically and genetically, Jews come from different ancestors indigenous to different parts of the world. Does Sand make his case from this perspective? No, not really. No one with any knowledge of the history of conversion in Judaism would deny that converts have been a part of the Jewish community since the Hellenistic-Roman period—the topic is a major focus of Shaye Cohen's work, for example—and there are even some known cases of mass conversion to Judaism by entire communities to support the idea that conversion was a significant factor in Jewish demographic growth. But Sand's thesis that the Jews have no unifying origin in antiquity leads him to stress the role of conversion in an exaggerated way.

Consider how Sand treats the origin of Ashkenazic Jews, Jews of Eastern European descent who now constitute a majority of the world's Jewish population. To demonstrate that Ashkenazic Jews do not originate from the Middle East—that is, that they do not descend from the Israelites or the Judeans of the Second Temple period—Sand dusts off an idea known as the Khazar theory, which claims that Ashkenazic Jews descend from a seminomadic Turkic people in southern Russia who converted to Judaism during the eighth century CE. Sand makes it appear as if scholars suppressed this hypothesis because it did not suit their Zionist agenda, but there is another explanation for why it has never gained much traction, and one that strikes me as more likely: it is just not that persuasive.

In a period lasting from the seventh century to the tenth, the Khazars ruled an empire that spanned the region between the Caspian and Black Seas; they left behind very little evidence and are mostly remembered today for the story that they converted to Judaism. Beginning in the nineteenth century, some scholars began to argue that Ashkenazic Jews descend from these converts, and the argument was picked up by various scholars over the course of the twentieth century. The scholar Abraham Pollack revived the theory in a book first published in Hebrew in 1944; various Russian language sources reference the story (Stalin himself seems to have been obsessed with it); the British Orientalist Douglas Morton Dunlop introduced the topic into mainstream English-language academic research in *The History of the Jewish Khazars* from 1954; and

Arthur Koestler's best-selling *The Thirteenth Tribe* from 1976 was the work that did the most to bring this idea to America. The Khazar theory has long been suspect among many scholars of Jewish history, because of its use in anti-Semitic and anti-Zionist polemics to attack the authenticity of Ashkenazic Jews and their connection to the land of Israel, but it is hard to say that it was ever suppressed. Bartal recalls that as a student he read about the Khazars in an encyclopedia consulted by almost every Israeli high school student in those days, and he even went back to check the reference to make sure his memory was correct: although the author of the encyclopedia article was unsure about how many Khazars had converted to Judaism, he describes the conversion as having important significance and requiring further research—an attitude hardly consistent with Sand's claim that Israeli scholars at the time were intent on expunging the episode from history.

What of the other possible explanation for the theory's marginalization: that it is just not a very good theory? A recent study by Shaul Stampfer, an expert in Eastern European Jewry, gives credence to such a possibility by reconsidering the Khazar theory and finding little evidence to support it. To be sure, there is nothing implausible about the idea that a Khazar king converted to Judaism in the eighth century CE, a story known to the medieval writer Yehuda Halevi and incorporated into his treatise *The Kuzari* from around 1140; but there is no firsthand evidence that can prove such an event took place. The story of the Khazar conversion surfaces only in sources from many centuries later, and there are no references to Khazar converts in any of the accounts written by Christians, Muslims, and Jews who visited Khazaria in the ninth and tenth centuries CE. Stampfer doubts that such a conversion ever happened, but even if it did, there is no way to show that it is the source of later Ashkenazic Jews—no way to know how large such a community was or what became of it after the fall of the Khazarian kingdom, and no sign of Turkic influence on the language and names of Eastern European Jews, as one would expect if they were the descendants of Turkic converts. There are, on the other hand, some compelling reasons to support the mainstream explanation for the origin of Ashkenazic Jews that Sand rejects, that their ancestors migrated to Eastern Europe not from the East but from

Western Europe, which expelled much of its Jewish population during the medieval period, and that the numbers of Ashkenazic Jews grew into the millions not because of a mass influx of converts but because of normal exponential demographic growth that can swell a population after a sufficient number of generations.

The problem with Sand's treatment of the Khazars is not just its one-sided representation of the evidence but the way he uses the theory to advance a certain representation of scholarship. I think it is fair to say, after everything we have seen in this book, that scholarship can be tendentious and blinkered in its perspective, but Sand's allegation of a scholarly plot to conceal the origin of the Jews does not jibe with reality: yes, one can point to how the ideologies of particular scholars shaped their work, but scholarship as a whole was not nearly as ideologically uniform as Sand would contend.

I do not see much point to speculating about why Sand would depict his scholarly predecessors in this way, but I would note that one of the reasons goes back to the model of national formation that he emulates. That approach to the origin of nations entails a top-down understanding of culture in which an intellectual elite— scholars, fiction writers, journalists, and others with the ability to shape people's thoughts and memories—creates a new form of self-identification that is then disseminated to the rest of the population. In other words, he is operating from an understanding of the nation that traces its formation to *inventors*, an intellectual elite with the know-how to engineer a certain form of identity, and Sand's effort to follow that model is at least part of the explanation for why scholars play such a central role in how he accounts for the origin of Jewish peoplehood.

The question I focus on in the rest of the chapter is whether it is possible, despite the glaring problems we have noted, that Sand has a point. Does the intellectual elite have the power or influence needed to reshape collective memory and identity in the top-down way this theory posits? We have struggled to locate the origin of the Jews in the ancient world. Does such an approach offer a way beyond that impasse by shifting the focus to the process of modern nation building? In the remainder of the chapter, I address these questions not by dwelling further on the shortcomings of Sand's argument, which his reviewers have done enough to expose, but

by reframing it as part of a larger debate over how nations originate. As we have noted, Sand comes from a particular school of
thought—the perspective associated with Gellner, Anderson, and
Hobsbawm—and the theory they introduced has been challenged
by more recent scholars who play down the novelty of the nation.
A review of this debate will help us to look beyond the particular
failings of Sand's argument, and to weigh the pros and cons of the
underlying model he builds on: the theory that *all* nations originated in modernity through acts of invention.

The Nation as Invention

What may be the most famous story of an invention in our own
day is the story of how Steve Jobs and Steve Wozniak invented the
Apple computer in a garage. According to the story as I have heard
it, Jobs and Wozniak manufactured the first fifty Apple I com-
puters in the garage of Job's childhood home in 1976. "It was just
the two of us," Jobs would later tell *Fortune* magazine during a tour
of the garage. "We were the manufacturing department, the ship-
ping department, everything." As has become clear in more recent
years, however, the story is not quite true. To be sure, there is a
real garage—the house at 2066 Crist Drive in Los Altos, California,
has been designated a historical landmark, and the first Apple I
computer sold from there was auctioned off in 2014 for $365,000—
but the story that it was created there, as Wozniak has recently
acknowledged, is a "bit of a myth": there was no design or manu-
facture there, and most of the work was done elsewhere. People
are drawn to the idea of a lone individual creating something new
through his own talent and heroic effort, but the truth behind the
garage story, as the business scholars Pino Audia and Chris Rider
have shown, reveals that inventions usually do not come out of the
blue that way; their inventors are usually indebted to earlier job
experiences and already existing organizations—what Wozniak and
Jobs learned from their time working for companies like Hewlett-
Packard and Atari, for example. The "garage legend," a variation of
the belief that something can be invented out of nothing, has led
many entrepreneurs astray, Audia and Rider argue, and would-be
inventors should attend more to what precedes the act of invention,

the history of earlier industries and social relationships from which it originates.

Although Sand does not understand the "invention" of the Jewish people as a heroic accomplishment, his narrative can be challenged on similar grounds. While there is plenty to criticize in Sand's account, what gives it its basic plausibility is the fact that it is simply applying a widely accepted model of nation formation to the Jewish people, the model championed by Gellner and many other scholars. But is the underlying model correct? Are nations "invented" out of scratch? The idea has certainly proven very influential—in fact, it is the dominant model for how to understand the rise of nations—but there are skeptics, scholars who contest its claim that nations are inherently modern and inherently fictitious.

The view of Gellner and others has since come to be known as the "constructivist" theory of nation: it tends to see nations as artificial, and very temporary. The opposing view, represented by scholars like John Armstrong, Anthony Smith, and Adrian Hastings, is described as "primordialism" or "perennialism," terms meant to convey the idea that the nation continues or emerges from something earlier. According to this perspective, the nation is not invented or created but grows, develops, or reawakens, a point primordialists try to demonstrate by tracing the antiquity of national identity, its persistence over a long period of time. From the constructivist perspective, the nation is artificial, mutable, and inherently modern. From the primordialist, it is natural, enduring, and ancient.

The constructivist view of the nation can be understood as a reaction to the primordialism of earlier racialized and Romanticized conceptions of ethnogenesis, but the modified primordialism of more recent scholarship is itself a reaction to constructivism, an effort to correct for what it regards as an exaggerated emphasis on the break between the modern and the premodern. It does not define the nation as an immutable entity that simply persists intact; its position, rather, is that the nation did not simply appear ex nihilo in modern times but emerged from premodern social relationships and forms of self-identity—that nations do indeed have navels that tie them to earlier ethnic groups. Part of what such scholars are trying to explain is why nationalism seems to have an enduring emotional grip on people that other modern ideologies like communism do not. As Anthony Smith notes, no amount of ideological indoctrination was able to instill an abiding feeling of identification with communism among the people of Eastern Europe even after fifty years, whereas nationalist sentiment persisted and even reasserted itself in a forceful way after the fall of communist rule. The primordialist answer for the enduring vitality of nationalism is that, in contrast to other ideologies like communism or liberalism, it builds on what Smith refers to as a "pre-existing framework of collective loyalties and identities."

One of the best examples of premodern nationalism, it turns out, is the Jews. Primordialists like Steven Grosby and Aviel Rosenwald have argued for the existence of a kind of nationalism among ancient Jews or Judeans, a sentiment defined not just by common religious commitment to the laws of Moses but by a strong sense of being part of a collective, of attachment to a particular place, and of sharing a common ancestry and history—all aspects of ancient Judean identity downplayed in Sand's account. One manifestation of this collective sentiment visible during the Second Temple period is reflected in the three annual festivals, Passover, Shavuot, and Sukkot, which drew thousands of pilgrims to Jerusalem every year. In the words of Philo of Alexandria, these were occasions when Jews who were otherwise strangers to one another were drawn together by a strong feeling of unity (*Special Laws* 1.70). That feeling of unity connected Judeans across their social, geographic, and class divisions, and it could express itself in a powerfully emotional way, stirring feelings of allegiance, obligation to fellow Judeans, protectiveness for the land of Judea, and self-sacrifice, as manifest during the Jewish revolt against the Romans, when many Judeans/Jews chose to die rather than surrender to the enemy. All this seems so similar to nationalism that the Jews are often cited in primordialist scholarship as a counterexample to the constructivist model, proof that nationalist sentiment need not be modern.

This debate between constructivists and primordialists, it should be emphasized, is not just about when the nation arose but about how. As we have noted, constructivists take a top-down approach to nationalism. It is initiated by an intellectual and political elite who use writing, technology, education, and civic rituals to instill a sense of national consciousness in a population otherwise fragmented.

The primordialists explain the feelings at work in nationalism in a very different way: those feelings are not manufactured but arise from naturally occurring emotions, the same feelings of attachment that we feel for our immediate family members now extended to a particular locality—the place where one is born—and backward in time to distant ancestors beyond one's parents and grandparents. A nation may not actually be that old, but the temporal extension of one's family relationships, the stretching of one's feeling of identification and attachment to distant generations, is what makes it *feel* primordial, something established long ago.

In contrast to constructivism, primordialism can explain why the nation elicits intense loyalty and self-sacrifice from people in a way that other ideologies cannot; at its base, it is rooted in the feelings we have for our closest kin and can thus elicit a similar intensity of attachment. This is also what allows primordialists to argue for the existence of the nation in premodern contexts. The changes wrought by modernity made it possible to stretch this intense feeling of attachment to a larger community beyond those one knows personally, but the process of identification involved does not require modernization because it arises from a common bonding process that develops within families and communities—the same process that leads other animals to favor their kin over nonkin.

In a certain sense, then, the difference between constructivism and primordialism corresponds to the difference between the artificial and the natural, and it is not surprising, therefore, that one of the things that primordialism objects to about constructivism, apart from its effort to make the nation very recent, is its use of the language of invention. In the past two or so decades, there have emerged a number of studies that have sought to emphasize the "limits" of invention, that is, they mean to minimize the plasticity of identity and tradition, to show that these are *not* things that people with power can simply make up or manipulate to advance their own interests.

We can illustrate this critique by looking at a response to the volume *The Invention of Tradition*, coedited by Hobsbawm and Ranger. In one of the essays in the volume, Ranger argues that the British who colonized Africa in the nineteenth century, looking to govern a population from a culture very different from their own, imported traditions from England and imposed them on their new subjects—harvest festivals, religious processions, an English conception of monarchic and customary rule. Ostensibly the colonizers were looking to respect local custom, but they were really inventing new traditions. Even the concept of the tribe was an invented tradition, Ranger argues. Prior to colonization, Africans did not belong to fixed tribes, participating in multiple social networks at the same time, and tribal affiliation was not as central to their identity as Europeans scholars supposed. It was actually colonization that froze the tribe into place as a rigidly bounded and hierarchical structure. While Ranger acknowledges that Africans tried to exert control over the newly created traditions for their own ends, for the most part he treats the invention of tradition as a tactic deployed by rulers to govern their subjects.

In an essay published twenty years later, Thomas Spear, a historian of Africa, called attention to a number of problems with this argument. (In fairness, he was preceded by an essay by Ranger, in which he expressed second thoughts about his own argument.) Spear counters that many of the traditions supposedly invented by Europeans actually built on indigenous precedents, and he strongly contests the assumption of African gullibility, passivity, and pliability. From his perspective tradition is not something the colonizers were able to fully control. Ill financed and poorly staffed, they were dependent on local authorities; their ability to innovate traditions was limited by what their subjects would recognize as legitimate; and they often acquiesced to practices they found objectionable, like witch doctoring, to avoid alienating the locals. European colonization had a significant impact on the customs of their subjects, changing them or giving them new meanings, but the colonizers did not create them from scratch, and they were far less able to manipulate tradition than scholars like Ranger assumed. For this reason, Spear concludes, it "makes little sense to talk about 'invention' in any meaningful sense of the word."

Some scholars have drawn a similar kind of conclusion about the invention of tradition in Israeli society. According to the perspective introduced by Hobsbawm and Ranger, the Zionist claim of continuity with the biblical past falls into the category of invented tradition: to quote Hobsbawm, "It is entirely illegitimate to identify the Jewish links with the ancestral land of Israel . . . with the desire to gather all Jews into a modern territorial state." But one does not have to conflate ancient and modern Israel to challenge the thesis that the link between them was an "invention" of an elite.

In a study that parallels Spear's treatment of African tradition, for example, Adam Rubin calls attention to the limits of invention in the Zionist community of prestate Palestine. Especially during the 1920s and 1930s, Zionist leaders grew anxious that they would be unable to integrate the flood of immigrants into the national community they were seeking to create. These migrants were coming to Palestine in great numbers not out of Zionist conviction but to escape persecution; they were an extremely heterogeneous population in terms of language, class, and religious background; many were still attached to the European cultures from which they had emigrated; and they lacked the national consciousness that was supposed to connect them to each other or to the Hebrew-speaking culture the Zionists were aiming to promote. In their efforts to address this challenge, Zionist leaders went to great lengths to foster a sense of a unified Hebrew culture, creating all manner of courses and publications, using radio and other media to broadcast their ideology, and creating new rituals to disseminate knowledge of Hebrew language and culture. Some even advocated for semicoercive measures to do so, calling for the ostracism of non–Hebrew speakers and the elimination of non-Hebrew publications. As heavy-handed as they were, however, these leaders did not simply impose their views. Although they themselves had rebelled against Eastern European Jewish life, the culture of Torah study, they realized they needed to embrace aspects of that culture if they were to reach the immigrants, and were thus compelled to recast their goals in the language of a religious tradition, the love of Torah, that was otherwise at odds with their secularism.

To some extent this case follows the model laid out by the nation as modern invention model—the Zionist leadership did try to inculcate a sense of nationhood that did not come naturally to the Jewish immigrants of the period. It is just that the concept of "invention" is not sufficient to convey the complexity of the process— the impediments and opposition that elites encounter when trying to impose a new tradition and that sometimes foil their efforts, and the ways in which they accommodate existing traditions. I do not want to push things too far in the opposite direction and minimize the impact of intellectual elites, but the work of Spear, Rubin, and other recent scholars suggests the inadequacy of the constructivist model as a way to understand the negotiation, the struggle, and the pushback that takes place between nationalists and the public they would turn into a nation.

In the light of this critique of constructivism, one can contest Sand's thesis even without having to call attention to its historiographical shortcomings. As an example, we can focus on one of the scholars whom Sand suggests is responsible for the invention of the Jewish people, the historian Ben-Zion Dinur (1884–1973). Dinur was one of the Zionist intellectuals concerned about creating a national consciousness among the new immigrants to Palestine. Rubin quotes a speech that Dinur gave at the Hebrew University in 1944, where he called for a way to unify the hodgepodge of discordant Jewish communities in Palestine that sometimes scarcely acknowledged each other as members of the same people:

> There are varying ethnic communities, classes, and standards of living, especially in the cities. The Ashkenazi doesn't consider the opinion of the Yemenite; the new immigrant that of the "sabra" [a Jew born in Israel or, at that point, Palestine]; neither of them that of the Polish Jews; the *halutzim* [Jews who migrated to Palestine during the final decades of the nineteenth century] disdain members of the Old Yishuv [Jews already in Palestine at the time of this immigration], while the latter sometimes doubt if the former are even part of *Kelal Yisra'el* [the macro-community of all Jews]. It is clear that there is no one public opinion, no uniform style of national life. . . . [I]t strikes me as comparable to a classroom of remedial education students abandoned by their teacher.

To address this situation, Dinur believed it was necessary to actively generate a sense of national consciousness among Jews, or as he might put it, to remind them of a history they had forgotten. As he wrote at a later point in his life: "If we want to be the heirs of the people of Israel, then we must instill those 4000 years of history into the heart of every person." The key, as suggested by Dinur's use of a classroom metaphor in the speech quoted above, was education, and he would go on to implement his ideas first as the head of the Jewish Teachers' Training College in Jerusalem from 1923 to 1948 and later as Israel's minister of education and culture between 1951 and 1955, in which capacity he endeavored to unify Israel's secular educational system, oversaw a redesign of the curriculum, and sought to shape public memory in various ways. Dinur qualifies as exactly the kind of intellectual required by the constructivist model, not only in his role as a scholar who emphasized the unity and continuity of the Jewish nation through his writing but as an educational leader and government minister in a position to actually institutionalize newly invented traditions.

And yet even someone with the influence of Dinur could not simply impose national consciousness in the way the nation-as-invention model requires. To begin with, it is not as if his efforts to shape Jewish collective memory were always successful. Having to work through a legislative process and a state bureaucracy raised obstacles, which is why some of his efforts to invent traditions—his proposal of secular Sabbath rituals and an Independence Day ritual modeled on the Passover seder, for example—were never implemented. Turning to his efforts as an education minister, it is true that he helped to impose state regulation over Israel's educational system, which remains centralized to this day under the control of an education minister who sets the goals of the national curriculum, but there are all kinds of ways that the impression of top-down control must be qualified and complicated. The situation Dinur was starting from was very disunified and discordant. Not only was there a difference between secular and religious education, and Jewish and Arab education, but there were even different secular education cultures within the Zionist movement—a "Labour" branch and a general education branch, teachers who wanted to emphasize national ideology and those who sought to minimize the impact of ideology—and he and subsequent education ministers have always had to contend with these or other differences. Indeed, the educational law Dinur introduced in 1953, which consolidated all these different streams into one system, was itself criticized across the ideological spectrum, the left fearing it gave too much influence to the right, the right, too much influence to the left. It was also criticized by fellow scholars: the philosopher of education

Zvi Adar (1917–1991) and fellow historians like Jacob Katz (1904–1998). While the law passed with the support of the centrist parties, the ideological differences did not simply disappear, resurfacing in a way that by the 1960s was beginning to fracture Dinur's plan to use education to foster unity.

We can illustrate this point by tracing the history of Israel's history curriculum. In 1956 Dinur published a Jewish history curriculum he developed that was meant to help ensure that the public would identify with "the glorious history of a People who was at the beginning 'one and unified.'" In their teaching of early Israelite history, for example, teachers were to emphasize "the unification of the tribes" in contrast to "the divisiveness of the Canaanites." Perhaps for a decade or two, such an approach generated the hoped-for unity, since there does not appear to have been much controversy about the history curriculum in the 1950s and 1960s, but then again, appearances can be deceiving. The new system largely left intact many of the divisions that had existed prior to the 1953 law. Those who designed the history curriculum eventually had to give up on creating common goals for the secular and religious education systems, and it became increasingly apparent that its Ashkenazic focus was exacerbating socioeconomic differences by treating in a dismissive way Jews who had emigrated from Arab countries (known as Mizrahi Jews) and Israeli Arabs. Tensions seemed to be boiling under the surface because, by 1968, the government realized it needed to do more to integrate Mizrahi and Ashkenazi students, though a reform plan was never fully implemented and may have even backfired, given research showing that Mizrahi alienation was only intensifying in the 1970s. For these and other reasons, fewer than twenty years after Dinur introduced his curriculum, history teachers were beginning to rethink the emphasis on national unity and began shifting their focus from building identification with the state to using history to develop analytic abilities.

When a new curriculum was introduced in 1975, for example, it still adhered to a Zionist narrative, but it played down the nationalism evident in the earlier curricula, and teachers were now advised to emphasize that "there are differing points of view that may be accepted, even in national matters." By the 1980s, as we have noted, Israeli historians were questioning the historical narratives that had been the touchstone of national consciousness, and even some of their ideas were making their way into the curriculum published in 1995. But it is not as if the reformers were simply able to impose their views either—the changes provoked a backlash from critics and government officials who saw them as anti-Zionist and sought to reassert the role of the school system as a way of cultivating national identity. Since around 2000, the school system has been lurching back and forth between the two educational approaches whenever the control of the government shifts from one party to the next. But that is precisely the point I am making—Israeli society has arguably always been too heterogeneous and too contentious for it ever to have been possible for an elite to simply impose a concept of unified Jewish peoplehood.

In the theory of nation formation advocated by the constructivists, the creation of a national consciousness *requires* the invention by intellectuals of a national historical narrative to foster the sense of unity, and the intervention of educators to change how people see themselves in relation to others. The efforts of Dinur would seem to bear out this thesis by showing that a consciousness of being part of a unified Jewish nation did not come naturally to the Jews who immigrated to Israel but was something that scholars and educators had to work to instill in them. At the same time, however, the mixed results of that effort, the opposition it provoked, and the attempts from within Israeli society to blunt or counter its nationalist agenda, illustrate the "limits" of such invention. Even as Dinur's plan for instilling national consciousness was being put into practice in the 1950s and early 1960s, there were evidently some who were alienated by such ideas. Sand himself was a student in the period when Dinur's history curriculum was being introduced, and clearly he did not learn from it the lessons he was intended to learn. (I cannot help but think that his strong aversion to the idea of the Jewish people comes from his own experience as a student in the school system that Dinur helped to bring into being—in one of his writings, *How I Stopped Being a Jew*, he even refers to his secondary school experience as a "nightmare.") While his hostility to the narrative that Dinur championed is certainly stronger than that of most Israelis, he was not the only one to try to break free from it: within a few decades, Israeli educators themselves were rethinking it and seeking more pluralistic alternatives.

My intention here is not to enter into the complex politics of Israeli education. My point is that the history of the idea of the Jewish people—the effort by scholars like Dinur to inculcate a sense of national identity—follows the constructivist model to some extent, but also illustrates one of the problems with this model: Intellectual elites are not in a position to simply impose their views on the public. They face opposition; scholars and educators do not agree among themselves; their efforts can provoke a backlash. It is true that states have significant power to impose changes on people's identity. They can divide people into ethnic categories, keep them separate educationally and politically, and use the educational system and civic rituals to try to instill solidarity. But even in the 1950s, when the State of Israel was perhaps most active in trying to consolidate the public's memory of its origin, the power of an official like Dinur was hemmed in by opposition from various ideological camps and by political and institutional constraints. The constructivist model requires a constructor—the intellectual, the teacher, the writer—who can summon the nation into being through ideas and words. Such a portrait is an exaggeration according to those critical of constructivism: the intelligentsia does not have as much control as this view ascribes to it, and it must often resort to negotiation, adjustment, and compromise.

To acknowledge the problems with constructivism is not to endorse primordialism, however, which is vulnerable to its own fair share of criticism. There have been many attempts to combine or compromise between constructivism and primordialism, but most accounts still fall into one camp or the other, and although the constructivist account of nations appears more popular among scholars than primordialism, the two approaches remain in a kind of standoff, rival explanations that expose one another's weaknesses but that cannot quite get the better of the other. We find ourselves stuck in yet another impasse. Because scholars have not resolved the larger debate over the origin of nations, and because no alternative way of thinking about the question has yet to supersede the constructivist and primordialist models as the basic options, there appears to be no way in the foreseeable future to finally resolve the debate over the origin of the Jewish people.

Choosing between Constructivism and Primordialism

If we cannot resolve the difference between constructivism and primordialism, and there is no clear path beyond them, perhaps we can at least gain some understanding of why scholars embrace one model over the other. In recent years there has been some attention to this question, and such research suggest that the reasons go beyond the intellectual arguments for and against each position. A scholar's preference for one approach over the other might be preconditioned by her or his background. Exploring the different explanations for why some scholars are constructivists and others are primordialists will not help us make a final judgment about whether the Jewish nation is a modern invention or not, but it may help us understand why different theories appeal to different people.

One way to understand the different preferences of scholars is geography: perhaps scholars from different cultures are drawn to one theory or another. The political scientist Adeed Dawisha argues something to this effect when he proposes that constructivism and primordialism arise from two distinct national traditions—an Anglo-French conception of nationhood and a German one. Dawisha argues that intellectuals from France and England, going back to the eighteenth century, tended to see the nation as a creation of the state. Neither the English nor the French originated from a homogeneous ethnic or linguistic population: they owed their sense of national unity to relatively powerful monarchies that had worked to impose unity, and this history encouraged thinkers to conceive the nation as an artificial construct brought about through state intervention. For German thinkers, on the other hand, the nation was an organic and naturally developing entity that had developed over a long period of time without the intervention of a state. For the French and the English, the nation existed by dint of a people's desire to continue a common life—the nation was a "daily referendum," in the famous phrase of the French nationalist Ernest Renan, and it could therefore be altered or go extinct if that was the will of the people. For German thinkers, the nation was rooted in nature, an expression of a common spirit that existed long before the rise of a unified state in Germany, a view that reflected the fact that the German sense of nationhood did in fact predate a unified German state, which did not exist until Bismarck's Prussia absorbed the other German states in 1871. Perhaps the difference between constructivists and primordialists comes down to whether they inherited an Anglo-French conception of nationhood or a German one.

One problem with such an explanation, however, is that it is not clear that Anglo-French and German nationalism can be distinguished so neatly—there are primordialist elements in French and English nationalism and constructivist elements in German nationalism, and certainly both strains can be found in Jewish nationalism. From Sand's book one might get the impression that Zionism was strictly primordialist, since it asserts the existence of a nation that has existed since ancient times, but Zionism also has a constructivist dimension, the kind that recognizes nationalism as a product of state intervention. Dinur was among those who combined both kinds of nationalism. While his view of the Jewish nation was clearly primordialist, casting it as something that had persisted throughout two thousand years of exile, he was also a constructivist to the extent that he recognized that the feeling of being a unified people was something that had to be created through top-down intervention. The continuity between the biblical past and the present existed only to the extent that Jews were aware of it. It was there to be found if one studied Jewish history, but one had to study that history to recognize it. The Jews had to be taught to be conscious of themselves as a nation. Hence the importance for Dinur of education, a way of instilling in a heterogeneous population not just the necessary historical knowledge but the feeling of identification and attachment required for individuals to awaken to their past, to feel themselves a part of the nation.

Another way to understand the preferences of scholars is to situate them in the light of their personal backgrounds and life experiences. A number of scholars have noted that some of the most important advocates of the constructivist theory have a similar background—they were Jews forced by the Nazis or other circumstances to move from one place to another, and their life stories and personal circumstances gave them reason to be suspicious of nationalism. An example is Ernest Gellner, who was born in Paris to Jewish parents from Bohemia, grew up in Prague, was driven by the Nazi threat to England, returned to Czechoslovakia later in the war, and eventually went back to England. The biographer John Hall speculates that his emphasis on the falsity of nationalism reflected his reaction as a Jew to the false charges against the Jews characteristic of many nationalist movements. Another scholar suggests that his constructivist leanings might have been shaped by his experience as a migrant who had to change his own identity several times over the course of his youth. A similar approach might be applied to Eric Hobsbawm, who was born to European Jewish parents in Alexandria, Egypt, and grew up in Austria and Germany before moving to England in 1933, the year Hitler came to power. His name should have been "Hobsbaum"—the spelling of his name was due to a clerical error on his birth certificate—but Hobsbawm embraced the change because, as he writes in his autobiography, it made it easier for him to live as a "non-Jewish Jew." Hobsbawm would go on to shun ethnic or religious particularism, becoming a lifelong cosmopolitan, and that view, reinforced by what he suffered at the hands of German nationalism and by his communist beliefs, is reflected in how he accounts for the origin of the nation, an account that casts the nation as a form of false consciousness that needs to be overcome.

If we were so inclined, we could apply a similar approach to other advocates of constructivism—the British historian Elie Kedourie (1926–1992), perhaps the earliest advocate of the nation as invention thesis, who was born to an Iraqi Jewish family, or Sand himself, born in a displaced person's camp in Austria to a non-Jewish father and Jewish mother. Is it relevant for understanding why these scholars were drawn to constructivism that they were exiles who never fully identified with nationalism or that they suffered at the hands of the most extreme form of nationalism?

Adding some credence to this possibility is a study conducted by a team of psychologists led by the late Peter Weinreich (1940–2016), which was an attempt to apply a social-psychological approach to the question of why some people are inclined to a primordialist position while others are not. Applying what Weinreich called Identity Structure Analysis, a way of understanding identity formation, they conclude in brief that people acquire primordialist sentiments early on as a part of the normal development of their identity, developing these feelings as an extension of the attachments they feel toward family members, but that some people go on to develop what they call "situationalism"—more or less a constructivist view of the nation—as a result of certain life experiences that lead them to question their primordialist feelings. Such experiences can include moving from one place to another or living in a state ruled by a succession of different nationalities, experiences that might lead a person to recognize that nations are not permanent realities, that they change over time, or that there is a way to identify oneself that goes beyond the nation. By applying this analysis to Gellner and Hobsbawm, we might argue that it was their experiences as outsiders or victims of nationalism gone amok that dislodged them from primordialist sentiment and set them on their way to constructivism.

Of course, it is a tricky business figuring out how scholars' biographies colored their scholarly conclusions, and there are other ways to understand a scholar's preference for one view over the other, such as politics, and more specifically in the case of the Jews, the politics of Jewish nationalism. In the case of a thinker like Hobsbawm, for example, there is clearly a connection between his constructivism and his anti-Zionism. For the cosmopolitan Hobsbawm, Zionism represented everything that was false and destructive about nationalism. There are other reasons to think that Zionism and its legitimacy are somewhere behind the position of other historians of the nation as well. The Middle East analyst Jonathan Spyer undertook a study of the primordialist-constructivist debate in Israel and found a striking correlation between the intellectual orientation of scholars and their political views. Primordialism appealed to Israeli scholars seeking to defend Jewish nationalism, those who believe it is a legitimate component of Israeli political life and want to see such nationalism endure; whereas constructivism is the model of choice for scholars who believe that Jewish nationalism is at odds with democracy and needs to come to an end. In Israel at least, the choice to be primordialist or constructivist is often tied to whether one is on the right or the left of the political spectrum, whether one embraces Zionism as integral to the State of Israel or advocates for a postnationalist conception of the state.

Spyer published this study before Sand published *The Invention of the Jewish People*, but it fits into this picture perfectly. Sand is quite forthright in saying that his goal is to support the rise of a postnational state that will include all its citizens equally, Jews and non-Jews. He rejects the primordialist conception of nationhood as racist, even going so far as to renounce his own Jewishness for that reason, and wants to see an Israel that undergoes the same transformation, becoming de-ethnicized. We do not need Spyer's analysis to see the politics at work in Sand's choice to follow a constructivist model.

There are thus at least two possible explanations for the embrace of a constructivist model, biographical and political, but a closer look suggests they need not be exclusive of the other. For as Weinreich and his colleagues note, the difference between a primordialist and a "situationalist" (i.e., constructivist) perspective correlates with different political views: those subjects who showed primordialist sentiments often empathized with nationalist parties, while "situationalists" tended to hold a far lower view of such parties. That aspect of their research suggests constructivism and post- or anti-Zionism may correlate with each other not because one comes from the other but because they both arise from a common psychological source—formative experiences in the scholars' backgrounds that shake them out of the primordialism to which they might otherwise have been predisposed.

There is little psychological research into what motivates scholars to hold the views they do. If there is anything to what Weinreich and his colleagues were suggesting, however, the debate between these positions—that is, the reason some scholars hold a constructivist view and others are primordialist—is not entirely rational, to the extent that the predisposition to hold one view or the other is rooted in experiences that precondition the direction in which reason develops. We have been pursuing the origin of the Jews as if it is a question to be resolved by weighing the different approaches and choosing among them, but our judgment about what qualifies as right, why one way of thinking seems more plausible to a given scholar than another, comes from a place we do not fully understand. It would take a very different kind of search for origin to illumine it: an inquiry into the prerational origin of how we think about origins.

CHAPTER EIGHT

Source Codes

THE GENETIC SEARCH FOR FOUNDERS

If the Romans hadn't commemorated their victory
In the Arch of Titus, we wouldn't know
The shape of the menorah from the Temple.
But the shape of the Jews we know,
Because they begat, and begat right up until me.

—YEHUDA AMICHAI

IN THE PAST few years, there has emerged a new form of primordialism that aims to push the origin of human history back into a
remote age. Most historians confine their study of the past to the
period of time that can be documented by textual sources, the past
four thousand years or so. The new primordialism pushes into a
much earlier period by using DNA and the brain's evolutionary
history to reconstruct demographic history, ancient social interaction, and other insights that illumine where people come from
and how they have evolved. We have seen that going back into the
distant past is not new in the study of the origin of the Jews. In
the nineteenth century linguistic paleontologists traced the origin
of the Jews to prehistoric Semites. The new primordialists should
not be confused with such scholarship, beginning with different assumptions and enlisting much more refined scientific methods, but
they have revived the project of tracing long-term continuities by

introducing new ways of recovering the ancestors of the Jews and tracing what they have bequeathed to later generations.

What made this new approach to the origin of the Jews possible is the field of population genetics, the branch of biology that studies the genetic composition of specific groups of people and the changes in that composition that arise over time—a field that has its roots in the early twentieth century but that has seen some dramatic advances in the seventy years since the discovery of the structure of DNA in 1953. This chapter summarizes what this research has revealed about the ancestry of the Jews, considers the critique of this research that has emerged in the past fifteen years or so, and broaches the question of whether a genetic approach offers a viable alternative to the constructivism that shapes how many contemporary scholars approach the question of the origin of the Jews.

If it is not obvious, I should acknowledge up front that I am not a geneticist and cannot claim any expertise in a field that requires rigorous scientific, mathematical, and computational training. What follows is from the perspective of an outsider to the field who is curious about its implications for the search we are trying to follow. I would note only that it is informed not just by reading but by direct engagement with geneticists involved in this kind of research, especially Noah Rosenberg, a population geneticist at Stanford University, whose work uses statistical methods, mathematical theory, and computer simulations to address various questions in human genetics and evolutionary biology. Rosenberg cannot be held accountable for any mistakes I have made in the following account, but he has helped me to overcome some of my ignorance and preconceptions. The critique of this kind of research has been sharp, to the point of questioning its legitimacy with suggestions that it is an attempt to revive the racialized understanding of Jewishness associated with Nazism. I describe the debate in as balanced a way as I can, taking the arguments of both sides seriously.

A Crash Course in Genetic History

Genomics is the study of genetic variation on a large scale across many different organisms. The field has been rapidly developing in the past few decades as it has improved its ability to follow the precise order of nucleotides within the DNA molecule and expanded its data set through large-scale testing. As a result geneticists have begun to construct a genetic history for the whole human species that illumines early humans' migration out of Africa and across the globe, and registers genetic mixing between different populations. Some observations fit with events known from historical sources, but many go beyond anything recorded in written sources, shedding new light on the history of human mating, population growth, migration, and other aspects of human evolutionary and demographic development. Jewish communities from around the world are among the populations studied in this way; indeed, they are one of the most intensively studied populations, and research in the past few decades has led to a number of new claims about their ancestry and geographic origin. To learn what such research has to say about the origin of the Jews—and more fundamentally, to understand how it is that a population's origin can be registered in a cell—it will help to situate them within a broader genetic history of human beings.

When the Human Genome Project—an international effort to map all of the twenty thousand or so genes in the human genome—was completed in 2003, the director of the project, Francis Sellers Collins, described the genome as a "history book, a narrative of the journey of our species through time." That narrative, crudely speaking, would tell something like the following story: At some point between one hundred and two hundred thousand years ago, there emerged in sub-Saharan Africa the ancestors of present-day humans, people who had to migrate as their numbers increased, conflicts emerged, or the environment pushed them out of one area and into another. For many thousands of years afterward, those migrations occurred within the continent of Africa, but then humans began moving outward from there, into the Middle East, Europe, and eventually reaching even remote places like Australia by around fifty thousand years ago. As they migrated from one place to another, people came to settle on different sides of geographical barriers that prevented interaction—mountain ranges, deserts, and bodies of water that made it difficult for people on either side of these barriers to meet and mate. Groups could also segregate themselves by avoiding contact with each other and mating only within their family or community, a practice anthropologists refer to as "endogamy."

It is this separation among different human groups that allowed them to develop in different directions, as reflected in the growing diversification of languages over the course of human history. Historical linguists have found that geographical separation, along with social separation, produces linguistic divergence relatively quickly. Within about six thousand years—two hundred generations, if one assumes the average time between two generations in a lineage to be about thirty years—proto-Indo-European has given rise to most of Europe's languages, along with languages in India and Central Asia. A similar process of diversification was taking place invisibly within the human cell as people migrated throughout Africa, and then eventually left Africa and spread to other parts of the world: over the centuries, the common genetic inheritance bequeathed to them by their common ancestors began to evolve in divergent directions as people separated from each other.

How exactly did this diversification take place? DNA molecules produce two identical copies of themselves. The process of copying is governed by proofreading mechanisms to make sure the copies are faithful to the originals, but sometimes copying mistakes sneak through, mutations that change the genetic composition of a person in usually biologically inconsequential ways but that add up over the generations in ways that can distinguish the genetic composition of those who come from one group from those coming from another group. (I say "usually" because such mutations can sometimes affect protein production in a way that leads to disease or some other change in the physical characteristics of an organism.) Geneticists represent the four chemical bases that make up a DNA sequence as the letters G (guanine), A (adenine), C (cytosine), and T (thymine), which are paired up with each other in various combinations. DNA has the capacity to replicate itself, decoupling the two strands of its double helix structure that each serves as templates for new strands that are combined with the original stands in two new DNA molecules. There are "proofreading" mechanisms that make sure there are no mistakes in the copied strands of DNA, but like the scribal mistakes that inevitably occur during the copying of a manuscript, there can be mistakes in the copying of DNA, the skipping or accidental repetition of chemical pairings that compose the DNA sequence—this is what is referred to as a "genetic mutation." Such mutations happen all the time, and rarely have an actual impact on the organism's health or its evolutionary development, but they mark the copy as ever so slightly different from its predecessor. Over the generations, as the replication process cycles on, these mutations accumulate, showing up at various points along the genome (a complete set of DNA sequences derived from the chromosome of a given species), just as scribal mistakes accumulate in a text as it is copied again and again. Not enough time has passed from an evolutionary perspective for different human populations to diverge genetically very much, even those who have had no contact with each other for thousands of years, but mutations happen with such frequency that even though, as confirmed by the Human Genome Project, the DNA sequence in humans is 99.9 percent the same in every individual, no two humans are exactly the same genetically.

It is that 0.1 percent of difference that is relevant to our story, because the analysis of these mutations is so precise now that genetics can identify within this small difference the divergent genetic histories of different populations. A mutation that begins within a single individual can spread throughout a population as that person mates, has children, and becomes the ancestor of multiple descendants, expanding into the population of a whole village or a specific geographic region. On the other hand, the barriers that separate populations from one another—the distance between communities settled far apart from one another, a mountain that impedes movement back and forth, the communication barrier that exists between people who speak different languages, or endogamy or other practices that restrict mating choices—can confine that mutation to a particular population, over time giving it a slightly distinctive genetic profile relative to other populations.

The separation between different populations was never complete enough, nor has there been enough time, from an evolutionary perspective, for the differences to make much of an impact on the common genetic profile that human beings share, and of course there have been innumerable migrations and other events that blur and complicate the picture. But even so, people's genetic ancestry leaves traces that allow scientists today not only to disentangle discrete genetic histories for different populations but also to discern genetic interconnections—for example, to connect the ancestry of individuals to particular geographic regions by matching their DNA to that of the modern population living in that region. One study in this vein, which was based on a sample of three thousand Europeans, found that it was able to correctly predict in this way the country of origin for individuals within a few hundred kilometers. In another recent study of two hundred Sardinian villagers, the researchers claim to have been able to use DNA analysis to correctly place 25 percent of them within their home villages and most of the rest within fifty kilometers of their village.

This capacity to connect people to presumed ancestors in the past, and to specific parts of the world, is what makes this kind of research relevant for understanding the origin of the Jews. Many Jews are born into their identity as Jews, inheriting their parents' DNA and thus what their parents inherited from their parents. What might the testimony of DNA tell us about the origins of Jewish communities? Do Jews share a common ancestry, as many have long believed? The field of population genetics has now reached a point where it is able to address these questions, not only producing many new studies of Jewish populations in different parts of the world but beginning to synthesize the resulting data into a larger picture, a genetic map of the worldwide Jewish population. What is emerging from such research is a genetic history of the Jews, a history that begins with certain small founding populations in prehistory or antiquity and develops through centuries of mating choices, population bottlenecks, migrations, and admixtures with other populations.

A good part of what follows in this chapter is a review of what this recent research has revealed about the origin of the Jews, but before we get to that, I take a step backward to situate the current research within a bigger history of its own. The methods of analysis being used today are of recent vintage, but current genetics research builds on earlier scholarship that goes back to the eighteenth century, scholarship that introduced some of the questions geneticists seek to address but failed to answer them in a convincing way. To fully appreciate what is new about current research, we need to understand how it is different from this earlier research conceptually, methodologically, and ethically. But there is a second reason to consider this history as well. In the final part of the chapter, we will be considering scholarly resistance to the genetic study of Jewish origins, a critique that has emerged from the fields of anthropology and the history of science. Part of the argument against such research is that genetics is reviving the scientific racism of nineteenth- and early twentieth-century scholarship, the kind of thinking used to justify the eugenics policies of the Nazis. To weigh the potential of genetics research as a way to understand the origin of the Jews, we need to factor in this disturbing history.

Biological Approaches to the Origin of the Jews

A biological approach to the question of Jewish origin predates the rise of genetics, but it is an open question where exactly to begin the history of this approach. Some would trace the origin of this approach to the period of the Spanish Inquisition in the fifteenth century, when Jewishness and Jewish traits were first conceived as something transmitted through "blood" relations, and when we have what are arguably the first race theories that attributed the distinctive qualities of the Jews to biological factors. Our focus here, however, is on the scientific study of the Jews, and that approach was developed in the eighteenth and nineteenth centuries, when biological inheritance in general became the subject of scientific inquiry. It was in this period, in the heyday of developmental thinking, that scientists began to treat the differences among humans on the model of how evolutionary biologists were seeking to understand the differences among animal and plant species, undertaking comparisons of different populations, amassing measurements and statistics, and trying to explain the differences in light of the developmental theories that were in consideration at the time.

The prehistory of genetic research, as it were, is the race science that developed in the eighteenth and nineteenth centuries and mostly relied on the methods of physical anthropology to address its questions. The German naturalist Johann Friedrich Blumenbach, briefly introduced in chapter 3, is considered the founder of this field, one of the first scholars to use science to understand human diversity. In contradistinction to the polygenism (the idea that humans developed independently from several unrelated ancestors) that some championed at his time, Blumenbach was a monogenist, believing that human beings were all members of one species. Within that species, however, he divided humans into five gradations or races distinguished by characteristics that he attributed to the effects of environment: Caucasians from Europe (known by that term because Blumenbach believed humans originated in the region of the Caucasus Mountains, in the zone between Europe and Asia) and four degenerated races, divided by geography and appearance, that had developed after humans moved to other regions, whom Blumenbach referred to as Mongolians, Ethiopians, Americans, and Malays. The Jews did not fit into his scheme very neatly. Blumenbach classified them with Caucasians, but he could not figure out why the traits that he thought distinguished the Jews from other Caucasians—traits supposedly acquired from their time in the East—had not disappeared when they moved to other environments. In many ways, Blumenbach's thinking was the opposite of what we might call racism. He thought humans were separated only by environment, not by inherent biological differences, and recognized there were many gradations between the admittedly arbitrary categories into which he sorted people. But he is remembered for introducing race as a scientific category and for pioneering the use of physical anthropology—especially the measurement of skull shape and size—that later scientists would rely on to sort peoples into racial types. Some would draw a direct line from his theories to genetic research, which, though it now rejects the category of race, is also concerned to measure and account for human biological variation and was even still using some of the racial categories introduced by Blumenbach ("Caucasoid," "Negroid," and "Mongoloid") into the 1980s.

By the second half of the nineteenth century, the conception of the Jews as a biologically distinct race had become widespread among scientists in Europe and the United States. Darwin's cousin Francis Galton (1822–1911) was a master of this kind of research, developing the use of large-scale data collection and statistical methods to establish and measure variation among humans. Among the techniques he applied in his work was composite photography, which, at the suggestion of his Australian Jewish student Joseph Jacobs (1854–1916), he used to help identify what he took to be the distinguishing characteristics of the Jews. Jacobs himself

FIGURE 7. Figurine found in Egypt by the archaeologist Sir Flinders Petrie and identified as a "Hebrew" based on the face's supposed physical resemblance to present-day Jews. *Source*: UC #33278. Reproduced courtesy of the Petrie Museum of Egyptian Archaeology, University College London.

would go on to use these photographs to argue for a common racial inheritance among Jews that had survived intact despite their dispersion to different parts of the world. A few tried to use archaeological evidence as well: the physician Cesare Lombroso (1835–1909), now remembered for his efforts to explain criminality as a result of physical and mental degeneration, took measurements of five putatively Jewish skulls found in a catacomb of Rome, believing they came from before the period of racial mixing; and Galton himself supported the work of the archaeologist Flinders Petrie in the hope that his study of ancient skulls and human figurines might show the persistence of racial traits from antiquity to the present (see Figure 7).

There were scholars in this period who rejected the classification of the Jews as a race. In a 1911 study of the subject, *The Jews: A Study of Race and Environment*, which was based on an analysis of Jewish immigrants in New York City as a sampling of the world-wide Jewish population, the physical anthropologist Maurice Fishberg (1872–1934) found so much physical heterogeneity among Jews from different regions that it made no sense to him to describe the Jews as a race. In the light of the evidence, he concluded,

> [T]he question of the origin of the Jewish "race" loses its significance. It is immaterial whether they were a homogenous ethnic type in their home in Palestine, or whether at the time of their consolidation into a national unit they were already a conglomeration of the diverse racial elements common at the time in Egypt, Palestine, Asia Minor and Mesopotamia. Nor is it important in this connection to make a pedantic effort to trace "the cradle of the Semites," as has been done by many authors, with the view to determining whether the ancient Hebrews were of Asiatic or African racial type.

What physical differences there were between Jews and non-Jews in a particular place were "less then skin deep," mostly the result of differences in dress and deportment and the social and economic differences between Jews and non-Jews. Franz Boas reached a similar conclusion in his study of Jewish immigrants in New York City, also arguing that it was impossible to distinguish Jews from non-Jews on biological grounds.

Boas, who would become one of the most important opponents of race science and racism in general, would go on to recognize that racial difference was in the eye of the beholder, that such difference was not based on real morphological differences but depended on the perceptions of the observer. The influence of his ideas helped to dismantle race as a scientifically valid explanation for human difference. But it is important to note that Fishberg and Boas reached these conclusions through the same research methods used by other scholars to argue that the Jews were a distinct racial type: the identification and measurement of physical and mental traits believed to be racially distinctive, statistical averaging to establish an ideal type, and comparisons with other racial types to measure the impact of interbreeding and environmental adaptation. Their research was criticized by scholars who believed that more precise methods might reestablish the stability of racial differences. This was the argument of Geoffrey Morant (1899–1964) and Otto

Samson (1900–1976), for example, in a study published in 1936, and they were by no means the only holdouts for an understanding of the Jews as a race (lest one judge Morant and Samson too harshly for defending the concept of race, it should be noted that the former was opposed to racism, later retracting his views on racial typologies, and the latter was a Jewish refugee from Nazi Germany). Despite mounting evidence that race science was an intellectual dead end, scholars continued to use its methods to reconstruct the racial history of the Jews, if not to identify them as a specific race, then to ascribe their physical and mental traits to racial mixing.

Of course nowhere was there more interest in this kind of research than in Nazi Germany. A notorious example is the German anthropologist Hans F. K. Günther (1891–1968), who played a major role in shaping the racial thinking of the Nazi Party. (Hitler owned six books by Günther and personally attended a lecture he gave at the University of Jena.) In a way Günther's conclusion was not that different from that of Fishberg and Boas; he too believed that the Jews did not descend from one particular race, but he put a very different spin on that observation. According to his analysis, the Jews descended from various non-European races, especially a Near Eastern race marked not only by distinctive physical traits—short heads, broad faces, excessive body hair, a distinctive nasal geometry, a certain smell—but also by ungovernability and a "commercial spirit." Racial mixing had fused these traits with those of other races in a way that could make them hard to recognize, but they could still be detected in present-day Jews, especially in their gestures and how they talked. Whereas Fishberg and Boas had concluded from such mixture that it made no sense to refer to the Jews as a race, Günther described the Jews as a hybrid *Volk*—not a race but a partially deracinated people—and for him that history explained why the Jews were a threat to Germans: continued racial mixing between Jews and Germans would further dilute the qualities that the German *Volk* had inherited from its Nordic ancestors (see Figure 8).

The Holocaust and the defeat of the Nazis discredited such research, and we are now in a position to recognize the absurdity of the reasoning involved, which depended on highly impressionistic and often anti-Semitic generalizations about what Jews looked like

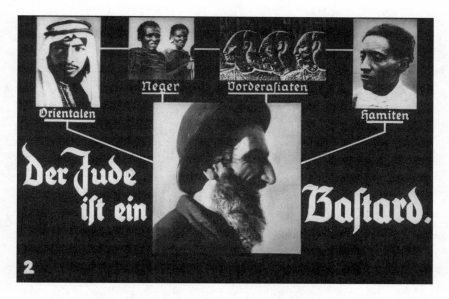

FIGURE 8. A Nazi propaganda slide of a Hitler Youth educational
presentation titled "Germany Overcomes Jewry," used to illustrate
the supposedly "bastardized" racial ancestry of the Jews.
Source: Copyright United States Holocaust Memorial Museum,
courtesy of Stephen Glick.

and how they behaved. But there is continuity between this earlier
race science and later genetic research. For one thing, it is not possible to draw a clear boundary between genetics and race science
prior to World War II: the study of human genetics, which began
in earnest after the rediscovery of Gregor Mendel's laws of inheritance in the early twentieth century, was another tool that a race
scientist or eugenicist might use, not replacing but supplementing
methods like anthropometrics, linguistics, and others used to understand the difference and interaction among different races. An
example is a study published in 1932 by Nicholas Kossovitch, the
leading blood-group anthropologist in France, which sought to address the question of the origin of modern Jews by undertaking
comparative blood analysis of the Jews in various locales. Blood
groups are different types of blood classified according to the presence or absence of inherited proteins and sugars on the surface
of red blood cells; they were relied on by geneticists to trace patterns of genetic inheritance until the final decades of the twentieth

century. (The scientists who established the heritability of blood groups based on research done during World War I, a Polish Jewish convert to Christianity named Ludwik Hirszfeld and his wife, Hannah, were later forced to move to the Warsaw Ghetto, where Hirszfeld organized antiepidemic measures before escaping with his family.) In retrospect, Kossovitch's work exemplifies a period of transition between race science to genetics: he used the kind of serological analysis of blood types that would continue to be used in postwar genetic studies, but he combined that with cranial measurements and other anthropometric observations typical of earlier race science, and framed his research in light of the racial theory of his day, casting his work as a response to the question, "Are modern Jews a race?"

Although Kossovitch's results also called into question the idea of the Jews as a biologically distinct group, the affinity between genetics and race science helps to explain the close alliance that was developing between geneticists and Nazis at the time of his study. In a recent history of that alliance, Sheila Faith Weiss argues that one reason German geneticists were drawn to the Nazis is that it was the one political party in Germany that made race—and hence inheritance—a focus. At a time when funding was scarce for genetics research, the Nazis provided them institutional support, and in turn, geneticists provided the Nazis with cutting-edge data that seemed to support their eugenics policies. One of the most infamous scientists associated with the Nazis' extermination of the Jews, Josef Mengele (1911–1979), was a genetics researcher who conducted his horrifying experiments on twins and other prisoners in Auschwitz with funding he secured with help from the director of the Kaiser Wilhelm Institute for Anthropology, Human Heredity and Genetics, Otmar Freiherr von Verschuer (1896–1969), who seems to have received blood samples for his laboratory in return. Such figures did not simply disappear after World War II. Günther, for example, continued to publish works that promoted voluntary sterilization and other eugenics practices into the late 1950s, and von Verschuer would go on to secure an important research position after the war. (Despite his suspicions, the investigator in charge of his case could not find enough evidence to prosecute von Verschuer as a Nazi collaborator; he was fined for his actions but not imprisoned, and was later granted a prestigious professorship at the University of Munich, where he founded an important center for genetics research.)

Indeed, it wasn't just specific researchers who continued on after the war; the race concept itself did not exactly vanish from the research either. After World War II there was a debate among scientists about the validity of race as a biological category, and it continued to be deployed in some genetics research into the following decades, as in the work of the Columbia University geneticist Theodosius Dobzhansky (1900–1975), a campaigner against racism but also an advocate for an updated concept of race. Even today, while certainly no one would defend the concept of race the Nazis had in mind, there is a debate among geneticists about the validity of using race as a way to describe genetic diversity: Geneticists know that the science does not support classifying humans into races, and many avoid such a categorization. Yet they argue that the use of racial categories as a shorthand description for differences among different populations can serve as a medically beneficial way to focus testing and treatment for genetically related diseases on the populations where such diseases are most common—a kind of practical and ethical argument. Critics argue, however, that such practice perpetuates racial thinking, and that such thinking continues to shape the research in less obvious ways.

We will return to that critique shortly, but it also needs to be noted that, as a field, postwar genetics worked hard to distance itself from race science for both scientific and ethical reasons. Many scientists already had a problem with Nazi-style race theorizing well before World War II, but in the wake of the Holocaust and the fall of the Nazis, race science was fully discredited as a pseudoscience, and even physical anthropology, while it survived as a field, suffered in reputation because of its association with such research. In the immediate aftermath of the war, in fact, scholars actively tried to dismantle race as a viable scientific category, an effort reflected in a document published in 1950 under the auspices of the United Nations: the UNESCO Statement on Race. The statement, whose coauthors included the anthropologists Claude Lévi-Strauss (who had to flee Vichy France in 1940 after being stripped of his citizenship because he was Jewish) and Ashley Montagu (also a victim of anti-Semitism as a Jew growing up in England), still accepted race as a valid categorization but sapped it of most of its explanatory power:

> National, religious, geographic, linguistic and cultural groups do not necessarily coincide with racial groups; and the cultural traits of such groups have no demonstrated genetic connexion with racial traits. Because serious errors of this kind are habitually committed when the term "race" is used in popular parlance, it would be better when speaking of human races to drop the term "race" altogether and speak of ethnic groups.

The statement goes on to note that while there is no scientific reason to think that inherited genetic differences are a major factor in producing the differences between cultures, there is evidence that whatever inborn differences might exist among groups are greatly overridden by individual differences and by environmental factors. Such a view was indebted to anthropology in the Boas tradition, but it was also greatly influenced by recent genetics research that showed the folly of relying on visible physical traits to classify people, established the biological commonality of all humankind, and demonstrated genetic interconnections that bridged across the cultural and social differences among people.

The UNESCO statement received its share of pushback from scientists who wanted to defend certain aspects of the race concept, including geneticists—and as we have noted, the field has yet to completely shake the specter of race as a continuing influence—but the turn against race was in tune with larger changes in postwar society. In the United States this was the age of the civil rights movement, when "ethnicity," a term meant to suggest culture rather than biology, fluidity rather than fixity, and equality rather than hierarchy, displaced "race" in how people categorized the Jews and other immigrant groups. In the scientific community, the burden of proof had shifted to those who wanted to prove a biological difference among races, and the antiracism position had powerful advocates among geneticists like Leslie Clarence Dunn (1893–1974) and Luca Cavalli-Sforza (b. 1922), along with scholarly allies in other fields, like Montagu, who prevailed in reshaping scientific culture—if not completely shedding it of the concept of race, at least rendering it largely meaningless for understanding human difference. That the antiracism ethos reflected in the UNESCO document—the emphasis on the commonality of human origins, the belief in the plasticity of the self, and the focus on environment rather than biology as the main cause of cultural difference—continues to prevail in genetics research is demonstrated by the fact that when racialist thinking surfaces now and then within the genetics community, it is widely denounced by other geneticists. (This was the response, for example, when in 2007 James Watson, codiscoverer of the structure of DNA, was quoted as saying that black Africans were not as intelligent as whites.) Although vestiges of race science continued into the postwar period, genetics research today has settled on a far more neutral alternative, the category of "population," an artificial grouping of people about whom information is sought—a category defined by geographic proximity or in some other way solely for research purposes, and which may or may not correspond to how people identify themselves. The inheritance that might hold such a population together biologically is not a set of visible and enduring physical traits that predetermine its propensities but miniscule, invisible, biologically inconsequential, and ever shifting mutations, the most faintly inscribed of biological signatures, only rarely associable with physical characteristics common to that group, and with no connection to mental capacity or cultural difference.

But despite this profound difference from race science, population genetics does carry forward a similar intellectual project. It does not purport to account for psychological or cultural differences among groups, but it too is an attempt to understand human difference and relatedness at a biological level. Race science accounted for human variation by moving from a smaller number of ancestors to a larger number of descendants, explaining their difference from one another by appeal to migration, intermixing, and social practices like endogamy. Despite its conceptual and methodological differences from race science, population genetics is also, ultimately, an attempt to track an increasingly ramified and intermeshed history of biological inheritance from remote ancestors to their present-day descendants. One of the more specific links between race science and genetics, in fact, is the prominent role that Jews play as a subject of research within each field. Even as race science was being discredited after World War II, the Jews were surfacing as a subject of genetic research, and there may be connections between the two kinds of research.

Some of the first postwar genetic studies of the Jews during the 1950s and 1960s were undertaken by physicians and geneticists in Israel, including major figures like Joseph Gurevitch (1898–1960), head of the clinical microbiological department at Hadassah hospital in Jerusalem and director of its blood bank; Chaim Sheba (1908–1971), first director of another major hospital in Israel now named for him; and Elisabeth Goldschmidt (1912–1970), the founder of genetic studies at the Hebrew University. Such scientists were presented with an unprecedented opportunity to compare Jews from different countries because in that period Jews were converging on Israel from so many different places. During the 1950s an estimated 70 percent of the country's Jewish population had been born elsewhere, with migration bringing Jews from Europe, North Africa, and the Middle East, and they were converging in Israel at exactly the time when population genetics was being energized by the discovery of new blood groups that gave geneticists a more precise way to demonstrate heredity. The use of blood groups, one of the few human traits that follow a clear-cut pattern of Mendelian inheritance, was found to offer a much more objective and precise way to study the genetic relations within and between different populations. It was already being used to study the Jews in the 1930s, but it was only in the 1950s that such data became more broadly accessible to geneticists through the publication in 1954 of a comprehensive reference work, Arthur Mourant's *The Distribution of the Human Blood Groups*. As a result there appeared in the 1950s and early 1960s a spate of Israeli genetic studies, usually conducted by medical doctors and motivated by an interest to understand the different frequencies of inherited diseases within different Jewish communities. There was even a major international conference on human population genetics held at the Hebrew University in Jerusalem in 1961, representing a pinnacle for the genetics research happening in this period.

It is not clear how conscious early Israeli geneticists were of continuing the kind of research conducted by race scientists just a few decades earlier. On the one hand, in keeping with the trauma suffered by so many Europeans Jews as a result of Nazi racial theories and the ethos articulated by the UNESCO statement, they rejected the racial language and eugenics orientation of such research. The German-born Goldschmidt refused even to visit Germany or speak German, and tried to prevent a major international conference on genetics from happening in Germany. On the other hand, as pointed out by the historian of science Nurit Kirsh, Goldschmidt, Gurevitch, and Sheba were all trained in prewar Central Europe, where they were likely influenced by race science. Kirsh suggests that it was from this intellectual tradition that they inherited their interest in using biology to establish the common origin of the Jews, and most specifically from the work of Zionist scientists like the Austrian Jewish physician Ignaz Zollschan (1877–1944), who drew on race science to argue for a move to Palestine as a way for Jews to overcome the harmful biological effects of living in an anti-Semitic Europe. At the same time this research was under way in Israel, other geneticists were focused on Jews living in other contexts. In 1953, for example, Leslie Dunn and his son undertook a genetic study of the Jewish community of Rome, and here too the history of science has uncovered intellectual continuities with earlier race science—this despite the fact that Dunn was a leading opponent of scientific racism and undertook his study of the Jews precisely to demonstrate that it was social behavior that shaped biology and not the other way around, as many race scientists had claimed. The question of how postwar genetics research relates to earlier race science is an ethically charged one, as critics use it to suggest genetics is perpetuating a new form of racism, and we will need to return to it later in this chapter.

The study of Jewish genetics in the 1950s and 1960s is the immediate precursor to the contemporary research we are interested in here. Replacing the concept of race with the less static and more flexible notion of population, it sought to place the Jews within a larger evolutionary history of humankind in which the transmission of genes from one generation to the next was greatly impacted by migrations to new places, geographic barriers, and linguistic, religious, and political behaviors that shaped reproductive choices. The Jews appeared as a particularly interesting case study both because they were known to be especially endogamous and because Jewish communities were so widely distributed across the globe, offering geneticists an opportunity to explore the effects of both isolation and intermixing (or "admixture" as many geneticists now prefer to describe interbreeding between two previously isolated groups). The evidence now available by this period—the discovery of dozens of blood types that were associated with particular genes—was far less impressionistic than the cranial measurements and other outwardly visible traits that race scientists relied on, proving sufficiently reliable that geneticists have continued to use such evidence to study Jewish populations until fairly recently. Also recommending the Jews as research subjects was the fact that they had a relatively well-documented history that made it possible in theory to understand the mating decisions reflected in the genetic data.

But we now know that the conclusions reached through such methods are very unreliable. The blood markers and other genetic markers they relied on were an improvement over anthropometrics, but they were still indirect—based on what genes produced rather than a reading of the genes themselves—and only a few hundred such markers were known. In the study of Jewish populations, in fact, they proved so imprecise that they supported inconsistent results. In 1979 there appeared two genetic studies, both involving researchers from Stanford, that addressed the same question—are the different Jewish populations from around Europe, the Middle East, and North Africa more genetically similar to one another, or were they more similar to the local non-Jewish populations among whom they resided? Both studies were very sophisticated for their time, but they yielded contradictory results. The one that involved the Stanford professor Sam Karlin (1924–2007), a mathematician known for his work in applying mathematics to population genetics, concluded that these populations were closer to each other than they were to the local non-Jewish populations; the other, involving the Stanford geneticist Cavalli-Sforza, reached the opposite finding, that Jewish groups were more similar to the local non-Jewish populations. Genetic study of Jewish populations was still relying on blood groups into the early 1990s.

In the time between the publication of these studies and now, there has been a methodological revolution in genetic studies. The change began in the 1970s, when Frederick Sanger (1918–2013), a two-time Nobel Prize winner, developed techniques to figure out the exact sequence of the chemical building blocks (A, G, C, and T) that compose the DNA molecule. But it was the automation of this sequencing process in the 1980s that unleashed a new wave of research by allowing scientists to identify hundreds of thousands of DNA sequence variations across the span of a cell's genetic makeup—in fact, scientists now have the ability to analyze the entire human genome thanks to the Human Genome Project. The dramatic increase in the number of markers, together with geneticists' increased computational power and more refined statistical tools, have made for a dramatic increase in analytic precision and nuance. It is now possible, for example, to discriminate between the paternal and maternal contributions to a person's genetic makeup through the analysis of the Y chromosome (transmitted from fathers to sons) and mitochondrial DNA (transmitted from mothers to children); and this, along with the ability to analyze the autosomal or non-sex-specific chromosomes inherited from both parents, have made it possible to read the DNA evidence with a high enough level of resolution that geneticists can now distinguish even very closely related populations from one another. Since the 1980s geneticists have also developed the ability to recover and analyze DNA evidence from skeletal remains and fossils, opening up another research frontier for understanding the course of human evolution and the genetic relationships between living people and the ancient populations from whom they descended.

This brings us into the present era of genetics research, a fast-developing field that has already had many consequences for the understanding of human evolution, prehistoric migration patterns, population growth over the millennia, and the effect of social behavior on genetic inheritance—not to mention what it has revealed about hereditary diseases. What precisely does this kind of research tell us about the origin of the Jews? The research we are focused on here began to appear in the late 1990s and has really picked up steam in the past decade. But even in that short period, it has been brought to bear on questions relevant to our inquiry, including the composition of the founding populations from which present-day Jews descend—who they were, where they lived or migrated from, and how long ago they lived. It is time now to examine some of what such research has discovered.

Y-Chromosomal Aaron and Other Jewish Genetic Founders

The work that initiated this most recent wave of genetics research—an initial study published by Michael Hammer, Karl Skorecki, and other geneticists in 1997, followed by another study a year
later that involved Mark Thomas, David Goldstein, and others—
was focused on the Cohanim, the caste of priests who once served
in the Temple. (*Cohanim* is the plural form of the Hebrew word
meaning priest; the singular form is *Cohen.*) Conducted at a time
when DNA sequencing was still relatively new and imprecise, their
research has been criticized for making too much of the evidence
it uncovered and even for mishandling it. There are other ways to
interpret the data, and the authors themselves have subsequently
revised their own conclusions, but their research garnered a lot of
excitement at the time: from members of religious communities
who hoped it would lead them to the Ten Lost Tribes of Israel or
that it would help them to reestablish the priesthood as they prepared for a third Temple; from genealogists who recognized a new
way to overcome the limits of the documents to which they were
confined; and from geneticists who saw in the study an intriguing
model for how DNA analysis might illumine questions of ancestry.
There were earlier studies of Jewish communities that tapped into
DNA sequencing techniques, but this research was to garner the
most headlines, and at least in the public's imagination, it inaugurated the current wave of research that I survey here.

Hammer and his colleagues' research into the Cohanim was a
kind of supercharged DNA paternity test. According to Jewish law,
membership in the Jewish community is based on maternal descent, but priestly descent is passed down paternally. The Torah
traces it back to Moses's brother, Aaron, who passed down the status to his male descendants. Whether or not Aaron ever actually
existed, there is evidence from Josephus and rabbinic sources that
priestly status was transmitted from father to son in the time of
the Second Temple and the following centuries. Since the Temple
no longer stands, there is not much for a priest to do these days,
and they were long ago eclipsed as religious leaders by the rabbi,
but being a Cohen still carries with it an honorific status, and that
status is still passed on from father to son.

But how many living Cohanim actually descend from such priests? Is there any way to verify such a lineage or to trace it back to antiquity? Cohen is one of the most common Jewish surnames in the United States today, but the transmission of the surname (such names having been adopted by or imposed on Jews only in the past few centuries) is not a reliable measure of priestly status. There are many people with the last name Cohen who are not even Jewish, and many people who have inherited priestly status but who have completely unrelated last names. I am not a Cohen myself, but I inherited the status of a Levite, a lower-level official in the Temple whose status was also passed on from father to son. I know my father inherited that status from my grandfather, but I have no idea how far back that status goes among earlier male ancestors. Something similar is true of many Jews who have inherited priestly status from their forebears, and it is conceivable that in the two thousand years between the end of the Temple period and the present, the line of inheritance was garbled in some way. According to Jewish law, the status of an adopted child is determined by the biological parents, but it is conceivable that some non-Cohen child was adopted into a priestly family and ascribed priestly status without being a biological descendant of the father, or that somewhere down the line a wife decided not to tell her priestly husband about an affair and passed the child off as his, or that some pretender simply faked priestly status to enjoy the honor that went with such a role. For much of their history, many Jews lived in small, tightly knit communities where it was probably difficult for a person to get away with faking being a Cohen, but a lot can happen in the span of two to three thousand years to scramble the genealogical and genetic picture.

For reasons we noted in our earlier discussion of claims of Davidic descent, it is difficult to verify priestly genealogy by appeal to written sources, but since priestly status is supposed to have been passed down from father to son, genetics might offer another way to verify such descent. If priestly status was transmitted through the paternal line, there would be mutations accumulating on the Y chromosomes of priests over the centuries that became part of what they passed down to their successors, and in theory it might be possible to trace those mutations back to the male from whom the whole line descends. This is what Hammer, Skorecki, and their colleagues wanted to test for, undertaking a study of self-identified Cohanim from Israel, the United States, and Britain to determine whether they shared a distinctive genetic inheritance that tied them to one another as co-descendants of a paternal lineage. In theory at least, descent from a common ancestor would have left a signal in the DNA of present-day descendants that a geneticist might be able to detect.

The focus of their analysis was an array of haplotypes found on the Y chromosomes of their subjects. A haplotype is a group of genes within an organism inherited from a single parent. Haplotypes on the male side tend to mutate at a relatively rapid rate, which means that when two males share a distinctive haplotype, that is evidence that they share a common ancestor in the relatively recent past. This is what Hammer, Skorecki, and their team discovered for self-identified priests: a haplotype that distinguished the Y chromosomes of a good number of Cohanim from that of non-priestly Jewish males. The Cohen Modal Haplotype, as this haplotype came to be known, was not found in many of the Cohanim tested, but it was present in about half of the test subjects, suggesting that a large number shared a common ancestor on their paternal side. The initial study had no way to identify this ancestor or determine when he lived, but since the haplotype showed up among both Ashkenazic and Sephardic Cohanim, its authors reasoned that it must have emerged before the split between the two populations sometime in the last millennium. The second study went further. Based on the assumption that mutations occur at a very standard rate, the authors of that study traced the differences among current priestly chromosomes to a point of convergence between 2,100 and 3,250 years ago—in other words, to an ancestor who could have been a Maccabean priest or one who served in Solomon's Temple or even conceivably Aaron himself (which is how this hypothetical ancestor came to be known as "Y-Chromosomal Aaron," a play on "Y-Chromosomal Adam," the hypothetical common paternal ancestor of all living people). Although there is no way to actually identify who the founder of this lineage was or determine when he lived except within extremely wide parameters, what made this study exciting for those interested in the historical implications of genetics was the possibility that DNA might speak to the ancient ancestry of the Jews.

Subsequent research has challenged this conclusion in a number of ways. One big problem is that the Cohen Modal Haplotype is found not only in priests but also among non-Jewish populations in Africa, the Middle East, and Europe. At first there were efforts to suggest such populations might also be descendant from the Hebrews, as in the famous case of the Lemba, an African tribe in Southern Africa (more about them a bit later). But it has since become clear that the original Cohen Modal Haplotype might have been common among Middle Eastern populations, not exclusive to the Jews or their Israelite ancestors.

This challenge to their findings, and the rapid methodological improvements in their field over the next decade, prompted the original researchers to try again, and they have since been able to refine their hypothesis. In 2009, a little more than a decade after the first study, Hammer, Skorecki, and a new team of colleagues undertook a more ambitious study, using a far greater number of markers on a larger sample size, and the results led them to a more nuanced conclusion. The original Cohen Modal Haplotype is indeed not specific to the Cohanim, surfacing in other Near Eastern populations, *but* a slightly mutated offshoot of this haplotype, an "extended Cohen Modal Haplotype," does seem distinctive to Jewish priests. The researchers were also able to illumine the lineages of the large number of other Cohanim who did not carry this haplotype by uncovering other haplotypes—twenty-one in all. Some of these alternative lineages were prehistoric in origin, others emerged more recently, but the researchers were able to salvage their original hypothesis by arguing that the most prevalent lineage, the one marked by the extended Cohen Modal Haplotype, probably went back to a founder in the period of the Jews' ancient Hebrew ancestors.

The research into this issue continues in a way that has compelled me to constantly update this description, and based on the most recent study that I have been able to locate, an Italian study from 2014 led by Sergio Tofanelli, it is not clear that Y-Chromosomal Aaron is going to hold up much longer. Tofanelli and his team reassessed the evidence and found that the extended

Cohen Modal Haplotype, the version that is supposed to distinguish Jewish priests, probably split off from an older Cohen haplotype far more recently than earlier geneticists concluded. Beyond the question of when the split occurred, the authors of this study make a larger point: figuring out the right mutation rate to apply is a hotly contested issue; mutation rates are not constant in the real world, and the longer the time span to a common ancestor, the harder it is to pinpoint a distinctive genetic signature or to accurately estimate the amount of time involved. It is impossible for a nonscientist like myself to evaluate the evidence and its analysis, but this most recent study gives one pause, questioning whether DNA evidence can be used to identify markers of ancient Jewish ancestry in the way that those who first identified the Cohen Modal Haplotype proposed. This will be welcome news to those skeptical of this kind of research—critics to be introduced in a few pages—and it illustrates how open-ended this kind of research is.

Despite such revisions and challenges, however, the genetic study of the Cohanim unleashed a new wave of research into the genetic history of the Jews that has been under way since around 2000, with geneticists using more and more refined methods to illumine the origin not just of particular lineages or communities but of the Jewish people in general. One of the most ambitious studies, research published in 2010 by the Israeli geneticist Doron Behar together with twenty other contributors, involved the analysis of whole-genome samples from fourteen different Jewish communities representing about 90 percent of the world's Jewish population. These samples were compared with genetic samples from sixty-nine neighboring non-Jewish populations, producing the most comprehensive and precise genetic profile of the worldwide Jewish population to date. The authors found that, genetically, most of the Jews sampled fell into three distinct subclusters that intermixed with the neighboring population but remained distinct enough to be distinguishable genetically from the surrounding population: (1) Ashkenazi, Sephardi, and North African Jews show genetic connections to both Middle Eastern and European populations; (2) Middle Eastern and Caucasian Jewish communities show genetic ties to the non-Jewish populations of those regions; and (3) Yemenite Jews formed their own subcluster. While this study demonstrated different ancestries for various populations—and different levels of admixture with non-Jews—it also showed evidence of commonality: with the exception of Ethiopian and Indian Jews, most contemporary Jews have a genetic connection to non-Jewish populations living in the Middle East. The most reasonable way to account for this finding according to Behar and his colleagues is to trace Jews in different communities to forebears who migrated from the Near East prior to the Jews' diffusion to different parts of the world, more or less what historians of the Jews have long claimed about their origin.

A few years after the publication of this study, its findings were challenged in an interesting way by the molecular biologist Eran Elhaik, who argued that the data actually supported a Khazar origin for Ashkenazic Jews. Since there are no more Khazars alive today, and no known Khazar descendants, Elhaik had to draw his samples from proxies—Armenians, Georgians, and Azerbaijani Jews from the South Caucasus region near where the Khazars are believed to have lived—and he found that 70 percent of European Jews and almost all Eastern European Jews cluster with these populations. In other words, Elhaik's analysis showed that the ancestors of Ashkenazic Jews do not hail from the Near East, as Behar and his team conclude, but from a population in the Caucasus, as argued by the Khazar theory.

There are reasons to be skeptical of how Elhaik approaches the question. He stakes a lot on the assumption that the present-day inhabitants of the region are the genetic descendants of the Khazars, but the particular populations he focuses on, Armenians and Georgians, happen to be a poor choice of proxy: they live in the southern region of the Caucasus, whereas the Khazarite kingdom was based in the north Caucasus and the region to the north of that. Rather than dismissing Elhaik's analysis on such grounds, however, Behar and his associates seized on it as a chance to refine their analysis. In a follow-up study, Behar and thirty coauthors compared a large collection of Jewish samples with the largest available genome-wide sample set from individuals living in the Khazar region, a sample that was far broader than Elhaik's and that factored in the population from the northern Caucasus as well as the south. Their findings confirmed a Middle Eastern connection for Ashkenazic Jewry: there was no substantial overlap with the present-day inhabitants of the Caucasus, south or north; instead, Ashkenazic Jews have ancestries that go back to the Middle East and European populations, with connections to Italian, Sephardic, and North African Jews, and to Mediterranean non-Jewish populations such as Cypriots and Italians. A more recent study by Shai Carmi and a team of other scientists, coming out of the Ashkenazic Genome Consortium led by the computer scientist Itzik Pe'er and the medical researcher Todd Lencz, shows that the founding population from which Ashkenazic Jews descend—a tiny population that around seven hundred years ago consisted of about three hundred fifty people—emerged from a mixture of European and Middle Eastern ancestries. Geneticists have not uncovered a "Jewish gene" or a single set of common ancestors that tie all Jews to one another, but to borrow a metaphor from Harry Ostrer, one of the scientists involved in the Ashkenazi Genetic Consortium, the Jews can be described at the genetic level as a tapestry, with no single genetic thread running through the whole tapestry, but with different Jewish populations woven together by various threads.

For some scholars, it is suspicious that genetic analysis would seem to be reaffirming what many Jews already believe about their origin. Sometimes, what the evidence reveals is that the actual biogenetic ancestry of people can be very different from what people think their ancestry is. Indeed, in one recent study, the researchers found that most Americans carry an ancestry outside their self-identified ethnicity. Is it possible that there is bias at work in the genetic study of the Jews, that researchers are predisposed to accept results that confirm what Jews believe about themselves, and to discount results at odds with that self-image? Possibly, but there have also been studies that suggest that in some contexts self-identity and genetically established ancestry can match up fairly well. That is what much of recent genetic research has been suggesting about the Jews: that there is a correspondence between what they believe about the origin of their ancestors and the genetic ancestry registered in their DNA, that they have an ancestry distinct from that of the non-Jews among whom they live, and that some of those ancestors came from the Near East.

Lest the reader think that such research merely affirms an already existing historical narrative, however, I would call attention to another recent study by Behar that challenges the traditional account of Ashkenazic Jewish history. In a 2003 study Behar argued that many Ashkenazic Levites have a different origin from the rest of the Ashkenazic population. According to the Bible, the Levites were one of the tribes of ancient Israel, the descendants of Jacob's son Levi, and they too passed their status down to their sons. Presumably then, the Y chromosomes of Levites would show something analogous to what was discovered on the Y chromosomes of Cohanim—evidence of a common paternal ancestry—but they do not: according to this study at least, there is no genetic evidence that the Levites among Sephardic and Ashkenazic Jews come from a common ancestry, as is the case for priests. Indeed, for more than 50 percent of Ashkenazic Levites, their ancestry seems different from that of other Ashkenazic Jews, appearing much more closely related to non-Jewish populations of Eastern European origin and without the Middle Eastern connection that surfaces in the genetic background of many Ashkenazic Jews. According to Behar and his coauthors, their ancestry goes back to a European male or a small number of such males in the past two thousand years, at a time close to the founding of the Ashkenazic population. It is even possible, they suggest, that the original founder of the lineage was a Khazar convert. Behar has subsequently backed off this conclusion, but the original study shows that he and his co-researchers are willing to entertain historical conclusions at odds with conventional thinking about the origin of the Jews if that is where the evidence leads them.

Not only has the DNA sequencing revolution made it possible to investigate the interrelations and geographic origins of diverse Jewish populations and vestigial castes; the analysis of mitochondrial DNA has now made it possible to tease out genetic history from the maternal side of people's genetic inheritance. Discovered in the 1960s, mitochondrial DNA is also directly inherited from a parent, but only from the mother, and it is thus something a person shares with his or her maternal line—the mother, grandmothers, great-grandmothers, and so forth, all the way back to the most recent common female ancestor to whom all living humans can be connected, "Mitochondrial Eve," who lived around 150,000 years ago. (Of course there were other females back then, but at some point their female descendants had only sons or had no children, thus ending their mitochondrial lineage.) Using this kind of evidence, geneticists have been piecing together a sex-specific genetic history of Jewish communities different from that gleaned from the Y chromosome alone.

Again, the Ashkenazic Jewish population—the most intensively studied of any Jewish population—offers an example of what such research reveals, though geneticists have been studying non-Ashkenazi Jewish populations as well. Several studies have now shown that many Ashkenazic Jews descend from a small number of maternal founders. According to Behar and his co-researchers, for example, 40 percent of today's Ashkenazic Jews descend from just four women. (The other 60 percent descend from numerous other maternal lineages.) The origin of these four maternal founders is a matter of dispute. Behar et al. believe that they originated in the Near East, but a 2013 study led by Martin Richards and his colleagues concluded that they originated not from the Middle East or the Caucasus for that matter, but from the Mediterranean and Western Europe, tentatively proposing that they might have been women converted to Judaism prior to the destruction of the Second Temple (a perhaps overly pious interpretation that never considers the possibility that these women mated with Jewish males without converting). Behar does not accept their conclusion, and the debate remains unresolved, but the research is continuing.

An even more recent analysis of mitochondrial DNA finds an imprint of an East Asian contribution to Ashkenazic Jews, perhaps from Chinese women encountered by Jewish traders on the Silk Road between 640 and 1,400 years ago. Work also continues on the maternal lines of Sephardic Jews. Research has rarely been able to distinguish between men and women in how it accounts for the origin of the Jews, and most accounts focus pretty much exclusively on male figures, be it Moses, Ezra, the Priestly source, the Maccabees, or the historians who supposedly invented the Jewish people in modern times. Genomics offers a way to recover a trace of the women involved in what happened, if not to uncover their identities then at least to detect their existence and distinguish their background from that of the male founders.

As a last example of what contemporary genetic research is telling us about the origin of the Jews, let me mention one other study that I learned about firsthand from one of its authors, a study that speaks to the fate of the legendary Ten Lost Tribes of Israel. According to the conventional historical account, the Jews descend from the tribe of Judah, one of the Twelve Tribes of Israel. The descendants of Judah and Levi survive to this day, but what happened to the other ten tribes? According to the Bible, they were deported during the Assyrian conquest of Canaan at the end of the eighth century BCE and were presumably assimilated into the populations of the places to where they were forced to move. But their fate remains unknown, inspiring an untold number of theories about their whereabouts and many claims that this or that people in Africa or Asia represent their descendants. Scholars have been trying to determine the whereabouts of the Ten Lost Tribes for centuries, and it might be that genetics can finally shed light on the question.

Another former colleague of mine from Stanford is Marc Feldman, director of the Morrison Institute for Population and Resource Studies and a renowned population biologist, and among his projects has been a study of the Samaritans, a contemporary community of about 750 people who live in Nablus and in Holon, a suburb of Tel Aviv. The Samaritans believe themselves descendants of the biblical Israelites—and more specifically the tribes of Ephraim and Manasseh, the sons of Joseph—but Jews have not traditionally accepted that claim. According to Josephus, the Samaritans were really descendants of the non-Israelite population resettled in the region of the northern kingdom of Israel by the Assyrians after they exiled the Israelite tribes who lived there, and their claim to be the descendants of the Israelites was a lie. When it was expedient to be identified with the Jews, the historian explained, the Samaritans professed descent from the Israelites, but when claiming kinship with the Jews was dangerous, as it was during the period when the Jews were being persecuted by the Greek king Antiochus IV, they showed their true colors by disavowing such an ancestry and declaring themselves to be foreign colonists. Samaritan chronicles, written in a much later period, tell a very different story, tracing their ancestry back to the biblical Israelites. Modern historians differ in how they describe their origin: some hew closer to Josephus's account, concluding that they originated as a breakaway Jewish sect during the Second Temple period;

others believe they might indeed descend from the ancient Israelites, as the Samaritans themselves claim.

The Samaritans have managed to survive into the present, and the State of Israel recognizes them as citizens and a legally protected minority, but their categorization in relation to Jews remains ambiguous in ways that have had legal and social implications. In 1992 the government briefly changed its policy, refusing to recognize them as Jews and classifying them as members of another religion, but then two years later reversed itself. While the Israeli state recognizes them as Jews, however, Orthodox religious authorities do not. In the Israeli system, the government defines citizenship status, but rabbinical courts have legal authority over the personal status of Jews (whether an individual is considered Jewish, for example, which is considered necessary if they are to marry someone who is Jewish according to Jewish religious law). These courts do not recognize the Samaritans as Jews, which means Samaritans cannot pursue matters of conversion, marriage, or divorce within the same juridical structure that governs the personal status of Jews. Samaritans still get married and divorced, but only as part of a separate de facto religious community not officially recognized by the state, and they cannot marry Jews within the rabbinical system and have faced unequal treatment from the Ministry of Religious Affairs in other respects as well. Their religious status remains legally fraught.

Thus there are real-world consequences at stake in determining the relationship between the Samaritans and the Jews, but the matter cannot be pursued using the methods that scholars normally use to illumine the origin of a people. Neither the historical documentation nor the excavation of the Samaritan sanctuary on Mount Gerizim (near present-day Nablus) has been able to resolve the origin of the Samaritans or their relationship to the Judean ancestors of the Jews. Hence the potential value of genetics. To clarify the ancestry of the Samaritans, the team that Feldman was part of analyzed samples from twelve Samaritans in comparison with samples from Jews of various backgrounds. Theirs was not the first genetic study of the Samaritans—there was an earlier study published in 2004—but Feldman's study took advantage of scientific and technological advances made since 2004, including methods like denaturing high-performance liquid chromatography and electrospray ionization/quadruple ion trap mass spectrometry.

What the analysis of the results revealed is that the Samaritan Y chromosomes were closest to those of Israeli Jewish priests (and also to Yemeni Jews and Bedouin)—in other words, the Samaritans share a genetic lineage with Jews that points to a common ancestry. According to this research, Josephus was wrong to have described the Samaritans as imposters, which does not mean the Samaritans are Jews, whatever we mean by that term, but that there might be something to the Samaritans' claim to be co-descendants of the ancient Israelites. Scholars have looked all over the world for descendants of the lost tribes of Israel. Genetics suggests that some of them might be living in a Tel Aviv suburb.

This kind of research is still very new: it seems to be updating itself all the time, and the conclusions described here are tentative and revisable—in fact some have already been revised. As an Ashkenazic Levite myself, I was bemused by the possibility that I might descend from a nomadic Turkic convert, but the feeling lasted only until I read a more recent study that has undone Behar's analysis by arguing that Ashkenazic Levites, like other Ashkenazic Jews, also descend from Near Eastern ancestors. But such revision is part of the scientific process, the way that it makes progress, and one gets the impression from reading this research that progress is possible, that the picture is going to become only clearer and clearer as scientists expand their databases and refine their techniques. Genetics has proven so successful as a historical tool that it is now vying with archaeology as the most exciting source of new data about the origin of the Jews. Indeed, some believe that it is far more reliable than archaeology—as an article in the Jewish periodical *The Forward* put it, "recreating history now depends not only on pottery shards, flaking manuscripts, and faded coins, but on something far less ambiguous: DNA."

Inheritance Disputes

But is genetic evidence "far less ambiguous" than other kinds of evidence? Not according to critics of this kind of research. In the immediate aftermath of the Holocaust, there was an alliance between geneticists and cultural anthropologists in the Boasian vein who came together to discredit race science, but the situation is different today: there are now anthropologists whose opposition to the research we have surveyed has led to a sort of counter-scholarship that not only questions the results of recent genetics research but challenges its underlying premises and its claim to objectivity. I have the feeling that this side would not choose me to represent their views any more than biologists would, but I want to describe their perspective as best I can in an effort to balance out the picture, to explain why, for all its precision and promise, genomics may not bring the clarity we seek.

For our purposes here, I would emphasize two main criticisms that have emerged over the past two decades: (1) the history of the genetic study of the Jews reveals disturbing continuities with earlier race science that suggest genetics has helped to rehabilitate racialized thinking and is marred by racial bias; and (2) as intriguing as this kind of research is, DNA makes for a very ambiguous kind of historical document, and it does not reveal what scientists have been claiming that it does. Let us consider each criticism in turn.

Among the scholars who have voiced the first kind of criticism is none other than Shlomo Sand, the author of *The Invention of the Jewish People*, who treats such research as a simple continuation of race science. "It is a bitter irony to see the descendants of Holocaust survivors set out to find a biological Jewish identity. Hitler would certainly have been very pleased." There is probably no more serious accusation to level against a field that has worked so hard to distinguish itself from race science, but in my view it is based on a caricature. The geneticists I have met or whose work I have read are not trying to develop a hierarchy of human groups based on perceived qualities; they are not seeking to discriminate against or eliminate the populations they study; and they are deeply opposed to racism, practicing the very science that discredited it as a biologically valid category. One of the geneticists I have had a chance to meet, a pioneer in the field of medical genetics named Arno Motulsky, was himself a refugee from the Nazis, departing Europe on the ill-fated MS *St. Louis*, which was turned away from the United States and nearly had to return its passengers to Germany. Fifty years before scholars like Sand were denouncing Jewish genetics for its "crude and dangerous racism," Motulsky was among those who tried to make sure it did not repeat the mistakes of earlier race scientists: "Population genetics is a discipline in whose name great outrages have been committed and possibly still can be committed," he warned his colleagues at the Jerusalem genetics conference in 1961. "This is a field that has dangerous implications, and this, I think, is something that we population geneticists should realize." It is upsetting to see geneticists like him branded as Hitler's accomplices.

Even so—and taking heed of Motulsky's warning—one can certainly understand scholars' concerns about the field and its potential implications, and the critics raise questions that we need to take seriously. Whatever the motives and aims of geneticists, their research is sometimes cited as support for racialist ideas, as illustrated by how the work of Noah Rosenberg was misappropriated by Nicholas Wade, a former *New York Times* science writer, who published a book on the topic of population genetics titled *A Troublesome Inheritance: Genes, Race and Human History* (2014). Wade uses the research of Rosenberg and other geneticists in a selective and misleading way to suggest that evolution and genetics can account for alleged mental differences among different populations, even offering an evolutionary explanation to account for the supposedly greater cognitive abilities of Jews. Some of his claims have been embraced by white supremacist websites. (Ironically, one of these websites, DavidDuke.com, uses Wade's book as an excuse to denounce Jewish scholars for denying the reality of race.) It is not as if geneticists like Rosenberg support such views—to the contrary, he protested against Wade's book in a letter submitted to the *New York Times* and signed by more than one hundred geneticists and biologists. But geneticists do not control how their work is interpreted by others, and as this case shows, there is a danger that it will be enlisted to provide a new rationale for the sort of racialized thinking that led to the eugenicist policies of the Nazis and racial segregation in the United States. While Sand's critique is overheated, it is perfectly legitimate to voice concern, especially with regard to how genetics is represented by the media and the ancestry testing industry.

A more fully developed and sophisticated version of this criticism appears in a recent study by the cultural anthropologist Nadia Abu

El-Haj titled *The Genealogical Science: The Search for Jewish Origins and the Politics of Epistemology.* Abu El-Haj is an anthropologist of science known for a controversial critique of Israeli archaeology as a form of Israeli state building and colonization, a work that embroiled her in one of the most publicly contentious tenure cases in the United States during the past decade. She followed up that work with a study of Jewish and Israeli genetics research into the origin of the Jews that aimed to expose the assumptions and biases implicit in such research and to critique the way it has been used politically and culturally by Zionists in Israel, American Jewish religious organizations, and a commercialized genetic testing industry. Genetics as she depicts it does not exactly reproduce the claims of race science—she notes important differences like the fact that contemporary scientists do not view biology as deterministic of who a person is and make a sharp distinction between the DNA they analyze and any physical or mental characteristics. But she emphasizes the continuities between race science and postwar Israeli genetics, and ultimately argues that contemporary research legitimizes a newly biologized conception of Jewish identity, though the conception of race that has emerged fuses a biological notion of identity with a neoliberal emphasis on personal autonomy—that is, the ability of individuals to define their own identity—and an embrace of multiculturalism. She reviews the Israeli research from the 1950s and 1960s and finds that it was influenced by bias against so-called Oriental Jews from the Middle East and by sheer indifference to Palestinians; and she finds other biases at work in the contemporary use of genetics to identify nonwhite groups in Africa and India as Jewish. Judging from the reviews that I have read, Abu El-Haj has convinced many readers that modern Jewish genetics research is a twenty-first-century race science, only now it is not anti-Semitic German scientists who are pursuing this kind of work but Israeli and Jewish American geneticists who are doing so, and at the expense of groups like the Palestinians.

To accept the critique of genetics as a revived form of race science, there are a lot of things one has to downplay or ignore. One has to minimize the critical role that geneticists played in discrediting the biological category of race after World War II. One has to disbelieve geneticists today when they distinguish their work from race science; and one has to discount important differences between the two kinds of science, including the differences between the concept of race and the notions of "population" or "cline" that have eclipsed it. While *The Genealogical Science* has not been challenged on factual grounds in the way her first book on archaeology was, reviewers like Yulia Egorova, an anthropologist herself, have questioned how it contextualizes its subject historically and anthropologically—for example, the book focuses on Jewish geneticists, assuming that their Jewishness is a core motivation of their scientific work, without framing them as part of the larger field of population genetics, which includes both Jews and non-Jews asking similar questions of other populations. Others have noted that Abu El-Haj does not give her subjects much of their own voice in her narrative, a methodological contrast with other anthropological studies of genetics research that are based on more extensive interviews with the geneticists themselves and on participant observation in the labs where they work.

But it also has to be acknowledged that Abu El-Haj's book reflects a criticism of population genetics that is not confined to that focused on the Jews. Similar arguments have been made about population genetics in general by Jenny Reardon, Duana Fullwiley, and many others who argue that the field was not as successful in distinguishing itself from race science as its practitioners believe. None of these scholars, including Abu El-Haj, is suggesting that genetics is a simple extension of the race science practices that led to Nazi eugenics; some, like Reardon, in her study of the ill-fated Human Genome Diversity Project (an effort initiated by Cavalli-Sforza to catalogue human genetic diversity), emphasize that the goal of the geneticists she studied was to fight racism and to benefit indigenous populations. But they argue that, good intentions notwithstanding, the scientists involved in the project did not fully overcome some of the assumptions they inherited from earlier science and brought to their work a range of race-based categories and assumptions that skewed the research and ultimately alienated the project from some of the communities it sought to serve. From what I have read, this view of genetics and its historical relationship to race science, a perspective that stresses the lines of continuity between the two fields, is common among the anthropologists who write about genetics research, and Abu El-Haj's argument is in line with this broader critique of the field.

A second critique of genetics research is one that has been made about archaeological evidence as well. Here too the evidence does not speak for itself: it has to be interpreted; and geneticists do not realize the extent to which their interpretations read into the evidence more than is really there. An example is another sensational genetics study from roughly the same period in which the Cohen study was conducted: the use of genetics to connect descendants of Thomas Jefferson's family with descendants of Sally Hemings, the slave with whom he was rumored to have had several children. Employing the same kind of analysis of Y-chromosome haplotypes used to identify the Cohen haplotype, DNA testing showed that Jefferson *or one of his close relatives* was the father of Hemings's son Eston. As Dena Davis has chronicled, that discovery was then spun in various ways. The Thomas Jefferson Memorial Foundation, which runs Monticello, accepted the president as the father, but in the same period, the separate Thomas Jefferson Foundation (sued by the other foundation for using a trademarked name) countered that the test established only a probability that Eston was fathered by one of two dozen Jefferson men known to be in Virginia at that time, and it pointed to Randolph Jefferson, the president's brother, as the more likely father. "Even if one could prove absolutely that Thomas Jefferson was the father of at least one of Hemings' children," Davis concludes, "there would still be differing ways of telling that story." Something similar is true of any attempt to reconstruct history from the genetic evidence for a given population: certainly for the Jews, such evidence does not track back to a single lineage or a single region of the world or a single period of time, and there is enough vagueness there that scientists can tell very different stories about the ancestry of the Jews, all of which can find support in the genetic record.

This is why, from the perspective of a critic like Abu El-Haj, the scientific rigor of the research involved in Jewish genetic history is beside the point. To become a genetic history, the data must undergo a process of emplotment, must be turned into a narrative, and that is where bias, stereotypes, and self-interest can slip in. That is true of history, archaeology, or any method we might use, but it is less obvious for geneticists, who are seen as more objective than these other kinds of scholars because of the scientific nature of their work. But even geneticists tend to favor certain narratives over others for reasons that have nothing to do with the science. For example, geneticists are inclined to think arborescently, to interpret the evidence inscribed into the DNA of Jewish populations as a tree that branches off in different directions from a common Middle Eastern root; but Abu El-Haj counters that the data, if read from a more neutral perspective, might more plausibly be conceived of as a bush too entangled to support any coherent narrative of origin.

If we follow Abu El-Haj's argument, the development of more refined genetic markers and the accumulation of data can never reveal a clearer historical picture because there is no history inherent in the genetic data itself: that history emerges only by reading the data in light of other sources of information; it can produce a linear narrative of common origin for the Jews—it can produce any narrative—only through a process of interpretation that is always going to simplify a more complicated reality. Geneticists often acknowledge that there is more than one way to interpret the evidence, but they support their particular hypothesis by arguing that it is the most "parsimonious," the simplest and most logical way of explaining the greatest number of observations. As Abu El-Haj points out, however, history does not always lend itself to parsimonious explanation: it is full of messy situations that may get overlooked in a simplistic linear narrative of descent.

Among the different kinds of genetic research discussed by Abu El-Haj, one is worth mentioning because it is vulnerable to both kinds of critique, a 2000 study of the Lemba people by Thomas, Skorecki, Goldstein, and others involved in some of the studies we have been surveying, along with the globe-trotting historian and adventurer Tudor Parfitt, then at the University of London. The Lemba, often referred to as the "Black Jews" of South Africa, are a population of an estimated fifty thousand Bantu-speaking people who live in Southern Africa. Although a good number are Christian and some are Muslim, many claim descent from Jews who migrated to Africa from a placed called Sena, which has been variously located in Yemen, Ethiopia, Judea, and Egypt. Fresh off their discovery of the Cohen Modal Haplotype, Thomas and his team analyzed 399 chromosomes from six different populations—the Lemba along with Sephardic and Ashkenazic Jews—and found that the Cohen Modal Haplotype was especially prevalent in one of the Lemba clans, the Buba, which is considered the oldest of the clans and has an important role in certain ritual performances. The results suggested that there might be some truth to the oral tradition that the Lemba descend from ancient Jewish exiles.

In keeping with her larger effort to cast genetics research as a continuation of race science, Abu El-Haj connects this research to the racism associated with South Africa, though the connection is indirect. Thomas's study built on an earlier study of the Lemba from the late 1980s conducted by Amanda Spurdle and Trefor Jenkins, which found that at least 50 percent of the Lemba chromosomes were of "Semitic" origin. For Abu El-Haj, the study's use of racial categories like "Semitic," "Negroid," and "Caucasoid" exposes its continuity with race science. In fairness to them, Spurdle and Jenkins managed to publish results that actually amounted to an argument *against* apartheid, undercutting the sharp distinction between black and white races on which its segregationist policies depended by demonstrating the *mixed* genetic ancestry of a black African group. But even if we acquit the scientists of outright racism, it must be acknowledged that Thomas and company's study built on research skewed in its conclusions by outmoded racialized categories

The Lemba study is also subject to the second kind of critique. As it happens, scholars have told another story about the Lemba, though one that is less well known than the genetic story. In 1997 Aviton Ruwitah, the senior curator of ethnography at the Museum of Human Sciences in Zimbabwe, published an article in which he argued that the Jewish origin of the Lemba was a modern invention. In Ruwitah's view, there are no unique physical, linguistic, or cultural traits that distinguish the Lemba from other neighboring ethnic groups, and it was far more likely that the Semitic-like customs that later scholars took to be Jewish in origin were actually picked up from Arab Muslim travelers. How then did the Lemba come to think of themselves as Jews? Ruwitah argues that the Lemba absorbed that origin story from their contacts with Western missionaries and scholars—another classic case of the invention of

tradition phenomenon where an indigenous African group inter-
nalizes an identity foisted on them by colonization.

Ruwitah undertook his study before the 2000 genetics study,
but according to Abu El-Haj, that research became a part of this
identity-construction process in its own right, further encouraging
the Lemba to identify as Jews. In the years since Thomas's study,
many Lemba have embraced a Jewish identity, undergoing conversion or sometimes even claiming that they had been keeping
their Jewishness in secret all along. This was a process triggered
by the genetic study, Abu El-Haj argues, which did not argue that
the Lemba were Jewish but drew the attention of an organization
called Kulanu, a Jewish nonprofit outreach organization that works
to help the Lemba and other "emerging" Jewish communities to
reclaim their Jewish identity and integrate into mainstream Jewish
life. The efforts of Kulanu do not involve merely recognizing lost
Jews and returning them to the fold, Abu El-Haj argues; the organization is creating new Jews in service to a project to build a more
multiracial Jewish community, to address the loss of Jews to assimilation, and to provide new Jewish settlers for the occupied territories. Abu El-Haj's point is similar to that of Judith Neulander with
respect to Stanley Hordes and his study of New Mexican crypto-
Jews: here too the modern researcher seems to have helped *invent*
a new kind of Jewish identity by making claims about a community's ancestry.

Since genetic history is a quickly developing field, one can imagine that it will someday be able to overcome some of the ambiguities and distortions identified by Abu El-Haj and other critics
of this kind of research. Even then, however, the basic issue that
Abu El-Haj points to will not go away, for it is built into the act
of treating DNA as a historical source. However large their data
sets, however sophisticated their analytic techniques, and however
abstruse the efforts to calculate mutation rates, geneticists will always need to rely on nongenetic evidence—written texts, oral traditions, interviews with subjects about who they are and where they
come from—to turn data into a coherent account of the past, which
means in turn that genetic history is susceptible to the same pitfalls
of interpretation that beset the other approaches we have considered. There is no way to know what genetics might yet reveal, but

according to Abu El-Haj and other critics, it is not going to get us much further in our quest to understand the origin of the Jews and may even lead us astray.

Approaching this debate from a vantage point outside of both genetics and anthropology, I struggle to judge who is right and who is wrong, or rather I struggle to understand how they both might be right, and I find it striking that there has not been much dialogue between the two perspectives. I have read many reviews of Abu El-Haj's work, but scarcely any have been written by geneticists themselves, perhaps a sign that they do not take her argument seriously or are not even aware of it. For their part, the anthropologists do not treat geneticists as intellectual equals either. Some are more empathetic than Abu El-Haj, spending more time with geneticists in their laboratories, but at the end of the day, they too do not address geneticists as fellow scholars but treat them as anthropological subjects: what these scientists are discovering about the histories of different populations, whether their research happens to ascertain the truth or not, does not matter from their perspective. Despite their differences, in other words, the two sides are not really debating each other or trying to address a common set of questions; they operate according to different epistemologies, as Abu El-Haj would put it; it is hard to know how to bridge their perspectives; and no side gets the last word in deciding which is the right way to think. From this outsider's perspective, it is thus unclear who to believe: whether the genetic research is truly revealing new and more reliable insights into the ancestry and origin of the Jews or whether the critics are right to be skeptical.

Fusion or Fission?

Someone torn between these perspectives might wonder whether it is possible to integrate them. We have seen that there was a time when cultural anthropologists and geneticists were allies against scientific racism, and there is a case to be made that the difference between geneticists and anthropologists today is not so unbridgeable. Many geneticists would not contest the central tenets of Abu El-Haj's position: many know that people's self-understanding is a social construct that may have little or nothing to do with who their ancestors were or where they lived; they acknowledge that the evidence is ambiguous and that the models and metaphors they use—the construction of phylogenetic trees, for example—can skew the interpretation of the evidence. Certainly scientists project their own perspective onto the evidence, but the scientific process assumes the possibility of bias and is designed to weed such distortion out over the long term. There is nothing to preclude the possibility of geneticists and anthropologists learning more from each other.

In my personal experience, however, a fusion of the two perspectives is not so easy. When I was at Stanford, Noah Rosenberg and I organized a series of talks on Jewish genetics through which we hoped to bring the two perspectives into conversation with each other, but we found it very difficult to do so. What I did not know then was that we were not the first scholars to attempt—and fail—at this kind of dialogue. In 1927 the German Jewish sexologist Max Marcuse organized an exchange published in the German medical journal *Die medizinische Welt* that was meant to put race scientists in conversation with anthropological critics, including no less a figure than Franz Boas himself, and the contributors there were not able to bridge their differences either. The problem is not just the challenge of how to communicate across fields or how to integrate different kinds of evidence but how to overcome an incommensurability of paradigms, a challenge that we still did not know how to overcome close to a century after Marcuse made his attempt.

A paradigm, as the philosopher of science Thomas Kuhn has explained, is not just a theory but something more deeply rooted than that, an underlying epistemological matrix that defines the kind of puzzles that are considered important and worth working on, as well as defining in advance what a successful solution to those puzzles would look like. Kuhn was focused on the difference between scientific paradigms from different periods of history. We are dealing with two contemporary paradigms that have been brought into a close encounter with each other through the study of Jewish genetic history but that are nonetheless as irreconcilable in their way as the thinking of Aristotle and Newton. It is possible to soften the difference between perspectives and to emphasize points of commonality, and there are ways in which each has developed in response to the other, but I suspect that even a redoubling of the effort to work more closely together will never completely close the gap because the underlying ways of thinking are incompatible.

If this description of the situation is correct, there is no way out of the impasse in which we find ourselves. One can imagine more progress on the genetics front—the accumulation of bigger data sets, more fine-grained observations—but that will not be enough to address the concerns that Abu El-Haj is voicing. One can also envision historians and anthropologists learning more about the study of Jewish genetics as a cultural practice, but it is hard to imagine geneticists ever fully accepting their critique since it basically argues that the field can never achieve the goal it has set out for itself—to treat DNA as a history book that tells the story of the human species. I would like to believe it possible to overcome this difference, but it is hard to see how that is going to happen unless one or the other side—or both—agrees to give up the way it thinks and reasons, and that seems unlikely.

The reader who has followed me this far might recognize that this is not the first time we have faced this kind of impasse. We ran into variations of the same problem when discussing recent efforts to merge different kinds of genealogy, processual and postprocessual archaeology, psychology and history, and constructivism and primordialism—a clash of paradigms that one can imagine being overcome only through the introduction of some new paradigm that has not yet been formulated. I have not been able to find a way to overcome this problem. All I can do is call attention to a question that it raises for our study, and one that cannot be ignored by those who would pursue this quest beyond where we have been able to go: Is there a way for scholars and scientists to truly progress in the search to understand the origin of the Jews when there is more than one way to think about the question and no possibility of reconciling the different perspectives?

Conclusion

Why is it that this thought comes back to me again and again and in ever more variegated colors? That formerly, when investigators sought out the origin of things, they always believed they would discover something of incalculable significance for all later action and judgment, that they always presupposed, indeed, that the salvation of man must depend on insight into the origin of things: but that now, on the contrary, the more we advance toward origins the more our interest diminishes.

—FRIEDRICH NIETZSCHE

THE JEWS HAVE ONE of the longest and most intensively studied histories of any population on earth, but the beginning of their history, how it is that the Jews came to be, remains surprisingly unsettled. What is the origin of the Jews? This book is an attempt to explore what scholars know—or believe they know—about how to answer that question. I cannot claim to have covered every theory or to have presented every piece of information, but I have tried to give some sense of how scholars think about the origin of the Jews, to sketch in how that thinking changes from period to period, to explore the differences among scholarly approaches, and to identify what makes the matter so difficult to resolve.

At the end of the day, however, it is not clear what we can say with any degree of confidence about the origin of the Jews. This is by no means to suggest that Jews lack an origin. We can be certain that at some point in the past, there were no Jews in the world, and now there are, and whatever it is that got us from one point to the other is what we've been looking to understand. But it is by no means clear that we can understand that process, at least not historically. Scholarship has produced many accounts of the origin of the Jews: some can be shown to be false; others stretch beyond what can actually be known; all are uncertain and subject to debate, and there seems to be no way beyond this impasse.

We have been treating origin as if it were something that can be investigated using the tools of history, anthropology, archaeology, and science, but it turns out to have many of the qualities of a religious concept like God: it is not simply hidden from view but seems to lie beyond our reach altogether, beyond observation, rational explanation, or even clear description. This is strange because we can point to processes of origination that happen all the time in the world around us—birth, growth, the construction of buildings, the formation of people through education, and the invention of new devices, and we know from science about evolution—but in a way, the familiarity of these other sorts of origin may have only misled scholarship, providing analogies that seem to explain what is happening but really only cover over the fact that we do not understand the process involved or even what it is that we are trying to understand. The history of the Jews has to start somewhere, but it is not clear whether, after many centuries of trying and failing to establish that starting point, scholarship has developed or will ever develop the ability to do so.

Knowing that this is a frustrating conclusion to have reached, I emphasize that to describe the search for the origin of the Jews as unresolved is not to deny all that scholars have discovered about ancient Jewish history over the past two centuries. If nothing else, scholarship has learned many things about how the Jews did *not* originate. Becoming less wrong is not the same as getting things right, however. Although scholarship has proven remarkably resourceful, coming up with a wide variety of theories and finding evidence in unexpected places, it is unclear whether all the effort has gotten us closer to understanding how the Jews originated. Indeed, it seems to me that the more scholars have learned, the more difficult it has become to reach any kind of conclusion.

How can it be that the search for the origin of the Jews has moved forward and backward at the same time, making things more obscure even as it yields more and more evidence? The reason I have offered has nothing to do with the Jews per se but is inherent in how scholars think about origin, a concept that becomes only more puzzling the more one dwells on it. Scholars in my field do not typically spend a lot of time examining their epistemological and metaphysical premises, but even if they did, it is unlikely that they would ever be able to resolve the ambiguities inherent in the concept of origin, for as we have seen, there is no consensus among scholars in any field about what an origin is or how to look for one. Our quest has taught us that if the origin of the Jews has eluded us, it is not because that origin is remote, invisible, or hard to access, or happens not to have left a trace of itself. It is because *the idea* of origin is inherently difficult to pin down.

Questioning the ontological status of origins is one of the defining moves of postmodernism, but the problems we have been struggling with here should not simply be identified with postmodernism, and they do not go away simply because, in some academic circles, there has been a kind of backlash against thinkers like Derrida. Scholars came to question the search for origin long before postmodernism, and there are many reasons to doubt our ability to ascertain origin that go beyond its critique, including good old-fashioned empirical reasons. In other origin-seeking fields, for example, some scholars have come to recognize that it requires a kind of fictional supplementation to turn the facts of history or science into an origin account. As the sociologist Robert Nisbet pointed out already in the 1960s, for example, no one actually sees the development of a society—all that we can establish are "the mingled facts of persistence and change"; and as he notes, the interpretation of these facts as a process of development seems to be based on a metaphor, an analogy with the growth of plants and animals. Something similar is true of all the different approaches we have considered: they too must rely on metaphor, borrow their plotlines from other fields of inquiry, and indulge in a lot of conjecture to fill in the gaps. We have been relying on historical inquiry to find something that does not exist within the realm of empirical investigation—a conclusion certain philosophers figured out some time ago but that somehow has still not penetrated the way many of us think about the question.

Needless to say, I have no way of predicting what scholars might discover in the future. The last three chapters have been focused on research since the 1990s, showing that the question of Jewish origin continues to attract scholarly interest even in an era shaped by the postmodern critique of origin, and perhaps continued research will lead to some result that overcomes the challenges with which we have been wrestling. That hasn't happened yet, however. Instead, the situation seems to be growing fuzzier, not clearer and more certain, with time. Even the recent findings of genetics research are already provoking critique, suggesting that this infusion of new data will not get us past the problems we have been confronting in this book. What makes the search for the origin of the Jews all the more challenging today is that the very act of seeking origins has grown suspect, giving rise to a genre of research that not only challenges the results of scholarly investigation but also questions scholars' objectivity and even their ethics. Future seekers of the origin of the Jews will not only have to contend with the elusiveness of the subject; if they are to incorporate everything that contemporary scholarship has to say about origins, they will also have to plunge into the depths of their own motivations and assumptions.

Lest I be misunderstood, I should be clear that none of this means that revisionists like Shlomo Sand are right when they propose a counter-narrative to what they describe as the conventional account of the origin of the Jews. Despite his efforts to discredit mainstream Jewish historiography, Sand has a lot in common with the scholars he criticizes, including the assumption that the origin of the Jewish people is hidden in the past in a way that only the scholarly elite can retrieve. In his case the origin he retrieves is polygenetic rather than monogenetic, recent rather than ancient, and arises from fabrication rather than developing naturally and gradually out of something earlier. But it too relies on a contested analogy of origination (invention) that simplifies the reality, and he recycles ideas that have an anti-Jewish pedigree (the Khazar hypothesis, the claim that the Jews are an artificial people). The conclusion I have reached, that there is something unresolvable about the question of the origin of the Jews, needs to be distinguished from a revisionism that seeks to displace one origin account of the Jews with yet another account.

If, despite all this, I am not quite ready to abandon the search, it is not because I have figured out some way beyond the impasse we have reached, but because I recognize that the question is a consequential one for many people, and that, from this vantage point at least, it will not suffice to simply leave the beginning of the Jewish story as unknowable. As we have seen, the search to understand the origin of the Jews is not merely a matter of intellectual interest but involves strong emotions, concerns, and interests and seems intertwined with people's sense of identity, their feeling of connection to others, and their sense of being rooted in the world. The feelings and motivations at work do not go away simply because scholarship pronounces the question moot. We must factor these existential, sociological, and political dimensions of the question into the equation as well.

The literary scholar Meir Sternberg, mentioned earlier in our discussion of the Habiru, makes a distinction that might help us to think about this question. Sternberg distinguishes between two kinds of informational lacunae in biblical literature—what he calls "blanks" and "gaps." Both represent an absence of information about the world described in the narrative. The blank is an incidental or trivial absence: the missing information is irrelevant for understanding the text, and readers may not even notice that it is missing. With a gap, by contrast, the missing information is considered of such importance that the reader will stop moving forward in the text to puzzle over it and to try to fill it in by doubling back and searching for clues within the preceding narrative. The blank "may be disregarded without loss; indeed must be disregarded in order to keep the narrative in focus," while gaps "demand closure," even if the narrative does not provide enough information with which to do so. A given reader may not notice a gap that the author has deliberately planted in the narrative or may see a gap where one was not intended by the author—as Sternberg notes, it is common for blanks to be elevated to "gaphood" and for gaps to be downgraded to "blankhood." Whether there by design or not, however, once a lacuna is recognized as a gap, it must be filled in, because the meaningfulness of the larger narrative depends on its resolution.

While Sternberg was speaking of literary texts, his distinction between blanks and gaps can be applied to the lost origin of the

Jews. Here, too, we are faced with a lack of information, and the options for supplying what is missing are similar as well: we can either hunt for clues that might allow us to infer what happened in the past, or use our imagination. But whether this particular hole in our understanding constitutes a gap or a blank—whether it is experienced as an absence that arrests us, compelling us to try to fill it in, or as an unknown of little consequence—is not a question that can be resolved through historical inquiry but requires an understanding of the mind in its interaction with the past: what it is that leads some people to recognize in the time before them a meaningful absence of information where others see nothing to wonder about.

From some perspectives, knowing the origin of a person or a thing is of little consequence—the facts of where a person comes from or how an object came to be are not considered relevant or important. For example, consider how certain twentieth-century French intellectuals came to view the origin of the Jews. By the eighteenth century there had developed in Europe an anti-Semitic caricature of the Jews as a rootless people, a people detached from any particular geographical or ancestral origin, without the connections of blood or soil that tied other nations to their pasts. As Sarah Hammerschlag has shown, this image of the rootless Jew was turned into a positive by Jean-Paul Sartre and other French intellectuals active after 1945, giving rise to the postmodern image of the Jew as the personification of uprootedness, a model or symbol for how to live in a world nomadically, without starting from a specific place or having firm ground to stand on. This positive revaluation of the rootless Jew emerges in the same intellectual context in which the postmodern critique of origin developed, and it is tempting to posit a relationship between the two developments, with the figure of the Jew becoming a symbol for a rootless, perpetually unsettled way of thinking embraced by these thinkers in a more general sense. In any case, it should not be a surprise that, in this context, for these thinkers, the historical question of the origin of the Jews was of no relevance, or was interesting only to the extent that it allied the Jews with a broader critique of rootedness.

One need not be a postmodern French intellectual to develop an indifference to origins. A survey sponsored by the online genealogy company Ancestry.com showed that one in three Americans could not name any of their grandparents, only 50 percent knew the name of more than one great-grandparent, and 27 percent did not know where their families lived before coming to America. Of course, a company like Ancestry.com has a stake in calling attention to what Americans do not know about their origins, but other research suggests that people are not simply ignorant about their origins for lack of knowledge but rather have reasons of their own for *not* wanting such information. In a study of what people in England thought about genealogical research, for example, the researchers found that the search for distant ancestors was indeed very meaningful for some of those surveyed, helping them to understand themselves or strengthening their connection to their family, but that a good number of others found such inquiry pointless: "Why one's ancestry should be a subject of such fascination nowadays is a mystery to me," wrote one man. "I just don't see how a blood link stretched by geography and time should still be so significant." Some recognize something narcissistic about the search. One respondent wrote, "What I think we are really doing though, is looking for clues about our own characteristics, seeing a flattering reflection in a tarnished mirror to pep up the ego." Others thought such information irrelevant for understanding who they were: "I'm not particularly interested in finding out more of my family tree, don't think it would help me to 'know who I am.' As far as I am concerned, I'm Me and that is enough." Still others did not want buried family secrets to come to light or worried that treasured family memories would be exposed as false: "Once the mystery of your past is revealed, there is no opportunity for fantasy—you can never be Russian royalty or the product of some great romance."

From other perspectives, however, the absence of information about one's roots is a deep and meaningful gap that compels a response. Psychologists describe the phenomenon of "genealogical bewilderment," an identity crisis that some adopted children undergo as a result of not knowing their biological parents or the circumstances of their conception. Something like genealogical bewilderment seems to be what motivates the children of Holocaust survivors to inquire into and reconstruct the lives of their parents before the war. In chapter 1, I mentioned a study by the sociologist

Arlene Stein, who learns from her interviews with these people that their quests to learn about the lost world their parents came from are really attempts to fill in gaps in their own life stories. To be sure, all these examples relate to origin in an intimate and immediate sense, looking back just a generation or two, but even in the realm of historical scholarship, in the search for an origin thousands of years ago, the motives that drive the search can be personal as well.

What made the question of Jewish origin such an insistent one for many of the scholars we have looked at was its perceived implications for their own identities as Europeans, Christians, Jews, cosmopolitans, Israelis, or Palestinians. These scholars believed that their answers to the question of Jewish origin addressed pressing questions of their times: Is it best to try to integrate Jews into Europe or to exclude them? How to resolve competing claims of indigenousness among Israelis and Palestinians? Present-day research is no different in this regard. Always there seems to be something beyond historical curiosity that motivates the scholarship: insecurity about the ambiguities of one's identity, the trauma of having been uprooted, a need to recover something that feels like it has been lost, a fear of being dislodged from one's place by another people, or profound discontent with some other origin account and what it implies about the present. It is to these kinds of considerations—the psychological, sociological, and political motives for scholarship—that we must look if we are to understand what makes the lost origin of the Jews appear as a relevant absence to scholars, why they see a mystery worth solving.

Why is it that, for some people, the absence of information about their origin is of little or no concern, while for others, the search for that knowledge can feel pressing, meaningful, a kind of moral imperative or a psychological compulsion? Are people from certain cultures or social backgrounds or with certain psychological predispositions or political leanings more impelled to search out their origins than others? I do not know the answer to these questions. As I noted in the introduction, many prominent scholars in the twentieth century, humanists and social scientists, came to see the search for origin as fruitless, inherently speculative, beside the point, or ideologically tainted. Indeed some described it as something worse than error, using religious terms like the "idol of origin" or "the cult of origins" to cast it as a kind of intellectual sin. But other research suggests that perhaps we do not yet fully understand what motivates people to be curious about origins. Recent social psychological research has shown that thinking about one's ancestors might have certain cognitive benefits, and anthropologists point to the social benefits of knowing who one's ancestors are; the perception of a shared ancestry can be key to a group's social solidarity, a reason to care about people beyond one's immediate family, and improve communication and relations within families. Clearly my own sensibilities have been shaped by scholarship's allergy to origins, but in my view scholarship has done a better job discrediting the concept of origin than understanding what motivates people to search for it.

As I think about who might read this book, I imagine that some number of readers find the lost origin of the Jews to be a meaningful absence—why else read a book like this?—and it is my empathy for them (or perhaps something stronger than that, my identification with them) that leaves me unsatisfied with where this search has led us. The inconvenient truth, however, is that there is no way for scholarship to close the gap. Scholarship has done a good job coming up with new evidence, and it is quite expert at debunking existing origin accounts for the Jews, but it has failed to generate an alternative narrative that can do the kind of work the Book of Genesis does in helping people to comprehend themselves and their places in the world. What we have seen suggests that leaning on scholarship to play the role of creation myth leads to claims that are tendentious at best, and sometimes quite destructive. This is the only honest way I can describe where the scholarly search for the origin of the Jews has led after so many centuries of effort, and yet I do not think it suffices to leave a hole at the beginning of Jewish history.

Of course, it is always an option to look beyond historical scholarship for answers. Genesis itself remains an option, and many people—perhaps most people—still prefer to look there or to other sacred myths to answer their questions about their origins. But as the reader likely realizes, there were good reasons that scholars questioned Genesis as an origin account, not just the well-known scientific ones but moral reasons as well: to accept Genesis as a historical account of origin is not just to accept that the world was created in six days; it is also to believe that women were created to serve men, and that certain people were destined to be the servants of other people. If the Bible had sufficed as an account of origin, it is true that we would not be stuck in this impasse, but personally, I would not want to pay the price that comes with embracing Genesis as the answer to our question.

All I can say by way of consolation is that this is not the first time in this study that we have been faced with an impossible impasse. We have encountered a number of different, sometimes antagonistic approaches to origin that cannot be reconciled or transcended— genealogy and antigenealogy, evolutionism and antievolutionism, constructivism and primordialism, processualism and postprocessualism, and the list goes on. Each perspective can continue on its separate trajectory and be satisfied with whatever progress it makes within its particular conceptual framework, but it exists in a world also inhabited by other paradigms, creating various kinds of intellectual stalemates that scholarship has yet to resolve. While we have not made headway beyond these impasses, we have encountered cases where someone operating from within one way of thinking becomes aware of the limits of his or her approach by engaging another way of thinking. Without taking away from the advances being made in fields like archaeology and genetics, I believe the most promising path forward in the search to understand the origin of the Jews lies in kindling—or rekindling—discontent with how scholars think about origins and encouraging thought that reaches beyond the contradictions of current paradigms.

Pinning one's hopes on a future paradigm shift is a concession that the lost origin of the Jews is not retrievable through any of the approaches that scholars now use to address the question. But to acknowledge this point is not to accede that we have made no progress. At the end of this quest, we are most certainly not back to the place where we started. We must suspend our search without reaching a destination, but by pushing the search for the origin of the Jews as far as scholarly inquiry can take us, wrestling with problems we cannot solve, and calling into question the very question that launched us, we have at least landed at a place from where we can appreciate that part of the mysteriousness of origins is why it is that we wonder about them.

More than a century ago, Friedrich Nietzsche recognized that the scholarly search for origin is a zero-sum game. The scholars he was referring to wanted to uncover origins that could ground their understanding of reality, but as the philosopher recognized, that is not the kind of origin their scholarship could deliver: the more it revealed about the origin of things, the less that origin seemed worth searching for. Something like this applies to the search for the origin of the Jews. All the advances we have surveyed—not just the textual, archaeological, and genetic discoveries but also the increased self-awareness about what it is that we mean by an origin— have made it only more difficult to reach a point in our quest where we can stop and feel that we have learned what we set out to learn. There have been insights along the way, but we are past the point where someone who follows the scholarship can have any reason to believe that it is someday going to yield a clear-cut answer. In truth, that possibility was probably lost from the moment people began to question the Genesis account many centuries ago, and given all the ways in which scholarship has fallen short since then, it seems a safe bet that it is never going to be able to clear things up.

But since this is not a conclusion likely to satisfy those who opened this book expecting to learn how the Jews originated, I want to conclude by suggesting another way forward, an alternative to giving up on the search altogether.

Of all the approaches we have examined in this book, the kind that in my view stands out as a potential path forward is genealogy. I don't have in mind genealogy as a method, the kind that entails searching through archives or conducting genetic tests. I mean a certain way of thinking about the search for origin, genealogy as a metaphor for an open-ended quest that, like the effort to follow an exponentially increasing number of ancestors backward in time, must move from the present moment into a past that grows increasingly complicated, many-sided, and hard to pin down. Even if there is some common ancestor or inaugural moment at the beginning of it all, genealogy can never get there because it confines itself to the documentable, to what can be proven, and it is just as likely to expose gaps in the evidence that cannot be filled as it is to answer our questions. All it can do, at best, is reveal partial and tentative answers, in a way that is halting, is always subject to critique, and has frustration built into it. In my view, this is the only kind of search that scholarship allows for, a search that grows more ramified, entangled, and daunting as it moves forward (if it can be said to move forward), but it does at least hold a door open for those not ready to give up.

It might be the case that we will never know for certain how to begin the story of the Jews; it might also be the case that the misleading or destructive effects of the search nullify anything that has been learned in the process. But I think something significant would be lost if scholars ever completely gave up. It is thanks to their research, after all, that we can now recognize the many *false* stories that have been told about the Jews' origin, and that insight is not to be dismissed. Nor should we be so quick to simply condemn the motivations that fuel this kind of research, which include the desire to locate Jews in a larger history of humanity and to demonstrate that they are something other than what people have assumed them to be. Scholars may have little hope of ever ascertaining the origin of the Jews, and maybe it is wrongheaded or delusional for them to develop that particular kind of intellectual aspiration, but there is something deep and perhaps primal about the aspiration to uncover that origin—it seems to originate from the same aspiration that produced Genesis itself, the need to understand who we are, how we came to be this way, and how we fit into the world. There would therefore be something sad and strange, something less human, about scholarship if it were ever to completely free itself of the attendant illusions, mature beyond its curiosity about where people come from, or give up altogether on trying to tell the story of their origin. I confess to still nursing the hope that, despite all the dead-ends we have come up against in this book, scholars will find ways to keep asking how the Jews originated. This is not because I expect them to ever break through to a definitive answer but because I value the humility that comes from recognizing that we do not know that answer and because, at the same time, I would lament the loss of a certain kind of ambition that modern-day scholarship has inherited from the myth-makers of old, the dream of being able to solve the enigma of beginnings.

ACKNOWLEDGMENTS

THOSE WHO HAVE UNDERTAKEN to research their family's roots may know that it does not take long before the quest to understand one's ancestry can become overwhelming. Count up the past ten generations—the tenth generation and all the intervening generations between then and now—and one's direct ancestors add up to around eight thousand people in total. Go back just another five generations, to around 1500, and one's cumulative ancestry at that point encompasses more than sixty-five thousand people. It is extraordinary how many souls it takes to produce a single human being. I have come to realize something similar is true when one produces a book: there are so many people to whom I am indebted for my ability to undertake this study, scholars, colleagues, friends, and family members—and the number of intellectual forebearers expands the more I think about things.

To single out just a few: there were two specific interactions that led me to undertake this book. The first is a friendship with Zvi Lederman and Shlomo Bunimovitz, archaeologists who direct the excavation at Tel Beth Shemesh in Israel. During the 1990s, as a young assistant professor at Indiana University, I worked with them to create a program that brought a few dozen students from IU to participate in their excavation, an experience that forced me to accept that I was not cut out to be an archaeologist but that was also an opportunity for many late-night discussions about archaeology, ethnogenesis, and other subjects that surface most explicitly in chapter 4. It was those conversations that first got me thinking about how scholars today account for the origin of peoples.

The second experience came after I moved to Stanford University, and had an opportunity to partner with Noah Rosenberg, a brilliant geneticist who had recently arrived to Stanford himself. After a meeting brokered by my colleague Vered Shemtov, we organized a series that aimed to bring geneticists, historians, anthropologists, and archaeologists into conversation about what genetic research can tell us about the Jews (this experience is the core of chapter 8). I would have been too intimidated to collaborate with someone of such scientific sophistication were Noah not so open, collaborative, and inquisitive in his own right, and I thank him for what I have learned from him.

Pushing further into the prehistory of this book, there are several other people I need to acknowledge for seminal conversations, advice, or feedback: John Efron (coauthor of the Jewish history textbook mentioned in the introduction where I was forced to think more precisely about where to start the history of the Jews), Amos Morris-Reich, Annette Yoshiko Reed, Stefan Schorch, Katharina Galor, James Redfield; Shahzad Bashir; and Ronny Miron. I also want to thank John Collins and Hindy Najman for the chance to present a version of chapter 8 at Yale University. In 2014, I moved to Penn to direct the Herbert D. Katz Center for Advanced Judaic Studies; and the greatest perk of that role, apart from working with the center's outstanding staff, is the chance to learn from the fellows hosted by the center each year. This book took shape during the fellowship years in 2014–2015 and 2015–2016—the first year devoted to the history of the academic study of the Jews; the second exploring intersections between Jewish studies and psychology. I cannot adequately express my gratitude for the chance to learn from so many generous-hearted scholars.

I also want to thank several people critical to the publication of the book. For many years, I have admired Fred Appel, an executive editor for Princeton University Press, for his role in producing so much excellent scholarship, and feel very lucky to be joining the list of authors who have had the opportunity to work with him and benefit from his support. There are a number of other people at Princeton University Press to whom I am indebted as well: editorial assistant Thalia Leaf who was helpful in countless ways—and a very patient troubleshooter; the production editor Jenny Wolkowicki, whose contributions are no less appreciated for being behind the scenes; an expert copy editor named Joseph Dahm, who helped me to overcome the limits of my writing; and the illustrations manager Dimitri Karentnikov whose efforts made it possible to include the images that appear in the book.

Mindy Brown helped me to prepare the manuscript at an earlier stage in the process, as did a diligent and resourceful graduate student at Penn, Alex Ramos. My thanks as well to Rabbi Ben Shull for his permission to reproduce an image of the illuminated family tree manuscript that inspired the book's cover (and appears at the beginning of the bibliographical commentary section). The tree was created between 1901 and 1911 by an artist named Joseph Judey, a refugee from Germany, and its surfacing a few years ago allowed Rabbi Shull to confirm his ancestry and connect with distant relatives. He and his family have since donated the tree to the Leo Baeck Institute, which also kindly gave its consent to use the image. I was initially drawn to the image because it conveyed to me the labyrinthine quality of origins, but I learned from Rabbi Shull that it has much deeper personal significance. See https://www.youtube.com/watch?v=S8z6W_HXQ4Q. Although we were not able to use the image itself for the book cover, it did loosely inspire its design by Jessica Massabrook, and I wish to convey my gratitude to her as well.

As in everything in my life, I am indebted to Mira Wasserman in ways that I can never adequately acknowledge.

The older I get, the more I realize what I learned from Liba Feuerstein, a beloved former teacher at Granada Hills High School in Los Angeles who passed away in 2013 as I was beginning to write this book. I have come to recognize her continuing influence in everything that I do as a reader and as a teacher, and this book is dedicated to her memory as a very belated expression of gratitude.

FIGURE 9. Illustrated family tree of Rabbi Ben Shull.
Source: Image courtesy of the Leo Baeck Institute, New York,
and with the permission of Rabbi Benjamin Shull.

THE FOLLOWING, offered in lieu of notes, is my way of acknowledging the scholarship to which I am indebted, and I also intend
it as a guide into various aspects of our topic that I could not adequately address within the main narrative. The bibliography offered here is by no means complete in its coverage of the scholarship, often only scratching the surface, but there should be enough
to allow interested readers to go beyond where I was able to go and
to help them more fully appreciate some of the questions and debates insufficiently addressed in the main narrative.

Introduction

The present book is by no means the first to address the question
of Jewish origin. For recent works that address this question, see
Christine Hayes, *The Emergence of Judaism* (Westport, CT: Green-
wood, 2006); Joseph Blenkinsopp, *Judaism, the First Phase: The
Place of Ezra and Nehemiah in the Origins of Judaism* (Grand
Rapids, MI: Eerdmans, 2009); Phillip Davies, *On the Origins of
Judaism* (London: Equinox, 2011). This book is not another historical reconstruction but an attempt to explore the thought processes of scholars as they seek to understand the origin of the Jews,
and to investigate the challenges that make that understanding so
elusive. A more relevant but unpublished precedent in that regard
is Ofri Ilani, "In Search of the Hebrew People: Bible Research in the
German Enlightenment, 1752–1810" (PhD diss., Tel Aviv University,
2012; in Hebrew).

Ancient Greek and Roman scholars speculated about the origin
of the Jews, but I will be addressing their ideas only in passing.
For discussion of what Tacitus and other ancient Greek and Roman
authors had to say on the subject, see Peter Schäfer, *Judeophobia:
Attitudes toward Jews in the Ancient World* (Cambridge, MA: Harvard University Press, 1997), 15–33. Tacitus's discussion of the different theories appears in his *Histories* 5.2–4 and is excerpted in

Menahem Stern, *Greek and Latin Authors on Jews and Judaism*, vol. 2 (Jerusalem: Israel Academy of Sciences and Humanities, 1980), 12–26.

For efforts to wrestle with the concept of origin, see Christopher Cherry, "Meaning and the Idol of Origins," *Philosophical Quarterly* 35 (1985): 58–69; A. C. Fabian, ed., *Origins: The Darwin College Lectures* (Cambridge: Cambridge University Press, 1988); Tomoko Masuzawa, *In Search of Dreamtime: The Quest for the Origin of Religion* (Chicago: University of Chicago Press, 1994); Paolo Spinozzi and Alessandro Zironi, eds., *Origins as a Paradigm in the Sciences and in the Humanities* (Göttingen: Vandenhoeck & Ruprecht, 2010); Russell McCutcheon, ed., *Fabricating Origins* (London: Equinox, 2015).

The cautionary notes against the search for origin cited here are drawn from Émile Durkheim, *The Elementary Forms of Religious Life: A Study in Religious Sociology*, trans. Joseph Ward Swain (London: Allen & Unwin, 1915), 8; Bronislaw Malinowski, *A Scientific Theory of Culture and Other Essays*, Malinowski Collected Works, vol. 9 (London: Routledge, 2009), 118; Marc Bloch, "The Idol of Origins," in Bloch, *The Historian's Craft* (New York: Knopf, 1954; repr., Manchester: Manchester University Press, 1992), 24–29. On the postmodern critique of origin, see John David Pizer, *Toward a Theory of Radical Origin: Essays on Modern German Thought* (Lincoln: University of Nebraska Press, 1995). A cognitive-narratological approach to origins and beginnings is developed by Eviatar Zerubavel, *Time Maps: Collective Memory and the Social Shape of the Past* (Chicago: University of Chicago Press, 2004). Wiktor Stoczkowski's study is *Explaining Human Origins: Myth, Imagination, and Conjecture* (Cambridge: Cambridge University Press, 2002). Amos Funkenstein, "The Dialectics of Assimilation," first appeared in *Jewish Social Studies*, n.s., 1.2 (1995): 1–14.

For more on the political dimensions of origins, see David Lowenthal, *The Heritage Crusade and the Spoils of History* (New York: Free Press, 1996); Joanne Wright, *Origin Stories in Political Thought: Discourses on Gender, Power, and Citizenship* (Toronto: University of Toronto Press, 2004); Catherine Nash, *Of Irish Descent: Origin Stories, Genealogy, and the Politics of Belonging* (Syracuse, NY: Syracuse University Press, 2008).

We will be filling in the nineteenth-century European context of the scholarly search for national origin as we go along, but for some of the background, see Richie Robertson, *The "Jewish Question" in German Literature, 1749–1939: Emancipation and Its Discontents* (Oxford: Oxford University Press, 1999). For more on how the Israeli-Palestinian conflict has manifested itself in scholarship, see Yoav Gelber, *Nation and History: Israeli Historiography and Identity between Zionism and Post-Zionism* (London: Vallentine Mitchell, 2011), and from a different point in the political spectrum, Nur Masalha, *The Bible and Zionism: Invented Traditions, Archaeology and Post-colonialism in Israel-Palestine* (London: Zed Books, 2007). Edward Said's study is *Beginnings: Intention and Method* (New York: Basic Books, 1975), and this work's interpretation by Massad is found in Joseph Massad, "Affiliating with Edward Said," in *Edward Said: A Legacy of Emancipation and Representation*, ed. Adel Iskander and Hakem Rustom (Berkeley: University of California Press, 2010), 23–49.

The concept of indigenousness merits more attention than I can give it. See Ronald Niezen, *The Origins of Indigenism: Human Rights and the Politics of Identity* (Berkeley: University of California Press, 2003). For a case study on the difficulties of establishing indigenous status for people in the Middle East, see Seth Frantzman, Havatzelet Yahel, and Ruth Kark, "Contested Indigeneity: The Development of an Indigenous Discourse on the Bedouin of the Negev, Israel," *Israel Studies* 17 (2012): 78–104. For biblical scholarship in service to a Palestinian claim of indigenousness, see Keith Whitelam, *The Invention of Ancient Israel: The Silencing of Palestinian History* (London: Routledge, 1996).

For readers curious about how I address (or avoid) the question of Jewish origin in the textbook I mention, see John Efron, Steven Weitzman, Matthias Lehmann, and Joshua Holo, *The Jews: A History* (Upper Saddle River, NJ: Prentice Hall/Pearson, 2008).

Chapter 1: Genealogical Bewilderment

For a recent study of the metaphor of roots that underlies both genealogical and etymological research, see Christy Wampole, *Rootedness: The Ramifications of a Metaphor* (Chicago: University of

Chicago Press, 2016). On "genealogical thinking," see Mary Bouquet, "Family Trees and Their Affinities: The Visual Imperative of the Genealogical Diagram," *Journal of the Royal Anthropological Institute* 2 (1996): 43–66; Sandra Bamford and James Leach, eds., *Kinship and Beyond: The Genealogical Model Reconsidered* (New York: Berghahn Books, 2009).

As an introduction to the concepts of genealogy and ancestry from a sociological perspective, I am indebted to Eviatar Zerubavel, *Ancestors and Relatives: Genealogy, Identity, and Community* (Oxford: Oxford University Press, 2012). Attempts to map out genealogy as an academic discipline include H. David Wagner, "Genealogy as an Academic Discipline," *Avotaynu* 22 (2006): 3–11; Arnon Herskovitz, "A Suggested Taxonomy of Genealogy as a Multidisciplinary Academic Research Field," *Journal of Multidisciplinary Research* 4 (2012): 5–21. To learn about the Board for Certification of Genealogists, see http://www.bcgcertification.org. My understanding of the role of the Internet in genealogical research depends on Rachel Jablon, *Virtual Legacies: Genealogies, the Internet and Jewish Identity* (PhD diss., University of Maryland, College Park, 2012).

On the challenges of establishing "descent from antiquity" (a generation-by-generation lineage connecting the living with specific ancestors in antiquity), see Anthony Wagner, *Pedigree and Progress: Essays in the Genealogical Interpretation of History* (London: Phillimore, 1975); Nathaniel Taylor, "Roman Genealogical Continuity and the 'Descents-from-Antiquity' Question," *American Genealogist* 76 (2001): 129–136.

Avotaynu: The International Review of Jewish Genealogy is published quarterly by Avotaynu, Inc., which also hosts a website with other kinds of resources, including an online index to the first twenty-four volumes. See http://www.avotaynu.com and a newly launched and more polished site, *Avotaynu Online*, at http://www.avotaynuonline.com. The International Institute for Jewish Genealogy and Paul Jacobi Center, based at the National Library in Jerusalem, was founded in 2004; its website can be found at http://iijg.org. For the genealogical study of the fourteenth-century Spanish town conducted by Maria Jose Surribas Camps, see her "A Brief History and Detailed Listing of the Jews of Tàrrega, Spain, Before and After the Black Death and Pogrom of 1348," *Avotaynu Online*,

http://www.avotaynuonline.com/2015/04/a-detailed-listing-of
-the-jews-of-tarrega-spain-before-and-after-the-black-death-and
-pogrom-of-1348/ (accessed May 30, 2015).

For more on the genealogies recorded in the Hebrew Bible, see
Marshall Johnson, *The Purpose of the Biblical Genealogies* (Eugene,
OR: Wipf & Stock, 1969); Robert Wilson, *Genealogy and History
in the Biblical World* (New Haven, CT: Yale University Press, 1977);
Ron Zadok, "On the Reliability of the Genealogical and Prosopo-
graphical Lists of the Israelites in the Old Testament," *Tel Aviv* 25.2
(1998): 228–254. On fictionalized genealogies from the Hellenistic
and Roman periods, see Erich Gruen, "Fictitious Kinships: Jews
and Others," in his *Rethinking the Other in Antiquity* (Princeton,
NJ: Princeton University Press, 2011), 277–307. The scholarship on
the (conflicting) genealogies of Jesus in the New Testament is too
extensive to cite, but for one recent study, see Jeremy Punt, "Politics
of Genealogies in the New Testament," *Neotestamentica* 47 (2013):
373–398. On Josephus's dubious genealogy, note Max Radin, "The
Pedigree of Josephus," *Classical Philology* 24 (1929): 193–196, and
for analysis of the role of genealogy (and the questions it raised
for the rabbis) in Talmudic literature, see Jeffrey Rubenstein, *The
Culture of the Babylonian Talmud* (Baltimore: Johns Hopkins University Press, 2003), 80–101; Moulie Vidas, "The Bavili's Discussion
of Genealogy in Qiddushin IV," in *Antiquity in Antiquity: Jewish
and Christian Pasts in the Greco-Roman World*, ed. G. Gardner and
K. Osterloh (Tübingen: Mohr Siebeck, 2006), 285–326.

On medieval Jewish claims to Davidic descent, I can recommend
Arnold Franklin, "Cultivating Roots: The Promotion of Exilarchal
Ties to David in the Middle Ages," *Association for Jewish Studies
Review* 29 (2005): 91–110; and his subsequent monograph *This
Noble House: Jewish Descendants of King David in the Medieval Is-
lamic East* (Philadelphia: University of Pennsylvania Press, 2013).
For the challenges of reconstructing the names and sequence of the
Exilarchs, key genealogical intermediaries between present-day
Jews and King David according to Sephardic tradition, see Moshe
Gil, "The Exilarchate," in *The Jews of Medieval Islam: Community,
Society and Identity*, ed. Daniel Frank (Leiden: Brill, 1995), 33–65.

Among many contemporary claims of Davidic descent, I focus
on Moshe Shaltiel-Gracian, *Shealtiel: One Family's Journey through*

History (Chicago: Chicago Review, 2005); and the website for the project known as "Davidic Dynasty," founded by Susan Roth: davidicdynasty.org. For other recent efforts to establish Davidic ancestry, see Arthur Menton, *The Book of Destiny: Toledot Charlap* (Cold Spring Harbor, NY: King David Press, 1996); Neil Rosenstein, *The Lurie Legacy: The House of Davidic Royal Descent* (New Haven, CT: Avotaynu, 2004). For a journalistic account of the effort to establish Davidic descent, see Nadine Epstein, "King David's Genes," *Moment Magazine*, March–April 2012, http://www.momentmag .com/king-davids-genes-2/ (accessed July 18, 2016). For evidence of such interest in the 1970s, note Arthur Kurzweil, "Finding Jewish Roots: Why Stop at King David," *New York Jewish Week*, July 24, 1977. On the documentary challenges of proving Davidic descent, see David Einsiedler, "Can We Prove Descent from King David?," *Avotaynu* 8 (1992): 29. Also relevant is the question of whether it is possible to establish descent from Rashi. See Jona Schellekens, "Descent from Rashi: A 'Mythological Charter,'" *Avotaynu* 19 (2003): 3–4. I make reference to a Charlap family newsletter that describes Bradman's research as confirmation of the Davidic lineage of the family: the newsletter can be found online at http://www .avotaynuonline.com/wp-content/uploads/2015/04/Charlap-11_3 .pdf (accessed May 15, 2016).

The inconclusive effort to find genetic evidence for the Shealtiel family's descent from David is recounted in Harry Ostrer, *Legacy: A Genetic History of the Jewish People* (Oxford: Oxford University Press, 2012), 105–106. Chapter 8 goes more deeply into genetics research, but I would note that the alliance between genealogical research and genetics is not recent: see E. S. Craighill Handy and Elizabeth Handy, "Genealogy and Genetics," *William and Mary Quarterly* 22.4 (1942): 381–388.

Contemporary interest in Jewish genealogy is often traced back to the 1970s—we have mentioned the works of Dan Rottenberg, *Finding Our Fathers: A Guidebook to Jewish Genealogy* (Baltimore: Random House, 1977); and Arthur Kurzweil, *From Generation to Generation: How to Trace Your Jewish Genealogy and Family History* (San Francisco: Wiley, 1980). But there was Jewish genealogical research much earlier in the twentieth century. See Arnon Hershkovitz, "Early Jewish Genealogical Research in Berlin and Jerusalem," *Avotaynu* 27 (2011): 23–26; Eric Ehrenreich, *The Nazi Ancestral Proof: Genealogy, Racial Science and the Final Solution* (Bloomington: Indiana University Press, 2007), which demonstrates that genealogical research was not always the innocuous avocation that it is today. (Under Nazi bureaucratic management it played a lethal role in identifying who was to be treated as a Jew.) For the case of Misha Defonseca, see Sharon Sergeant, "The Myth of Impossible Proof: Modern Genealogy Methods and a Holocaust Fraud," *Association of Professional Genealogists Quarterly* 23 (2008): 65–71.

Turning to the "constructivist" approach to genealogical claims, I mention several works that played a formative role in the development of this approach: The citation from Max Weber comes from his *Economy and Society: An Outline of Interpretive Sociology*, ed. Guenther Roth and Claus Wittich (Berkeley: University of California Press, 1978), 389; His views are developed by Maurice Halbwachs, *On Collective Memory*, ed. Lewis Coser (Chicago: University of Chicago Press, 1992); and Fredrik Barth, *Ethnic Groups and Boundaries: The Social Organization of Culture Difference* (Boston: Little, Brown, 1969). As for the application of this approach to genealogies in particular, I would call attention to David Henige, *The Chronology of Oral Tradition: Quest for a Chimera* (Oxford: Clarendon, 1974), which explores the manipulation of information in African royal genealogies; and David Schneider, *A Critique of the Study of Kinship* (Ann Arbor: University of Michigan Press, 1984). For recent studies of "genealogical imagination," see Andrew Shryock, *Nationalism and the Genealogical Imagination: Oral History and Textual Authority in Tribal Jordan* (Berkeley: University of California Press, 1997); and Maria Elena Martínez, *Genealogical Fictions: Limpieza de Sangre, Religion, and Gender in Colonial Mexico* (Stanford, CA: Stanford University Press, 2008).

For the findings of Stanley Hordes, including his effort to counter the criticisms of Judith Neulander, see his *To the End of the Earth: A History of the Crypto-Jews of New Mexico* (New York: Columbia University Press, 2008). The website of the Society for Crypto-Judaic Studies, which he helped to found, can be accessed at http://cryptojews.com (accessed July 20, 2016). Among those who have defended Hordes, see Seth Kunin, "Juggling Identities among the Crypto-Jews of the American Southwest," *Religion* 31 (2001): 41–61.

On Spain's recent offer of citizenship to the descendants of Jews expelled from Spain, see Rick Gladstone, "Many Seek Citizenship Offered to Sephardic Jews," *New York Times*, March 19, 2014, http://www.nytimes.com/2014/03/20/world/europe/many-seek-spanish-citizenship-offered-to-sephardic-jews.html?_r=0 (accessed July 20, 2016). There may be a problem with the Spanish government's decision to fast-track citizenship for any Jew whose ancestors were expelled from Spain: although Sephardic Jews compose around 10 percent of the world Jewish population (the term "Sephardic" is often used in reference to Jews who descend from those expelled from Spain), a scientist named Joshua Weitz has calculated that nearly all Jews today might have a genealogical connection to Spanish Jews, whether or not they identify as their descendants. See Joshua Weitz, "Let My People Go (Home) to Spain: A Genealogical Model of Jewish Identities since 1492," *PLOS ONE* 9.1 (2014): e85673: http://journals.plos.org/plosone/article?id=10.1371/journal.pone.0085673.

For Judith Neulander's skeptical response to Hordes research, see Judith Neulander, "Crypto-Jews of the Southwest: An Imagined Community," *Jewish Folklore and Ethnology Review* 16.1 (1994): 64–68; and Neulander, "The New Mexican Crypto-Jewish Canon: Choosing to be 'Chosen' in Millennial Tradition," *Jewish Folklore and Ethnology Review* 18.12 (1996): 19–58. For a more recent study in a similar vein, see also Jonathan Freedman, "Conversos, Marranos, and Crypto-Latinos," in *Boundaries of Jewish Identity*, ed. Susan Glenn and Naomi Sokoloff (Seattle: University of Washington Press, 2010), 188–202. For an account of her debate with Hordes, see Barbara Ferry and Debbie Nathan, "Mistaken Identity? The Case of New Mexico's 'Hidden Jews,'" *Atlantic*, December 2000, http://www.theatlantic.com/magazine/archive/2000/12/mistaken-identity-the-case-of-new-mexicos-hidden-jews/378454/ (accessed February 10, 2016). Neulander, it should be noted, is also skeptical of Hordes's use of genetics to support his genealogy, coauthoring a genetic study that sought to refute his use of this kind of evidence. See Wesley K. Suton, Alec Knight, Peter Underhill, Judith Neulander, T. Todd Disotell, and Joanna

Mountain, "Toward Resolution of the Debate Concerning Purported Crypto-Jews in a Spanish-American Population: Evidence from the Y Chromosome," *Annals of Human Biology* 33 (2006): 100–311.

In the section on the use of genealogy as a critique of origin, the discussion focuses on Gilles Deleuze and Félix Guattari, *A Thousand Plateaus*, trans. Brian Masumi (Minneapolis: University of Minnesota Press, 1987), 1–25 (for the rhizome/Internet comparison, see Vincent Miller, *Understanding Digital Culture* [London: Sage, 2011], 26–29); Michel Foucault, "Nietzsche, Genealogy, History," in *Language, Counter-Memory, Practice: Selected Essays and Interviews by Michel Foucault*, ed. Donald Bouchard (Ithaca, NY: Cornell University Press, 1977), 139–164; Catherine Nash, "Genealogical Identities," *Environment and Planning D: Society and Space* 20 (2002): 27–52; Daniel Boyarin and Jonathan Boyarin, "Diaspora: Generation and the Ground of Jewish Identity," *Critical Inquiry* 19 (1993): 693–725; Arlene Stein, "Trauma and Origins: Post-Holocaust Genealogists and the Work of Memory," *Qualitative Sociology* 32 (2009): 293–309.

Chapter 2: Roots and Rootlessness

One aim of this chapter is to explore how scholars sought to recover the "prehistory" of the Jews prior to the biblical period, and that project was tied to the emergence of the category of prehistory in the nineteenth century. For background on the concept of prehistory, see Donald Grayson, *The Establishment of Human Antiquity* (New York: Academic Press, 1983); Christopher Chippindale, "The Invention of Words for the Idea of 'Prehistory,'" *Proceedings of the Prehistoric Society* 54 (1988): 303–314; Alice Prehoe, "The Invention of Prehistory," *Current Anthropology* 32 (1991): 467–476.

The history of the scholarly category of the Semite in the same period has to be pieced together from a range of articles and books. Gil Anidjar's *Semites: Race, Religion, Literature* (Stanford, CA: Stanford University Press, 2008) is suggestive but does not pursue the origin of this category much beyond a description of Renan's views and the category's demise after the Holocaust. The category of Semite was derived from the name Shem, the oldest son of Noah. Jews have long identified themselves as the descendants of Shem through their Israelite ancestors, but certain non-Jewish interpreters understood them to be the descendants of Japhet or Ham, and according to the historian Benjamin Braude, Christian Europeans did not make a connection between Jews and Shem until after 1400. (Had the history of biblical interpretation taken a different turn, we might be fretting today about a resurgence of anti-Japhetism.) See Benjamin Braude, "The Sons of Noah and the Construction of Ethnic and Geographic Identities in the Medieval and Early Modern Periods," *William and Mary Quarterly* 54 (1997): 103–143.

The German *semitisch* was introduced as a linguistic category by Schlözer in an essay published in the leading Oriental studies journal of the day: August Ludwig von Schlözer, "Von der Chaldäern," in *Repertorium fuer biblische und morgenlaendische Literatur*, vol. 8, ed. J. G. Einhorn (Leipzig: Weidmanns Erben und Reich, 1781), 113–176. For more on the development of Semitic/Semite as a linguistic category, see Yaakov Grundfest, "On the History of the Classification of Semitic Languages," in *History of Linguistics, 1993*, ed. Kurt Jankowsky (Amsterdam: John Benjamins, 1995), 67–74; Maurice Oleander, *The Languages of Paradise: Aryans and Semites, a Match Made in Heaven*, trans. Arthur Goldhammer (Cambridge, MA: Harvard University Press, 1992); and Martin F. J. Baasten, "A Note on the History of Semitic," in *Hamlet on a Hill: Semitic and Greek Studies Presented to Prof. T. Muraoka on the Occasion of His Sixty-Fifth Birthday*, ed. Baasten and W. T. Van Peursen (Leuven: Peeters, 2003), 57–72 (my thanks to John Huehnergard for this reference). For a current understanding of the origin of the family of languages known as Semitic, see Edward Lipinski, *Semitic Linguistics in Historical Perspective* (Leuven: Peeters, 2014), 2–3. Smith's reconstruction of early Semitic religion was published posthumously as *Lectures on the Religion of the Semites* (London: Adam and Charles Black, 1894). The quote questioning the conflation of the racial and the linguistic in the use of the term "Semite" comes from Hilary Richardson, "The Semites," *American Journal of Semitic Languages and Literatures* 41 (1924): 1–10.

Intertwined with the scholarly category of Semite is the category of Aryan, whose history is discussed in Léon Poliakov, *The Aryan Myth: A History of Racist and Nationalist Ideas in Europe* (New York: New American Library, 1977); Dorothy Figueira, *Aryans,*

Jews, Brahmins: Theorizing Authority through Myths of Identity (Albany: State University of New York Press, 2002); and Stefan Arvidsson, *Aryan Idols: Indo-European Mythology as Ideology and Science*, trans. Sonia Wichman (Chicago: University of Chicago Press, 2006). The description of Aryan-related scholarship as "myth plus footnotes" is from Bruce Lincoln, *Theorizing Myth: Narrative, Ideology, and Scholarship* (Chicago: University of Chicago Press, 1999), 215.

The field of linguistic paleontology was founded by Adolphe Pictet through his work *Les Origines indo-européennes, ou, Les Aryas primitifs: Essai de paléontologie linguistique*, 2 vols. (Paris: Cherbuliez, 1859–1863). Though the term has gone out of fashion, research in this field continues. See Colin Renfrew, *Archaeology and Language: The Puzzle of Indo-European Origins* (Cambridge: Cambridge University Press, 1987), esp. 42–74; John Bengston, ed., *In Hot Pursuit of Language in Prehistory* (Amsterdam: John Benjamins, 2008); and David Anthony, *The Horse, the Wheel, and Language: How Bronze Age Riders from the Eurasian Steppes Shaped the Modern World* (Princeton, NJ: Princeton University Press, 2008).

For more on etymology, see Yakov Malkiel, *Etymology* (Cambridge: Cambridge University Press, 1993). Davide Del Bello, *Forgotten Paths: Etymology and the Allegorical Mindset* (Washington, DC: Catholic University of America Press, 2007), traces the history of etymology from antiquity through Isidore to postmodern scholarship. On the relationship between etymology and genealogy in antiquity, the Middle Ages, and the early modern period, see R. Howard Bloch, *Etymologies and Genealogies* (Chicago: University of Chicago Press, 1983); Marian Rothstein, "Etymology, Genealogy, and the Immutability of Origins," *Renaissance Quarterly* 43 (1990): 332–347. On the early modern use of etymology to understand the origin of nations, see Angus Vine, "Etymology, Names and the Search for Origins: Deriving the Past in Early Modern Europe," *Seventeenth Century* 21 (2006): 1–21, from whom I take the citations to Camden and Bodin. Friedrich Diez introduced a "critical" approach to etymology in his *An Etymological Dictionary of the Romance Languages*, trans. T. C. Donkin (London: Williams and Norgate, 1864), from a German work first published between 1836 and 1844.

The identity of the Habiru and their relationship to the Hebrews has generated an overwhelming number of studies since the two terms were first identified. Among those I draw on are Hugo Winckler, "Die Hebräer in den Tel-Amarna Briefen," in *Semitic Studies in Memory of Rev. Dr. Alexander Kohut*, ed. George Kohut (Berlin: Calvary & Co., 1897), 605–609; Moshe Greenberg, *The Hab/piru* (New Haven, CT: American Oriental Society, 1955); Nadav Na'aman, "Habiru and Hebrews: The Transfer of a Social Term to the Literary Sphere," *Journal of Near Eastern Studies* 45 (1986): 271–288; and Ann Killebrew, "Hybridity, Hapiru, and the Archaeology of Ethnicity in Second Millennium BCE Western Asia," in *A Companion to Ethnicity in the Ancient Mediterranean*, ed. Jeremy McInerney (New York: Wiley, 2014), 142–157.

Winckler's identification of the kingdom of Mitanni with its Hurrian population as the first Indo-Aryan state is found in Hugo Winckler, "Die Arier in den Urkunden von Baghaz-koi," *Orientalistische Literaturzeitung* 13 (1910): 289. On possible intersections between the Hurrians and the Habiru, see Ephraim Speiser, "Ethnic Movements in the Near East in the Second Millennium BCE: The Hurrians and Their Connections with the Habiru and the Hyksos," *Annual of the American Schools of Oriental Research* 13 (1931–1932): 13–54. (Speiser, incidentally, rejected the association of the Hurrians with the Aryans and undercut the Habiru/Hurrian contrast by describing the Hurrians as fellow "wanderers" of the Habiru.) For an English translation of the Amarna letters, see William Moran, *The Amarna Letters* (Baltimore: Johns Hopkins University Press, 2000). The excerpt cited from an Amarna letter about the Habiru is based on his translation on 265–266. Anson Rainey voices skepticism about the equation of Habiru with Hebrew in his review of Oswald Loretz's *Habiru–Hebräer: Eine soziolinguistische Studie über die Herkunft des Gentiliziums 'ibrî vom Appellativum ḥabiru* (Berlin: De Gruyter, 1984), in *Journal of the American Oriental Society* 101 (1987): 539–551.

An illuminating discussion of the influence of race theory on Assyriology in this period is Jerrold Cooper, "Sumerian and Aryan: Racial Theory, Academic Politics, and Parisian Assyriology," *Revue de l'histoire des religions* 210 (1993): 169–205. Also relevant for understanding Winckler's intellectual context are Suzanne Marchand,

German Orientalism in the Age of Empire: Religion, Race, and Scholarship (Cambridge: Cambridge University Press, 2009), esp. 212–251; and Steve Holloway, ed., *Assyriology, Orientalism, and the Bible* (Sheffield: Sheffield University Press, 2006).

Adolf Wahrmund's work on the Jews as nomads, first published in 1887, is *Das Gesetz des Nomadenthums und die heutige Juden-herrshaft* (repr., Munich: Deutscher Volks-Verlag, 1919). I take the citation from his work from Sander Gilman, "Aliens versus Predators: Cosmopolitan Jews vs. Jewish Nomads," in *The German-Jewish Experience Revisited*, ed. Steven Aschheim and Vivian Liska (Berlin: De Gruyter, 2015), 59–74, esp. 68. On the nationalist and anti-Semitic views at work in the scholarship of Friedrich Delitzsch, see Bill Arnold and David Weisberg, "A Centennial Review of Friedrich Delitzsch's 'Babel und Bibel' Lectures," *Journal of Biblical Literature* 121 (2002): 441–457. For Werner Sombart's description of the Hebrews as "restless, wandering Bedouin" (a quality that he invokes to account for the Jews' alleged affinity for capitalism), see his *The Jews and Modern Capitalism*, trans. M. Epstein (New York: E.P. Dutton, 1913).

Turning to Saussure and his rejection of linguistic paleontology, the most relevant chapter of his *Course in General Linguistics* is titled "The Contribution of Language to Anthropology and Prehistory." See Ferdinand de Saussure, *Course in General Linguistics*, ed. Charles Bally and Albert Sechehaye (New York: Philosophical Library, 1959), 222–227. For an introduction to his thinking, see Paul Bouissac, *Saussure: A Guide for the Perplexed* (London: Continuum, 2010). Saussure's rejection of Pictet's effort to reconstruct a lost mother tongue is touched on in Oleander, *Languages of Paradise*, 99–101, but Saussure did not completely rebuff the teachings of his mentor. See John Joseph, "Root and Branch: Pictet's Role in the Crystallization of Saussure's Thought," *Times Literary Supplement* 5258 (2004): 12–13. The citation from Saussure about his youthful enthusiasm for linguistic paleontology is taken from Robert Godel, "Souvenirs de F. de Saussure concernant sa jeunesse et sus études," *Cahiers Ferdinand de Saussure* 17 (1960): 12–26, 16, as cited in Anna Morpurgo Davies, "Saussure and Indo-European Linguistics," in *The Cambridge Companion to Saussure*, ed. Carol Sanders (Cambridge: Cambridge University Press, 2004), 9–29, esp. 14.

Meir Sternberg's study is *Hebrews between Cultures: Group Portraits and National Literature* (Bloomington: Indiana University Press, 1998). To illustrate the influence of Saussure's perspective on how scholars of Jewish studies think about the words that Jews use to identify themselves, I have mentioned several recent studies of the category "Jew" and its relationship to its linguistic antecedents. The article that sparked the debate was Adele Reinhartz, "The Vanishing Jews of Antiquity," published in the online review *Marginalia* on June 24, 2014: http://marginalia.lareviewofbooks .org/vanishing-jews-antiquity-adele-reinhartz/ (accessed December 5, 2015)—and various responses can be found at the same website. For another example of what I take to be a Saussurean approach to the meaning of "Jew," see Ishay Rosen-Zvi and Adi Ohir, "Goy: Toward a Genealogy," *Dine Israel* 28 (2011): 69–122. My own view on the relationship between *iudaios* and "Jew," or at least the position I adopt in this book, follows Annette Reed's contribution to the discussion, "*Iudaios* Before and After 'Religion,'" http://marginalia .lareviewofbooks.org/ioudaios-religion-annette-yoshiko-reed/, which calls on scholars to be more self-reflective about the narratives of origin implicit in their translation choices; and Daniel Schwartz, *Judeans and Jews: Four Faces of Dichotomy in Ancient Jewish History* (Toronto: University of Toronto Press, 2014), which makes a case for shifting from one term to the other to bring out different aspects of Judean/Jewish identity. See also Cynthia Baker, *Jew* (New Brunswick, NJ; Rutgers University Press, 2017).

Chapter 3: Histories Natural and Unnatural

For background on developmental/evolutionary thinking, see Peter Bowler, *Evolution: The History of an Idea* (Berkeley: University of California Press, 1983); Robert Nisbet, *History of the Idea of Progress* (New York: Basic, 1980); and Misia Landau, *Narratives of Human Evolution* (New Haven, CT: Yale University Press, 1991). On the concept of degeneration, see Daniel Pick, *Faces of Degeneration: A European Disorder* (Cambridge: Cambridge University Press, 1989).

On Darwin's impact on how people conceptualized origin, I have learned much from Gillian Beer, *Darwin's Plots: Evolutionary*

Narrative in Darwin, George Eliot, and Nineteenth-Century Fiction (Cambridge: Cambridge University Press, 1983). Darwin was not completely uninterested in the question of how life first originated, but he felt that the science of his day did not allow for a resolution of the question. See Juli Pereto, Jeffrey Bada, and Antonio Lazcano, "Charles Darwin and the Origin of Life," *Origins of Life and Evolution of the Biosphere* 39 (2009): 395–406. Darwin's reference to "innumerable miraculous creations" comes from his *The Variation of Plants and Animals under Domestication*, vol. 1 (London: John Murray, 1868), 12. His reference to the Jews appears in Charles Darwin, *The Descent of Man and Selection in Relation to Sex* (London: John Murray, 1871), 240. Darwin discusses "living fossils" in *The Origin of Species by Means of Natural Selection, or the Preservation of Favored Races in the Struggle for Life* (London: John Murray, 1859), 107 and 486.

Turning to biblical studies, we have mentioned several key figures from the eighteenth and early nineteenth centuries prior to Darwin and Wellhausen who conceived of the origin of Jews as happening in stages or through an ongoing process like degeneration. For more on these scholars, see Jonathan M. Hess, "Johann David Michaelis and the Colonial Imaginary: Orientalism and the Emergence of Racial Anti-Semitism in Eighteenth-Century Germany," *Jewish Social Studies* 6 (2000): 56–101; John Rogerson, *Old Testament Criticism in the Nineteenth Century: England and Germany* (London: SPCK, 1984). On De Wette, see James Pasto, "Islam's 'Strange Secret Sharer': Orientalism, Judaism, and the Jewish Question," *Comparative Studies in Society and History* (1998): 437–474 (from which I take the passage from De Wette's *Biblische Dogmatik Alten und Neuen Testaments* [Berlin: Reimer, 1831]); and Pasto, "W. M. L. de Wette and the Invention of Postexilic Judaism: Political Historiography and Christian Allegory in Nineteenth-Century German Biblical Scholarship," in *Jews, Antiquity, and the Nineteenth-Century Imagination*, ed. Hayim Lapin and Dale Martin (Potomac: University of Maryland Press, 2003), 33–52. These articles draw on Pasto's unpublished dissertation, from which I learned much: "Who Owns the Jewish Past? Judaism, Judaisms, and the Writing of Jewish History" (PhD diss., Cornell University, 1999).

On the Jews as a developmental anomaly—a "living fossil" or an atavism—I cite several sources: Johann Friedrich Blumenbach, "On the Natural Variety of Man," in *The Anthropological Treatises of Johann Friedreich Blumenbach*, ed. T. Bendyshe (London: Longman, Green, Longman, Roberts and Green, 1865), 234; Jakob Friedrich Fries, *Über die Gefährdung des Wohlstands und Charakters der Deutschen durch die Juden* (Heidelberg, 1816), 10; Maurice Fishberg, *The Jews: A Study of Race and Environment* (New York: Charles Scribner's Sons, 1911), 82; Richard Andree, *Zur Volkeskunde der Juden* (Bielefeld and Leipzig, 1881), 24–25.

Julius Wellhausen's *Prolegomena zur Geschichte Israels*, 2nd ed. (Berlin: Reimer, 1883) was translated very soon afterward into English by J. Sutherland Black and Allan Menzies as *Prolegomena to the History of Ancient Israel* (Edinburgh: Charles and Adam Black, 1885), which also includes a reprint of Wellhausen's article on Israel originally published in vol. 13 of the 9th edition of *Encyclopedia Britannica*, 306–412.

An overview of Wellhausen's method within its nineteenth-century context is Reinhard Kratz, "Eyes and Spectacles: Wellhausen's Method of Higher Criticism," *Journal of Theological Studies* 60 (2009): 381–402; see also the essays published in Douglas Knight, ed., *Julius Wellhausen and His Prolegomena to the History of Israel*, Semeia 25 (Atlanta: Society of Biblical Literature, 1983). For the intellectual background of Wellhausen's approach, see Lothar Perlitt, *Vatke und Wellhausen: Geschichtsphilosophische Voraussetzungen und historiographische Motive für die Darstellung der Religion und Geschichte Israels durch Wilhelm Vatke und Julius Wellhausen* (Berlin: De Gruyter 1965), which treats his relationship to Darwinism and other developmental theories and his preference for the natural over the artificial; and Diane Banks, *Writing the History of Israel* (London: T & T Clark, 2006), 50–75.

The Documentary Hypothesis has long provoked dissent, some of it from Jewish or Israeli scholars who had a different view of the Jews than Wellhausen did. Even a scholar who for the most part accepted the conclusions of Wellhausen's analysis, Siegmund Maybaum (1844–1919), placed the Pentateuch's sources in a different historical trajectory that cast Judaism in a more positive light. (For more on Maybaum and other Jewish critics of the Documentary

Hypothesis, see Ran HaCohen, *Reclaiming the Hebrew Bible: German-Jewish Reception of Biblical Criticism* [Berlin: De Gruyter, 2010].) An influential challenge to Wellhausen's narrative came from Yehezkiel Kaufmann (1889–1963), who began his scholarly career in Palestine in 1928 and became a professor of Bible at the Hebrew University in 1949; he transmitted his views to later Israeli scholars like Menahem Haran, Avi Hurvitz, and others, who developed additional arguments for placing the Priestly source in the pre-exilic period. For more on the reaction against Wellhausen among Israeli biblical scholars, see Yaacov Shavit and Mordechai Eran, *The Hebrew Bible Reborn: From Holy Scripture to the Book of Books—A History of Biblical Culture and the Battles over the Bible in Modern Judaism* (Berlin: De Gruyter, 2007).

For what we know about the Persian period of Jewish history, see W. D. Davies and Louis Finkelstein, eds., *The Cambridge History of Judaism*, vol. 1: *The Persian Period* (Cambridge: Cambridge University Press, 1984); Hugh Williamson, *Studies in Persian Period History and Historiography* (Tübingen: Mohr Siebeck, 2004); Oded Lipschitz and Manfred Oeming, *Judah and the Judeans in the Persian Period* (Winona Lake, IN: Eisenbrauns, 2006); and Jon Berquist, *Approaching Yehud: New Approaches to the Study of the Persian Period* (Atlanta: Society of Biblical Literature, 2007). For the limits of what we know about this period, see Sara Japhet, "Can the Persian Period Bear the Burden? Reflections on the Origins of Biblical History," in *From the Rivers of Babylon to the Highlands of Judah: Collected Studies on the Restoration Period* (Winona Lake, IN: Eisenbrauns, 2006), 342–352. Peter Frei's attempt to give the Persian Empire a role in the codification of the Torah appears in English as "Persian Imperial Authorization: A Summary," in *Persia and Torah: The Theory of Imperial Authorization of the Pentateuch*, ed. James Watts (Atlanta: Society of Biblical Literature, 2001), 5–40. For criticism of this theory, see, for example, Lisbeth Fried, "Did Ezra Create Judaism?," in *Marbeh Hokmah: Studies in the Bible and the Near East in Loving Memory of Victor Avigdor Hurowitz*, ed. S. Yona et al. (Winona Lake, IN: Eisenbrauns, 2015), 171–184.

For the theory that the Jews originated in India, I mention two sources: (1) an account attributed to Aristotle's disciple Clearchus, known from a citation in Josephus's work *Against Apion* 1.176–183 (for commentary on this passage, see Menahem Stern, *Greek and Latin Authors on Jews and Judaism*, vol. 1 [Jerusalem: Israel Academy of Sciences and Humanities, 1974], 47–52); and (2) a nineteenth-century study that aims to draw (farfetched) parallels between rabbinic and Sanskrit literature, Friedrich Nork, *Braminen und Rabbinen, oder Indien das Stammland der Hebräer und ihrer Fabeln* (Meissen: Goedsche, 1836). On the scholarly identification of India as the homeland of the Aryans, see Thomas Trautman, *Aryans and British India* (Berkeley: University of California Press, 1997); and Edwin Bryant, *The Quest for the Origins of Vedic Culture: The Indo-Aryan Migration Debate* (Oxford: Oxford University Press, 2001). On the shift from India to Persia as the homeland of the Aryans, see Arvidsson, *Aryan Idols*, 52–53; and for more on European perceptions of Iran, see Mostafa Vaziri, *Iran as Imagined Nation: The Construction of National Identity* (New York: Paragon House, 1993).

By the end of the twentieth century, scholars had grown more wary of invoking Persian influence to explain Judaism. See James Barr, "The Question of Religious Influence: The Case of Zoroastrianism, Judaism, and Christianity," *Journal of the American Academy of Religion* 53 (1985): 201–235. But the theory is making a comeback in the study of rabbinic literature. For the role of the Aryan myth in modern Iranian self-understanding, see Reza Zia-Ebrahimi, "Self-Orientalization and Dislocation: The Uses and Abuses of the 'Aryan' Discourse in Iran," *Iranian Studies* 44 (2011): 445–472: David Motadel, "Iran and the Aryan Myth," in *Perceptions of Iran: History, Myths and Nationalism from Medieval Persia to the Islamic Republic*, ed. Ali Ansari (New York: I.B. Tauris, 2014), 119–146.

The conflict between Wellhausen and Eduard Meyer is recounted in Reinhard Kratz, *Das Judentums im Zeitalter des Zweiten Tempels* (Tübingen: Mohr Siebeck, 2004), 6–22; and Blenkinsopp, *Judaism, the First Phase* (mentioned in the bibliography for the introduction), 28–32. The debate between Wellhausen and Meyer is an example of how scholars' different interpretations of the evidence relate to different conceptualizations of origin. Wellhausen's description of the origin of Judaism reflects what Max Weber called an immanent evolutionary approach; it posits a process driven mostly by internal impulses. The actors in the *Prolegomena* are the Israelites/Jews themselves, while external players like the Persians are relegated to the margins. Meyer, on the other hand, stressed the role of external events as a necessary catalyst. See Max Weber, "A Critique of Eduard Meyer," in *Max Weber: Collected Methodological Writings*, ed. Hans Bruun and Sam Whimster (London: Routledge, 2012), 139–168, esp. 148; and for further discussion of Meyer's views, note Stefan Hauser, "History, Races, and Orientalism: Eduard Meyer, the Organization of Oriental Research, and Herzfeld's Intellectual Heritage," in *Ernst Herzfeld and the Development of Near Eastern Studies, 1900–1950*, ed. Ann Gunter and Stefan Hauser (Leiden: Brill, 2005), 505–559. Wellhausen's description of the Elephantine community as a vestigial form of Israelite religion comes from *Israelitische und jüdische Geschichte*, 10th ed. (repr.; Berlin: De Gruyter, 2004), 176–178.

Finally, some references that bear on the issue we address at the end of the chapter—the demise of a developmental approach to the origin of the Jews. Wellhausen's impact on subsequent biblical scholarship, including his declining influence, is surveyed in Ernest Nicholson, *The Pentateuch in the Twentieth Century: The Legacy of Wellhausen* (Oxford: Oxford University Press, 1998); David Carr, "Changes in Pentateuchal Criticism," in *Hebrew Bible/ Old Testament: The History of Its Interpretation*, vol. 3, pt. 2, ed. Magne Sæbø (Göttingen: Randenhoeck and Ruprecht, 2015), 433–466. Some of the strongest attacks on the Documentary Hypothesis have come from European scholars, and the work of the German scholar Rolf Rendtorff (1925–2014) is often cited as an example. See his study, *The Problem of the Process of Transmission in the Pentateuch*, trans. John Scullion (Sheffield: JSOT Press, 1990). A more recent generation has sought to revive the hypothesis in modified form (see, for example, Joel Baden, *The Composition of the Pentateuch: Renewing the Documentary Hypothesis* [New Haven, CT: Yale University Press], 2012), but it no longer uses source criticism to reconstruct the origin of Judaism.

For representative examples of the so-called minimalist approach to biblical history, which treats Israel as depicted in the Bible as the work of Persian-period Judean imagination, see Philip Davies, *In Search of Ancient Israel* (Sheffield: Sheffield

Academic, 1992); Thomas Thompson, *Early History of the Israel- ite People: From the Written and Archaeological Sources* (Leiden: Brill, 1992); and the aforementioned Keith Whitelam, *The Inven- tion of Ancient Israel.* On the emergence of an antievolutionist or postevolutionist perspective in social and cultural anthropology, see Robert Nisbet, *Social Change and History* (Oxford: Oxford University Press, 1969), the source for the quote that opens the chapter, from 3–4; Robert Carneiro, *Evolutionism in Cultural Anthropology: A Critical History* (Boulder, CO: Westview, 2003); Stephen Sanderson, *Evolutionism and Its Critics* (Boulder, CO: Paradigm, 2007). On the work of Stephen Jay Gould as a post- modern revision of evolutionary theory, see Murdo McRae, "Ste- phen Jay Gould's (Post)Modernism," *Interdisciplinary Literary Studies* 1 (2000): 215–227.

Chapter 4: A Thrice-Told Tel

For more on the use of archaeology to understand ancient Israel- ite or biblical history, see John Bartlett, ed., *Archaeology and Bib- lical Interpretation* (London: Routledge, 1997); William Dever, *Who Were the Ancient Israelites and Where Did They Come From?* (Grand Rapids, MI: Eerdmans, 2003); Brian Schmidt, ed., *The Quest for the Historical Israel* (Atlanta: Society of Biblical Litera- ture, 2007). The results of Petrie's excavation at Tel El-Hesi have been reprinted as W. M. Flinders Petrie, *Tell El Hesy (Lachish), Hyksos and Israelite Cities* (1891; repr., Cambridge: Cambridge University Press, 2013).

The current expedition at Beth Shemesh got under way in 1990, and its directors, Zvi Lederman and Shlomo Bunimovitz, have pub- lished the results of their research in a number of different essays, including Shlomo Bunimovitz and Zvi Lederman, "A Border Case: Beth-Shemesh and the Rise of Ancient Israel," in *Israel in Transi- tion*, 2 vols., ed. Lester Grabbe (London: T & T Clark, 2008), 1:21– 31; and Bunimovitz and Lederman, "Canaanite Resistance: The Philistines and Beth Shemesh—A Case Study from Iron I," *Bulle- tin of the American Schools of Oriental Research* 364 (2011): 37–51. They also have a major volume on the excavation *Tel Beth-Shemesh: A Border Community in Judah—Renewed Excavations, 1990–2000.*

The Iron Age, Monograph Series of the Institute of Archaeology of Tel Aviv University (Winona Lake, IN: Eisenbrauns, 2016).

This chapter is also meant as an introduction to the concept of ethnogenesis. Three studies are often cited for their seminal role in developing the contemporary conception of ethnogenesis: Lester Singer, "Ethnogenesis and Negro-Americans Today," *Social Research* 29 (1962): 419–432, which I describe in the main narrative; William Sturtevant, "Creek into Seminole," in *North American Indians in Historical Perspective*, ed. Eleanor Leacock and Nancy Oestrich Lurie (New York: Random House, 1971), 92–128; and, though it does not use the term "ethnogenesis," Fredrik Barth, *Ethnic Groups and Boundaries: The Social Organization of Cultural Difference* (Bergen: Universitetsforlag, 1969). As noted, however, the term "ethnogenesis" has an earlier history that goes back to the nineteenth century. See J. H. Moore, "Cultural Evolution: Ethnogenesis," in *International Encyclopedia of the Social and Behavioral Sciences* (Amsterdam: Elsevier, 2001), 3045–3049. With its more recent meaning, the concept has been adopted by archaeologists working in a range of places; see T. M. Weik, "The Archaeology of Ethnogenesis," *Annual Review of Anthropology* 43 (2014): 291–305. Lederman and Bunimovitz were not the first to apply the concept of ethnogenesis to ancient Israel. See Avraham Faust, *Israel's Ethnogenesis: Settlement, Interaction, Expansion, and Resistance* (London: Equinox, 2006).

This chapter relies for its history of the excavation of Tel Beth Shemesh on the accounts provided by Bunimovitz and Lederman, but it is also indebted to the study of the history of archaeology. Those interested in the history of biblical archaeology might read Neil Asher Silberman, *Digging for God and Country: Archaeology, Exploration, and the Secret Struggle for the Holy Land* (New York: Knopf, 1982); Peter Roger Stuart Moorey, *A Century of Biblical Archaeology* (Cambridge: Lutterworth, 1991); Thomas Davis, *Shifting Sands: The Rise and Fall of Biblical Archaeology* (Oxford: Oxford University Press, 2004); Raz Kletter, *Just Past? The Making of Israeli Archaeology* (London: Equinox, 2006).

Duncan Mackenzie published some of his findings in "Excavations at Ain Shems (Beth-Shemesh)," *Palestine Exploration Fund Annual* 1 (1911): 41–94. For an account of Mackenzie's work at

Beth Shemesh, see Nicoletta Momigliano, *Duncan Mackenzie: A Cautious Canny Highlander and the Palace of Minos at Knossos* (London: Institute of Classical Studies, University of London, 1999), esp. 85–122. An important development for understanding the history of the site's excavation is the recent publication of Mackenzie's lost field report from the third and final season at Tel Beth Shemesh. See Duncan Mackenzie, Zvi Lederman, Shlomo Bunimovitz, and Nicolette Momigliano, *The Excavations of Tel Beth Shemesh, November–December 1912* (London: Routledge, 2016). For Mackenzie's account of the origin of the Aegean race, see Duncan Mackenzie, "Cretan Palaces and the Aegean Civilization. II," *Annual of the British School at Athens* 12 (1905/1906): 216–258.

Arthur Evans' description of the people of Philistia as a mixture of Semitic and Minoan racial stock can be found in Arthur Evans, *The Mycenean Tree and Pillar Cult and Its Mediterranean Relations* (London: Macmillan, 1901), 33. An example of how the two cultures intermixed in his mind was a "Mycenean Beth Shemesh" discovered on Crete, a pillar that he believed played a role in a solar cult and which he compared to the religious use of pillars documented in the Bible (*Mycenean Tree*, 71–77). For Giuseppe Sergi's similar account of racial history, see his *The Mediterranean Race: A Study of the Origin of European Peoples* (London: Walter Scott, 1909).

For more information about the Philistines who settled in Canaan in the twelfth century BCE, see Carl Ehrlich, *The Philistines in Transition: A History from ca. 1000–730 BCE* (Leiden: Brill, 1996); Assaf Yassur-Landau, *The Philistines and Aegean Migration at the End of the Late Bronze Age* (Cambridge: Cambridge University Press, 2010).

The results of the second expedition at Beth Shemesh were published as five volumes in the period between 1931 and 1939. The most relevant volumes for our purpose are those cowritten with George Ernest Wright, *Ain Shems Excavations (Palestine), Part IV (Pottery)* (Haverford, PA: Haverford College, 1938), and *Part V (Text)* of the same series, from 1939. Grant's publications on Palestinians include his *The Peasantry of Palestine: The Life, Manners, and Customs of the Village* (Boston: Pilgrim, 1907). His use of the concepts of race and racial mixing to describe the history of the Philistines, Canaanites, and Hebrews can be found in Elihu Grant,

The Orient in Bible Times (Philadelphia: J.B. Lippincott, 1920), written before his expedition to Beth Shemesh.

Among the twenty books and thousand articles and reviews published by William Foxwell Albright, those I draw on here include *From the Stone Age to Christianity: Monotheism and the Historical Process* (Baltimore: Johns Hopkins University Press, 1940) and *Yahweh and the Gods of Canaan: A Historical Analysis of Two Contrasting Faiths* (Garden City, NY: Doubleday, 1968). Albright addressed finds from Beth Shemesh directly in "The Seal of Eliakim and the Latest Preexilic History of Judah, with Some Observations on Ezekiel," *Journal of Biblical Literature* 51 (1932): 77–106 and "The Beth Shemesh Tablet in Alphabetic Cuneiform," *Bulletin of the American Schools of Oriental Research* 173 (1964): 51–53. For studies of Albright's life and scholarship, including additional bibliography, see Peter Feinman, *William Foxwell Albright and the Origins of Biblical Archaeology* (Berrien Springs, MI: Andrews University Press, 2004); Peter Machinist, "William Foxwell Albright: The Man and His Work," in *The Study of the Ancient Near East in the 21st Century: The William Foxwell Albright Centennial Conference*, ed. Jerrold Cooper and Glenn Schwartz (Winona Lake, IN: Eisenbrauns, 1996), 385–403; and Burke Long, *Planting and Reaping Albright: Politics, Ideology, and Interpreting the Bible* (University Park: Pennsylvania State University Press, 1997), whose effort to deconstruct the self-representation of Albright exemplifies the backlash against Albright and his positivistic approach that emerged in the decades after his death in 1971.

My discussion of the field's move away from the Albrightean paradigm mentions several studies. Kathleen Kenyon reported the results of her work at Jericho in *Digging Up Jericho: The Results of the Jericho Excavations, 1952–1956* (New York: Praeger, 1957). German scholarship that challenged Albright's approach included Manfred Weippert, *Die Landnahme der israelitischen Stämme in der neueren wissenschaftlichen Diskussion* (Göttingen: Vandenhoeck & Ruprecht, 1967). Turning to the United States, the scholarship of William Dever is a turning point in the breakdown of the Albrightean paradigm. See William Dever, "What Remains of the House That Albright Built?," *Biblical Archaeologist* 56 (1993): 25–35; and

Dever, "Archaeology, Ideology, and the Quest for an 'Ancient' or 'Biblical' Israel," *Near Eastern Archaeology* 61 (1998): 39–52.

Mendenhall's theory (introduced in "The Hebrew Conquest of Palestine," *Biblical Archaeologist* 25 [1962]: 65–87) was subsequently developed by Norman Gottwald, *Tribes of Yahweh: A Sociology of the Religion of Liberated Israel, 1250–1050 BCE* (Maryknoll, NY: Orbis, 1979). The gradual settlement theory goes back to the German scholars Albrecht Alt and Martin Noth. Note, for example, Albrecht Alt's 1925 essay translated as "The Settlement of the Israelites in Palestine," in *Essays on Old Testament History and Religion* (Oxford: Blackwell, 1966), 133–169, but its theory of Israelite origin was revived in more recent times through the archaeological work of Israel Finkelstein, as reflected in *The Archaeology of Israelite Settlement* (Jerusalem: Israel Exploration Society, 1988).

The differences between processual and postprocessual archaeology are discussed in Michael Shanks and Ian Hodder, "Processual, Post-processual, and Interpretive Archaeologies," in *Reader in Archaeological Theory: Post-processual and Cognitive Approaches*, ed. David Whitely (London: Routledge, 1998), 69–95. Bunimovitz has reflected on how postprocessualism has influenced his perspective in "Cultural Interpretation and the Bible: Biblical Archaeology in the Postmodern Era," *Cathedra* 100 (2001): 27–46 (in Hebrew). The self-reflexivity characteristic of postprocessualism has encouraged a new wave of scholarship that aims to contextualize biblical and Israeli archaeology as a form of social and political practice. See, for example, Nadia Abu El-Haj, *Facts on the Ground: Archaeological Practice and Territorial Self-Fashioning in Israeli Society* (Chicago: University of Chicago Press, 2001), a controversial work that criticizes Israeli archaeology, including the archaeology of Israelite origins, as an extension of the process of Israeli state building and settlement of Palestinian territory; Rachel Hallote and Alexander Joffe, "The Politics of Israeli Archaeology: Between 'Nationalism' and 'Science' in the Age of the Second Republic," *Israel Studies* 7 (2002): 84–116.

Chapter 5: Thought Fossils

For overviews of psychohistory, see David Stannard, *Shrinking History: On Freud and the Failure of Psychohistory* (Oxford: Oxford University Press, 1980); and Saul Friedlander, *History and*

Psychoanalysis: An Inquiry into the Possibilities and Limits of Psychohistory (New York: Holmes & Meier, 1978). To balance out the skepticism of these works, note the more optimistic treatment of the field in Cristian Tileagă and Jovan Byford, eds., *Psychology and History: Interdisciplinary Explorations* (Cambridge: Cambridge University Press, 2014), which includes the essay by Joan Scott, "The Incommensurability of Psychoanalysis and History," 40–66, to which I refer at the end of the chapter. The quotation opening this chapter is from Smith Ely Jelliffe and Elida Evans, "Psoriasis as an Hysterical Conversion Symbolization," *New York Medical Journal* 104 (1916): 1077–1084.

When referring to Freud's *Moses and Monotheism*, I am following the translation by Katherine Jones, wife of Ernest Jones, who consulted with Freud directly: Sigmund Freud, *Moses and Monotheism*, trans. Katherine Jones (London: Hogarth, 1939). The other work by Freud important to this chapter is *Totem and Taboo*, first published in English in the translation of A. A. Brill (New York: Moffat, Yard, & Co., 1918). *Moses and Monotheism* has become an object of renewed scholarly interest since the 1990s, especially after the publication of Yosef Yerushalmi's *Freud's Moses: Terminable and Interminable* (New Haven, CT: Yale University Press, 1991). The works I have consulted include Ilse Grubrich-Simitis, *Early Freud and Late Freud: Reading Anew Studies on Hysteria and Moses and Monotheism*, trans. Philip Slotkin (London: Routledge, 1997); Richard Bernstein, *Freud and the Legacy of Moses* (Cambridge: Cambridge University Press, 1998); Peter Schäfer, "The Triumph of Pure Spirituality: Sigmund Freud's Moses and Monotheism," *Jewish Studies Quarterly* 9 (2002): 381–406; Ruth Ginsburg and Ilana Pardes, eds., *New Perspectives on Freud's Moses and Monotheism* (Tübingen: Niemeyer, 2006); Franz Maciejewski, *Der Moses des Sigmund Freud: Ein unheimlicher Bruder* (Göttingen: Vandenhoeck and Ruprecht, 2006); Jay Geller, *On Freud's Jewish Body: Mitigating Circumcisions* (New York: Fordham University Press, 2007). Salo Baron's review of *Moses and Monotheism* appears in *American Journal of Sociology* 45 (1939): 471–477.

Criticism of Freudian theory is too extensive to cite, but examples include Paul Robinson, *Freud and His Critics* (Berkeley: University of California Press, 1993); and Todd Dufresne, ed., *Against Freud: Critics Talk Back* (Stanford, CA: Stanford University Press,

2007). When referring to the lack of scientific support for repression, I base myself on David Holmes, "The Evidence for Repression: An Examination of Sixty Years of Research," in *Repression and Dissociation*, ed. Jerome Singer (Chicago: University of Chicago Press, 1990), 85–102; Lawrence Patihis et al., "Are the 'Memory Wars' Over? A Scientist-Practitioner Gap in Beliefs about Repressed Memories," *Psychological Science* 25 (2014): 519–553. The research on this topic continues. A recent study showing the brain has a mechanism for hiding fear-inducing memories from itself is Vladimir Jovasevic et al., "GABAergic Mechanisms Regulated by miR-33 Encode State-Dependent Fear," *Nature Neuroscience* 18 (2015): 1265–1271.

For more on Freud's interest in archaeology, prehistory, and antiquity, in addition to Assmann, see Lis Møller, *The Freudian Reading: Analytical and Fictional Constructions* (Philadelphia: University of Pennsylvania Press, 1991), 31–56; Simon Price, "Freud and Antiquities," in *Psychoanalysis in Its Cultural Context*, ed. Edward Timms and Ritchie Robertson (Edinburgh: Edinburgh University Press, 1992), 132–137; Michael Shortland, "Powers of Recall: Sigmund Freud's Partiality for the Prehistoric," *Australasian Historical Archaeology* 11 (1993): 3–20; Stephen Barker, ed., *Excavations and Their Objects: Freud's Collection of Antiquity* (Albany: State University of New York, 1996); and Richard Armstrong, *A Compulsion for Antiquity* (Ithaca, NY: Cornell University Press, 2005).

The relationship between Freud's phylogenetic approach and the racial science of his day is discussed in Sander Gilman, *Freud, Race, and Gender* (Princeton, NJ: Princeton University Press, 1993), 12–48; Eliza Slavet, *Racial Fever: Freud and the Jewish Question* (New York: Fordham University Press, 2009). Here and there in *Moses and Monotheism*, Freud alludes directly to race science, referring to Francis Galton, for example, the scientist who sought to measure differences among humans in an effort to determine the effect of heredity on people's physical and psychological traits. See Nathan Roth, "Freud and Galton," *Comprehensive Psychiatry* 3 (1962): 77–83.

Freud was not the first to entertain an Egyptian origin for Judaism—the idea went back to the seventeenth and eighteenth centuries and to thinkers like the German poet and scholar

Friedrich Schiller (1759–1805). Isaac Bernays (1792–1849), grand-father of Freud's wife, developed a version of this argument under a pseudonym. For a history of this interest in ancient Egypt as the origin of monotheism, see Jan Assmann, *Moses the Egyptian: The Memory of Egypt in Western Monotheism* (Cambridge, MA: Harvard University Press, 1988); and on the eighteenth-century theory of Moses's Egyptian origin, see Martha Helfer, *The Word Unheard: Legacies of Anti-Semitism in German Literature and Culture* (Evanston, IL: Northwestern University Press, 2011), 23–56. A more immediate precedent for Freud's study was Karl Abraham's study of Akhenaten, which Freud read but, to his discredit, did not acknowledge. For an English translation, see "Amenhotep IV: A Psychoanalytic Contribution to the Understanding of His Personality and of the Monotheistic Cult of Aton," in the posthumous collection *Clinical Papers and Essays on Psycho-Analysis* (London: Hogarth, 1955), 262–290.

Jan Assmann has developed his ideas about Akhenaten and Moses in a number of publications. In addition to *Moses the Egyptian*, other relevant English publications include Jan Assmann, *The Price of Monotheism* (Stanford, CA: Stanford University Press, 2009), and *From Akhenaten to Moses: Ancient Egypt and Religious Change* (Cairo: American University in Cairo Press, 2014). As acknowledged by Assmann, there have been earlier efforts to read Manetho's account as a reminiscence of Akhenaten: Eduard Meyer, *Aegyptische Chronologie* (Leipzig: Heinrichs, 1904), 92–95; and Donald Redford, "The Hyksos Invasion in History and Tradition," *Orientalia* 39 (1970): 1–51, esp. 44–50. Assmann's essay, "Collective Memory and Cultural Identity," from which I draw the quote about his view of social memory, appears in *New German Critique* 65 (1995): 125–133.

Two recent studies illumine Assmann's approach to Akhenaten and Moses: Geoffrey Winthrop-Young, "Memories of the Nile: Egyptian Traumas and Communication Technologies in Jan Assmann's Theory of Cultural Memory," *New German Critique* 96 (2005): 103–133; and in the same issue Claudia Berger, "Imperialist Fantasy and Displaced Memory: Twentieth-Century German Egyptologists," 135–169. Akhenaten (or Ikhnaton, as Freud spelled his name) became a celebrity in the decades following the rediscovery of Amarna, as did family members like his son Tutankhamen. The history of how Akhenaten has been imagined since his rediscovery is recounted in Dominic Montserrat, *Akhenaten: History, Fantasy, and Ancient Egypt* (London: Routledge, 2000).

Manetho's writing has been published in translation by William Waddell, *Manetho* (Cambridge, MA: Harvard University Press, 1980). For a study of Manetho's account, see Russell Gmerkin, *Berossus and Genesis, Manetho and Exodus* (London: T & T Clark, 2006). Among those who read Manetho's narrative as a parody or inversion of the Exodus story is Amos Funkenstein, *Perceptions of Jewish History* (Berkeley: University of California Press, 1993), 36–38. But other scholars believe that it was really Josephus, through his paraphrase of Manetho, who added the Jews to the narrative. See Erich Gruen, "The Use and Abuse of the Exodus Story," *Jewish History* 12 (1998): 93–122. I did not lay out the evidence for my claim that Manetho's description of Osarsiph's sacrileges might reflect a common ancient Near Eastern trope used to discredit enemy rulers and usurpers, but I gather some of the evidence for that trope in Steve Weitzman, "Plotting Antiochus's Persecution," *Journal of Biblical Literature* 123 (2004): 219–234.

Among those at the forefront of the effort to update psycho-analysis in light of neuroscience is the Nobel Prize–winning scientist Eric Kandel. See Eric Kandel, "A New Intellectual Framework for Psychiatry," *American Journal of Psychiatry* 155 (1998): 457–469; and Edith Laufer, ed., *On the Frontiers of Psychoanalysis and Neuroscience: Essays in Honor of Eric R. Kandel* (New York: Guilford, 2012). But one should also note skeptics like Elisabeth Wilson, "Another Neurological Scene," *History of the Present* 1 (2011): 149–169; and Nima Bassiri, "Freud and the Matter of the Brain: On the Rearrangements of Neuropsychoanalysis," *Critical Inquiry* 40 (2013): 83–108.

On the intergenerational transmission of trauma, note M. Gerard Fromm, ed., *Lost in Transmission: Studies of Trauma across Generations* (London: Karnac, 2012). For research that casts doubt on the transmission of trauma, especially beyond the second generation, see Abraham Sagi-Schwartz et al., "Does Intergenerational Transmission of Trauma Skip a Generation? No Meta-analytic Evidence for Tertiary Traumatization with Third

Generation of Holocaust Survivors," *Attachment and Human Development* 10 (2008): 105–121. On the possibility that the effects of trauma are biologically heritable, see Rachel Yehuda, Martin Teicher, Jonathan Seckl, Robert Grossman, Adam Morris, and Linda Bierer, "Parental Posttraumatic Stress Disorder as a Vulnerability Factor for Low Cortisol Trait in Offspring of Holocaust Survivors," *Archives of General Psychiatry* 64 (2007): 1040–1048; and note also an overview of the research by Natan Kellermann, "Epigenetic Transmission of Holocaust Trauma: Can Nightmares Be Inherited?," *Israel Journal of Psychiatry and Related Sciences* 50 (2013): 33–39.

For the postmodern responses to Freud that I cite at the end of the chapter, see Jacques Derrida, *Archive Fever: A Freudian Impression* (Chicago: University of Chicago Press, 1996); Edward Said, *Freud and the Non-European Other* (London: Verso, 2003); David Carroll, "Freud and the Myth of Origin," *New Literary History* 6 (1975): 513–528.

Chapter 6: Hellenism and Hybridity

The touchstone for this chapter is Shaye Cohen, *The Beginnings of Jewishness: Boundaries, Varieties, Uncertainties* (Berkeley: University of California Press, 1999), especially the essay "From *Ethnos* to Ethno-Religion," 109–139. For other recent studies of the Jewish-Hellenistic period, see Lee Levine, *Judaism and Hellenism in Antiquity: Conflict or Confluence?* (Seattle: University of Washington Press, 1998); John Barclay, *Jews in the Mediterranean Diaspora: From Alexander to Trajan (323 BCE–117 CE)* (Berkeley: University of California Press, 1999); John Collins, *Between Athens and Jerusalem: Jewish Identity in the Hellenistic Period* (Grand Rapids, MI: Eerdmans, 2000); Troels Engberg-Pedersen, ed., *Paul Beyond the Judaism/Hellenism Divide* (Louisville, KY: John Knox, 2001); Erich Gruen, *Heritage and Hellenism: The Reinvention of Jewish Tradition* (Berkeley: University of California Press, 2002).

For more on the symbolic resonance of Hellenism and Hebraism within European culture, see Yaacov Shavit, *Athens in Jerusalem: Classical Antiquity and Hellenism in the Making of the Modern Secular Jew* (London: Littman Library of Jewish Civilization, 1997);

Tessa Rajak, "Jews and Greeks: The Invention and Exploitation of Polarities in the Nineteenth Century," in the volume of her collected essays *The Jewish Dialogue with Greece and Rome* (Leiden: Brill, 2001), 535–557; and Miriam Leonard, *Socrates and the Jews: Hellenism and Hebraism from Moses Mendelssohn to Sigmund Freud* (Chicago: University of Chicago, 2012).

I should note some of the primary sources I draw on in this chapter. Citations of Philo and Josephus come from the standard Loeb editions of their work, published by Harvard University Press. The quote from Isocrates's *Panegyricus* is cited from Cohen, *Beginnings of Jewishness*, 132.

I suggest that Cohen's theory might account for some of the religious practices that surface for the first time during the Hasmonean period—the use of the ritual bath or *mikveh*, now attested by some 850 excavated examples in Palestine from the Hellenistic and Roman periods, and the wearing of *tefillin*, first attested by evidence found among the Dead Sea Scrolls. The origin of these practices remains unclear, but recent scholarship situates their emergence in the Hellenistic period and sees Greek influence at work. See Yonatan Adler, "The Archaeology of Purity" (PhD diss., Bar Ilan University, 2011); Yehuda Cohn, *Tangled Up in Text: Tefillin and the Ancient World* (Providence, RI: Brown Judaic Studies, 2008). For the practice of fastening the text of Homer to oneself, see Saul Lieberman, *Hellenism in Jewish Palestine* (New York: Jewish Theological Seminary, 1962), 108n50; and note the recommendation of the second-century Roman physician Quintus Serenus Sammonicus to treat recurrent fevers by placing under the patient's head the fourth book of the *Iliad* (R. Pepin, *Quintus Serenus [Serenus Sammonicus] Liber Medicinalis* [Paris: Presses Universitaires de France, 1950], 47, no. 48, line 13).

In addition to Hellenism, another focus of this chapter is hybridity as a way of conceptualizing origin. See Deborah Kapchan and Pauline Strong, "Theorizing the Hybrid," *Journal of American Folklore* 112 (1999): 239–253; Peter Wade, "Hybridity Theory and Kinship Thinking," *Cultural Studies* 19 (2005): 602–621. Postcolonialist studies of hybridity routinely invoke Homi Bhabha's reconceptualizing of the term in *The Location of Culture* (London: Routledge, 1994), and for further discussion of postcolonialist approaches to hybridity, see Anjali Prabhu, *Hybridity: Limits, Transformations and Prospects* (Albany: State University of New York, 2012). I refer to several recent efforts to develop an alternative to hybridity as a description/explanation of Hellenistic culture. These include Andrew Wallace-Hadrill, *Rome's Cultural Revolution* (Cambridge: Cambridge University Press, 2008), 9–14 (proposing "bilingualism" as a model); Stephanie Langin-Hooper, "Problematizing Typology and Discarding the Colonialist Legacy: Approaches to Hybridity in the Terracotta Figurines of Hellenistic Babylonia," *Archaeological Review from Cambridge* 28 (2013): 95–113 ("entanglement"); Rachel Mairs, *The Hellenistic Far East: Archaeology, Language, and Identity in Greek Central Asia* (Oakland: University of California Press, 2014), 185–187.

Turning to the history of the study of the Hellenistic period, Johann Gustav Droysen's formulation of the Hellenistic age was developed in several works: *Geschichte Alexanders des Grossen*, first published in 1833 (repr., Herausgeber: Literaricon, 2015), and now available in translation by Flora Kimmich, *Johann Gustav Droysen: History of Alexander the Great* (Philadelphia: American Philosophical Society, 2012), and his never completed history of Hellenism, published in 1836 and 1843 as *Geschichte des Hellenismus*, vol. 1: *Geschichte der Nachfolger Alexanders* (Cambridge: Cambridge University Press, 2011). Arnaldo Momigliano's reflections about Droysen are found in "J. G. Droysen between Greeks and Jews," *History and Theory* 9 (1970): 139–153. For more on Droysen's conception of the Hellenistic age, his educational views, and his approach to history, see Robert Southard, *Droysen and the Prussian School of History* (Lexington: University Press of Kentucky, 1995); Arthur Assis, *What Is History For? Johann Gustav Droysen and the Functions of Historiography* (Oxford: Berghahn, 2014).

Henry Fischel's interest in the parallels between ancient Jewish and Greek culture is reflected in his *Rabbinic Literature and Greco-Roman Philosophy: A Study of Epicurea and Rhetorica in Midrash* (Leiden: Brill, 1973). I could have mentioned a number of other Jewish scholars from the same period with similar interests—Victor Tcherikover (1894–1958), David Daube (1909–1999), and Moses Hadas (1900–1966)—but Henry was the one I knew personally. The publications of Elias Bickerman mentioned in the chapter include

The God of the Maccabees: Studies on the Meaning and Origin of the Maccabean Revolt, trans. Horst Moehring (Leiden: Brill, 1979) and *From Ezra to the Last of the Maccabees* (New York: Schocken, 1949). For a biography of Bickerman, see Albert Baumgarten, *Elias Bickerman as a Historian of the Jews: A Twentieth-Century Tale* (Tübingen: Mohr Siebeck, 2010). Shaye Cohen's tribute appears as "Elias J. Bickerman: An Appreciation," *Jewish Book Annual* 40 (1982–1983): 162–165.

For more on *Bildung*, see W. H. Buford, *The German Tradition of Self-Cultivation: "Bildung" from Humboldt to Thomas Mann* (Cambridge: Cambridge University Press, 1975); David Sorkin, "Wilhelm von Humboldt: The Theory and Practice of Self-Formation (*Bildung*), 1791–1810," *Journal of the History of Ideas* 44 (1983): 55–73. On the value and ambivalence of *Bildung* for Jews, see David Sorkin, *The Transformation of German Jewry, 1780–1840* (New York: Oxford University Press, 1987); George Mosse, *German Jews Beyond Judaism* (Bloomington: Indiana University Press, 1985); Shulamit Volkov, *Germans, Jews and Antisemites: Trials of Emancipation* (Cambridge: Cambridge University Press, 2006), 248–255. On the role of the Greeks and Hellenism for European intellectuals, see Damian Valdez, *German Philhellenism: The Pathos of the Imagination from Winckelmann to Goethe* (New York: Palgrave, 2014). Eliza Butler's critique of the German preoccupation with the Greeks is E. M. Butler, *The Tyranny of Greece over Germany* (Cambridge: Cambridge University Press, 1935). The speech where Hegel describes Greek learning as a "secular baptism" can be found in G. W. F. Hegel, *Early Theological Writings*, trans T. M. Knox (Philadelphia: University of Pennsylvania Press, 1971), 321–330.

My information about the description of clean-shaven Jews as "German" comes from Nancy Sinkoff, *Out of the Shtetl: Making Jews Modern in the Polish Borderlands* (Providence, RI: Brown Judaic Studies, 2004), 199–200. On Joseph II's effort to ban Jewish beards, see Raphael Patai, *The Jews of Hungary: History, Culture, Psychology* (Detroit, MI: Wayne State University Press, 1996), 216. That Bickerman registered the parallel between Antiochus's decrees and Joseph's edicts is clearly indicated by *God of the Maccabees*, 29, where he quotes the classicist Theodor Mommsen's description of Antiochus as "this caricature of Joseph II."

For readers curious about Hellenistic education, my discussion draws on Henri-Irénée Marrou, *A History of Education in Antiquity* (Madison: University of Wisconsin Press, 1956; first published in French in 1948); Teresa Morgan, *Literate Education in the Hellenistic and Roman Worlds* (Cambridge: Cambridge University Press, 1998); and Raffaella Cribiore, *Gymnastics of the Mind: Greek Education in Hellenistic and Roman Egypt* (Princeton, NJ: Princeton University Press, 2001). Martin Hengel emphasizes the impact of Greek influence on Jewish education in *Judaism and Hellenism: Studies in Their Encounter in Palestine during the Early Hellenistic Period* (Philadelphia: Fortress Press, 1974), 1:65–78. An important source from beyond Palestine is the writings of Philo: see F. H. Colson, "Philo on Education," *Journal of Theological Studies* 18 (1917): 151–162; Erkki Koskenniemi, "Philo and Classical Education," in *Reading Philo: A Handbook to Philo of Alexandria*, ed. Torrey Seland (Grand Rapids, MI: Eerdmans, 2014), 102–128. Shaye Cohen's study of the connections between Greek and rabbinic education is "Patriarchs and Scholarchs," *Proceedings of the American Academy for Jewish Research* 48 (1981): 57–85.

At the end of the chapter, I contrast Cohen's explanation for the beginnings of Jewishness with another recent theory proposed by Daniel Boyarin. I am referring to Daniel Boyarin, "The Christian Invention of Judaism: The Theodosian Empire and the Rabbinic Refusal of Religion," *Representations* 85 (2004): 21–57.

Chapter 7: Disruptive Innovation

Shlomo Sand, the focus of this chapter, has developed his argument in several publications, including *The Invention of the Jewish People*, trans. Yael Lotan (London: Verso, 2009); *The Invention of the Land of Israel: From Holy Land to Homeland*, trans. Geremy Forman (London: Verso, 2012); and *How I Stopped Being a Jew*, trans. David Fernbach (London: Verso, 2014). For reviews, see Israel Bartal, "Inventing an Invention," *Ha'aretz*, July 6, 2008; Anita Shapira, "The Jewish People-Deniers," *Journal of Israeli History* 28 (2009): 63–72; Derek Penslar, "Shlomo Sand's 'The Invention of the Jewish People' and the End of the New History," *Israel Studies* 17 (2012): 156–168.

The term "Jewish people" or "Jewish peoplehood" has a different connotation in an American setting than it does in an Israeli setting. As Sand uses the term (*ha'am hayehudi* in Hebrew), the word "people" is synonymous with "nation," a collective associated with a particular language and territory and realizing its will in the context of a state. In the American setting, under the influence of Reconstructionist and Reform Judaism, the term "Jewish peoplehood" identified American Jews with Jews in Israel but was not synonymous with "nation"—in fact, it functioned as an alternative to "nation," referring to a group detached from language, territory, or state. See Noam Pianko, *Jewish Peoplehood: An American Innovation* (New Brunswick, NJ: Rutgers University Press, 2015).

Sand's book gives us a reason to briefly explore the Khazar theory, an attempt to explain the origin of Ashkenazic Jews. For a recent review of the evidence that concludes the hypothesis has little to support it, see Shaul Stampfer, "Did the Khazars Convert to Judaism?," *Jewish Social Studies* 19 (2013): 1–72. For a different interpretation of the evidence, see Peter Golden, "The Conversion of the Khazars to Judaism," in *The World of the Khazars: New Perspectives*, ed. Peter Golden, Haggai Ben Shammai, and András Róna-Tas (Leiden: Brill, 2007), 123–163. While there is not enough evidence to settle the debate over the Khazar theory (and this includes genetic evidence discussed in chapter 8), it is possible to study what motivates those who advocate for the theory. For an attempt to reconstruct Arthur Koestler's motives, see Robert Blumstock, "Going Home: Arthur Koestler's Thirteenth Tribe," *Jewish Social Studies* 48 (1986): 93–104. Koestler develops the theory in *The Thirteenth Tribe: The Khazar Empire and Its Heritage* (London: Hutchinson, 1976). On the theory's connection to Russian anti-Semitism, see Victor Shnirelman, "The Story of a Euphemism: The Khazars in Russian Nationalist Literature," in Golden, Ben Shammai, and Róna-Tas, *World of the Khazars*, 353–372.

This chapter is also an attempt to probe the "constructivist" approach to the origin of nations and its debate with "primordialism." For important articulations of the constructivist thesis, the three most cited studies are Ernest Gellner, *Nations and Nationalism* (Oxford: Blackwell, 1983); Benedict Anderson, *Imagined Communities: Reflections on the Origin and Spread of Nationalism*

(London: Verso, 1983); and Eric Hobsbawm, *Nations and Nationalism since 1780* (Cambridge: Cambridge University Press, 1992). Hobsbawm's description of Zionism as illegitimate appears on 48. The quote from John Milton comes from his *The History of Britain*, published in 1670, which can be found online at https://www.dartmouth.edu/~milton/reading_room/britain/text.shtml (accessed July 21, 2016).

For the primordialist perspective, see Edward Shils, "Primordial, Personal, Sacred and Civil Ties: Some Particular Observations on the Relationships of Sociological Research and Theory," *British Journal of Sociology* 8 (1957): 130–134; Clifford Geertz, "The Integrative Revolution: Primordial Sentiments and Civil Politics in the New States," in *Old Societies and New States: The Quest for Modernity in Asia and Africa*, ed. Geertz (New York: Free Press, 1963), 107–113; John Armstrong, *Nations before Nationalism* (Chapel Hill: University of North Carolina Press, 1982); Anthony D. Smith, *The Ethnic Origin of Nations* (Oxford: Blackwell, 1986); Pierre van den Berghe, "A Socio-biological Perspective," in *Nationalism*, ed. John Hutchinson and Anthony Smith (Oxford: Oxford University Press, 1994), 96–102; Adrian Hastings, *The Construction of Nationhood: Ethnicity, Religion, and Nationalism* (Cambridge: Cambridge University Press, 1997); Aviel Roshwald, *The Endurance of Nationalism: Ancient Roots and Modern Dilemmas* (Cambridge: Cambridge University Press, 2006).

On the evidence for "nationalism" among ancient Israelites or Jews, see Steven Grosby, "The Chosen People of Ancient Israel: Why Does Nationalism Exist and Survive?," *Nations and Nationalism* 5 (1999): 357–380; David Goodblatt, *Elements of Ancient Jewish Nationalism* (Cambridge: Cambridge University Press, 2006). And for reservations about projecting nationalism onto antiquity, Steve Weitzman, "On the Political Relevance of Antiquity: A Response to David Goodblatt's *Elements of Ancient Jewish Nationalism*," *Jewish Social Studies* 14 (2008): 165–172. For a critique of primordialism more generally, see Jack Eller and Reed Coughlan, "The Poverty of Primordialism: The Demystification of Ethnic Attachments," *Ethnic and Racial Studies* 16 (1993): 183–202.

Another body of research relevant for understanding Sand's argument is the scholarship on the "invention of tradition." The concept was introduced to scholarship by Eric Hobsbawm and Terence Ranger, eds., *The Invention of Tradition* (Cambridge: Cambridge University Press, 1983), and since the appearance of that work, many studies with similar titles have appeared—e.g., V. Y. Mudimbe, *The Invention of Africa* (Bloomington: Indiana University Press, 1988); Adam Kuper, *The Invention of Primitive Society* (London: Routledge, 1988); Werner Sollers, ed., *The Invention of Ethnicity* (Oxford: Oxford University Press, 1989), etc. For the critique of invented tradition, see Gaurav Desai, "The Invention of Invention," *Cultural Critique* 24 (1993): 119–142; Thomas Spear, "Neo-traditionalism and the Limits of Invention in British Colonial Africa," *Journal of African History* 44 (2003): 3–27; M. Ozan Erözden, "The Practical Limits of Inventing Traditions: The Failed Reinvention of the *Sinjska Alka*," *Nations and Nationalism* 19 (2013): 475–492. Another kind of critique of the invented tradition thesis comes from members of indigenous communities who protest having their traditions depicted as invented—and hence inauthentic—by outside scholars. See Jocelyn Linnekin, "Cultural Invention and the Dilemma of Authenticity," *American Anthropologist* 93 (1991): 446–449; Charles Briggs, "The Politics of Discursive Authority in Research on the 'Invention of Tradition,'" *Cultural Anthropology* 11 (1996): 435–469.

For more on the garage myth, see Pino Audia and Christopher Rider, "A Garage and an Idea: What More Does an Entrepreneur Need?" (University of Illinois at Urbana-Champaign's Academy for Entrepreneurial Leadership Historical Research Reference in Entrepreneurship), http://ssrn.com/abstract=1501554 (accessed May 16, 2016). Steve Wozniak's admission that the garage story was "a bit of a myth" appears in an interview with Brandon Lisy, "Steve Wozniak on Apple, the Computer Revolution, and Working with Steve Jobs," *Business Week*, December 4, 2014, http://www.bloomberg.com/news/articles/2014-12-04/apple-steve-wozniak-on-the-early-years-with-steve-jobs (accessed May 16, 2016).

To illustrate the failure of top-down invented traditions in Israel, I draw on Adam Rubin, "'Turning Goyim into Jews': Aliyah and the Politics of Cultural Anxiety in the Zionist Movement, 1933–1939," *Jewish Quarterly Review* 101 (2011): 71–96. For other reservations about the concept of invented tradition as applied to Israel, see

Yitzhak Conforti, "Zionist Awareness of the Jewish Past: Inventing Tradition or Renewing the Ethnic Past?," *Studies in Ethnicity and Nationalism* 12 (2012): 151–171.

My discussion of Ben-Zion Dinur and his efforts to instill unified national consciousness among Israelis during the 1950s relies on Ariel Rein, "Ben Zion Dinur: The Historian as the Educator of a Nation," in *Education and History: Cultural and Political Connections*, ed. Rivka Feldhay and Immanuel Etkes (Jerusalem: Zalman Shazar Center, 1989), 377–390 (in Hebrew); Uri Ram, "Zionist Historiography and the Invention of Modern Jewish Nationhood: The Case of Ben Zion Dinur," *History and Memory* 7 (1995): 91–124. My account of what happened to the history curriculum after Dinur synthesizes material from Shlomo Swirski, *Politics and Education in Israel: Comparisons with the United States* (New York: Falmer Press, 1999); Yossi Dahan and Gal Levy, "Multicultural Education and the Zionist State—The Mizrahi Challenge," *Studies in Philosophy and Education* 19 (2000): 423–444; Yitzhak Conforti, "Alternative Voices in Zionist Historiography," *Journal of Modern Jewish Studies* 4 (2005): 1–12; Amos Hofman, "The Politics of National Education: Values and Aims of Israeli History Curricula, 1956–1995," *Journal of Curriculum Studies* 39 (2007): 441–470; Tsafrir Goldberg and David Gerwin, "Israeli History Curriculum and the Conservative-Liberal Pendulum," *International Journal of Historical Learning, Teaching and Research* 11.2 (2013), http://www .history.org.uk/resources/secondary_resource_6445_149.html. I am also indebted to Israel Bartal for sharing a draft of a paper on the topic that draws on his experience as chair of the senior high school history curriculum for the state educational system between 1995 and 2003: "Schoolbooks, Politics of Culture, and Israeli 'Collective Memory.'" The paper is an English version of a Hebrew essay that appears as Israel Bartal, "History, Memory and Education: The Israeli Case, 2003," in *Army, Memory, and National Identity*, ed. Moshe Naor (Jerusalem: Magnes Press, 2007), 161–177.

In the second half of the chapter, I suggest that some scholars have been trying to find a way beyond the debate between constructivism and primordialism. I am referring to studies like Andrew Sayer, "Essentialism, Social Constructivism, and Beyond," *Sociological Review* 45 (1997): 453–487; Rogers Brubaker and Frederick

Cooper, "Beyond Identity," *Theory and Society* 29 (2000): 1–47; and Bonny Ibhawoh, "Beyond Instrumentalism and Constructivism: Reconceptualizing Ethnic Identities in Africa," *Humanities Today* 10 (2010): 221–230. In a different corner of academia—the field of social psychology—the plasticity of the self is something scientists are still trying to understand. Note, for example, the research project being directed by Emmanouil Tsakiris, "The Plasticity of the Self: Experimenting with Self-Identity in the Face of Change," http://erc.europa.eu/plasticity-self-experimenting-self-identity -face-change (accessed May 30, 2016).

When exploring why some scholars prefer constructivism and others primordialism, I was drawing on information and ideas gleaned from Andrzej Walicki, "Ernest Gellner and the 'Constructivist' Theory of Nation," *Harvard Ukrainian Studies* 22 (1998): 611–619 (which briefly links Gellner's views to his migrant background); John Hall, *Ernest Gellner: An Intellectual Biography* (London: Verso, 2010); Eric Hobsbawm, *Interesting Times: A Twentieth-Century Life* (New York: Pantheon, 2003); Adeed Dawisha, "Nations and Nationalism: Historical Antecedents to Contemporary Debates," *International Studies Review* 4 (2001): 3–22; Alexander Joffe, *Zion as Proxy: Three Jewish Scholars of Nationalism on Zionism and Israel* (Jerusalem: Leonard Davis Institute for International Relations, Hebrew University, 2007); Peter Weinreich, Viera Bacova, and Nathalie Rougier, "Basic Primordialism in Ethnic and National Identity," in *Analyzing Identity: Cross-Cultural, Societal and Clinical Contexts* (East Sussex: Routledge, 2003), 115–169; and Jonathan Spyer, "Theories of Nationalism: The Israeli Experience as a Test Case," *Israel Studies Forum* 20 (2005): 46–68.

Chapter 8: Source Codes

The chapter emerged from a lecture series organized with Noah Rosenberg at Stanford in an effort to put geneticists in dialogue with scholars of Jewish studies. Some of the presentations have been published in Noah Rosenberg and Steven Weitzman, eds., "From Generation to Generation: The Genetics of Jewish Populations," *Human Biology* 85 (2013).

Several books have appeared in recent years that introduce the field of Jewish genetic history. These include Jon Entine, *Abraham's Children: Race, Identity, and the DNA of the Chosen People* (New York: Grand Central, 2007); David Goldstein, *Jacob's Legacy: A Genetic View of Jewish History* (New Haven, CT: Yale University Press, 2008); Harry Ostrer, *Legacy: A Genetic History of the Jewish People* (Oxford: Oxford University Press, 2012). While Jews are by no means the only population studied in this way, they have received a lot of attention, perhaps even a disproportionate amount relative to other groups, for reasons discussed in Daphna Birenbaum-Carmelli, "Prevalence of Jews as Subjects in Genetic Research: Figures, Explanation, and Potential Implications," *American Journal of Medical Genetics, Part A* 130 (2004): 76–83.

This chapter also explores the critique of genetics research among anthropologists and historians of science, focusing on Nadia Abu El-Haj, *The Genealogical Science: The Search for Jewish Origins and the Politics of Epistemology* (Chicago: University of Chicago Press, 2012). Among many reviews and responses to this work, I found helpful Yulia Egorova's review in the *Anthropological Quarterly* 85 (2012): 967–971; Petter Hellström, "Genetic Diaspora, Genetic Return," *Studies in History and Philosophy of Science Part C* 44 (2013): 439–442; Susan Kahn, "Who Is a Jew? New Formulations of an Age-old Question," *Human Biology* 85 (2013): 919–924.

The study of Jewish genetic research is part of a broader vein of anthropological scholarship that approaches genetics as a cultural, social, or political practice. Compare Paul Brodwin, "Genetics, Identity, and the Anthropology of Essentialism," *Anthropological Quarterly* 75 (2002): 323–330; Sander Gilman, ed., *Race in Contemporary Medicine* (London: Routledge, 2007); Jennifer Reardon, *Race to the Finish: Identity and Governance in the Age of Genomics* (Princeton, NJ: Princeton University Press, 2004); Duana Fullwiley, *The Enculturated Gene: Sickle Cell Health Politics and Biological Difference in West Africa* (Princeton, NJ: Princeton University Press, 2011); Catherine Nash, *Genetic Genealogies: The Trouble with Ancestry* (Minneapolis: University of Minnesota Press, 2015).

Abu El-Haj was not the first to subject Jewish genetic research to critical examination. For earlier studies, see Raphael Patai with his daughter, geneticist Jennifer Patai, *The Myth of the Jewish Race* (New York: Scribner's Sons, 1975); Katya Azoulay, "Not an Innocent Pursuit: The Politics of a 'Jewish' Genetic Signature," *Developing World Bioethics* 3 (2003): 119–126; Susan Kahn, "Are Genes Jewish? Conceptual Ambiguities in the New Genetic Age," in *The Boundaries of Jewish Identity*, ed. Susan Glenn and Naomi Sokoloff (Seattle: University of Washington Press, 2010), 12–26; Shelly Tenenbaum and Lynn Davidman, "It's in My Genes: Biological Discourse and Essentialist Views of Identity among Contemporary American Jews," *Sociological Quarterly* 48 (2007): 435–450. Sand's remark that the genetic study of the Jews would have pleased Hitler is taken from *Invention of the Jewish People*, 319.

For attempts to wrestle with the challenges of treating DNA as a historical document, see Dena Davis, "Genetic Research and Communal Narratives," *Jurimetrics* 42 (2002): 40–49 (the source of my information about the genetic controversy surrounding Thomas Jefferson); Yulia Egorova, "DNA Evidence? The Impact of Genetic Research on Historical Debates," *Biosocieties* 5 (2010): 348–365; the studies in Keith Walloo, Alondra Nelson, and Catherine Lee, eds., *Genetics and the Unsettled Past* (New Brunswick, NJ: Rutgers University Press, 2012); Noa Kohler and Dan Mishmar, "Genes as Jewish History? Human Population Genetics in the Service of Historians," in *Race, Color, Identity: Rethinking Discourses about "Jews" in the Twenty-First Century*, ed. Efraim Sicher (New York: Berghahn, 2012), 234–246. Francis Collins's description of the human genome as a "history book" can be found at https://www.genome.gov/12011238/an-overview-of-the-human-genome-project/ (accessed July 21, 2016).

For more on the history of race and race science as it relates to the Jews, see Iris Idelson-Shein, *Difference of a Different Kind: Jewish Constructions of Race during the Long Eighteenth Century* (Philadelphia: University of Pennsylvania Press, 2014); John Efron, *Defenders of the Race: Jewish Doctors and Race Science in Fin-de-Siècle Europe* (New Haven, CT: Yale University Press, 1994); Mitchell B. Hart, ed., *Jews and Race: Writings on Identity and Difference, 1880–1940* (Waltham, MA: Brandeis University Press, 2011). For an important recent work in German, see Veronika Lipphardt, *Biologie der Juden: Jüdische Wissenschaftler über "Rasse" und Vererbung, 1900–1935* (Göttingen: Vandenhoeck & Ruprecht, 2008).

The connections between race science before World War II and postwar genetics are a much-researched topic. For the shift in scientific culture, see William Provine, "Geneticists and the Biology of Race Crossing," *Science* 182 (1973): 790–796, who interviewed geneticists active between 1930 and 1950 about their changing attitudes. On how various fields distanced themselves from race science after 1945, see Amos Morris-Reich, "Taboo and Classification: Post-1945 German Racial Writing on Jews," *Leo Baeck Institute Yearbook* (2013): 1–21. It is important to note that there was resistance to race science even prior to World War II, as documented in Elazar Barkan, *The Retreat of Scientific Racism: Changing Concepts of Race in Britain and the United States between the World Wars* (Cambridge: Cambridge University Press, 1993). For studies that stress continuity between race science and postwar genetics research, see S. O. Y. Keita and Rick Kittles, "The Persistence of Racial Thinking and the Myth of Racial Divergence," *American Anthropologist* 99 (1997): 534–544; Snait Gissis, "When Is 'Race' a Race? 1946–2003," *Studies in History and Philosophy of Science, Part C* 39 (2008): 437–450; Veronika Lipphardt, "Isolates and Crosses in Human Population Genetics: Or, a Contextualization of German Race Science," *Current Anthropology* 53 (2012): 69–82. Although recognizing race as a social construct, the field is still struggling with its use as a way of categorizing people. See Sheldon Krimsky and Kathleen Sloan, eds., *Race and the Genetic Revolution* (New York: Columbia University Press, 2011).

Fishberg's study of the Jews as a race question is Maurice Fishberg, *The Jews: A Study of Race and Environment* (London: Walter Scott/New York: Charles Scribner's Sons, 1911). The quotation comes from p. 515. Boas's study is Franz Boas, *Changes in the Bodily Form of Descendants of Immigrants* (New York: Columbia University Press, 1912). For a critique of their work, see Geoffrey Morant and Otto Samson, "An Examination of Investigations by Dr. Maurice Fishberg and Professor Franz Boas Dealing with Measurements of Jews in New York," *Biometrika* 28 (1936): 1–31. I mention a study from the 1930s that combines the methods of race science with the blood group analysis used in genetics research: N. Kossovitch and

F. Benoit, "Contribution a l'etude anthropologique et serologique des juifs modernes," *Revue anthropologique* 42 (1932): 99–125.

On the alliance between genetics and Nazism, see Alan Steinweis, *Studying the Jew: Scholarly Antisemitism in Nazi Germany* (Cambridge, MA: Harvard University Press, 2006); Sheila Faith Weiss, *The Nazi Symbiosis: Human Genetics and Politics in the Third Reich* (Chicago: University of Chicago Press, 2010). On the views of the Nazi race scientist Hans Günther (compared and contrasted with those of Franz Boas on race), see Amos Morris-Reich, "Project, Method and the Racial Characteristics of the Jews: A Comparison of Franz Boas and Hans F. K. Günther," *Jewish Social Studies* 13 (2006): 136–169.

On the UNESCO statement against scientific racism, see Michelle Brattain, "Race, Racism and Antiracism: UNESCO and the Politics of Presenting Science to the Postwar Public," *American Historical Review* 112 (2007): 1386–1413; Anthony Hazard, *Post-war Anti-racism: The United States, UNESCO, and "Race"—1945–1968* (New York: Palgrave Macmillan, 2012). The UNESCO statement against race can be found at http://unesdoc.unesco.org/images/0012/001229/122962eo.pdf (accessed May 30, 2016).

For more on Israeli research into the genetics of the Jews during the 1950s and 1960s, see Nurit Kirsh, "Population Genetics in Israel in the 1950s—The Unconscious Internalization of Ideology," *Isis: A Journal of the History of Science* 94 (2003): 631–655; Nurit Kirsh, "Genetic Studies of Ethnic Communities in Israel: A Case of Values-Motivated Research at Work," in *Jews and Sciences in German Contexts*, ed. Ulrich Charpa and Ute Deichmann (Tübingen: Mohr Siebeck, 2007), 181–194. On Elisabeth Goldschmidt, see Kirsh, "Geneticist Elisabeth Goldschmidt: A Twofold Pioneering Story," *Israel Studies* 9 (2004): 71–105. I have mentioned an international conference held in Israel in 1961 that represents a culmination of research in Israel until that point; the volume that came out of the conference is Elisabeth Goldschmidt, ed., *The Genetics of Migrant and Isolate Populations* (New York: Williams & Wilkins, 1963). On the intersections of early Zionist ideology and race science, see R. Falk, "Zionism, Race, and Eugenics," in *Jewish Tradition and the Challenge of Darwinism*, ed. Geoffrey Cantor and Marc Swetlitz (Chicago: University of Chicago Press, 2006), 137–162;

Dafna Hirsch, "Zionist Eugenics, Mixed Marriage, and the Creation of a 'New Jewish Type,'" *Journal of the Royal Anthropological Institute* 15 (2009): 592–609. Since the association of Zionism with race is highly charged politically, two historical notes are in order: (1) Race in the period prior to World War II was not necessarily seen by Zionist thinkers as predeterministic, nor was it necessarily accompanied by the goal of segregating Jews from Palestinians. For some, it offered an argument for coexistence by revealing kinship between Jews and Arabs, as in the thinking of the Zionist sociologist Arthur Ruppin. See Amos Morris-Reich, "Arthur Ruppin's Concept of Race," *Israel Studies* 2 (2006): 1–30. (2) Nazi racial doctrines changed Zionist thinking about race beginning in the 1930s. Note, for example, the shifting attitude toward race in the thinking of the anthropologist Ignaz Zollschan, who went from championing race science to leading an international campaign against Nazi racism, as discussed in Paul Weindling, "The Evolution of Jewish Identity: Ignaz Zollschan between Jewish and Aryan Race Theories, 1910–1945," in Cantor and Swetlitz, *Jewish Tradition and the Challenge of Darwinism*, 116–136.

On Leslie Dunn's study of the Jews of Rome, see Leslie Dunn and Stephen Dunn, "The Jewish Community of Rome," *Scientific American* 196 (March 1957): 118–128; and for discussion, Veronika Lipphardt, "The Jewish Community of Rome: An Isolated Population? Sampling Procedures and Bio-historical Narratives in Genetic Analysis in the 1950s," *Biosocieties* 5 (2010): 306–329.

Moving into the 1970s, I mention two contradictory studies of Jewish genetics from 1979. These were Sam Karlin, Ron Kenett, and Batsheva Bonné-Tamir, "Analysis of Biochemical Genetic Data on Jewish Populations: II. Results and Interpretations of Heterogeneity Indices and Distance Measures with Respect to Standards," *American Journal of Human Genetics* 31 (1979): 341–365; and Dorit Carmelli and Luca Cavalli-Sforza, "The Genetic Origin of the Jews: A Multivariate Approach," *Human Biology* 51 (1979): 41–61. I have also come across at least one book on the subject from this period as well: Arthur Mourant, Ada C. Kopeć, and Kazimiera Domaniewska-Sobczak, eds., *The Genetics of the Jews* (Oxford: Clarendon, 1978). Mourant is known for producing a major reference work that helped map blood groups across populations and ethnic groups, *The Distribution of the Human Blood Groups* (Oxford: Blackwell, 1954).

To understand the changes that have set in since the 1990s, see an overview written by one of the pioneers of this new phase of genetics research, Luca L. Cavalli-Sforza, "The DNA Revolution in Population Genetics," *Trends in Genetics* 14 (1998): 60–65; and for a more recent account of what such research has told us about human origins, see Eugene Harris, *Ancestors in Our Genome: The New Science of Human Evolution* (Oxford: Oxford University Press, 2015). On the ability of recent genetic research to pinpoint people's places of origin, see John Novembre et al., "Genes Mirror Geography within Europe," *Nature* 456 (2008): 98–101; Eran Elhaik et al., "Geographic Population Structure Analysis of Worldwide Human Population Infers Their Biogeographic Origins," *Nature Communications* 5 (2013): 1–12. (The lead author, Eran Elhaik, also produced the study supporting the Khazar theory of the Ashkenazic Jewish population.)

On the Jews in particular, I will mention only studies I refer to in the narrative. For the original genetic studies of Jewish priests, see Karl Skorecki et al., "Y Chromosomes of Jewish Priests," *Nature* 385 (1997): 32; Mark Thomas, Karl Skorecki, and Haim ben-Ami, "Origins of Old Testament Priests," *Nature* 394 (1998): 138–140. Criticism of this research comes from Avshalom Zoossmann-Diskin, "Are Today's Jewish Priests Descended from the Old Ones?," *Homo: Journal of Comparative Human Biology* 51 (2000): 156–162. For the authors' revision of their thesis (the *extended* Cohen Modal Haplotype), see Michael Hammer et al., "Extended Y Chromosome Haplotypes Resolve Multiple and Unique Lineages of the Jewish Priesthood," *Human Genetics* 126 (2009): 707–717. For the most recent—and highly skeptical—contribution to this debate, see Sergio Tofanelli et al., "Mitochondrial and Y-Chromosome Haplotype Motifs as Diagnostic Markers of Jewish Ancestry: A Reconsideration," *Frontiers in Genetics* 5 (2014): 384.

On the attempt to construct a kind of worldwide genetic profile of the Jewish people, see Doron Behar et al., "The Genome-Wide Structure of the Jewish People," *Nature* 466 (2010): 238–242; Harry Ostrer, "The Population Genetics of the Jewish People," *Human Genetics* 132 (2013): 119–127. Elhaik's revival of the Khazar hypothesis appears as Eran Elhaik, "The Missing Link of Jewish European Ancestry: Contrasting the Rhineland and the Khazarian Hypotheses," *Genome Biology and Evolution* 5 (2013): 61–74. Behar's refutation appears as Behar et al., "No Evidence from Genome-Wide Data of a Khazar Origin for the Ashkenazi Jews," *Human Biology* 85 (2013): 859–900. For an overview of the debate, see Noah Kohler, "Genes as a Historical Archive: On the Applicability of Genetic Research to Sociohistorical Questions: The Debate on the Origins of Ashkenazi Jewry Revisited," *Perspectives in Biology and Medicine* 57 (2014): 105–117.

For the study that traces the matrilineal ancestry of many Ashkenazic Jews to four founding women, see Doron Behar et al., "The Matrilineal Ancestry of Ashkenazi Jewry: Portrait of a Recent Founder Event," *American Journal of Human Genetics* 78 (2006): 487–497, which built on Mark Thomas et al., "Founding Mothers of Jewish Communities: Geographically Separated Jewish Groups Were Independently Founded by Very Few Female Ancestors," *American Journal of Human Genetics* 70 (2002): 1411–1420. Behar's conclusions that these maternal founders had Near Eastern ancestry has now been challenged by Marta Costa et al., "A Substantial Prehistoric European Ancestry Amongst Ashkenazi Maternal Lineages," *Nature Communications* 4 (2013), article number 2543, http://www.nature.com/ncomms/2013/131008/ncomms3543/full/ncomms3543.html (accessed March 28, 2016). Behar rejects their analysis but has not yet published a response.

On the ancestry of Ashkenazic Levites, see Doron Behar et al., "Multiple Origins of Ashkenazi Levites," *American Journal of Human Genetics* 73 (2003): 768–779. For a critique of how this research was conducted, see A. Zoossmann-Diskin, "Ashkenazi Levites' 'Y modal haplotype' (LMH)—An Artificially Created Phenomenon?," *Homo* 57 (2006): 87–100. For a self-revision of the earlier view, see Siiri Rootsi et al. (including Behar), "Phylogenetic Applications of Whole Y-Chromosome Sequences and the Near Eastern Origin of Ashkenazi Levites," *Nature Communications* (2013), article number 2928, http://www.nature.com/ncomms/2013/131217/ncomms3928/full/ncomms3928.html (accessed March 28, 2016).

Genetic study of Ashkenazic Jews has been given a recent boost by the Ashkenazi Genome Consortium. See http://

ashkenazigenome.org. For some of the research coming out of this initiative, see Shai Carmi et al., "Sequencing an Ashkenazi Reference Panel Supports Population-Targeted Personal Genomics and Illuminates Jewish and European Origins," *Nature Communications* 5 (2014), article number 4835, http://www.nature.com /ncomms/2014/140909/ncomms5835/full/ncomms5835.html (accessed July 18, 2016). Although less studied than the Ashkenazic population, Jewish communities from the Middle East and North Africa have received some attention from geneticists. See Noah Rosenberg et al., "Distinctive Genetic Signatures in Libyan Jews," *Proceedings of the National Academy of Science of the United States of America* 98 (2001): 858–863; Christopher Campbell et al., "North African Jews and Non-Jewish Populations Form Distinctive, Orthogonal Clusters," *Proceedings of the National Academy of Science of the United States of America* 109 (2012), http://www.pnas.org /content/109/34/13865.full. The Sephardic population has received more attention partly as a result of the appearance of "crypto-Jews" in recent years. See Susan Adams et al., "The Genetic Legacy of Religious Diversity and Intolerance: Paternal Lineages of Christians, Jews, and Muslims in the Iberian Peninsula," *American Journal of Human Genetics* 83 (2008): 725–736; Felice Bedford, "Sephardic Signature in Haplogroup T Mitochondrial DNA," *European Journal of Human Genetics* 20 (2012): 441–448; Inês Nogueiro et al., "Echoes from Sepharad: Signatures on the Maternal Gene Pool of Crypto-Jewish Descendants," *European Journal of Human Genetics* 23 (2015): 693–699; W. Sutton et al., "Toward Resolution of the Debate Regarding Purported Crypto-Jews in a Spanish-American Population: Evidence from the Y Chromosome," *Annals of Human Biology* 33 (2006): 100–111.

For genetic study of the Samaritans, see P. Shen et al., "Reconstruction of Patrilineages and Matrilineages of Samaritans and Other Israeli Populations from Y-Chromosome and Mitochondrial DNA Sequence Variation," *Human Mutation* 24 (2004): 248–260; Peter Oefner et al. (including Marc Feldman), "Genetics and the History of the Samaritans: Y-Chromosomal Microsatellites and Genetic Affinity between Samaritans and Cohanim," *Human Biology* 85 (2013): 825–838. On the legal and social challenges of being Samaritan in Israel, see Mordecai Roshwald, "Marginal Jewish

Sects in Israel (II)," *International Journal of Middle East Studies* 4 (1973): 328–354.

The discussion of the genetic history of the Lemba draws on Amanda Spurdle and Trefor Jenkins, "The Origins of the Lemba 'Black Jews' of Southern Africa: Evidence from P12F2 and Other Y-Chromosome Markers," *American Journal of Human Genetics* 59 (1996): 1126–1133; Mark Thomas et al., "Y Chromosomes Traveling South: The Cohen Modal Haplotype and the Origins of the Lemba—The 'Black Jews of South Africa,'" *American Journal of Human Genetics* 66 (2000): 674–686. Tudor Parfitt has written extensively about the case and reflected on how the genetic findings (and their description in the media) affected Lemba self-identification: see Tudor Parfitt, "The Lemba: An African Judaising Tribe," in *Judaising Movements: Studies in the Margins of Judaism*, ed. Parfitt and Emanuela Trevisan-Semi (London: Routledge, 2002), 39–52; and with Yulia Egorova, *Genetics, Mass Media, and Identity: A Case Study of the Genetic Research on the Lemba and Bene Israel* (London: Routledge, 2006). Besides Abu el-Haj's critique of this research, see A. Ruwitah, "Lost Tribe, Lost Language? The Invention of a False Lemba Identity," *Zimbabwea* 5 (1997): 53–71. On the connection between the Lemba and the American Jewish community, see Noah Tamarkin, "Genetic Diaspora: Producing Knowledge of Genes and Jews in Rural South Africa," *Cultural Anthropology* 29 (2014): 552–574. For a genetic study that raises doubts from a scientific perspective, see Himla Soodyall, "Lemba Origins Revisited: Tracing the Ancestry of Y Chromosomes in South African and Zimbabwean Lemba," *South African Medical Journal* 103 (2013): 1009–1013.

Do people's perceptions of their ancestry correspond to the genetic ancestry recorded in their genes? There is plenty of evidence that self-reported ancestry and genetic ancestry need not and often do not coincide. See, for example, Katarzyna Bryc et al., "The Genetic Ancestry of African-Americans, Latinos, and European Americans across the United States," *American Journal of Human Genetics* 96 (2015): 37–53. But on the other hand, people's understanding of their ancestry and their genetically estimated biological ancestry need not be completely unrelated to each other, and there is recent research that indicates that in some contexts the two can match up in a significant way. See Hua Tang et al., "Genetic Structure, Self-Identified Race/Ethnicity, and Confounding in Case-Control Association Studies," *American Journal of Human Genetics* 76 (2005): 268–275; Andres Ruiz-Linares et al., "Admixture in Latin America: Geographic Structure, Phenotypic Diversity and Self-Perception of Ancestry Based on 7342 Individuals," *PLOS Genetics* 10.9 (2014), http://journals.plos.org/plosgenetics/article?id=10.1371/journal.pgen.1004572 (accessed July 20, 2016).

I mention a controversial book by the journalist Nicholas Wade, which has provoked a backlash from geneticists for misrepresenting their research as support for a revived form of racial history that uses genetics to account for traits like Jewish intelligence. The book is Nicholas Wade, *A Troublesome Inheritance: Genes, Race and Human History* (New York: Penguin, 2014). The protest letter from Rosenberg and colleagues appears at https://cehg.stanford.edu/letter-from-population-geneticists (accessed June 28, 2016). For an example of how Wade's book has been incorporated into anti-Semitic discourse, see http://davidduke.com/jews-race-nicholas-wade-jewish-supremacism-attempts-guard-gates-science/ (accessed June 28, 2016). On the prehistory of Wade's claims about the higher cognitive abilities of Jews, see Sander Gilman, "'The Bell Curve,' Intelligence, and Virtuous Jews," *Discourse* 19 (1996): 58–80.

This chapter might have given the impression that concern about genetic ancestry research comes only from outside the field of genetics, but that needs to be corrected since the field itself has called attention to the problems and voiced concerns. See, for example, the warning against genetic ancestry testing from the American Society of Human Genetics: http://www.ashg.org/pdf/ASHGAncestryTestingStatement_FINAL.pdf (accessed July 20, 2016). Also pertinent is the commentary of Charmaine Royal et al., "Inferring Genetic Ancestry: Opportunities, Challenges, and Implications," *American Journal of Human Genetics* 86 (2010): 661–673, which recommends ways to responsibly pursue such research.

Conclusion

The conclusion touches on what motivates us to seek out information about lost ancestors and distant lands of origin. One area of relevant research we have mentioned is the study of "genealogical bewilderment," the identity problems suffered by adopted or foster children as a result of not knowing their birth parents. First proposed by H. J. Sants ("Genealogical Bewilderment in Children with Substitute Parents," *British Journal of Medical Psychology* 37 [1964]: 133–142), the concept suggests that humans have an innate need for information about their heredity, but note that this concept has been challenged. See Kimberly Leighton, "Addressing the Harms of Not Knowing One's Heredity: Lessons from 'Genealogical Bewilderment,'" *Adoption and Culture* 3 (2012): 63–106. The evidence that there might be cognitive benefits to thinking about ancestors comes from Peter Fischer et al., "The Ancestor Effect: Thinking about Our Genetic Origin Enhances Intellectual Performance," *European Journal of Social Psychology* 41 (2011): 11–16. On the social benefits of knowing one's ancestry, see Eviatar Zerubavel's book, *Ancestors and Relatives*, noted in the bibliography for chapter 1; Anne-Marie Kramer, "Kinship, Affinity and Connectedness: Exploring the Role of Genealogy in Personal Lives," *Sociology* 45 (2011): 379–395 (interesting for what it suggests about the meaningfulness of searching for ancestors but also the source of my quotations from people who believe that such research is pointless or narcissistic); Amy Smith, *Tracing Family Lines: The Impact of Genealogy Research on Family Communication* (Lanham, MD: Lexington Books, 2012). An unexpected font of research is tourism studies, which has taken an interest in why people seek out lost ancestors and homelands because of the implications for understanding consumer behavior. See, for example, Nina Ray and Gary McCain, "Personal Identity and Nostalgia for the Distant Land of Past: Legacy Tourism," *International Business & Economics Research Journal* 11 (2012): 977–989; Philip Pearce, "The Experience of Visiting Home and Familiar Places," *Annals of Tourism Research* 39 (2012): 1024–1027.

I draw the distinction between blanks and gaps from Meir Sternberg, *The Poetics of Biblical Narrative* (Bloomington: Indiana University Press, 1987), 235–237. On the rootless Jew, see Sarah Hammerschlag, *The Figural Jew: Politics and Identity in Postwar French Thought* (Chicago: University of Chicago Press, 2010). A description of the 2007 Ancestry.com study can be found at http://blogs.ancestry.com/circle/?p=2102 (accessed October 23, 2016). The link to the study itself appears to have gone dead.

The citations at the beginning of each chapter come from the following sources: **Introduction**, Hannah Arendt, *Responsibility and Judgment* (New York: Schocken Books, 2003), p. 260; **Chapter 1**, Henry Wieneck, *The Hairstones: An American Family in Black and White* (New York: St. Martin's Griffin, 1999), p. 275; **Chapter 2**, Ferdinand de Saussure, *Course in General Linguistics* (trans. Wade Baskin; eds. Perry Meisel and Haun Saussy; New York: Columbia University Press, 1959), p. 222; **Chapter 3**, Robert Nisbet, *Metaphor and History: The Western Idea of Social Development* (New Brunswick, NJ, Transaction Publishers, 2009), pp. 3–4; **Chapter 4**, Robin George Collingwood, *An Autobiography and Other Writings* (Oxford: Oxford University Press, 2013), p. 122; **Chapter 5**, Smith Ely Jelliffe and Elida Evans, "Psoriasis as an Hysterical Conversion Symbolization," *New York Medical Journal* 104 (1916): 1077–1084; **Chapter 6**, Christoph Wieland as cited in Rudolf Vierhaus, "Bildung," *Geschichtliche Grundbegriffe* (eds. O. Brunner et al.; Stuttgart: Klett, 1972), p. 518; **Chapter 7**, John Milton, *The History of Britain. That Part Especially, Now Called England* (London: R. Wilks, 1818), p. 1; **Chapter 8**, Yehuda Amichai, "I Feel Just Fine in My Pants," from *The Selected Poetry of Yehuda Amichai* translated and edited by Chana Bloch and Stephen Mitchell. Copyright © 1996 by University of California Press. Reprinted by permission of the publisher; **Conclusion**, Friedrich Nietzsche, *Daybreak: Thoughts on the Prejudices of Morality* (eds. Maudemarie Clark and Brian Leiter; Cambridge: Cambridge University Press, 1997), p. 30.

A NOTE ON THE TYPE

{⚊⚊⚊⚊⚊}

THIS BOOK has been composed in Miller, a Scotch Roman typeface designed by Matthew Carter and first released by Font Bureau in 1997. It resembles Monticello, the typeface developed for The Papers of Thomas Jefferson in the 1940s by C. H. Griffith and P. J. Conkwright and reinterpreted in digital form by Carter in 2003.

Pleasant Jefferson ("P. J.") Conkwright (1905–1986) was Typographer at Princeton University Press from 1939 to 1970. He was an acclaimed book designer and AIGA Medalist.

The ornament used throughout this book was designed by Pierre Simon Fournier (1712–1768) and was a favorite of Conkwright's, used in his design of the *Princeton University Library Chronicle*.